Ritual and Mantras:
Rules Without Meaning

Ritual and Mantras:
Rules Without Meaning

FRITS STAAL

MOTILAL BANARSIDASS PUBLISHERS
PRIVATE LIMITED • DELHI

First Indian Edition: Delhi, 1996

Published by arrangement with Peter Lang Publishing, Inc.

First published as *Rules Without Meaning: Ritual, Mantras and the Human Sciences*

ISBN: 81-208-1411-8 (Cloth)
ISBN: 81-208-1412-6 (Paper)

Also available at:

MOTILAL BANARSIDASS
41 U.A. Bungalow Road, Jawahar Nagar, Delhi 110 007
120 Royapettah High Road, Mylapore, Madras 600 004
16 St. Mark's Road, Bangalore 560 001
8 Camac Street, Calcutta 700 017
Ashok Rajpath, Patna 800 004
Chowk, Varanasi 221 001

FOR SALE IN INDIAN SUBCONTINENT ONLY

PRINTED IN INDIA
BY JAINENDRA PRAKASH JAIN AT SHRI JAINENDRA PRESS, A-45 NARAINA, PHASE I, NEW DELHI 110 028 AND PUBLISHED BY NARENDRA PRAKASH JAIN FOR MOTILAL BANARSIDASS PUBLISHERS PRIVATE LIMITED, BUNGALOW ROAD, DELHI 110 007

For Wichai

Contents

Part IV. The Human Sciences

FIGURES

TABLES

Preface

Philosophers tell us that no sharp boundary can be drawn between innate knowledge and knowledge based upon experience. This is not surprising for knowledge that is innate in individuals may have been acquired by the species over a period of time. This description applies not only to animal instinct, but also to knowledge of the rules of ritual and mantras that are studied in this book. Often innate and unconscious, they lead a life of their own, independent of religion, society and language. But how can ritual and mantras be governed by rules that lie beyond the human sciences and the study of religion?

It took a long time before I recognized the nature of this question and its many puzzling overtones. For more than a decade, I had been engaged in the study of the 1975 performance of the Vedic *Agnicayana* ritual by Nambudiri brahmins in South India. The result was published in 1983 in two illustrated volumes entitled *AGNI—The Vedic Ritual of the Fire Altar*. In the course of this work, it dawned upon me that these data were extraordinary, and that no one knew how to account for them. Relevant specialists—Indologists, anthropologists, psychologists, or scholars of religion—offered no conceptual tools that I could use. If I wanted to go beyond mere description and offer explanations, I had to strike out on my own. My efforts are not completed but there is enough for others to continue, with or without me.

Although the core of this book is the discussion of ritual and mantras in parts II and III, I stumbled upon related issues that could not remain unmentioned. It now looks to me as if we have been skirting the tips of an iceberg which is almost entirely under water. But can we be certain it is an iceberg we have been skirting? Are we above or below the surface, and surface of *what*? When I don't know my way about, am I climbing, diving, or riding waves that elude identification? Or am I on a summit, with distant views hidden behind thick and near-permanent clouds? Part IV shows that the landscape or seascape remains mysterious. The compasses and maps displayed in Part I may not be reliable. What seems certain is that we have to put together what is not generally put together.

Ritual and mantras have been strangely neglected in the theoretical sciences. Socrates questioned everything, from Greek grammatical usage to the existence of Gods. He paid attention to dreams and oracles, but not to ritual. When Plato tells us that Socrates sacrifices a cock or a hen, at home or on an altar of the state, he performs this rite automatically, without recognizing the need for an explanation, much as we would switch on our favorite channel.

"Mantras" have also been ignored; outside the counter-culture, the term is not even English. Although there are seventy million of them according to a Sanskrit text, their forms and uses are totally unexplained. The eighteenth century Danish missionary Bartholomaeus Ziegenbalg discovered a few in Malabar on the south west coast of India. Most Indian mantras originated in the Vedas and have since become virtually indestructible. They are not yet fashionable like the silk road, used by imperial China to export, in addition to silk, porcelain, lacquers, furs, cinnamon, vermilion and tea. But what was the emperor of China content to receive in return for these riches? Apart from marihuana and Ganges water (still smuggled to Mongolia), primarily one commodity: *mantras*. Unchanging in ever changing contexts of language, religion and society, generally kept secret and guarded jealously, mantras travelled from India not only throughout Southeast Asia and Indonesia, but crossed the Himalayas from Kashmir into Central Asia and China (first century A.D.), went on to Korea (fourth century) and Japan (sixth century), and ascended the Tibetan plateau (eighth century). They have now reached California where they fetch high prices. All transactions take place behind a smoke-screen of labels such as "Hindu," "Buddhist," "Tantric," "Taoist," and, belatedly, "shaman," labels originating from the outside. Ritual and mantras are still basic features of the civilizations of Asia. The only American response is glossolalia.

The *Frontispiece* of this book (photograph by Adelaide de Menil) illustrates one of its main theses: that ritual is transmitted not only without meaning, but often without language. Cherumukku Vaidikan Vasudevan *Akkitiripad* (a title he acquired by performing the *Agnicayana* more than thirty years ago) shows his son Vallabhan how to perform the *Nihnava* rite. This mysterious rite is performed twice daily, in the morning and afternoon, during several consecutive days. The ritual patron and several of his priests place their hands on a bundle of grass, which lies to the west of the altar. The position of the hands is different in the two surviving traditions. According to the Kauṣītakins, it should be as follows:

Morning: left hand palm down; right hand on left hand with palm up;

Afternoon: left hand palm up; right hand on left hand with palm down.

The Taittirīya tradition calls for different positions:

Morning: left hand palm up; right hand on left hand with palm down;

Afternoon: right hand palm up; left hand on right hand with palm down.

The Plate illustrates the first of these positions: the father is about to place his right hand on the left. The rite is mentioned below (pages 74, 85, and 93), described in my book AGNI (I: 358–59, 366–67) and discussed by Pamela MacFarland in "Ritual Language Dismantled" (to be published in *Le rituel. Actes du colloque du centénaire de L'Ecole Pratique des Hautes Etudes, Section des Sciences Religieuses*).

Rules without Meaning is not only based on AGNI but is also related to three of my earlier books and four that are more recent or about to appear. Ritual and mantras are independent of religion in ways similar to mysticism, the subject of *Exploring Mysticism: A Methodological Essay* (University of California, 1975). Ritual and mantras were studied in ancient India as described in *The Science of Ritual* (Bhandarkar Oriental Research Institute, 1982). These studies were connected with Indian linguistics which is the subject of my *Reader on the Sanskrit Grammarians* (MIT, 1972). Parts I and IV include material touched upon in *Over zin en onzin in filosofie, religie en wetenschap* (Meulenhoff, Amsterdam, 1986). Chapters 4 through 6 are supplemented by *Universals: Essays in Indian Logic and Linguistics* (University of Chicago Press, 1988a) which Chapter 5 overlaps slightly. Some portions of the book correspond to *Jouer avec le feu: Pratique et théorie du rituel védique* (*Publications de l'institut de civilisation indienne*, Paris, 1989). Chapter 28C should be supplemented with *Kailas. Center of Asia* (University of Chicago Press, 1988b).

The materials of Parts II and III have been approached from various angles in a series of special studies (for details, see the Bibliography). While Chapters 7 through 11 derive from AGNI, an early version of Chapter 12 appeared under the title "Ritual Syntax" in the Ingalls Festschrift of 1980 (*Sanskrit and Indian Studies*, edited by M. Nagatomi, B. K. Matilal, J. M. Masson and E. C. Dimock, Jr., and published by D. Reidel Publishing Company, Dordrecht). Parts of Chapter 13 appeared in "The Meaninglessness of Ritual" (*Numen. International Review for the History of Religions* 1979, edited by M. Heerma van Voss, E. J. Sharpe and R. J. Z. Werblowsky, and published by E. J. Brill, Leiden) and parts of Chapter 14 in "Rites That Make No Sense" (*The Communication of Ideas: 10th International Congress of Anthropological and Ethnological Sciences*, edited by J. S. Yadava and V. Gautam in 1980, and published by Concepts Publishing Company, New Delhi). Chapters 15 and 16 include material from "The Search for Meaning: Mathematics, Music and Ritual" (*American Journal of Semiotics* 1984, edited by

Thomas Sebeok). A related version was published by Elemire Zolla in *Conoscenza Religiosa* (1983) under the title: "Ritmo nel rito." Portions of Chapters 18, 20, 21A and 22 overlap "Vedic Mantras", edited by H. P. Alper for *Understanding Mantras* and to be published in 1988 by the State University of New York Press, Albany. Chapter 19 appeared under the title "Moon Chants, Space Fillers and Flow of Milk" in the Sreekrishna Sarma Felicitation Volume, *Surabhi*, printed in 1983 at Kalakshetra Publications Press, Tiruvanmiyur, Madras. Chapter 23 corresponds to an article of that title in the *Journal of the American Oriental Society* (1985), edited by Ernest Bender. Chapters 24 and 25 share parts with "The Sound of Religion" also published in *Numen* (1986) and forthcoming in a different form in the volume of essays in honour of Milton Singer, edited by Michael M. Ames and Murray Leaf and to be published by the *Centre for South Asian Studies* at the University of Toronto.

Chapter 26 is extracted from my monograph of 1982 of that title, already mentioned. Chapter 27 includes fragments from "The Fidelity of Oral Tradition and the Origins of Science" (*Mededelingen der Koninklijke Nederlandse Akademie van Wetenschappen, Afd. Letterkunde*, Nieuwe Reeks, Deel 49, No. 8, published by the North-Holland Publishing Company, Amsterdam/Oxford/New York 1986). Chapter 28 incorporates material from "Substitutions de paradigmes et religions d'Asie" (*Cahiers d'Extrême Asie* 1985, edited by Hubert Durt for the Ecole Française d'Extrême-Orient, Section de Kyoto). Chapter 30A corresponds to parts of a contribution entitled "Ritual, Mantras and the Origin of Language" to the Professor R. N. Dandekar Felicitation Volume *Amṛtadhārā*, edited by S. D. Joshi and published by Ajanta Publications, Delhi (1984).

I am grateful to the editors and publishers of these publications for permission to use them in the preparation of this book. Fragments have also been presented in various stages of completion or incompletion to audiences at Amsterdam, Berkeley, Berlin, Haverford, Kyoto, Leiden, Madras, Nanterre, New Delhi, Oxford, Paris, Santa Barbara, Sydney, Utrecht, and other places. At the University of California, Berkeley, my courses on the philosophy of religion and on the philosophies of India have reflected phases of the development of my thinking.

I am grateful to friends and colleagues who have commented on earlier drafts and without whom errors, mistakes and misjudgments would be more numerous and glaring. Paul Attinello, Hubert Durt, Robert Goldman, Mark Juergensmeyer and Pamela MacFarland have commented on the published or forthcoming articles mentioned which acknowledge their assistance. I am especially grateful to Morris Halle who read an earlier version of Chapters 4 through 6 and explained to what extent I was out of touch with recent developments in linguistics—an ignorance, I am afraid, that is not yet cured. My principal debt is to Harold Arnold who read the pre-final version in its entirety, corrected mistakes and gave me the benefit of his judicious comments on matters of detail and substance.

Contemporary technology has replaced the support of secretaries and the pleasure of thanking them. But new developments bring new pitfalls. When I was preparing the bibliography, with temperatures soaring in the upper eighties, my printer broke down. The work was completed owing to prompt assistance rendered by Rand Morimoto and Scott Tachiki of *Computer Options*, to both of whom I express my thanks.

My final gratitude goes to Donald Wiebe who invited me to write this book for the *Toronto Studies in Religion* of which he is the General Editor. A similar book addressing another audience could have been written in a different vein. The data are sufficiently rich for the accent to have been placed on philosophy, language, music, ethology, sociobiology, semiotics, cognitive psychology, the sociology of knowledge, the future, or something else more directly related to the present needs of humanity. This might have resulted in a different book, more readable, relevant and welcome. No doubt, a book like this should be written before long. My book has followed its own course but the direction it has taken suggests that I am the person least suited to have been its author. I am not a student of religion, anthropologist, or specialist in any of the fields of study I have been foolhardy enough to comment on. I take comfort from Arthur Waley's translation—a Bloomsbury version—of the twentieth chapter of Lao Tzu's *Tao Te Ching*:

> I droop and drift, as though I belonged nowhere.
> The world is full of people that shine;
> I alone am dark.

All men and women huddle together in religious communication. I alone am outdated, without context, abstracting formulas from thick description, pressing ancient wisdom only to be left with bare bones.

> All men have enough and to spare.
> I alone seem to have lost everything.
>
> All men can be put to some use.
> I alone am untractable and boorish.

September 15, 1987 FRITS STAAL

A note on the pronunciation of Sanskrit

THE Sanskrit vowels, pronounced as in Italian or Japanese, are short (*a, i, u, ṛ, ḷ*) or long, viz. twice as long as the short ones (*ā, ī, ū, ṝ, e, o, ai, au*). The consonant *r* is pronounced as in Italian, while the vowels *ṛ* and *ḷ* contain a vocalic element similar to the short *i* in the third syllable of English *ability*. Among the consonants, there are a series of dentals (*t, th, d, dh, n, s*) and a corresponding series of retroflexes or cerebrals (*ṭ, ṭh, ḍ, ḍh, ṇ, ṣ*). The former are produced when the tip of the tongue touches the teeth (as in French), the latter when it is bent backward and touches the palate (the English pronunciation of *t, d, n, s* is more or less in between). In the case of Sanskrit *s* and *ṣ*, the tongue points in the same directions, but breath passes over it. The palatals are pronounced when the tongue touches the front of the palate: *c* as in English *chair*, *j* as in *jar*, *ñ* as in Spanish, and *ś* as in *sheet*. The aspirates (*kh, gh, ch, jh, ṭh, ḍh, th, dh, ph, bh*) are pronounced with a clearly audible release of breath following the consonant: *th* like in *ant-hill*, *dh* like in *bald-head*, etc. The *ṃ* expresses nasalization of the preceding vowel, and the *ḥ* sounds like an *h* followed by a short echo of the preceding vowel (*agniḥ* as *agnih*[i]). The other consonants are pronounced as in English.

★

Unlike in English, there is in Sanskrit a difference between the stem of a noun (e.g. *dhyāna-, dhīti-, karman-*) and the Nominative case, which is used when the noun functions syntactically as the subject of the sentence (e.g. *dhyānam, dhītiḥ, karma*). I generally refer to nouns by using their stem form, but some of the sources I quote use the Nominative case form.

Part I

Methods, Meanings and Rules

Introductory Note

This book proposes a series of related hypotheses that help to understand and explain ritual and mantras. Part I introduces the approach I have adopted and its philosophical and linguistic presuppositions. This approach is scientific in that it is based upon the assumption that ritual and mantras can be studied like other objects and are not beyond the pale of an investigation that is empirical and rational and therefore akin to science. Adopting a scientific approach does not imply that ritual and mantras can be fruitfully or interestingly studied with the help of, for example, quantitative, statistical or behavioristic methods. I assume, simply, that the data can be isolated and set forth clearly after which rational hypotheses can be formulated to account for them. The hypotheses I present are concerned with a variety of other topics, including religion, mythology, language, music, and ritualization among animals. Part IV places the results in a wider perspective and discusses the status of a human science under which they fall.

Ritual and mantras have been studied by textual scholars, anthropologists and scholars of religion. All contribute essential data but none have explained why people engage in ritual activities and chant, recite, or meditate on mantras. Scholars of religion have reacted to unsuccessful positivistic and other reductionist suggestions by advocating self-proclaimed non-scientific methods, like those inspired by philosophical movements such as phenomenology or hermeneutics. These methods describe and interpret, but they do not seek to explain. Among the reasons given for the need of such special methods is the circumstance that man is different from everything else and that man studying himself as a subject is different from man studying anything else as an object. We shall take a closer look at the reasoning that lies behind these assumptions in Part IV.

Promising results, mostly in the area of human language, have been reached in the human sciences without resorting to the use of such unscientific methods. No definite conclusions have been reached in the areas of ritual and mantras, but the reason is that these have not been studied within such a perspective. I believe that a promising point of departure for the study of our topics lies in the human sciences. This belief is not an unshakeable or metaphysical conviction; it is a matter of method, that is, of trial and error. Nor does it imply that we must follow some existing approach within the human sciences. If we place ritual and mantras within the wider domain of human activities and competences, and relate them to other features and characteristics of the human animal, we have gained some insight and perspective and are perhaps on our way to a more adequate understanding.

1

Meanings and Rules in the Human Sciences

In the analysis of ritual and mantras, two concepts play an important part: *meaning* and *rules*. To understand these concepts is not easy since they have been ceaselessly discussed and continue to be controversial in modern philosophy and linguistics. The six chapters of Part I attempt to sketch this two-fold background in an abbreviated and simplified manner. Although this will necessitate some detailed discussion, my only purpose is to explain well-established results that are relevant to the investigation into ritual and mantras. Four topics are of particular relevance and their rough outline will provide some idea of the direction in which the argument will move us.

First, we shall learn that a characterization of the scientific method, first given by philosophers—specifically, empiricists and early positivists—and so widely accepted outside their circles that it is now a common assumption, is a caricature that represents only a few of the methods that scientists actually use. This observation is not confined to meanings and rules, but is pertinent to their study.

Second, we shall see why the home of meaning is language. That is, "meaning" is a concept that applies primarily to certain features of language, and only derivatively, or metaphorically, to other things. Whether we should say that, within the domain of language, meaning pertains to "utterances," "statements", "propositions," "sentences," or something else, is a topic that has been much discussed and is worth discussing; but it is not our problem. We shall see that logicians have related meaning to truth and that philosophers have tried to go beyond this.

Third, we shall learn that "meaning," although primarily linked with expressions of language, need not automatically be a property of all members of that class: for some expressions of language are meaningless.

The first three topics, taken together, may be described as a thumbnail sketch of what is living and what is dead in the much maligned philosophy of positivism.

Fourth, we shall see that the notion of "rule," which is primarily used in logic and linguistics, is basic for the understanding of many human activities, not only in those restricted areas where "the rules *are* the game;" that rules are primarily descriptive and only derivatively prescriptive; and finally, that recent philosophic scepticism with regard to their use and understanding need not be taken too seriously.

Since "meaning" is primarily discussed in philosophy and "rules" in linguistics, I shall start with philosophy and deal with linguistics afterwards. I apologize to the practitioners of both disciplines for they will probably find much that is not to their liking. And much in this account must remain sketchy. My aim, however, is not to provide introductions to philosophy or linguistics, but to give the background needed to prevent misunderstandings of the explorations that follow. The hypotheses I shall formulate are, like all scientific hypotheses, amenable to improvement and modification. They will need to be checked with other data than that I have considered, and be subjected to further conceptual analysis and rational argumentation. My reference to linguistic concepts has led some scholars to characterize my methods as "linguistic." This is misleading for I shall show that neither ritual nor mantras are languages: hence, linguistic methods in the strict sense are unlikely to be helpful. My approach shares with linguistics the recognition that the object of study is concerned with rules and, though profoundly human, is amenable to scientific study.

Finally, a remark about terminology. The English uses of "science" and "scientific" are different from the corresponding uses in German, Dutch, or French. In English, these terms are chiefly applied to the "exact" sciences, that is, the mathematical and natural sciences. In German, *Wissenschaft* expresses an "exact" and yet more flexible concept and the same holds for the Dutch *wetenschap* and the French *science*. None of these European terms exclude the humanities. It is ironic that many American scholars of religion have adopted continental philosophies such as phenomenology and hermeneutics that are critical of science whereas many European scholars of religion continue to refer to their discipline as a science. To use the term "human science" in English may suggest a controversial novelty: an application of scientific methods to the study of the human animal. In other languages, the expression "human science" raises no eyebrows.

2

The Empiricist Caricature of Science

Empiricism may be defined in the words of Thomas Aquinas, who accepted this view and attributed it to Aristotle, as the doctrine that nothing is in the intellect which was not previously in the senses. It is contrasted with rationalism, which may be defined in various ways but always stresses that some knowledge is innate. For Plato, rationalism was connected with certainty: it meant that sense knowledge (because of the changeability of the world of the senses) lacks the certainty that rational knowledge (for example, mathematical knowledge) possesses. For Kant, who tried to combine empiricism and rationalism, all knowledge starts *with* knowledge of the senses but it does not start *from* that knowledge.

If the empiricist doctrine is correct and all knowledge starts *from* the senses, the question arises as to how more general knowledge is acquired. The obvious answer seems to be: through generalization. David Hume seems to have subscribed to this view: according to him, every general hypothesis is a generalization from observed instances. Such a generalization is often referred to as induction. According to John Stuart Mill, even mathematical knowledge, which most philosophers regard as deductive, is based upon induction for it consists of very highly confirmed generalizations from experience. Early positivists, such as Auguste Comte, espoused similar views.

The question whether induction is justified has plagued many philosophers. I am inclined simply to follow Plato's lead and be satisfied that empirical knowledge is never or rarely certain. The exceptions generally contain conceptual terms, regard particulars, or both: for example, "Paris is the capital of France."

Nelson Goodman (1955, Chs. 3 and 4) has argued that induction can never lead to certain knowledge by introducing a predicate *grue* which means "*blue* before time *t* and *green* after time *t*." Now if all topazes found before time *t* were found to be blue, were they *blue* or *grue*? And what about the question: is the next emerald to be examined after time *t*, *grue* or *green*? We cannot give absolutely certain answers to these questions. But we can say this: *grue* is an artificial and far-fetched predicate (Goodman calls it: "less well-entrenched"), and *blue* and *green* are not. Therefore, it is more likely that the topazes were *blue* and that the emerald will be *green*. These answers are probably correct and I find them satisfactory provided we remember that quite a few improbable statements have turned out to be true.

The view that general knowledge arises through generalization from observed instances is untenable. Why did such a view arise at all? To answer this question we have to go back to the beginnings of Western philosophy. The philosophical theories of Plato and Aristotle were based upon a double reflection on the place of man in the universe and the data of contemporary science. The latter comprised in particular mathematics and physics as they were being developed by Greek scientists and by the philosophers themselves. Thus Plato's theory of ideas or forms was related to mathematical notions on the one hand and conceptual analysis on the other. During the Western middle ages, further logical and conceptual precision was gained, but respect for the data of science declined as is shown by the fact that scientific knowledge beyond what was known to the ancient Greeks was rarely taken into account.[1]

This is not an overstatement. It may be illustrated by the relatively simple example of geography. Greek scientific cartography reached its greatest height with Ptolemy (second century C.E.). After Ptolemy, map making was replaced by religious cosmography that had no basis in fact. Only after 1300 did geography begin to develop again. Joseph Needham compared this Western development with the history of geography in China: at first, the Chinese had nothing of the quality of Ptolemy (or even Herodotus or Strabo) at times contemporary with them; but during the gap between the third and thirteenth centuries, when European learning stood still, the Chinese were progressing

Modern philosophy tried to make a new beginning and re-establish its links with science. But the sciences, especially the natural sciences, went their own way and became rapidly independent of philosophy. Descartes and Leibniz were among the last Western philosophers who were creative scientists. After them, adequate knowledge of the mathematical and physical sciences became virtually impossible for any non-specialist to attain. Philosophers remained conversant with the humanities and the history of philosophy for another century or two.

Empiricists and positivists were right in emphasizing that philosophy could not make any progress unless it took into account what knowledge the sciences provided. But they went wrong in two respects: they emphasized only the natural sciences, whose successes had been the most spectacular, and attributed to these the "scientific method of generalization" that was a product of their imagination. This attribution was due to the very gap between philosophy and sciences, the existence of which they decried. Their caricature of the scientific method was widely adopted. Many critics of science—phenomenologists, for example—based their criticism upon it.

The philosopher and scientist Alfred N. Whitehead pointed out that many scientific discoveries result from imaginative speculation that does not begin, but ends with observation. He illustrated this with the discovery of the planet Pluto "in order to avoid the suspicion of biased selection," since Pluto was the most widely publicised recent discovery at the time of his writing (1930: Whitehead 1933, reprint 1942:150). I shall instead discuss the discovery of Neptune which is even more apposite.

Hegel had stated *a priori* that there were seven planets shortly before the eighth, Neptune, was discovered. Legend has it that he reacted to the discovery when it was reported to him by saying: *Umso schlimmer für die Tatsachen* ("so much the worse for the facts"). The discovery of Neptune was connected with the discovery of irregularities in the orbit of the planet Uranus

---

steadily and toward the end of that period were far ahead of the Europeans (Needham 1959, III:512-532; cf. also Staal 1988b).

that led Bessel and other astronomers to postulate the existence of a hypothetical center of gravity by which they could be explained. Two astronomers calculated its probable position: J. C. Adams in Cambridge and U. J. J. Le Verrier in Paris. Challis examined the relevant photographic plates and saw a speck of light in the area of the heavens in which Adams had predicted the planet would be found, but did not recognize the planet. J. G. Galle in Berlin detected it much later (in 1846) at a short distance from where Le Verrier had predicted it would be found. Thus Neptune was discovered.

It is clear that the discovery of Neptune was neither in line with Hegel's pronouncements, nor in accordance with the empiricist and early positivist account of how science works. For if "generalization from experience" were all that astronomers aspired to, they should have been satisfied with the description of the orbit of Uranus and would not postulate centers of gravity elsewhere. True, Uranus' orbit looked irregular from the point of view of a specific scientific expectation, and was a deviation in those terms. But the formula describing it was adequate and elementary. As Whitehead remarked (1952: 153), "there is a motive of unrest which urges scientists beyond mere satisfaction with the simple description, beyond even the *general* description. It is the desire to obtain the *explanatory* description which may justify the speculative extension of Laws, beyond actual, particular instances of observation."

Recently, philosophers of science such as Thomas Kuhn and Paul Feyerabend have argued that scientific discoveries do not take place in any regular fashion. Whitehead already knew that; he stated clearly what Kuhn reiterated and is now widely accepted:

> The advance of any reasonably developed science is twofold. There is the advance of detailed knowledge within the method prescribed by the reigning working hypotheses; and there is the rectification of the working hypothesis dictated by the inadequacies of the current orthodoxy (Whitehead 1942:258).

This view of science is supported by the history of science not only in the West but also in India (see Staal, 1988a). The empiricist-positivist account of scientific method is one-sided, limited, and generally incorrect.

Another widespread error is that science contradicts the "metaphysical" distinction between appearance and reality that Bertrand Russell referred to as "one of the distinctions that cause most trouble in philosophy." He was thinking, probably, of Hegelians such as F. H. Bradley whose "Appearance and Reality" of 1893 was influential in philosophical circles in Britain when he was young. The distinction between appearance and reality, however, is basic to scientific analysis. The most interesting results in science are hypotheses about the existence of entities such as elementary particles or fields that *are not* directly observed but are assumed to be "real" in order to account for "appearances" that *are* observed such as tables, movements and other events that take place in the macroscopic universe.

Squeamishness about unobservables, then, comes not from scientists but from philosophers. Since natural scientists went about their work without paying attention to philosophy, mistaken ideas about scientific method had little effect on them. But these same ideas had a devastating effect on the humanities and the social sciences that were groping for a methodology and therefore paid attention to philosophy. As a result, empiricist and positivist phobias and strictures have prevented progress in these disciplines. We shall examine in this regard Emile Durkheim's account of religious phenomena which does not include mysticism because it was regarded as based upon unobservables. The situation in linguistics at the beginning of the century, and in some parts of psychology even at present, is similarly restrictive. Bloomfield, for example, confined himself to utterances that are observed and defined language as "the totality of utterances that can be made in a speech community," a mistaken view abandoned by the Indian grammarians more than two thousand years ago (Chapter 5). Behaviorism is still favored by many social scientists who are under the impression that it is "scientific." Chomsky observed that a profitable debate on the subject has become difficult: "The behaviorist position is not an arguable matter. It is simply an expression of lack of interest in theory and explanation" (1965: 193 note 1).

The following accounts of ritual and mantras are not restricted by these empiricist and positivist prohibitions; their aim is the opposite, namely, to pave the way for adequate and interesting theories and explanations. That such explanatory machinery may be unobservable is a fact about theory formation. Ritual and mantras can only be accounted for when unobservables are taken into account. Even a description in terms of structures goes beyond the linear concatenation that is observed (Chapter 12). Sometimes the data themselves are unobservable: some mantras are not recited or chanted, but gone through mentally. Priests put down bricks in a specific order which is "in their head." Some rites and recitations can only be adequately described by taking into account *what has been omitted* (Chapters 11C, 27). This is not behaviorism even in the extended sense used by Quine and others which includes "dispositions to behavior."

It is instructive to see what physicists do as distinct from what philosophers say they do. I shall discuss examples taken not from contemporary physics, which may be uncharacteristically imaginative, but from the entrenched areas of classical physics. Georg Joos' "Theoretical Physics" of 1934 introduces electromagnetism in the following terms:

> Two different methods are employed in the theoretical treatment of electrical and magnetic phenomena. The first method starts with macroscopically measurable quantities and describes mathematically the relationships between such quantities found by experiment. An enormous range of phenomena may be brought within the scope of this method in the form of a system of differential equations. The integration of these equations for particular cases then permits us to answer, by rigorous calculation, a large number of questions, including many of technical importance. This method employs only experimental laws and their mathematical consequences; it is therefore entirely free from hypothesis and cannot come into conflict with experience. Since it makes no assumptions whatsoever concerning the structure of electrical charges or

> of matter, we call this the continuum theory, or the field theory. Nevertheless, it was soon recognized, that a large number of very striking phenomena, e.g. those of electrolysis, are entirely left out when this point of view is taken. In order to explain these phenomena, we must make assumptions concerning the structure of matter and of electrical charges. We cannot verify these assumptions by direct observation, but only by testing their consequences. This second method will be called the atomistic method. While the continuum theory will be treated first, we shall nevertheless not attempt to exclude all reference to atomistic concepts; on the contrary, we shall occasionally avail ourselves of a side-glance at the atomistic picture of the phenomena for greater vividness (Joos 1947 reprint:249).

After 200 pages filled with electro-magnetic equations and their discussion, Joos introduces the theory of heat:

> The Theory of Heat, like the Theory of Electricity, may be developed from two different points of view. The phenomenological method employs only concepts like temperature, quantity of heat, &c., which are taken from the macroscopic world of observations and which can be measured directly. The laws thus obtained have the advantage of being free from hypothetical assumptions. On the other hand, in the Theory of Heat, e.g. in connexion with the Law of Entropy, we feel the need of a deeper 'explanation.' Such an explanation, deeper because more vivid, is furnished by the atomistic, statistical view. Here again, as in the electrical case, we find that although we develop the theory separately from the two sides, it will often prove advantageous, while we follow one line of approach, not to shut our eyes completely to the other (Joos 1947: 457).

Joos was a physicist and not a philosopher. He is clear when he deals with equations but careless with regard to words and conceptual issues. For example, he calls "theory of heat" two different things, of which only the second refers to the theory of heat. Similarly unhelpful is his belief that the best justification for theory and hypothesis is "vividness." He places "explanation" within quotation marks that appear to be apologetic. But it is significant that Joos refers to the non-theoretical approach that he describes first, as "phenomenological." This shows how the areas of physics that conform to the requirements of empiricism and positivism which are also those of phenomenology, constitute only a first step and are followed by theoretical and explanatory accounts that do not conform to these strictures. The empiricist, positivist, behaviorist, and phenomenological critiques, by confining themselves to the antechambre, have missed the most interesting areas of the interior.

This assemblage of thinkers has belatedly been joined by "ordinary language" philosophers. They, too, reject the "metaphysical" distinction between appearance and reality, and try to avoid speculation that goes beyond the phenomena. All these philosophers advocate that one should limit oneself to ordinariness, surfaces and appearances. Phenomenologists confine themselves to the world of everyday experience (Husserl's *Lebenswelt*, in French: *le monde vécu*); ordinary language philosophers to ordinary language; both criticize science because it makes use of abstraction, formalization and theory construction. Wittgenstein, for example, after rejecting his own logico-positivistic views in favor of a new ordinary language philosophy, wrote: "And we may not advance any kind of theory. There must not be anything hypothetical in our considerations. We must do away with all *explanation*, and description alone must take its place" (Wittgenstein 1958:47). Historians of philosophy have not failed to note that Wittgenstein agrees with the phenomenologists in their "espousal of description divorced from explanation" (Munson 1962). I have elsewhere discussed this remarkable convergence in contemporary philosophy that is largely due to its alienation from science (Staal 1975: Chapter 4).

In 1961, a meeting at Royaumont brought together representatives from continental phenomenology and Anglo-American analytical philosophy. The proceedings were published in *La philosophie analytique* (Beck, ed., 1962). At that time it was not yet fashionable to try to reconcile and harmonize trends from different philosophical camps (cf. Chapter 30B). Gilbert Ryle remarked that "Husserl always wrote as if he had never met a scientist and never heard a witty remark." Van Breda, the editor of the *Husserliana*, reacted strongly: he did not doubt that Husserl lacked a sense of humor—"I am paid to be aware of it"—but he insisted that Georg Cantor and David Hilbert were among Husserl's most intimate friends and that Max Planck was ringing his doorbell practically every other day. Father van Breda's veracity is beyond dispute, but it puts Husserl's imperviousness to the scientific ideas that surrounded him in an even harsher light.

Among later positivists, the so-called logical positivists remained empiricists but abandoned the extreme insistence on observables. A. J. Ayer, in his *Language, Truth and Logic* of 1936, often regarded as a typically empiricist and positivist manifesto, agreed "with the rationalists that the process by which scientific theories come into being is often deductive rather than inductive" (page 137). Logical positivism, which paid increasing attention to scientific theory and explanation, was brought to Chicago by Rudolf Carnap and influenced American philosophers such as Quine. Its point of departure had been that "scientific" statements must be liable to verification or falsification. Logical positivists first proposed that the meaning of an empirical statement was "the method of its verification or falsification." In the case of the "analytical" statements of logic, truth depends on meaning alone, which implies that they tell us nothing about the world. However, direct "verifiability" was found to be non-existent or impossible in many interesting cases. Karl Popper insisted on "falsifiability", but it soon became clear that a counter-example calls for an explanation, but need not invalidate a theory. Quine holds that it is impossible to clearly demarcate between analytical and empirical statements, that individual statements are not decidable and that our theory as a whole, or all our theories together, "impinge on experience only along the edges" (Quine 1953:42; often elucidated, e.g., Quine 1981:39–40). On such a view there is no clear distinction between truths that depend on meaning and matters of fact, or between natural science, logic and speculative metaphysics. This is a far cry from the original empiricist and early positivist caricature of the so-called scientific method, and probably closer to the truth.

3

The Positivist Critique of Meaning

If centrality admitted of degrees, the problem of meaning might be regarded as the most central problem of contemporary philosophy. It came into prominence when positivism reacted against the more pompous claims and expressions of metaphysical speculation that preceded it. The ancient Greek philosophers provided not only the main themes of Western thought but also a logical terminology by means of which these could be expressed and discussed. For the Greeks, clarity of thought and of language had always been important. Socrates' interest in definitions illustrated these concerns which were further developed by Plato's conceptual analysis and strengthened by Aristotle's logic. These kinds of analysis and especially formal logic were further developed during the Western middle ages, as we have already noted.

The modern philosophers who tried to make a new beginning and to reestablish the links with science, continued to follow the Socratic tradition and pay attention to precision and logic. But formal logic began to decline. With Leibniz as a lone exception, it went downhill and reached a nadir around 1800. By that time philosophers had already lost contact with science; with logic also gone, they began to cultivate ideas of the Romantic period, noted for its interest in art and religion and its dislike of science and logic. Romantic ideas were beneficial to some of the human sciences, especially the slowly burgeoning science of language (Chapter 6). But they also initiated a reign of obscurantism from which we have not yet recovered and in the wake of which contemporary religious romanticism thrives. The greatest among the obscure philosophers, Hegel, could claim that the development of reality was the unfolding of an Absolute Idea without adding precision, clarification or argument; for although its claims were expressed in voluminous publications, these were virtually unintelligible. In Greek philosophy, obscurity had existed, but it remained exceptional. Heraclitus, whom Hegel regarded as an important predecessor, had been singled out for being *σκοτεινός* or "obscure." It took twenty-three centuries, however, for obscurity to become a fashion. Lack of concern for clarity or logic did not prevent Hegel from being influential. On the contrary, it was the main cause of that influence.

The posivitist critique of meaning can be illustrated with the help of almost any sentence written by Hegel. The following passage in his philosophy of religion is more remarkable than many because it incorporates an attempt at "clarification":

> The Jewish God does not attain to the consummation of spirit. 'To attain the consummation of spirit' means precisely that subjectivity should offer itself up as infinite: this absolute antithesis is the outermost extremity of spiritual appearance and negative, infinite return; (that is, it is) subjectivity, and precisely *this* subjectivity; (it is) an individual for the intuiting consciousness (Hegel 1827,III:48; English translation by R.F. Brown, P.C. Hodgson, and J.M. Stewart with the assistance of H.S. Harris, 1985,III:113).

Positivists asked: what meaning do such expressions convey? Sentences cannot be understood in isolation, but that does not imply that no criteria need to be observed for meaning to be conveyed. In the above passage, for example, what is meant by "means precisely"? What is "offer itself up as infinite"? There is declared to be an "absolute antithesis," but of what? How can it "offer itself up as infinite" and also be "infinite return"? That this subjectivity is *this* subjectivity does not add information to its already having been called subjectivity. Even the team of translators (to whom the additions within parentheses are due) have not cleared up these difficulties.

According to the positivists, the kind of criteria needed in order for sentences to convey meaning are similar to the explicit or implicit principles of language that prevent expressions such as "mistakes felt bemuse although" or "(a +) p =." Such expressions convey no meaning because they are not *well-formed*. Hegel's sentences were also lacking in well-formedness, but of a different, semantic kind.

Syntactic well-formedness is a clear concept in the case of the artificial language of mathematics, but it also applies to ordinary language. The expression "(a +) p =" is not well-formed because expressions that contain "+" or "=" are only defined when those symbols occur between two expressions, as in "a + b" or "a = b." The expression "a +" is a fragment that is not well-formed and therefore does not convey meaning. Similar principles or rules account for the fact that "mistakes felt bemuse although" is ungrammatical. Any imaginative person can think of an interpretation for such an expression and poets do not fail to produce them; but unlike an English sentence, this sequence of four words does not possess an interpretation that follows from the structure of English and that any speaker of English will unhesitatingly accept. This lack of meaning is due to obvious circumstances, for example, that most English sentences contain a main verb. Either "felt" or "bemuse" would be suitable candidates, but their juxtaposition, without intervening connective, makes no sense. Similarly, "although" is only used to relate one clause to another, but in the example under discussion there is only one clause.

The expression "spinach wept wet history" is different from "mistakes felt bemuse although" in that it does not seem to be *syntactically* wrong: it has one main verb, a subject, and an object preceded by a qualifier. All is in accordance with the rules of syntax and yet, it does not make any sense. Here the lack of well-formedness is not *syntactic* but *semantic*. It is easy to specify what went wrong in this particular example. The causes lie in the structure of the English vocabulary which abounds in facts such as the following: "spinach" is not an agent but the subject of "wept" must be an agent; "history" is not a physical object but "wet" must qualify such an object.

Critiques of meaningless language are not only found in Western philosophy. The Buddha similarly objected to the question "where does the saint go after death?" which he regarded as "not fitting" and therefore "to be set aside" (*ṭhapanīya*) in the same way as "in which direction has the fire gone after it has gone out?" (*Majjhima-nikāya* 1.483–488). The notion of "non-fitting" or "semantically anomalous" plays an important role in early Buddhist philosophy (see e.g. Jayatilleke 1963). These problems were also formulated in more systematic and positive terms. In Indian theories of language, "semantic compatibility" (*yogyatā*) plays a similar role and is distinguished from "syntactic compatibility" (of different kinds: e.g. *ākāṅkṣā*). Examples given by Indian theorists of expressions that lack semantic compatibility include *anginā siñcati*, "he wets it with fire"; those that lack syntactical compatibility include *gaur aśvaḥ puruṣo hastī* "cow horse man elephant" (see e.g. Kunjunni Raja 1963:157,164–166; Staal 1969 = 1976).

Rudolf Carnap objected to Martin Heidegger's *Nichts nichtet*, "nothing nothings" on kindred grounds. But even if such expressions should be "set aside," it does not follow that the problem they may hint at ceases to exist. For with regard even to such expressions, we are in a position to ask meaningful questions: not merely whether they are well-formed, and how they convey meaning if they do, but also, if they don't, whether they suggest a meaning that can be expressed in a more intelligible manner by other expressions. Conversely, clarity is not enough. There must be something of interest to convey as well. Clarity of expression is a necessary, not a sufficient condition for philosophy and science. Plato, Aristotle, Descartes, Leibniz, Spinoza or Hume did not only offer ideas and theories for discussion but offered them in such clear terms that we are in a position to discuss them. The Greek concern for definitions corresponds to the Indian notion of *sūtra*, developed in order to express meaning clearly, unambiguously and "without embellishment" (Chapters 5 and 26).

The contrast between philosophy on the one hand, and religion or poetry on the other, lies partly in this concern with meaning. The early stages of religion are characterized by the fact that "meaning" is assigned to a variety of entities, e.g., rivers, mountains, trees or the sky. Poetry expresses similar sentiments metaphorically. Ordinary usage preserves such beliefs, semi-seriously, for it is common and normal to talk about "the meaning" of a sunset, life, the universe or man. "Man Makes Sense," the title of a reader in anthropology (Hammel and Simmons 1970), is understandably popular. Following the positivist critique of obscurity, however, most contemporary philosophers accept that meaning is not the kind of commodity that can be assigned to everything; it is primarily, a property of linguistic expressions. This explains the "linguistic" phase in contemporary philosophy and the recent importance of linguistics. This development (which also occurred in India) explains the gap between philosophy and science on the one hand, and religion on the other; for meaning, minimized by the former two, is maximized by the latter.

If "meaning" belongs to expressions of language, it is natural to assume that these expressions *refer* to reality directly and, as it were, "depict" it. Frege had improved the medieval insight that some terms mean without referring. His famous examples are "morning star" and "evening star," expressions with a difference *sense* that *refer* to the same planet. The most precise and powerful theory of reference and truth was developed by Alfred Tarski.

3A. Ludwig Wittgenstein

In his first book, the *Tractatus Logico-Philosophicus* (1922), Wittgenstein stated that the expressions of language are elementary or composite. Elementary expressions describe *atomic facts*, are true when those facts exist, false if they don't, and consist of series of names that directly refer to things. Composite expressions are *truth functions* of elementary expressions, constructed from the latter with the help of logical connectives such as *not*, *and*, and *or*. The truth or falsity of composite expressions is completely determined by the truth functions of the elementary expressions which they comprise. A composite expression which is true independent of the elementary expressions of which it consists (e.g., "*p* or not-*p*," where *p* stands for any expression), is called a tautology. According to Wittgenstein, logic consists of such tautologies, which "do not say anything about the world and thus have no factual content." Logic, therefore, is without reference and, in a sense, meaningless (Naess 1965:16). Since many philosophical expressions cannot be constructed from elementary expressions, their truth value is undetermined and they are therefore meaningless as well. This holds *a fortiori* for statements that claim to refer to the ineffable. For that of which we cannot speak we must remain silent.

Criticism of this account came from different directions. J. L. Austin objected to the thesis that all statements of language must be true or false. Tarski had not made that assumption but Wittgenstein's treatment suggested it. Austin pointed to a fact well known to philologists and students of language, that many utterances of language do not conform to this thesis: questions, commands, expressions of hope and, perhaps, belief, and utterances by which something is not only *said* but also *done*. Austin included among the latter "ceremonial" statements such as salutations or baptizing a ship: when it is called "Queen Elizabeth," it is not given a description which may be characterized as true or false, but a name. Other conventions must hold. The person baptizing must be qualified to do so, unlike a person who says "2 × 2 = 4." "Suppose," says Austin,

> that you are just about to name the ship, you have been appointed to name it, and you are just about to bang the bottle against the stem; but at that very moment some low type comes up, snatches the bottle out of your hand, breaks it on the stem, shouts out 'I name this ship *Generalissimo Stalin*,' and then for good measure kicks away the chocks. Well, we agree of course on several things. We agree that the ship certainly isn't now named the *Generalissimo Stalin*, and we agree that it's an infernal shame . . . (Austin 1961:226–227).

Austin suggested that some of the expressions that are used under such circumstances are not "true" or "false", but "felicitous" or "unfelicitous." The utterances of language which, in saying, *do* something, he dubbed "performative utterances."

Following Smart (1965), Quine has been critical of Austin's notion because Tarski's account works equally well for performatives:

> "I bid you good morning" is true of us on a given occasion if and only if, on that occasion, I bid you good morning. A performative is a notable sort of utterance, I grant; it makes itself true; but then it is true. There are good reasons for contrasting and comparing performatives and statements of fact, but an animus against the truth/false fetish (a reference to Austin 1962:150) is not one of them (Quine 1981:90).

The fiercest critic of Wittgenstein's first book was Wittgenstein himself. In his second book, published thirty years later and entitled *Philosophical Investigations* (1953), Wittgenstein showed that expressions of language rarely consist of names that refer to things. Words have a variety of functions and it is a cause of philosophical confusion to assume that they all function like *names*. Sentences, therefore. do not depict reality in any direct or straightforward fashion. Expressions that are similar in syntactic or *grammatical* structure are often different in semantic or *logical* structure. Wittgenstein attributed to Bertrand Russell the insight that the apparent logical form of proposition need not be its real one. Although such insights were new to philosophers and were heralded as revolutionary, they have never been rare in classical linguistics. The eighteenth century grammarian Du Marsais, for example, showed that "I have an idea" and "I have a book," despite their identical syntactic structure, have different semantic structures, and should not only be interpreted differently, but also in a different manner. When Wittgenstein made his famous declaration that the meaning of a word often lies in its *use* he echoed what the Latin grammarians, and many schoolmasters following them, had always known: *verba valent usu*, "words derive their meaning from their use." The Sanskrit grammarians linked this insight with their criticism of commentators who believed, as many people still do, that the meaning of a word is based upon its etymology; this is incorrect because *yogād rūḍhir balīyaḥ*, "usage is stronger than etymology." The Sanskrit grammarians also distinguished clearly between *logical* and *grammatical* form (see Kiparsky and Staal 1969; now republished in Staal 1988a: 184–281).

These developments explain why philosophy became entangled in questions that resort under a more specialized scientific discipline, namely, linguistics. Western linguistics did not have ready answers to many questions about usage or about the distinction between logical and grammatical structure since it was itself relatively undeveloped and had suffered, as we shall see in Chapter 6, from unnecessary strictures and prohibitions. The question how meaning is expressed in a particular language is not a philosophical question(although it possesses philosophic features and implications), but an empirical question about the "semantics" of that language or about a "universal semantics" that applies to all languages.

The difference between logical and grammatical categories does not coincide with that between semantic and syntactic structures. Syntactic structures often express differences that traditional grammarians would have called "logical." This is illustrated by the following pair of sentences, made famous by Noam Chomsky:

John is eager to please (1)

and

John is easy to please (2)

These two expressions differ with respect to one word; to be precise: the second syllable of a word. This much is apparent when we restrict ourselves to "surface" features. However, once we analyze their structure, we discover a great deal more. In both sentences, "John" is the grammatical subject. But (1) and (2) express meaning in a different manner and have different syntactic structures. In (1), "John" is the logical subject of the sentence, which recurs in related expression such as "John's eagerness to please." In (2), "John" is the logical object, which recurs in "to please John is easy", "it is easy to please John," etc. If we reverse these structures, we obtain ungrammatical results which I shall mark, in linguistic fashion, with the asterisk * :

* "John's easiness to please"
* "to please John is eager"
* "it is eager to please John."

Though these expressions have been obtained by analogous processes, it is not clear what meaning, if any, may be assigned to them. Something similar holds for expressions such as "fearful cream" and "spinach wept wet history," which are syntactically well-formed but semantically unacceptable.

The positivist critique of meaning led to the insight that the meaninglessness of certain metaphysical statements constitutes a special case of the meaninglessness that linguists try to explain in natural languages. The assistance of linguistics is valuable because obscurity is not necessarily a mark of lack of thought or insight. Descartes' first exposition of analytical geometry was extremely obscure and is still very difficult to read even at present when every schoolboy is familiar with the subject. The critique of meaning, therefore, reduces to three parts: obscurity remains undesirable because it obfuscates the distinction between what makes sense and was does not; since sometimes sense turns out to be concealed, everything that is obscure should not immediately be "set aside"; linguistic and semantic analysis is necessary to find out which is which.

3B. Martin Heidegger and Hans-Georg Gadamer

I shall illustrate these observations with a brief discussion of two obscure philosophers; in the first instance, but not in the second, sense can be detected. The first is Martin Heidegger.

When he wrote down the phrase *das Nichts nichtet*, "nothing nothings," to which Carnap, Ayer and others objected, Heidegger was not unaware of the strangeness of the expression. He had already introduced other similar ones into his philosophy. At the end of the Introduction to *Sein und Zeit* of 1927, he wrote that for performing the task he set himself, not merely words were lacking but above all, "grammar:" we need only compare certain passages in Plato's *Parmenides* or in Aristotle's *Metaphysics* with a narrative from Thucydides, to realize to what extraordinary formulations the Greeks were subjected by their philosophers. "And since the forces are essentially weaker, and the area of being that should be unlocked is ontologically much more difficult than what the Greeks had before them, the circumstantiality of concepts and the harshness of expression will accordingly increase" (Heidegger 1953:39).

We should be charitable in accordance with a principle of Quine (uncharitably discussed in Staal 1988a: *Introduction*) and assume that Heidegger tried to convey meaning. Later in *Sein und Zeit*, Heidegger actually makes a proposal that reflects a critical analysis of linguistic usage and is not different in character from the critical observations linguistic philosophers had offered. He argued that it is misleading to ask, with regard to our own being, "What" (is it)? Since our being is always our own and as such unique, we must ask "Who?" This implies that the Aristotelian *categories*, which arose from an analysis of questions of the form "what?", cannot be used. Heidegger therefore introduces a new kind of characterizations of being, which he calls *Existenzialien*, "existentials." In his introductory chapters he tried to clarify the distinction between "existentials," which deal with our own being, and "categories,", which deal with other being. I shall not follow this exercise further, but it is not surprising to find that new expressions, including verbal neologisms such as the *nichten* of "das Nichts nichtet," emerged from it.

Whether it is true that our own being is fundamentally different from other being because it is "always our own," is a topic to which we shall return: for it is related to the doctrine that the humanities (or *Geisteswissenschaften*) are fundamentally different from the natural sciences (*Naturwissenschaften*) and require a different method of study (Chapter 29). As for the new "grammar" that Heidegger needs, it is not far-fetched or prohibited to abandon ordinary language and introduce new languages that use a different grammar. The best examples of such artificial languages are the languages of mathematics. There are various misapprehensions here, however. It is not true, for example, that there is only one such language, and that it deals with "quantity" and not with "quality." On the contrary, mathematical languages come in great variety and if we have specific needs it is often possible to construct an artificial language that meets these needs. Einstein, for example, used the language of "tensor analysis" to express relationships he needed in his general theory of relativity, and which he happened to have studied.

The use of artificial languages is mostly confined to the natural sciences and is largely responsible for their success. The rise of modern science in the sixteenth and seventeenth centuries is due precisely to this application of mathematics to the study of nature (for an interesting discussion of why this did not happen in China, where both mathematics and the natural sciences were highly developed, see Needham 1959:150–168). The application of artificial languages, is not confined to the natural sciences. It has been useful in economics and especially in logic and linguistics. It could be used in logic because it was in some respects based upon Aristotle's categories: the expression *P(x)*, "*x* is *P*," for example, reflects Aristotle's distinction between subject and predicate, as does the notion of a function expressed by "f(x)." In mathematics and physics, this one-place function is generalized to many-place functions such as "$f(x_1, \ldots, x_n)$."

It is likely that an artificial mathematical language could be constructed to express whatever is clear in Heidegger's "existentials." To abstract a notation from verbal notions, use could be made of the λ-operator introduced by the logician Alonzo Church. This operator enables us to abstract a feature from a compound expression, and introduce and employ it elsewhere. Such operators may be used to construct a language that expresses meaning intelligibly in a systematic manner, unlike an isolated expression such as "das Nichts nichtet."

Carnap's criticism of that expression was therefore justified:

for such an expression is helpful and productive only if it is well-formed and functions within the context of a well-defined language. To create such a language is not only common in mathematics or physics. Among philosophers, Aristotle, Leibniz, and even Spinoza, not to mention Peano, Frege, Russell and Whitehead, tried to construct such artificial languages. In Heidegger, the expression Carnap criticized may not be meaningless but remains an isolated curiosity, liable to spread confusion rather than illumination. Heidegger's entire development bears this out: for he never attempted to provide "general accounts" that could be studied within the framework of a general language. On the contrary, he refused to accept any truth that is independent of "human being" (*Dasein*): "the laws of Newton, the principle of noncontradiction, any truth whatsoever is only true as long as *Dasein* is . . . before Newton's laws were discovered, they were not true;" to which he added, curiously (for Heidegger has never evinced sympathy for intuitionism, which exludes the principle of the excluded middle), "that does not however imply that they were false" (Heidegger 1953: 226).

My second example illustrates an obscure philosopher who, however charitably we analyze his expressions, does not seem to yield sense. This takes us closer to contemporary problems for it is concerned with "hermeneutics," a topic that will be discussed later (Chapters 29 and 30 A–B). The exposition of hermeneutics in Gadamer's *Wahrheit und Methode* ("Truth and Method") of 1960 exemplifies meaninglessness better than Hegel, Heidegger, or any other contemporary philosophy with which I am familiar.

Gadamer's "philosophical hermeneutics" combines Heidegger with Husserl's phenomenology and Dilthey's distinction between *Natur-* and *Geisteswissenschaften* to provide a new philosophical foundation for the *Geisteswissenschaften* by means of a theory of interpretation. Gadamer makes a surprising move to begin with: he accepts only one kind of method—that of the natural sciences. He characterizes this method in the same terms as empiricists and positivists have done before him: it is the caricature of scientific method in its pristine form. Gadamer rejects it, good for him; and since it was the only method he recognized; he rejects all method.

This move sounds radical but Gadamer is not the radical type of philosopher we see in Heidegger. Heidegger was radical in style and substance. The difference in style between Gadamer and Heidegger is illustrated by their manner of referring. In Heidegger references are scarce, and limited to Plato, Aristotle, Aquinas ("Thomas von A."), Nietzsche, Husserl, and a few others including increasingly in his later work, the classical German poet Hölderlin (1770–1843) who wrote, for example:

> *Nah ist*
> *und schwer zu fassen der Gott,*
>
> ("Close, and difficult to grasp, is the god.")

These lines (the first of *Patmos*) introduce a being similar to *Dasein*: in *Sein und Zeit*, almost beyond reach, but in Heidegger's later work always already "there" (*da*). This notion resembles the Vedāntic concept of *brahman*, an entity beyond everything that is also identified with my *self*. In Heidegger, we meet not only with references, but also with momentous put-downs, for example, of Descartes, Dilthey or Kierkegaard: "they have not advanced beyond X" is a typical Heideggerian form of critique in which elementary insights that fit the case are substituted for "X". Whatever the force of these criticisms, to be quoted by Heidegger is tantamount to immortality. Awesome and difficult to grasp are the differences of opinion between philosophers thus depicted. When Heidegger differs with Aristotle, his prose takes on the purple glow of a combat between giants, a collision between mountain massifs as in Japanese Sumo.

To be quoted by Gadamer is nothing special. He refers to the *haute burgeoisie* of European, especially German, culture. Great names rank with contributors to *Festschrifte*, and since texts are the primary objects of "hermeneutics," this is not surprising. Hermeneutics had been introduced into textual and historical interpretation by Dilthey (Chapter 29). It plays an important role in Heidegger, but shares its name with Aristotle's small treatise *De Interpretatione*, in Greek: περὶ ἑρμηνείας. Here Aristotle was concerned with topics such as subject and predicate, affirmation and negation, modalities, etc. That the negation of the sentence is the negation of its predicate, is first stated there. This inspired the logical notation Russell and Whitehead introduced in the *Principia Mathematica* that logicians have adopted: for "~(P(x))" is the same as "(~P)(x)" so that it is sufficient to write "~P(x)."

Gadamer's hermeneutics attributes to logic and natural science "unassailable and anonymous authority." As it happens, science, like the number of planets, is not unassailable; it is subject to revision. It is also not anonymous: we speak of "Euclid's Fifth Postulate," "Fermat's Last Theorem," "Planck's constant," and "Einstein's Theory of Relativity." It has no authority at any rate among scientists, who know that it is provisional and never the last word. Having set up his straw man, Gadamer contrasts him with hermeneutics. The latter does not act piecemeal, but "aims at totality," just as learning Serbo-Croatian is more than "going through a dictionary of words."

We shall return to the chief notion of hermeneutical analysis: *Verstehen*, for which "understanding" is too general a translation and "empathy," too narrow. According to Gadamer, *Verstehen* Calvinism is "to be like a Calvinist." He adds that this concept does not exist in the natural sciences. It is true that we are not birds, trees or stars, and most of us are not Calvinists; but we are animals, bodies, objects, substances, and consist of cells, molecules and atoms. Gadamer also stresses that *Verstehen* includes, but science excludes "intuition," "emotion," or "feeling," which, as a matter of fact, play an important role in the discovery or invention of scientific theories although they are not part of the theories themselves. But Gadamer wishes to make the difference between the sciences and humanities as large as possible and in so doing does not hesitate to place the humanities in a light that must seem disturbing to their best practitioners. For on his account, *Verstehen* as applied to a text is arbitrary: "Normative concepts such as the author's intention or the original reader's understanding represent in fact nothing but empty slots, which may be filled with *Verstehen* as the occasion arises" (Gadamer 1965:373).

If *Verstehen* can put meaning in all openings, like putty, we may interpret Gadamer according to our wish. He seems to intend this, for "language is speculative . . . in as far as the finite possibilities of the word are correlated to the intended sense as a trend toward infinity" (page 444). This means, as is seen from the context, that an expression of language does not mean what it says, but points to an infinity of things unsaid. Gadamer restricts this poly-interpretability again in what must be proclaimed the star sentence of his work, "in propositions, the meaning horizon of what is actually to be said is concealed with systematic exactitude" (*ibid.*). This means that a sentence always conveys the opposite of what is says.

Such a scenario brings to mind Aristotle's characterization of the principle of non-contradiction as a principle with which one cannot disagree without accepting it (*Metaphysica* Γ). Either one disagrees with what Gadamer says, in which case one must agree with what he means; or one agrees with what he says by disagreeing with its meaning. One must in all cases agree and disagree, and Gadamer's originality lies in this combination. He has adopted from the positivist-empiricist tradition its most monumental error—the caricature of the scientific method—and failed to heed its most valuable contribution—the critique of meaninglessness. And this philosophy aims at instructing us about interpretation!

4

Linguistic Background

The history of linguistics does not begin in Greece but in India. The proper way to introduce the subject would therefore be to start there and mention the West only when Indian ideas were introduced into European speculations about language. This would conflict with prejudices of long standing, e.g., that science is an exclusively Western development, and be misleading because it would not explain why Indian ideas were so long and consistently misunderstood in the West. I shall therefore begin and proceed in the conventional manner with Western antiquity, turn to India on reaching the stage of Western development when Indian ideas were beginning to be introduced, and return to the West after surveying Indian linguistics. This sketch contributes to the present investigation because we shall later study the Indian science of ritual, which is closely related to Indian linguistics but has no counterpart among Western sciences (Chapter 26).

In Western Antiquity, the Alexandrian school of Dionysius Thrax (around 100 B.C.E.), extended by Apollonius Dyscolus, adopted a conception of grammar in which words were regarded as the smallest functional units of language and were considered indivisible like atoms. The only smaller units which the Greek grammarians recognized were *letters*. They referred to these by means of the Greek term *στοιχεῖον* which is the same as the word for "element" Euclid used in the title of his work on geometry, "The Elements." His commentator, the Neoplatonist Proclus, a metaphysician and mathematician, commented on this similarity:

> Just as an utterance in language consists of first principles that are the most simple and indivisible, and each word λέξις and each speech λόγος is built up from those, similarly there are certain theorems that precede all of geometry, constitute principles for the theorems that follow, extend over all, and provide proofs for many special cases; they are called *elements* (ed. Friedlein, 1873:72).

That the ancient Greek science of grammar did not develop is partly due to the fact that letters are not in any significant sense the elements from which words are constructed. What they do is provide information about spelling. The confusion between grammar and spelling has pervaded European ideas about language for many centuries and is still occasionally to be found. The same holds for the related misconception that grammar is a prescriptive discipline which determines correct usage.

The confusion between grammar and spelling existed on a different level in China, where writing characters has always been a more complex and significant matter than in languages that use an alphabetic system. In the Far East in general, calligraphy occupies a central place in art and civilization. It is a "*Gesamtkunstwerk*" that would have appealed to Richard Wagner if he had been able to appreciate how it integrates painting, sound, meaning and harmony. The Chinese conception of language is permeated by the art of writing as is illustrated by the efforts of Chinese Buddhist monks to understand Sanskrit. They thought that this knowledge consisted in learning how to write and how to pronounce the written language. In Chinese, both tasks are immense, and when one has completed them, one has in the process mastered a language with which one was already familiar to begin with. In Sanskrit, on the other hand, both tasks are simple. Having mastered the Sanskrit alphabet and its pronunciation, the Chinese believed that they knew the language; and when they repeatedly noticed that they did not, they were at a loss to explain why. A curious circumstance supported their assumption: many Sanskrit texts they looked at abounded in mantras that happened to conform to their idea of language. For knowing how to derive the recitation of a mantra from the way it is written is almost all there is to know about it.

In Europe, the concept of grammar of the Alexandrian school "endured with little real change for more than ten centuries" (Robins 1976:18). The Greek grammarians were replaced by Latin grammarians such as Priscian and Donatus, but their outlook and methodology remained the same. A new science of grammar prospered between the twelfth and fifteenth centuries, and inspired theories and philosophies of grammar for a few more centuries. Important innovations were due to the *Modistae*, who constructed grammars in the late thirteenth and early fourteenth centuries in line with logic and semantics or "the mode of signifying" (*modus significandi*; see, e.g., Bursill-Hall 1971). These efforts depended on philosophy, especially Aristotelian categories and logic which had been introduced earlier into medieval philosophy. The notion of "rule" (*regula*) was introduced from logic along with these other notions, but its use remained largely confined to logical rules of deduction such as occur in Aristotelian syllogistics. With the help of this conceptual apparatus, the "grammarians" triumphed over the humanistic schools of the "authors" who had been more textually oriented. But a more scientific and empiricist approach was introduced into Western linguistics only after the discovery of Sanskrit.

New data about language, and a concomitant turn to empiricism, were needed to transform Western ideas about language into a science. The new data arrived, but the resulting empiricism followed Hume and adopted the caricature of scientific method we have reviewed above. If Western scholars of language had adopted the rationalism of the Indian grammarians, which was embodied in their notion of rule, linguistics could have been related to logic and mathematics in a fruitful manner. Instead, Western scholars abandoned logic and concentrated on texts. This limitation, combined with positivism, was fruitful in historical and comparative philology and phonology, but prevented progress in pure linguistics for another two centuries.

At the end of the eighteenth century, Sir William Jones (1746–1794) discovered that Sanskrit, the classical language of India, was related to the languages of Europe. This discovery, and the promulgation of the facts of that relationship, marked the beginning of scientific philology. Facts about Sanskrit and fragments of Sanskrit grammars in Latin had existed earlier, as did scattered information about Indian linguistics. Filippo Sassetti (1540–1588), for example, was impressed by the Indian discovery that different sounds are produced by the various movements of the mouth and the tongue, a fact unknown in the West. Sassetti attributed the large number of sounds in Indian languages to the widespread custom of chewing betel leaves and areca nuts (Staal 1972:30). But such hypotheses were of no significance compared to the birth of "comparative grammar" which was the work of Franz Bopp.

The first European who knew Sanskrit well was Sir Charles Wilkins (1749?–1836), whose "Grammar of the Sanskrita Language" was published in 1808. In that grammar, he used the Indian method of analyzing words into smaller units. Bopp learned this technique from Wilkins' grammar and used it in his "Systems of conjugation in Sanskrit compared with those in the Greek, Latin, Persian and Germanic languages" of 1808. With the help of his Indian techniques, Bopp was able to compare related languages for the first time in a systematic and scientific manner (Thieme 1982/1983:3).

In order to evaluate the Indian contribution to linguistics and the lively controversies that followed its adoption by Western linguists and philosophers, we shall now turn to linguistics in India and return in Chapter 6 to the sequel of linguistic studies in Europe that led to contemporary linguistics.

5

The Origins of Linguistics in India

The origin of linguistics in India is connected with the oral transmission of the Vedas. It is customary in Western anthropology and related disciplines to distinguish between "literate" and "nonliterate" societies, and to regard the former as more advanced and civilized. But in India, there was no system of writing during the Vedic period, and scientific linguistics would not have developed if writing had been known (see below, pages 371–372). In order to safeguard the accurate transmission of the Vedas, the continuous (*saṃhitā*) form of recitation, called *Saṃhitāpāṭha*, which corresponds to the flow of speech in spoken language, was dissolved into its constituent elements and the concomitant modifications were studied. The *sandhi* junctions or euphonic combinations between these elements were analysed. At first, attention went primarily to words (called *pada*) although some stems and endings were discovered and similarly "separated". The "word-for-word" recitation, set up alongside the Saṃhitāpāṭha, was called Padapāṭha.

The Saṃhitāpāṭha and Padapāṭha were related to each other by means of *rules*. That such rules need to be numerous and complex can be imagined from the following example:

SAṂHITĀPĀṬHA: órv aprā ámartyā niváto devỳ udvátaḥ / /
PĀDAPĀṬHA: / ā́ / urú / aprāḥ / ámartyā / ni-vátaḥ /
devī́ / ut-vátaḥ / /
"the immortal goddess has pervaded the wide space,
the depths and the heights."

I shall, by way of illustration, formulate three rules that are needed to express the relationship between these two modes of recitation. I shall not formulate these rules in the same manner in which this was done in India, for this would involve more Sanskritic detail than is needed or wanted in the present context. I shall use instead the expression of a rule by means of an *arrow* adopted in modern linguistics. This can be shown to be equivalent in all relevant respects to the expressions used by the ancient Indian authors (Staal 1965a). A rule which is formulated with the help of such an arrow, for example:

$$A \rightarrow B,$$

may be read as: "replace A by B," or "substitute B for A." I shall use another symbol, the "+" sign expressing *immediate succession* or *concatenation*, without defining it, but its use will be obvious. It should be borne in mind, lastly, that my rendering of these rules makes use of the customary transliteration of Sanskrit into the Roman alphabet which is in some respects different from the exclusively *oral* methods of expression used by the ancient Indians (see Chapter 27).

The first rule may now be formulated as:

$$a + u \rightarrow o. \qquad (1)$$

This rule expresses that the "*o*" of "*orv*" in the Saṃhitāpāṭha is substituted for the combination of "*ā*" and the first "*u*" of "*uru*" in the Padapāṭha.

The second rule explains the "*v*" of "*orv*", but it cannot be simply formulated as:

$$u \rightarrow v,$$

for this would entail that *all* occurrences of "*u*" are replaced by "*v*". This rule applies only when its context is restricted, as in:

$$u \rightarrow v \text{ when } a \text{ follows.} \qquad (2)$$

The third rule similarly explains "*devy*":

$$i \rightarrow y \text{ when } u \text{ follows} \qquad (3)$$

Rules (2) and (3) look similar; they express, in fact, a correspondence that holds in similar circumstances. It may be expressed with the help of a generalization from (2), (3), and other rules in something like the following form:

vowel → *corresponding semi-vowel* when a different vowel follows. (4)

Attached to each of the Vedic schools was a *Prātiśākhya* which aimed at a complete description with the help of rules of the derivation of the Saṃhitāpāṭha from the Padapāṭha of that school. These works studied a few, well-defined grammatical topics such as sandhi and accent, always with reference to a specific corpus, and discussed the notion of rule that developed over the centuries. Rules such as (1), (2) and (3) are common in this literature. But rules of a more general form such as (4) were only beginning to be formulated.

The earliest Padapāṭha, that of the Sāmaveda or Veda of Songs, was composed around 1,000 B.C.E. At roughly the same time, the sentences and verses of the Vedas, especially the Rigveda, were set to music and transformed into mantras for use in ritual. For this purpose, the sounds of the original were not only taken apart and analysed, but also transformed into other sounds. These modifications were also formulated by rules. Some of these conformed to sound correspondences needed or postulated by the grammarians. Other sound transformations had nothing to do with language structure but were necessitated by the requirements of melody. We therefore find linguistically meaningful rules such as those that transform *i* into *e* or *agni*, "fire", into its Vocative case or mode of address: *agne*, as well as linguistically meaningless rules such as those that transform *agni* into melodic forms like *o-gna-i*.

Linguistics was adumbrated in the Prātiśākhyas but originated in the tradition of grammatical analysis of which the oldest extant work is the Sanskrit grammar of Pāṇini (6th or 5th century B.C.E.), generally referred to as the *Aṣṭādhyāyī* or "Eight Chapters." In this work, which consists of almost 4000 brief rules called *sūtra*, the interest has shifted from the fixed corpus of Vedic recitations to the living domain of spoken Sanskrit. The grammar was not prescriptive but descriptive and based upon empirical data: it did not legislate what does or does not belong to Sanskrit, but took the forms of language from usage. Pāṇini's commentator Patañjali (ca. 150 B.C.E.) explained this: when you need pots, you go to a potter; but when you need words, you don't go to a grammarian; you go to the people who speak the language.

When the grammarian is a native speaker (the only case considered in ancient India), the language is always already available to him. If he wants to form the plural of a noun, he does not have to look for it in a recitation or a text; he knows it because he knows his native language. His task is to postulate and formulate rules that account for all the forms he knows and encounters, and for their various uses. A difference between the Prātiśākhyas and the grammars of Pāṇini and the other Indian linguists, therefore, is that the former confined themselves to finite collections of utterances (*uccāraṇa*) such as were transmitted in the Vedas, whereas the latter studied the infinitely many sentences (*vākya*) that make up any living language.

The insight that language is infinite was formulated by Patañjali in a colorful passage that deserves to be quoted in full:

> Now if grammatical expressions are taught, must this be done by the recitation of each particular word for the understanding of grammatical expressions—for example, should we recite the grammatical forms *gauḥ*, "cow," *aśvaḥ*, "horse," *puruṣaḥ*, "man," *hastī*, "elephant," *śakuniḥ*, "kite," *mṛgaḥ*, "deer," *brāhmaṇaḥ*, "brahmin?" No, says the author [that is, Patañjali], this recitation of each particular word is not a means for the understanding of grammatical expressions. For we have a tradition which describes how Bṛhaspati addressed Indra during a thousand divine years going over the grammatical expression by enunciating each particular word, and still did not attain the end. With Bṛhaspati as the professor, Indra as the student, and a thousand divine years as the period of study, the end could not be attained; so what of us at the present day, who when we live in full live at most a hundred years? . . . The recitation of each particular word, therefore, is not a means for the understanding of grammatical expressions. How, then, must grammatical expressions be understood? Some work containing general and particular rules has to be composed (*Mahābhāṣya*, ed. Kielhorn, 5.23–6.3).

This passage refers implicitly to the practice of "enumeration" (*saṃkhyā*) which was adopted in the Prātiśākhya literature and which is characteristic of the least scientific and most popular of the later philosophic systems, accordingly referred to as "Sāṃkhya." But since the forms of language are infinite, they cannot be described by enumeration, but must be characterized in a more systematic and scientific manner, that is, by "general and particular rules" (*sāmānyaviśeṣaval lakṣaṇam*). In this last expression, Patañjali used the term *lakṣaṇa* which is a common synonym for *sūtra* or "rule."

The infinity of language is a feature of language that, in the West, had been known to logicians, but to which the classical or medieval grammarians did not pay attention. A simple example is concatenation by means of a connective such as "and". If "A" and "B" are grammatical expressions, and certain other conditions are also met, "A *and* B" is also a grammatical expression. Thus we can form "fathers and mothers," "fathers and mothers and sisters and brothers," etc. In English there is a rule, applicable to the written form of the language, that replaces all but the first occurrences of "and" by a comma, and other languages have similar devices that may effect changes in expressions of the form "A and B and C and. . . . " But expressions of this latter form have to be postulated in the first place if we wish to explain any others that express concatenation or conjunction.

In Sanskrit, indefinitely large expressions are formed in various ways but the most striking is nominal composition. The collection of animals referred to by Patañjali, that in English could be referred to by the conjunction: "cows, horses, men, elephants, kites, deer and brahmins" is in Sanskrit referred to by a single nominal compound: *gauraśvapuruṣahastīśakunimṛga-brāhmaṇāḥ*, in which the single elements are concatenated in accordance with rules. Pāṇini's grammar describes such rules and many others that account for the infinity of language.

It is sometimes objected that such an explanation is inappropriate because language is not "really" infinite: sentences or other linguistic expressions are not literally infinitely long since the human life span is finite. The point of such an analysis is, however, that it generates a structure for which it is impossible to fix an upper limit or boundary. For any sentence *S*, "He said that *S*" is also a sentence, and this process may be re-iterated indefinitely. The Netherlands constitution is formulated without making use of periods, as an enumeration of hundreds of legal principles separated by semicolons, following the opening phrase: "WE, Beatrix, Queen of the Netherlands, etc., have ordained . . . " followed by several hundred pages of text, formulated in the form of a single sentence. No one has objected to the Netherlands constitution because of this special feature; it is accepted as a meaningful, albeit lengthy, sentence. That in spoken language an upper bound seems to be necessary and may be actually determined is a different matter. It is not a matter of linguistic *competence* but due to limitations of memory and other restrictions that are of a psychological nature and belong to what is today called *performance*. We shall return to this feature (Chapter 21C).

In logic and mathematics, the generation of infinitely many forms by a single, finite rule, has long been known. The kind of rule that effects such an apparent miracle is called *recursive*. Such a rule produces infinitely many forms because it can be applied to its own output. A simple example is:

$$A \rightarrow AB.$$

If this rule is applied to the "A" that occurs on the right, we obtain:

$$(AB)B,$$

and if we re-iterate the process, we obtain, omitting the parentheses:

ABBB, ABBBB, ABBBBB, ABBBBBB, etc.

Pāṇini did not explicitly name or discuss such recursive rules in his grammar but he made use of them in a variety of contexts. His grammar is a device that generates an infinite class of correct expressions of Sanskrit; it is, therefore, what is presently called, following Noam Chomsky, a *generative grammar*.

Pāṇini's grammar analyzed words systematically into smaller

units such as roots, stems, suffixes, prefixes and infixes. Some of the latter were set up for grammatical purposes and attached to forms to indicate that certain grammatical operations had to be applied. Such markers are nowadays called "meta-linguistic" and Pāṇini recognized their special and separate status. The connexions between nouns, verbs and other forms were dealt with in his grammar by systems of relations, the most important of which were "grammatical relations" called *kāraka* that operate on different levels. In this context, the distinction between what we referred to as logical and grammatical relations (page 24), was discovered and analysed.

Adopting a modern terminology, the origin of linguistics in India may be characterized in approximate terms by saying that the phonetic and phonological investigations of the Prātiśākyas, which were piecemeal and *ad hoc*, were extended and the results supplemented with similar investigations pertaining to morphology, syntax and semantics, all combined in a single generative grammar of spoken Sanskrit. The main innovation was a methodology that developed the familiar concept of rule into something more abstract and led to the study of categories of rules, rule systems and rule order. This was possible because Pāṇini's rules were formalized in a manner that corresponds to mathematical formalization in the West. Metarules governed the use of "metalinguistic" markers and explained and facilitated the application and operation of the rules and the order in which they had to be applied. Some of these formulated what appear to be obvious matters, like some of Euclid's axioms and theorems. For example, a metarule stated that the meta-linguistic markers have to be removed from the finally derived forms. An example from English may illustrate this. If we describe the formation of the past tense by introducing a "*suffix -ed*" the past tense of *work* is not:

**worksuffixed*

(where the asterisk "*" denotes ungrammatically), but:

worked.

A general metarule could generate correct results that would otherwise have to be obtained by particular rules of the form:

**worksuffixed → worked.*

Such a metarule would include the linguistically more interesting, but methodologically similar rule:

**dosuffixed → did.*

Since the rules were ordered, an important metarule safeguarded the consistency of the grammar by specifying that "in case of contradiction between two rules, the latter (in the order of rules adopted by the grammar) prevails." Other logical terms and distinctions necessitated by the grammar were also introduced, e.g., the distinction between use and mention and between object-language and meta-language.

In order to give an idea of the use and function of some of these rules and rule-systems I shall discuss a simplified and abbreviated derivation of the Sanskrit sentence:

devadattaḥ pacaty odanam, (5)
"Devadatta is cooking rice"

(see Kiparsky 1982:2 and following; Staal 1982:8–9). The derivation may appear to be arbitrary and *ad hoc*, but that is because it cannot demonstrate the most powerful feature of the system: namely, that methods of analysis that apply to this specific sentence also apply to infinitely many others. Active sentences such as (5) are not more basic than their passive counterparts "rice is being cooked by Devadatta," or related nominalizations such as: "Devadatta, a cooker of rice," "rice, cooked by Devadatta," "the cooking of rice by Devadatta," "Devadatta's cooking of rice," etc. All of these were regarded as alternative realizations of the same underlying structure. In each case, a specific path of rules leads to a specific result. I shall follow one such path.

In order to derive any sentence we have to take account of the leading principle of the *kāraka* system expressed by the metarule 2.3.1: *anabhihite*, "if not (already) expressed." This means that every *kāraka* relation must be expressed by the morphology, but no *kāraka* may be expressed more than once.

The derivation begins by selecting items from the lexicon and deciding on a semantic relation between them. To the nominal items, gender and number are assigned, and to the verbal roots, a time reference. We select *devadatta-* as "independent agent," *odana-* as "agent's principal goal," and for the verbal root *pac-*, reference to "ongoing time." If we had chosen differently, we could derive one of the related expressions mentioned before, e.g., the passive.

The rules will now specify which abstract, "meta-linguistic" or "grammatical" markers have to be attached to the lexical items. These enable us to attach subsequently the "real" nominal and verbal endings, but also entail the application of other rules that are necessary for the correct forms to be obtained. For the active form, an "infix" *SaP* and the ending *tiP* are attached to the verbal root. (In expressing these markers I use capitals, which could not have been done in the grammar of Pāṇini which was orally transmitted and composed: see end of Chapter 27). After the grammatical elements "*S*" and "*P*" have done their job, they are deleted (in accordance with a metarule already referred to) and the form *pacati* is obtained. The "goal" function is expressed by assigning the accusative ending *-am* to the nominal item that bears that function. The "agent" function is expressed by assigning the instrumental ending *-ena* to the nominal bearing that function.

Now the leading principle that nothing is expressed more than once comes into play. In the present derivation, the verb endings have been chosen to express the agent. The goal is therefore not yet expressed, and so it receives the accusative ending *-am*. The agent, however, is already expressed and cannot now be assigned an instrumental ending. The ungrammatical form:

**devadattena pacaty odanam*,
* "by Devadatta is cooking rice"

is thereby correctly blocked. Instead, a rule steps in which assigns the nominative case when only the notion of nominal stem, gender and number remain to be expressed. Applying it to *devadatta-*, the correct form *devadattaḥ* results.

Indian linguistics did not maintain the high level that Pāṇini had introduced. We still find it in Patañjali, three centuries later, for he did not hesitate to criticize Pāṇini when the occasion arose. But he also began to twist the use of Pāṇini's rules to account for new forms that Pāṇini had not known because they had come into being only later in the course of the natural development of Sanskrit. Originally, Pāṇini's grammar was based on the spoken language of his compatriots. In due course, it became prescriptive and came to be looked upon as an arbiter of correct Sanskrit, thus arresting its natural development. By that time the Indian sciences had entered a period of scholasticism which corresponds to some extent to that of the Western Middle Ages.

The notion of rule was permanently introduced into the traditional sciences including philosophy. Its uses and varieties increased and their discussion continued over the centuries. In the thirteenth century C.E., a *sūtra* was defined as "consisting of few syllables, not leading to doubt, containing the essence of a topic, fully expicit, without embellishment and faultless" (cf. Renou 1956:53–59 and 1963). Such a "definition" may provide beginners with a first inkling of the subject, but when it was formulated, sciences dealing with rule-governed activities had existed for almost two thousand years.

6

Contemporary Linguistics and Rules

Chomsky argued in his *Cartesian Linguistics* of 1966, that Descartes introduced into European speculation on language the view that human language does not merely serve a communicative function, but is an instrument for the free expression of thought and for expressing appropriate responses to new situations. Chomsky's thesis has been the subject of a series of important reviews (Harman 1968, Zimmer 1968, Lakoff 1969, Salmon 1969), some of them critical (especially Aarsleff 1970), but its substantial correctness is not now in question. According to Chomsky, the Cartesian emphasis on the creative aspect of language use found its most forceful expression in Wilhelm von Humboldt's attempt to develop a comprehensive theory of general linguistics. Von Humboldt emphasized that the infinity of language is expressed by finite means, and in so doing formulated the theoretical foundation for recursive rules without formulating such rules himself. He played, however, an important role in the reception of Indian ideas that led to the slow birth of linguistics in the West.

The origin of the Western science of linguistics developed from Bopp's adoption of the methods of the Indian grammarians mentioned at the end of Chapter 4. Bopp's work immediately led to a controversy which was, in essence, a discussion about methodology and empiricism. After publishing his comparative grammar, Bopp wrote a Sanskrit grammar, which he dedicated to Wilhelm von Humboldt, and a "Comparative Glossary of Sanskrit." August Wilhelm von Schlegel wrote in a letter to von Humboldt of 1829: "Mr. Bopp certainly has grammatical sense; if only he had studied the Indian grammarians more diligently, if he did not always try to be original when it is inappropriate, he would have been able to do something really good."

The real target of the criticism was Bopp's view that the Indian grammarians had created many forms, "that are not real roots, but are the stems of verbs derived from nouns." By "not real," Bopp meant that these forms are not forms of the Sanskrit language but had been postulated by the grammarians. The majority of scholars dissented. Niels Westergaard, for example, explained in 1841:

> There are many roots we do not know from nouns derived from them, and of which we cannot establish the use from classical passages and books. For this reason there are people who claim that such roots have never existed in the language at all, but have merely been invented—I wouldn't know why—by the grammarians. But such an assertion is astonishing, given the fact that so little is known of Indian literature (in Staal 1973:54).

The methodological discussion between Bopp and Schlegel about the issues of empiricism and postulated elements was overshadowed by the dispute about the value of the study of the Indian grammarians. We have seen that Schlegel defended the need for such study which Bopp had questioned, at least to some extent. The issue about empiricism was better understood by von Humboldt who wrote to Schlegel, also in 1829:

> In one respect, basic to Bopp's view, I differ from him. He regards the roots as grammatical abstracts. But I consider them to be ancient words which disappeared when language became increasingly inflected. I admit that the Indian grammarians, who use them with few exceptions merely as scientific tools, freed them from other sounds or subjected them to other sound changes in order to transform them into pure sources from which the forms of language originate. I am therefore always searching for the appearance of these roots in Asian languages other than Sanskrit, and have discovered something, but not a great deal (in Staal 1973:62).

This passage shows that von Humboldt accepted unattested forms postulated by the Sanskrit grammarians not if they were "abstracted," "scientific tools," but only if they were "real" sources, that is, forms of Sanskrit, or another language, that generate other expressions of the language. It is likely, therefore, that his ideas about the creative use of language were inspired not only by "Cartesian linguistics" and by the general emphasis on creativity that characterizes the Romantic period, but were also influenced by the Sanskrit grammarians' creation of artificial, metalinguistic elements which von Humboldt interpreted as "ideal forms."

During the second half of the nineteenth century the study of Sanskrit began to flourish, first in India and later in Europe. Ramkrishna Gopal Bhandarkar studied the historical development of Sanskrit and determined which stage of its development corresponded to the state of the language described by Pāṇini and other grammarians. Kielhorn, Liebich and others contributed further to this kind of research. But there were also sceptics, although not among specialists of the Indian grammatical tradition. Theodor Benfey, for example, claimed in the *Introduction* to his Vedic grammar of 1874 that the Indians had left us on the one hand (in the Vedas), "the most beautiful language without a grammar based upon it," and on the other hand (in Pāṇini), "the most beautiful grammar without the language upon which it is based." The main proponent of the view that there existed a "grammarians' Sanskrit" which was "a thing of grammatical rule merely, having never had any real existence as a language" was the first important American Sanskritist, William Dwight Whitney (1827–1894).

Whitney emphatically rejected the "reality" of the roots given by the Sanskrit grammarians. In his own *Sanskrit Grammar* (first published in 1879, and still regularly reprinted), he never accepted a root unless he had found it in a text. Needless to say, Whitney's grammar did not follow Pāṇini's grammar, which his *Preface* attacked for its "highly artful and difficult form of about four thousand algebraic-formula-like rules in the statement and arrangement of which brevity alone is had in view, at the cost of distinctness and unambiguousness" (page xi).

The most important contributions by Pāṇini and the Indian grammatical tradition were not the analysis of words into smaller units, the postulation of abstract elements, or the view that language is more than the finite portion or corpus of data that we come across, important as these insights are. Their greatest contribution was the invention of the notion of *rule* that made all these discoveries possible and accounted for other new insights as well. The production and interpretation of infinitely many forms, for example, can only be based upon a finite system of rules. Early in the nineteenth century, von Humboldt had understood the importance of "finite means" by which infinite forms are generated; but he referred to rules only occasionally and did not produce anything like a generative grammar. It took another century-and-a-half before attempts were made to construct such grammars, or fragments of grammars, with the help of rules.

How could Whitney, an excellent Sanskrit scholar who was also the leading American linguist of the second half of the nineteenth century, have missed the central contribution of the Indian grammarians? The reason is that in all his grammatical work, including the *Sanskrit Grammar* of 1879, Whitney was not inspired by Pāṇini but by the empiricism of the Prātiśākhya literature that had been discarded by Pāṇini and his successors. It is therefore misleading to claim that Whitney "did not discredit and slight the old Hindu grammarians because of any lack of acquaintance with them . . . He published not only the Atharva-Veda-Prātiśākhya but also a similar edition of the Taittirīya-Prātiśākhya . . . " (Seymour in Sebeok 1966,I:416). Whitney's studies of the Prātiśākhya literature supports and accounts for his narrow empiricism and explains his adherence to their restrictive scientific method which happened to coincide with the caricature of science we studied in Chapter 2.

That the approach of the Prātiśākhya literature led to Whitney's outlook in linguistics is supported by his own declarations. Whitney checked the completeness of the statements of the Prātiśākhyas with the Vedic corpus they purported to describe and found, to his satisfaction, complete agreement. For example, commenting on the passage of the Taittirīya Prātiśākhya which described the conversion from dental *n* in the *Padapāṭha* to retroflect *ṇ* in the *Saṃhitāpāṭha*, he notes: "I have not discovered in the Saṃhitā any case of a lingual nasal arising in the conversion of the pada text into saṃhitā which is not duly provided for in this chapter" (Whitney 1871:180; cf. also 281). Such observations do not show that Whitney understood the Sanskrit grammarians; on the contrary, they confirm that he did not.

Whitney was very influential, especially in the United States, and the empiricist outlook of twentieth century American linguistics is not intelligible without that influence. In Europe, knowledge of the Indian grammarians remained relatively strong and the Romantic perspective that was beneficial to linguistics continued for some time. Kielhorn's pupil Bruno Liebich, for example, devoted a chapter of his monograph on Pāṇini to Whitney's views and gave a spirited defense of Pāṇini's method. He pointed out that a grammarian, who studies his mother tongue, need not confine himself to forms encountered in texts, for he is in a position to reproduce all possible linguistic forms whenever he needs them *by reflection*—just as a scientist may at any time obtain through experimentation what it would take him a long time to find in nature.

Modern linguistics originated, finally, when de Saussure reacted against the diachronic considerations that characterized historical and comparative philology and phonology, and advocated a synchronistic approach that looked at language as a system. This led to the rediscovery of structures that Pāṇini had discovered two and a half thousand years earlier. De Saussure was not impressed by the Sanskrit grammarians about whom he knew little, because he associated them with the language which was the bulwark from which diachronic philology had developed. But Pāṇini's method had been equally synchronistic as de Saussure's albeit for a different reason: he looked upon Sanskrit as eternal and unchanging. This illustrates in passing how erroneous beliefs may lead to solid scientific achievements.

6A. Noam Chomsky

Building on the vast amount of information that had been collected by historical and comparative phonologists throughout the nineteenth century, Trubetzkoy and Jakobson developed synchronistic phonology which led to Jakobson's discovery of distinctive features, first published in 1938 but "not generally discussed in the professional literature until the 1950s in spite of the fact that Jakobson continued to write about them all through the intervening period" (Halle 1983:85–86). A little later, in the late 1950s, Noam Chomsky began to study grammatical rules systematically and in a principled manner. Chomsky was influenced by Zellig Harris, who attempted formalization although he did not use rules, and was familiar with the uses of rules in logic and mathematics. He discovered later that the notion of a rule as a postulated, hypothetical entity, is closely related to the rationalist conception of human language which had also been the Indian view and the opposite of Whitney's empiricist and Prātiśākhya-inspired thesis that "language in the concrete sense is the sum of words and phrases by which any man expresses his thought" (Whitney 1874:372 in Chomsky 1964:22).

Chomsky noted in the first book for which he became widely known ("Syntactic Structures" of 1957), that the more careful proposals for the development of linguistic theory, due to Bloch, Harris, Hockett, Wells and others, attempted to "construct a grammar of the language directly from the raw data." These attempts were perfect embodiments of Hume's empiricist view in epistemology that every general hypothesis is a generalization from observed instances (above, page 7). Chomsky added: "I think that it is very questionable that this goal is attainable in any interesting way, and I suspect that any attempt to meet it will lead into a maze of more and more elaborate and complex analytical procedures that will fail to provide answers for many important questions about the nature of linguistic structure" (Chomsky 1957:52–53). Chomsky continued to develop generative and transformational grammar and in so doing demonstrated the inadequacies inherent in the empiricist account of scientific method.

In the late fifties, Chomsky, presumably, did not know the work of Pāṇini or the Indian grammarians, and the importance they attached to *rules*. In 1961, he published an article "On the notion 'rule of grammar' " in a volume of symposia in applied mathematics entitled *Structure of Language and Its Mathematical Aspects*. Here he defined and discussed several concepts he had already used in his linguistic work, such as context-free rules, context-sensitive (or context-restrictive) rules, non-recursive, left-recursive, right-recursive, nested dependency, branches, self-embedding nodes, and degrees of self-embedding. Of this battery of concepts, context-sensitive or context-restrictive rules were used by Pāṇini and defined and formulated in essentially the same manner as was done by Chomsky (Staal 1965a; republished, 1988a: 171–180). The rules (2), (3) and (4) (pages 38–9) are context-sensitive rules of this type. Through systematic uses of this array of methods and techniques Chomsky transformed the traditional European speculations about language and the insights of philology, a respectable branch of scholarship, into linguistics and brought this new science to the forefront of contemporary scientific attention.

Chomsky postulated abstract structures and used rules to derive from these first syntactic structures, and subsequently two different levels of representation, one semantic and one phonetic. Among the rules he used the so-called transformational rules became especially known. These rules are somewhat similar to context-sensitive rules, but the context they depend on is larger and more complex. In context-sensitive or context-restrictive rules, the only context that is taken into account is what immediately precedes or follows. This applies, for example, to the "initial vowel" immediately following the element that undergoes substitution in rules (2), (3) and (4).

In the sixties and after, transformational rules were used to account for a large variety of facts in syntax and phonology. They have now been replaced by other mechanisms such as case marking, thematic role assignment, binding of variables, etc.

Whatever their precise form, such mechanisms which involve rules of varying complexity, must account for facts that depend on distant contexts such as pronominalization. In the four English sentences:

> The fact that I hate John does not worry him
> The fact that I hate him does not worry John
> John is not worried that I hate him
> He is not worried that I hate John,

The pronoun "him" in the first three refers to "John," but the pronoun "he" in the fourth does not. Such simple facts known to every user of the language exhibit complex relationships that are now explained by the rules of "binding theory" (Chomsky 1986:164–184). I shall continue to refer to transformations since they can be represented by simple tree-shaped diagrams or "trees," which can also be used to represent ritual structures (Chapters 10–12). To what extent the newer mechanisms apply to ritual structures can be decided when more is known about both.

Some critics argued that transformational rules are simple and ordinary and express relationships of a familiar type that is only to be expected. The philosopher Hilary Putnam claimed that they are "abbreviations," and the linguist Charles Hockett that they are "analogies" (page 438). These criticisms are well taken provided we postulate that these "abbreviations" or "analogies" have all the extraordinary properties that Chomsky had used to define transformations. For there is nothing obvious or natural about transformational rules or any of the newer rules that have taken their place.

Chomsky has emphasized, quite to the contrary, that there is no a priori necessity for human languages to be organized in this complex way. The specific rules and structural properties that characterize phonology and syntax are nontrivial, far from obvious, and restricted by abstract principals of a highly restrictive, complex and intricate kind. Insight in this complexity constitutes one of the most remarkable general results of contemporary linguistics. It demonstrates that the human mind is not the *tabula rasa* that might be expected if the brain were an empty bowl.

With its myriad rules, the *Aṣṭādhyāyī* supports the result that human language is not a simple or trivial device. Pāṇini's grammar is a generative grammar, as we have seen. It is not a transformational grammar but it introduced levels of analysis and distinguished between "deep" or underlying structures and "surface" structures derived from them with the help of rules (Kiparsky and Staal 1969). However, Pāṇini's grammar and the generative grammars or fragments of grammars that have been written in the wake of Chomsky's discoveries—foremost among them, Chomsky and Halle's *Sound Structure of English* of 1968—are so similar in spirit, method, organization and results, that a conclusion follows which goes beyond the achievements of linguistics or any other particular science: namely, that linguistics and therefore science is not a Western invention but a universal discovery of humanity.

6B. Chomsky *versus* Wittgenstein

Rules have also been discussed in contemporary Western philosophy and I shall end this outline with a brief reference to the resulting controversies. Wittgenstein was sceptical about the possibility and the precise meaning of "following a rule." His account of these problems is meandering and confusing, but it starts out clearly. He begins (cf. *Philosophical Investigations* 1953:185) with simple cases, e.g., a pupil is taught to write down a sequence of numbers:

2, 4, 6, 8, 10, 12 . . . .

Wittgenstein asks: how far does the student have to go in order for us to say that he has "understood the rule"? The above numbers may seem to suffice, but only at first sight. Let us suppose we have doubts. We will give him exercises, say, up to 1000. Now we ask him to continue and he writes:

1004, 1008, 1012, 1016, . . .

"We say to him: 'Look what you've done?'—He doesn't understand. We say: 'You were meant to add *two*: look how you began the series?" But he apparently assumed that the rule meant: "Add 2 up to 1000, 4 up to 2000, 6 up to 3000, and so on."

I shall not follow the lengthy discussions which Wittgenstein devoted to such cases and which have led to an extensive discussion in contemporary philosophy. It would be tempting to say that their importance is restricted by the circumstance that Wittgenstein remained, until the end of his life, "a boy doing sums" (the expression is adapted from Anscombe 1959:171). Recently, Wittgenstein's puzzles have been analyzed by Saul Kripke (1982), and this analysis has in turn been discussed by Chomsky (1986). I have no wish to even try to improve upon these admirable interpreters, and just as Chomsky assumed that Kripke's Wittgenstein was the genuine article and referred to him as "Wittgenstein." I shall extend the assumption and refer to Chomsky's Kripke's Wittgenstein as "Wittgenstein." In Chomsky's words, Wittgenstein's "skeptical paradox about rules" is briefly the following:

> Given a rule R, there is no fact about my past experience (including my conscious mental states) that justifies my belief that the next application of R does or does not conform to my intentions. There is, Wittgenstein argues, no fact about me that tells me whether I am following R or R′, which coincides with R in past cases but not future ones. Each application of a rule is 'a leap in the dark.' My application of a rule is 'an unjustified stab in the dark. I apply the rule *blindly*' (Chomsky 1986:225).

What is formulated as if it were Chomsky's chief critique sounds uncharacteristically subdued: "There may be" (with reference to following a rule) "a question as to *how* we do it, but there seems little doubt that we do it. Furthermore, none of this seems to have much if any utility in our lives" (Chomsky 1986: 229). That we follow rules is clear, and Wittgenstein seems only to have argued that we cannot give a clear conceptual account of this. "Utility," however, is not an important consideration in the evaluation of scientific theories. Chomsky's substantial critique is contained in his comment on a simple example:

> At a certain stage of language growth, children characteristically overgeneralize: They say *sleeped* instead of *slept*, *brang* (on the analogy of *sang*) instead of *brought*, and so forth. We have no difficulty in attributing to them rules for formation of past tense, rules that we recognize to be different from our own (Chomsky 1986:227).

This passage shows several things. First of all, the children who use these forms may not know what rules they are following. They may not be aware of them in the same way in which we are aware of them. It is not certain, moreover, that they form *brang* on the analogy of *sang*. But it is the best hypothesis we can come up with and in that respect not different from any scientific hypothesis, only simpler than most. Like all others, it may have to be rejected as soon as we find a better theory.

Now as to our own awareness of what rules we follow ourselves. We are not ordinarily aware of the fact that when we use *slept* we are deviating from a general rule which describes that the past tense in English is formed by affixing the ending *-ed*. Perhaps we were aware of this at first, when we had just realized that *slept* is irregular in this manner. Later we may have forgotten about it although if anyone were to ask us about the rule we are following this is probably what we would say. However, we may be wrong in the same sense with respect to the rule *we* are following as with respect to the rule the children were following. Our guess has the character of a scientific hypothesis, and if a better one is forthcoming, we would accept it. For example, a much more *general* rule may account for the formation of the past tense of verbs such as *sleep* in English.

Wittgenstein demonstrated that we cannot be absolutely certain about a rule that we are following in our more or less unconscious usage of language. However, we can never be certain about unobservables, about the future or the past. The sun is likely to rise to-morrow but then, it might not. Perhaps it did not rise around 1000 B.C.E. on the day that Joshua fought the battle of Jericho when the sun and moon stood still. The uncertainty about rules is not different from the problem of induction and from Nelson Goodman's puzzles already referred to (above, page 8). Measures of probability and certainties of less than 100% are marks of observables and unobservables and, since we cannot be certain, we are entitled to be sceptical. We do the best we can; that is, we look for the most likely hypothesis. As soon as a likelier one than the one we now possess has been found, the one we possess is no longer the most likely and must be rejected. This insight is as old as Plato's *Timaeus*.

Many interesting things may be said about rules and done with them as Pāṇini and Chomsky, among others, have demonstrated. Wittgenstein's scepticism is concerned with our awareness or knowledge of rules; it tells us nothing special about rules. It is anyway not clear what Wittgenstein means by a clear account. In the areas we shall study in Parts II and III, I am involved with rules, but the clearest account I can come up with is often not very clear, which does not imply that we should simply abandon those areas.

Rules are important and interesting because they express regularities. When we come across regularities we postulate rules to account for them. There are similarities and differences in this respect between different areas of experience: in physics, biology and the human sciences. Rules are in some respect like the principles and laws we postulate in the physical sciences to account for observed regularities. One difference is that we may be conscious of applying or following rules. But often we are not, and in those cases we are in a position to guess or postulate.

Since there has been some confusion about "the meaning of rules" I shall end this chapter with some comments on *rules of semantics*. These assign meanings to linguistic expressions and although not too much is known about them, they seem in some respects similar in type to the rules of phonology and syntax. We may ask what is the *meaning* of such rules. But that question is not different from such questions as what the rules say, what their functions and domains of application are, what they effectively do, etc.

How do semantic rules assign meaning? There is no general answer to that question. Different expressions of a language such as English get meanings assigned to them in different ways. A few words refer to things, e.g., the expression "this chair" generally refers to a particular thing (but not in the very sentence I am now typing on the key-board). "A chair," "any chair," "some chair" are different; they seem to be some kind of stand-ins or variables. "The chair" may even refer to a Platonic idea. "Chairs" can do many of these things.

By contrast, "and" never refers to a thing. It is defined in context, or recursively: that is, "A and B" is defined in terms of "A" and "B." Hence we have to postulate a metalinguistic *and*. But even if this analysis seems to apply to the "and" in "John and Mary went for a walk" it does not apply, at least not in the same manner, to the "and" in "John and Mary married." The case of "John and Bill married" is different again, in most states.

"Slept" derives its meaning from "sleep" but it refers to a past event. "In" often expresses situation or locality, and some things Pāṇini said about the locative in Sanskrit apply to "in." But not in such expressions as "in spite of" where the three constituent words contribute to the meaning in a manner that is different from most other words.

A system of rules that assigns meanings to the expressions of a language is therefore a rich and complex system, and need not be less complicated than a branch of astrophysics. The main difference seems to be that, for the time being, the branches of astrophysics have received more attention and nothing exists so far that even comes close to a complete semantics for English. For Sanskrit, we have at least Pāṇini who is surprisingly, though not entirely, complete (cf. Thieme 1982/83:6–9). For English semantics, we have a discussion of many interesting cases in such works as Quine 1960. For English phonology, we have a mine of information in Chomsky and Halle 1968 but even this book is primarily interested in facts that shed light on general linguistic theory and does not discuss irregularities and exceptions.

There are many kinds of rules, and innumerable rules that are postulated to account for the ways meanings are conveyed. But we have learned that not everything in the universe must of necessity have a meaning. We don't ask zoologists about the meaning of elephants. To refer to the meaning of rules is not prohibited but can easily be misleading and confusing, and it is clearer and more helpful to our understanding to say that such rules as we have discussed are without meaning. Another way of saying this is that the logic of "meaning" and the grammar of "meaning" are not the same; and the same holds for "rules." Their being meaning rules implies that they are about meaning but it does not imply that they have meaning. These being cups for drinking implies that we drink from them but it does not imply that we drink them.

Part II

Ritual

Introductory Note

The account of ritual that will be outlined here is based upon the study of a specific type of ritual: Vedic ritual. This raises a number of questions. For example, to what extent does the nature of this particular ritual influence or limit the nature of the theory? I shall revert to these questions later when their answers, given the proper context, will be more easily recognized (see Chapter 30C). However, a related problem should be briefly referred to at the outset. What is ritual? Don't we have to start with a definition of ritual before we can understand it or pave the way for a theory of ritual?

The demand for such a definition seems straightforward and uncontroversial; and yet, it is based upon confusion. "Ritual" is a fashionable term, and many things have been called ritual. The power of Shakespearean drama is called "ritual," curses and dances are regarded as ritual, and in any museum of ancient art, items of which the use or function is not known are dubbed "ritual objects." Jack Goody (1977) has shown that anthropologists have called almost anything ritual. He refers to an author who includes among rituals, "coronations, funerals, Christmas, dances, football, theatre, gymnastics, brass-bands, pop festivals, student demonstrations." Adds Goody: "Include elections, schools, work groups and the rituals of family living, and you have covered much of social life in Britain to-day" (1977: 26). Goody concluded that the term "ritual" is best avoided.

The confusion I referred to does not lie in the uncertainty that surrounds and almost seems to characterize the extension of the concept of "Ritual." The confusion lies in demanding *first*, a definition and assuming that a theory of the defined object can be given only *afterwards*. It is possible that there exist areas of experience where such a relationship between definitions and theories prevails. Examples come to mind from mathematics: having defined a circle, we may ask what its properties are or derive theorems about its relation to other similarly defined figures. In general, however, especially in an empirical science, the situation with regard to an unknown area of experience is different. We have intuitions about what rituals are but we do not precisely *know* what they are. In order to know it we need a theory first, and not the other way round. Different people have different intuitions even though there may be a common core or a family resemblance upon which linguistic usage is based. When we read: "the president's speech was ritual," we vaguely know what is intended here: the president went through the movements of giving a speech because the circumstances required it but did not say anything important or significant. It is not clear that it will be profitable to add all such cases of linguistic usage onto a heap, and seek to extract a definition for what they have in common. My guess is, that they have nothing nontrivial in common, that even a family resemblance is hard to establish and that the definition, if it can be derived, will turn out to be uninteresting. Dictionaries, which use such methods, illustrate this lack of insight. The Concise Oxford Dictionary, for example, defines "ritual" in terms of "rite," and says about "rite": "a religious or solemn observance." What then are we to do?

First of all, we should be led by our intuitions for those are all we have; but they should be based upon familiarity with the area in which we expect to find something. We should not concentrate on borderline or doubtful cases; these can be dealt with later. We will, accordingly, reject most of the cases discussed by Goody: a few people have called these rituals, many have rejected them and we don't know our way about. We should then select some clear and uncontroversial cases about which everybody agrees that they are ritual. For these we should try develop a theory, and this can be done by any means within our power. For theories cannot be "derived" from data as in the caricature of Chapter 2; they are inspired by ideas, musings, and other exercises of the imagination. Once formulated, they should be clear enough to be subjected to tests and experimentation.

If we are unable to develop a theory, this may simply be due to personal limitations; but there may be more interesting reasons. For example, there may not be a single concept to which our intuition refers. For even though we should start with intuitions in an area where nothing else is available, intuitions are not infallible. The concept of "religion," for example, for which most Western languages have a word and for which we possess, accordingly, an "intuition," may not be a universal concept; hence it may not be possible to set up an interesting theory of religion (Chapter 28).

Once we have arrived at a theory which accounts for an area of experience that is generally accepted as falling within the domain of a word—say, "ritual"—we are in a position to check our intuitions and consider the borderline cases. If we find that some are accounted for by our theory, we include them and accept them as rituals; if not, we reject them. For example, if we find that, according to our theory, commencement exercises are rituals, but football matches are not, we are in a position to discuss some advantages and disadvantages of our theory. If the final result is satisfactory and exhibits general features or structures that are interesting and lead to further investigations, insights or predictions, we have reason to be optimistic. Perhaps we can, at that stage, set up a definition of "ritual" that is in accordance with the theory and that enables us, if it is "operational," to recognize whether any object presented to us is or is not a ritual.

Bertrand Russell has summarized this approach to theory formation in simple terms: "Instinct, intuition, or insight is what first leads to the beliefs which subsequent reason confirms or confutes" (1953:19). This implies that definitions do not come in the beginning, but in the end. Definitions, moreover, may be left implicit in a theory: for to explicate them—which is always possible in accordance with a logical theorem due to Evert Beth and generalized by William Craig (see Beth 1959:288–293)—may yield nothing but unmanageable phrases.

So we shall proceed as follows. We will start with Vedic ritual which comprises data of which no one has denied that they come under ritual. There are, moreover, Indian terms which demarcate this domain and distinguish it from other things (e.g., Sanskrit *yajña*). We shall discuss characteristics and properties of Vedic ritual and then sketch a proposal for a theory. Subsequently we shall try to find out whether the proposed hypothesis is applicable to other undoubted rituals, and to things of which some people have claimed that they are rituals, although others have been doubtful. This latter undertaking will be an extensive enterprise, and we shall be concerned only with a first beginning. New data will be needed to test our hypothesis and, if necessary, change or abandon it.

7

Vedic Ritual

More than three thousand years ago, small groups of semi-nomadic peoples crossed the mountain regions that separate Central Asia from Iran and the subcontinent of India. They spoke an Indo-European language, which developed into Vedic, and imported the rudiments of a social and ritual system. Like other speakers of Indo-European languages, they celebrated fire, called Agni, and like their Iranian relatives, they adopted the cult of Soma—a plant, probably hallucinogenic, which grew in the high mountains. The interaction between these Central-Asian adventurers and earlier inhabitants of the Indian subcontinent gave birth to Vedic civilization, named after the four Vedas, oral compositions that have been transmitted by word of mouth to the present day. The Vedas depict Vedic religion, in the words of Louis Renou (1953:29), as "first and foremost a liturgy, and only secondarily a mythological or speculative system."

The four Vedas are directly connected with the ritual they depict because portions of three of them are recited and chanted as part of these ritual performances. The first of these three is the Rigveda, a collection of poems, hymns and invocations reflecting myths, rites, battles and insights of many kinds; its verses are *recited*. The second is the Sāmaveda which consists mostly of parts of the Rigveda set to music; its songs are *chanted*. The Yajurveda consists of verse and prose: both forms are recited in the ritual, the latter being largely devoted to the description and interpretation of its acts. The three Vedas were transmitted orally (Chapters 5 and 27). The fourth or Atharvaveda, in some respects similar to the Rigveda, probably reflects a different stratum of society. It is only distantly related to Vedic ritual.

There are two basic types of Vedic ritual: Śrauta and Gṛhya. The former is generally older and more complex; it is sometimes called "traditional," "public" or "solemn." The latter comprises domestic or life-cycle rites such as the ceremonies performed at birth, initiation, marriage or death. The Śrauta rituals were primarily dedicated to Agni and Soma. Offerings of clarified butter and other vegetable and animal substances, including libations of juice extracted from the stalks of the Soma plant, were poured or thrown into sacrificial fires installed on altars. The recitations and chants that accompany the ceremonies are generally derived from sentences or bits and pieces from the Vedas and are called *mantras*, a term originally used to distinguish the versified sections of the Vedas from the prose passages called *brāhmaṇa*. They will be studied in Part III.

The simplest Śrauta ritual is the Agnihotra, still performed by several hundred brahmins in India. It consists of an oblation of milk offered every morning and evening by a householder with the optional assistance of a priest. Many Śrauta performances required the execution of multifarious activities by up to seventeen priests, each attached by birth to one of the branches or schools into which the Vedas were subdivided. The rites were performed by the priests on behalf of and for the benefit of a *Yajamāna* or "ritual patron," a distinguished personage (sometimes a king). The contribution of each priest or group of priests to each of the Vedic rituals was formulated in precise detail in a manual that belonged to his school. These manuals, the Śrauta Sūtras, composed between approximately the eighth and the fourth centuries B.C.E., are the primary source for our knowledge of Vedic ritual. They will be studied in Chapter 26.

One of the most elaborate Vedic rituals was called Agnicayana, the "piling of Agni." The verbal root *ci-* from which *cayana* is derived means "pile up, arrange, order, construct." During the performance of this ritual, which originated around 1,000 B.C.E., a large altar in the shape of a bird was piled up from more than a thousand bricks in five layers, called *citi* (from the same verb), of approximately two hundred each. The bricks fell into specific groups, had different names and shapes and were each deposited in a specific order and "with a specific mantra," that is, while a specific mantra was recited. It we had to characterize this ritual in terms of its historical origin, we should say that it constituted a purely Indian development, distinguishable in this respect from the cult of Agni which was Indo-European and from the cult of Soma which was Indo-Iranian.

Though Vedic ritual contained popular as well as more exotic or extravagant elements, it was confined to an elite of professionals who spent much of their life learning and preserving its oral tradition. These experts became the brahmins of India. Performances must have been relatively common for at least five centuries, from about 1,000 to 500 B.C.E. Then Vedic ritual began to decline and new cultures and traditions rose to prominence. Though Hinduism and Buddhism are replete with Vedic elements, they belong to another age. "Hinduism" (put between quotes because it is not a single or unitary unit: see below, pages 397–398) continued to look upon the Vedas as its source, formally transmitted by the brahmin members of its highest caste, regarded as an eternal revelation, "of nonhuman origin," and no longer understood. Among later philosophies, the Vedānta or "End of the Vedas," reacted against the ritual and subordinated it to philosophy, but it retained ritual elements and continued to bask in the ancient glory of the Vedas. Buddhism rejected the Vedic heritage, the authority of brahmins and the supremacy of Vedic ritual. In due course it evolved its own hierarchies and ceremonies, incorporating again Vedic rites. Vedic fire ceremonies became part of the Buddhist tradition and were exported all over Asia. The "piling" (*cayana*) of the Vedic fire altar was transformed into the Buddhist *caitya* (from the same root *ci-*) or *stūpa* (Tibetan: *chöten*). Originally a funeral pile, it became the primary cult-symbol of Buddhism throughout Asia.

Fragments and features of Vedic rites survive to the present day in India in the Gṛhya or domestic ceremonies of high caste Hindus, for example, in marriage ceremonies. Performances of the larger Vedic Śrauta rituals were revived several times, e.g., during the Gupta period in North India and during the Chola and Vijayanagara dynasties of the South. However, these extensive rituals are heard of less and less. A text of the eleventh century declared that they were no longer performed.

India, however, is a land of miracles. In Kerala, a distant corner in the southwest of the subcontinent, far away from the original home of Vedic civilization in the northwest, a few families among the isolated and orthodox community of Nambudiri brahmins have maintained their traditional Vedic heritage and continue to perform two Soma rituals: the Agniṣṭoma, or "Praise of Agni," which lasts five days, and the Agnicayana or "Agni," which lasts twelve days and continues through some of the nights whence its other name: Atirātra or "over-night." The Nambudiri performances are not artificial or scholarly reconstructions (as have taken place in some parts of northern India), nor are they the results of recent revivals. As in other parts of southern India, the tradition is authentic and alive. The rituals are performed as they have been learned from teachers, who have learned it from their teachers, and so on. We are able to reconstruct the lineage until we reach the ancient Śrauta Sūtras, from which contemporary performances deviate only in detail, thereby confirming what is also obvious from other sources: namely, that the contemporary tradition is based upon the same tradition as is reflected in these texts.

One such Atirātra-Agnicayana was performed in a small village in Kerala in 1975. For the first time it was attended by outsiders, filmed, photographed, recorded and extensively documented. Robert Gardner and I produced from 20 hours of rough footage a 45-minute film, "Altar of Fire." A more extensive version is presently being prepared in collaboration with Philo Bregstein. With the help of the two chief Nambudiri ritualists, C. V. Somayajipad and Itti Ravi Nambudiri, I prepared a definitive account of the ceremonies as they took place in 1975, illustrated with photographs by Adelaide de Menil. This account was published in two volumes in 1983 under the title: "Agni—The Vedic Ritual of the Fire Altar." This book, which will be referred to as AGNI, contains the empirical data upon which most of the discussions, proposals, hypotheses and theories of the following pages are based.

Vedic ritual is not only the oldest surviving ritual of mankind; it also provides the best source material for a theory of ritual. This is not because it is close to any alleged "original" ritual. Vedic ritual is not primitive and not an *Ur*-ritual. It is sophisticated and already the product of a long development. But it is the largest, most elaborate and (on account of the Sanskrit manuals) best documented among the rituals of man. Hubert and Mauss, who noted these facts in 1899, used the Vedic animal sacrifice as source material for the construction of a ritual paradigm ("un schème abstrait du sacrifice") in their "Essai sur la nature et la fonction du sacrifice." However, they did not know that these rituals are still performed, and many data were inaccessible to them. They also erred in concentrating on *sacrifice*, a term that I shall confine to a ritual in which an animal is ritually killed. But all ritual is not sacrifice. The Vedic Śrauta rituals consist of a hierarchy: *four* basic rituals that involve oblations of milk, rice or barley (the most important of these are the Full- and New-Moon Ceremonies); *one* ritual that involves animal sacrifice; *seven* varieties of Soma rituals; and finally the Agnicayana which incorporates one or more occurrences of most of these others (AGNI I:40–54).

There are other ritual traditions in which animal sacrifice plays a relatively subordinate role. Foremost among these is the Taoist ritual tradition, which vies with the Vedic in its degree of elaboration and complexity and is also equally well documented. Although not as old as the Vedic, it preserves and incorporates earlier ritual traditions of China. It also survives to the present day, in particular in Southern Taiwan where it was discovered and studied by Kristofer Schipper. This tradition is compared with the Vedic in other publications (Schipper and Staal 1988 and forthcoming).

Because of the Indian and Chinese facts, I have adopted the general term "ritual" rather than the more limited notion of "sacrifice." This is in accordance with the prevailing usage in anthropology, at least in most of its English manifestations. Contemporary theorists on ritual from other backgrounds sometimes use the term "sacrifice." Walter Burkert has explained this preference but is aware of its possible limitations:

> Turning to the special problem of sacrifice, and thus limiting the scope of inquiry, let us concentrate on the area of study with which most of us are familiar—namely animal sacrifice in Jewish, Greek and Roman religion, including its sublimation in Christian theology. This does not forbid us to look for similarities and divergences in other cultures, though such evidence will not decisively corroborate or falsify the findings. Whether the sacrifice we choose is a typical or a very special case is another question. I do not wish to contradict Frits Staal's claim that the most promising field for ritual studies is the Indian and Chinese tradition (Hamerton-Kelly 1987:162).

8

The Agnicayana Ritual

Since the Agnicayana-Atirātra will provide us with the bulk of our empirical data, a brief description of this ritual is in order (cf. the "Bird's-eye view of the Agnicayana" in AGNI I:55–58).

The ritual takes place inside an enclosure within which various altars are constructed:

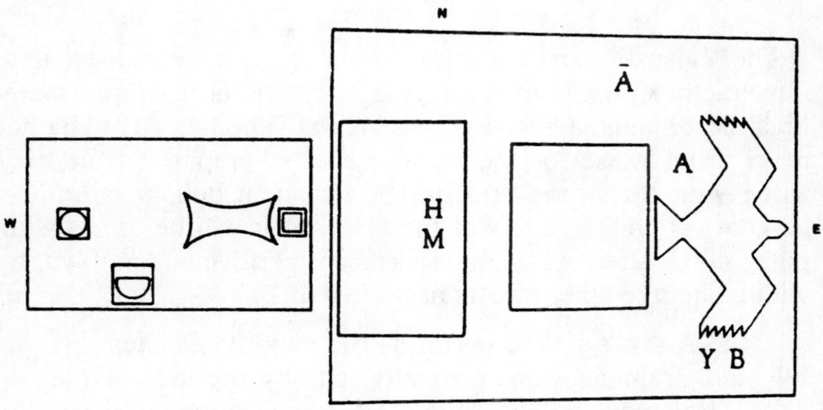

Figure 1
The Ritual Enclosure

The smaller enclosure to the west contains at its western extremity the circular domestic altar on which the domestic fire will be installed and on which the oblations are cooked. At its eastern end is the square offering altar on which the offering fire will be installed: this is the fire in which the oblations are offered.

To the south is the semi-circular southern altar on which the southern fire will be installed.

The larger enclosure to the east, trapezoid in shape, is constructed later; it will be referred to as the Great Altar space. At its eastern end, a new offering altar will be constructed in the shape of a bird with its head facing east. The old offering altar in the western enclosure will now become the new domestic altar, and fire will be carried from the old to the new offering altar and installed there. The two rectangular areas inside the Great Altar space have specific functions: the larger one, to the west, is the hall of recitation; and the smaller one, to the east, is connected with the preparation of Soma and called the Soma hall.

The Agnicayana performance of 1975 took twelve days and the main rites were distributed as follows.

First Day

The Yajamāna and his priests enter the ritual enclosure in an introductory procession, carrying in clay pots the three sacred fires the Yajamāna has kept burning in his home. The ukhā pot, main ritual vessel of the Agnicayana, is prepared from clay, along with the heads of a horse, a man, a bull, a ram and a he-goat, as well as a few of the bricks that will be used for the piling of the alter. An animal sacrifice is performed for Vāyu, the wind. The five chief priests are selected:

the Adhvaryu who performs the majority of rites;
the Brahman who, generally, sits by the side of the Yajamāna, supervising the rites but without participating;
the Hotā who recites from the Rigveda;
the Udgātā who chants from the Sāmaveda;
the Sadasya who is in charge of the hall of recitation.

The priests formally enter the smaller enclosure; this is called *adhyavasāna*. Fire is produced by friction from two pieces of wood. An iṣṭi rite is performed: this rite reflects the basic pattern of the full- and new-moon ceremonies, and is used on various occasions (Chapter 9A). Here it marks the consecration (*dīkṣā*) of the Yajamāna, which follows immediately after it. During his consecration, the Yajamāna crawls onto the skin of a black antelope, a turban is tied around his head, he is given a staff, and he closes his fists. From the consecration on the first day until the final bath on the twelfth day, the Yajamāna should sit on the antelope skin and carry the staff. Neither he nor his wife should go outside the ritual enclosure. The Yajamāna should generally keep his fists closed and refrain from speaking (except for the prescribed recitations), from bathing, sexual intercourse, and certain kinds of food. At the end of the consecration, the Yajamāna picks up the ukhā pot, which is filled with fire, and takes three steps with it. He wears a golden breast plate.

Second Day

The mahāvīra pot is prepared from clay. This vessel will be used during the repeated performances of the Pravargya rite, a pastoral ceremony during which hot milk is prepared and offered to the Aśvin twins, divine young men who ride the wind.

Third Day

A tree is cut and a sacrificial pole is made from it. Animal victims will be tied to it and other rites performed around it. To the east of the old enclosure, in which the three altars have already been made, the measurements of the Great Altar space and of the bird-shaped offering altar are laid out (see Figure 1).

Fourth Day

In the place of the old offering altar, the new domestic altar is piled up from five layers, each consisting of 3 × 7 rectangular bricks. The Adhvaryu consecrates each brick on behalf of the Yajamāna with mantras. The offering fire is installed on the domestic altar and fire from the ukhā pot is added to it. An introductory iṣṭi (*prayāṇīyeṣṭi*) is performed. Outside the enclosure, Soma stalks are bought from a merchant. They are measured, placed on a bullock skin, and transported on a Soma cart. King Soma is installed on a throne to the south of the new domestic = old offering altar, and a guest iṣṭi (*ātithyeṣṭi*) is performed in his honor. The Yajamāna and his priests touch a plate with clarified butter, ceremonially pledging not to harm each other (*tānunāptra*). The Yajamāna and his priests, except the chanters of the Sāmaveda, sprinkle the Soma with mantras; that is, they recite mantras over it which mention the act of sprinkling. The Subrahmaṇya priest of the Sāmaveda recites for the first time his invitation to Indra, king of the gods, other gods and brahmins, urging them to attend the forthcoming Soma pressing on the tenth day. The first Pravargya is performed, followed by a sequence of rites called Upasad, followed in turn by lesser rites including Nihnava or "Hiding Rite" (Frontispiece, pages xv, 85 and 93). The ground is prepared for constructing the new offering altar. It is plowed and seeds are sown. Several items are buried in the ground, including a replica of a tortoise, the ukhā pot, a golden image of a man and the five animals heads. Two hundred bricks, of various shapes and sizes, are placed on the ground in specific order, making up the first layer of the bird altar. A "naturally perforated" or "porous" stone is placed in the center. All bricks are consecrated with mantras by the Adhvaryu on behalf of the Yajamāna. The Pravargya and Upasad ceremonies follow.

Fifth Day

After the morning Pravargya, Upasad, Nihnava, etc., the second layer of 200 bricks is laid and consecrated, followed by the evening Pravargya, Upasad, Nihnava. etc. The shapes and configurations of the bricks have one pattern on the first, third and fifth layer; and another on the second and fourth.

Sixth Day

After the morning Pravargya, Upasad, Nihnava, etc., the third layer is laid and consecrated, with a naturally perforated stone in the center, followed by the evening Pravargya, Upasad, Nihnava, etc.

Seventh Day

After the morning Pravargya Upasad, Nihnava, etc., the fourth layer is laid and consecrated, followed by the evening Pravargya, Upasad, Nihnava, etc.

Eighth Day

After the morning Pravargya etc., the fifth layer is laid with a "naturally perforated" stone in the center. The Yajamāna recites a sequence of mantras which express the wish that the bricks turn into cows. A long, continuous oblation of milk, sesame seed, and other substances is made for Rudra and the Rudras on the westernmost brick of the northern wing of the bird. The Udgātā sings chants around the bird, and a strong man pours a continuous stream of water from a pitcher three times around the altar. The evening Pravargya, Upasad, and Nihnava follow.

Ninth Day

After morning and evening Pravargya, Upasad, and Nihnava, now performed for the last time, the mahāvīra pot and other implements used in the Pravargya are placed on the new offering altar in the shape of a man. Agni fire is carried forth in a pot from the new domestic to the new offering altar and is installed in its center. A long, continuous oblation of clarified butter is made into this new offering fire through a large bamboo ladle. This oblation, called "Flow of Wealth" (*vasor dhārā*), is followed by numerous other offerings and oblations. The hall of recitation is prepared along with its six hearths, each associated with a priest. Now Agni and Soma are carried forth together and the Agnīṣomīya animal sacrifice is performed. The Subrahmaṇya priest, standing between the Yajamāna and his wife, chants his invitation to the Soma pressing for the last time.

Tenth to Twelfth Day

The tenth day is the Soma pressing day, and from now on ceremonies will continue throughout the next two days and nights. After the Hotā's morning recital (*prātaranuvāka*), which starts long before sunrise, the morning pressing of Soma begins and the first Soma oblations are offered. Two chanters, four other priests and the Yajamāna crawl in snakelike procession onto the altar, where they make an oblation into the offering fire. They then move to a place to the north of the altar where three chanters sing their first chant, "the ouside chant for the purified Soma." Numerous rites are performed, many simultaneously, overlapping and/or temporarily interrupted by others. Fires are installed on the hearths in the hall of recitation. Eleven goats are sacrificed.

The priests enter the hall of recitations where the Soma juice is drunk. The Hotā recites his first *śastra* recitation from the Rigveda. Four "Soma sequences" follow, each consisting of a Sāmaveda *stotra* chant, a Rigveda *śastra* recitation, Soma offering and Soma drinking (Chapter 9B). From now on, all recitations and chants, each marked by formal features of considerable complexity, take place in the hall of recitation. Soma offerings are made into the offering fire and the remnants are drunk in the hall of recitation.

At the midday pressing, the Grāvastut priest recites, blindfolded, Rigveda verses in praise of the Soma pressing stones (page 374). Five Soma sequences follow. Then the priests are offered *dakṣinā*, a ritual fee, and the Yajamāna is anointed as in the royal consecration. After the third pressing, another pair of Soma sequences is gone through, then three more, then a single especially mysterious one ("the sixteenth"), three nocturnal rounds of four, and a finale in the early morning of the twelfth day, bringing the total number up to twenty-nine. On this last day, two copious Soma offerings are made for Indra. Ancestral rites are performed as well as expiation rites for errors or omissions that were made or might have been made. The alliance between the Yajamāna and his priests is dissolved (*sakhyavisar-*

jana). The Yajamāna, his wife, and the priests have the final bath (*avabhṛtha*), a concluding iṣṭi (*udayanīyeṣṭi*) is performed and a final goat is sacrificed. This is followed by a departure rite (*udavasāna*). The Yajamāna returns home in ceremonial procession with his wife and the three fires which he installs on his home altars so as to perform the evening and morning Agnihotra rites for the rest of his life as a householder.

9

Basic Rites

Among the numerous ritual sequences that occur repeatedly in the Agnicayana and in other Vedic Śrauta rituals are the Iṣṭi and the Soma sequence. In the preceding section, we have briefly indicated where, in what surroundings and under what circumstances some of these occur. The Iṣṭi is important not only as a structural element but also because its basic manifestation occurs in the Full- and New-Moon Ceremonies. The number and nature of Soma sequences defines the Soma rituals. Because both of these are important structural elements we shall describe the Iṣṭi and Soma sequence in greater detail. They may be called the elements (*στοιχεῖα*) of Vedic ritual (page 33).

9A. The Iṣṭi

The iṣṭi culminates in an offering of rice or barley cakes. The Yajamāna and his wife are assisted by four priests: the Adhvaryu of the Yajurveda who performs the ritual acts; the Hotā who recites from the Ṛigveda; the Brahman who supervises the rites without participating; and the Agnīdhra or "kindler." An iṣṭi is preceded, accompanied and followed by numerous accessory rites, but its basic structure consists in a brief series of acts that follow each other in rapid succession. The subdivision of these acts into elements is fixed, but their numbering and grouping together is to some extent arbitrary. In the following description of the iṣṭi paradigm, six elements are grouped in three episodes of two elements each, which is a natural manner of subdivision:

EPISODE I.
Element 1. The Adhvaryu commands the Hotā to address the deity, e.g., Agni, by saying: "Address Agni!"

Element 2. The Hotā addresses or invites Agni by reciting verses from the Ṛigveda.

EPISODE II.
Element 3. The Adhvaryu exclaims to the Agnīdh: "Make (him) hear!"
Element 4. The Agnīdh shouts: "Be it so! May he hear!"

EPISODE III.
Element 5. The Adhvaryu commands the Hotā to recite his main recitation, the *yājyā* ("offering verse") by saying: "Say the *yājyā* for Agni!"
Element 6. The Hotā begins the *yājyā* by murmuring: "Earth! Air! We who say the *yājyā* . . ." and then recites verses from the Rigveda, ending with the exclamation: "May (Agni) lead (the offerings to the gods)!" At the last syllable, which the Hotā shouts at the top of his voice, the Adhvaryu makes the offering by throwing or pouring it into the fire, and the Yajamāna pronounces his "renunciation": "This is for Agni, not for me!"

Some of the elements or parts of elements in this structure are fixed (e.g., 3, 4, and the exclamation in 6). Others contain variable units, or are themselves variable. In 1 and in the renunciation in 6, the name Agni may be replaced by another, but in the exclamation in 6 it is always Agni who is understood. The verses from the Rigveda in 2 and 6 vary. As a result of these and other variations, there are many different iṣṭis. All have the same structure, but they have different names and address different gods with different verses. The large rituals contain many iṣṭis, which occur either in sequence, or inside other units themselves inserted within the larger rituals.

The structural relations between the six elements in the three episodes can be described in various terms and from various points of view. From the point of view of the Hotā, who recites twice, the structure of the configuration of six elements is:

$$A\ R - B\ C - D\ R'.$$

From the point of view of the Adhvaryu, who issues a command three times, it is:

$$R\ A - R'\ B - R''A'.$$

The iṣṭis constitute the paradigm for one type of ritual performance. Other forms are obtained by extending or modifying the basic form. In the animal sacrifice, for example, there is an additional officiating priest, the Maitrāvaruṇa, and Episode I of the basic structure is extended with one element, as follows:

Element 1. The Adhvaryu commands the Maitrāvaruṇa to command the Hotā to address the deity.
Element 1′. The Maitrāvaruṇa commands the Hotā to address the deity.

The rest is the same.

9B. The Soma Sequence

All the larger Soma rituals are characterized by sequences of rites that I have called "Soma sequences" (AGNI I:49, 54, 599, 608, etc.). Each Soma ritual is defined by a specific number of these sequences. The Agniṣṭoma consists of twelve Soma sequences: five at the morning pressing, five at the midday pressing, and two at the third (or evening) pressing. The Atirātra consists of 29 such sequences. The number is not symbolic, but arrived at by computation: the Atirātra is constructed from the Agniṣṭoma by first modifying some of its twelve Soma sequences; and then adding to them: three, one (the "sixteenth"); three nocturnal rounds of four; and one final sequence. Thus 12 + 3 + 1 + 12 + 1 = 29 (above, page 76).

Each Soma sequence consists of a chant (*stotra*) from the Sāmaveda; a recitation (*śastra*) from the Rigveda; Soma offerings to the deities; and Soma drinking by the Yajamāna and some of his priests. Each of these four episodes consist of several smaller rites and other elements, some of them fixed, and others variable. Here follows a simplified description of the four episodes and their constituent elements:

EPISODE I. CHANT (by three chanters)
Element 1. The Adhvaryu (or his assistant, the Pratiprasthātā, depending on certain circumstances: see AGNI I:625) hands two blades of *darbha* grass to the Udgātā, main chanter of the

Sāmaveda, while reciting: "You are the bed for the coupling of Ṛk and Sāman — for the sake of procreation!"

Element 2. The Adhvaryu or Pratiprasthātā continues with a recitation in which the sound HIṂ, certain gods and chanters occur, and which ends with: "OM! Chant!"

Element 3. The three chanters, facing west, north, and south, intone the chant which begins with HIṂ and consists of three sequences in each of which are triple repetitions of certain lines, depending on which chant it is. This complex pattern is marked with the help of sticks placed on a piece of cloth. Each chant consists of an addition of five pieces, in some of which the original syllables of the verse are "hidden" by lengthened "*o*" 's. Numerous other rules are followed (see AGNI I:602, etc.).

Element 4. Yajamāna and Adhvaryu recite together a piece called "Chant Milking" (*stutadoha*).

EPISODE II. RECITATION (by Hotā, Maitrāvaruṇa, Bṛāhmanācchaṃsin, or Acchāvāka)

Element 1. The Hotā (or one of the other priests) recites a piece called "prior light" (*puroruc*). Without making any pause, in fact, without taking breath, this leads into:

Element 2. The main recitation. This is marked by triple repetition of the first and last verse, taking breath only at certain junctions, etc. There are other insertions by the reciter (e.g., "Let us both recite!") and by the Adhvaryu. The latter, called "salutation" (*pratigara*) are inserted when the reciter produces his lengthened "*o*" 's.—Caland and Henry (1906, I: 232, note 8), generally dauntless, referred to these as "bizarres contorsions liturgiques."

Element 3. The Hotā adds a piece called "Recital Strength" (*ukthavīrya*).

Element 4. Yajamāna and Adhvaryu recite together a piece called "Recitation Milking" (*śastradoha*).

Element 5. The Yajamāna adds another piece, which has no name but which I shall translate for the sake of illustration:

> The ritual has been, has been produced,
> it is born, it has grown,
> it has become king of the gods.
> May it turn us into kings,
> may we be masters of wealth!

EPISODE III. SOMA OFFERING.

This is in some respects like an iṣṭi. It involves an offering, an offering verse (*yājyā*). and ends in the exclamation: "May (Agni) lead (the offerings to the gods)!"

EPISODE IV. SOMA DRINKING

Element 1. Each priest who is about to drink addresses the Adhvaryu with: "Adhvaryu, invite me"

Element 2. The Adhvaryu replies: "You are invited!"

Element 3. The priest drinks and recites from the Rigveda, touching his face and heart at certain points.

Element 4. The Adhvaryu recites a long piece from the Yajurveda, called "Long Drink" (*dīrghabhakṣa*).

This concludes the simplified description of a Soma sequence. Again, some elements are fixed, others are variable, and there is a certain amount of overall variation which it is not necessary to describe in the present context. Some Soma sequences are more complicated than the type outlined here, others are simpler. Some deviate considerably, e.g., the sixteenth (Chapters 17 and 18: (5)).

10

The Structure of Ritual

The description of the Agnicayana in Chapter 8 is considerably abbreviated and simplified; it omits many rites and ceremonies which are less important although we shall mention some of them later. Of the more important ceremonies, only the Iṣṭi and the Soma Sequence have been described in greater detail (in Chapter 9). In AGNI, a fuller description of the entire Agnicayana or Atirātra takes up about 500 pages, and even there, various rites and rituals have been omitted because they had already been described in other works. The summaries in Chapters 8 and 9 should suffice, however, to gain a first understanding of the structure of the ritual.

A cursory inspection of the description shows that some rites occur at the beginning and again at the end of others. For example, the construction of each layer of the altar is "surrounded" by performances of Pravargya and Upasad in the morning and in the evening, as follows:

Pravargya - Upasad - Layer - Pravargya - Upasad. (1)

In the process of this "surrounding," Pravargya and Upasad are regarded as a unit (the Nihnava and other lesser rites are included but I shall disregard them). For if they were considered as two independent rites, the process could be executed in two steps, first surrounding the layering by one rite, and then surrounding the result by another, as in:

(Pravargya - (Upasad - Layer - Upasad) - Pravargya) (2)

Both structures, exemplified by (1) and (2), are frequent, but the second is more common. These same structures are found among recitations. For example, at the beginning and end of each consecration of a layer of the Agnicayana altar, the Adhvaryu recites Taittirīya Saṃhitā 5.7.9.1a followed by Taittirȳa Saṃhitā 5.7.8.1a. The structure is of the same form as (1) and the two recitations, obviously, belong together in that order. We know this without taking the content of the recitations or rites into account; a mere inspection of the structure of (1) suffices. Such an argument is, as we shall see, a *syntactic* argument.

If we refer to the two recitations from the Taittirīya Saṃhitā together as B, and to all the intervening recitations (adding rites, if we wish) as A, we would notice that the recitations called B are the same on each layer, but the sequences of A are different, at least in part. The general structure, however, is always the same and may be expressed as:

B A B. (3)

This accounts for (1) if "B" is interpreted as "Pravargya - Upasad." It accounts for (2) if applied twice, interpreting "B" first as "Upasad" and then as "Pravargya." (3) is recursive and exhibits the feature of self-embedding (page 53). Such structures have long been recognized by students of Vedic ritual although they have not been expressed in this form. Heesterman, for example, describes the *odana* ritual of preparing a rice stew which is subsequently eaten by the priests, and occurs repeatedly: "we find the odana prescribed both at the beginning and at the end of the horse sacrifice" (1983:88). The structure "odana—interval—odana" is again of the form (3).

In all such cases we have an identical element at the beginning and at the end of a rite. There are numerous cases where the activities at the beginning and end of a rite are related to each other but are not identical. Hubert and Mauss (1909) drew attention to some facts that are well known to ritualists, viz., that the final bath (avabhṛtha) at the end corresponds to the consecration (dīkṣā) at the beginning, and the concluding offering (udanīyeṣṭi) similarly corresponds to the introductory offering (prāyaṇīyeṣṭi), the departure (udavasāna) to the entrance (adhyavasāna), the dissolution (sakhyavisarjana) to the alliance (tānūnaptra), and so forth. In all these cases, a large number of rituals intervene between these initial and final rites.

In lesser rites, we often find the same structure. For example, within the Full- and New-Moon Ceremonies, the main oblation (pradhānahoma) is preceded by oblations called ājyabhāga and followed by an oblation called sviṣṭakṛt. The ājyabhāgas are in turn preceded by "fore-offerings" (prayāja) and the sviṣṭakṛt is followed by "after-offerings" (anuyāja). In the Soma sequences, each śastra recitation is preceded by puroruc and followed by ukthavīrya (see Chapter 9B, Episode II: Element 2 occurs between Elements 1 and 3). The puroruc is often preceded by a recitation called āhāva ("Let us both recite!"; omitted in Chapter 9B because it does not occur in all cases), and the ukthavīrya is followed by śastradoha (Element 4). Similarly, there are recitations preceding and following each stotra chant (Elements 2 and 4 surround 3 in Episode I). These examples can be extended almost indefinitely.

A moment's reflection will show that numerous simple human activities are of the same form. If a rite takes place within an enclosure, the priest performing the rite has first to enter the enclosure, and after completing it, leave. Similarly, when going to a concert, one first goes to the concert hall, which is followed by entering the building, listening, leaving, and returning, in that order. In ritual, such structures are repeated and extended indefinitely.

As in this nonritual example, both the main oblation of an iṣṭi and the śastra recitation function as a center for two pairs of initial and final acts. The sequence in which the two initial rites or recitations occur is reversed or mirrored in the two final rites or recitations—as in (2), above page 85. This general structure is found on many levels and can be applied to units of various sizes. Let us represent five initial rites by $A_1, \ldots, A_5$. They occur in the following order at the beginning of the Agnicayana:

A_1 introductory procession
A_2 adhyavasāna
A_3 dīkṣā

A_4 prāyaṇīyeṣṭi
A_5 tānūnaptra

Now let us denote each corresponding final rite by the same symbol, adding an asterisk, as follows:

A_1^* return home
A_2^* udavasāna
A_3^* avabhṛtha
A_4^* udayanīyeṣṭi
A_5^* sakhyavisarjana

The order in which these rites are gone through is the following:

$$A_1A_2A_3A_4A_5 \ldots A_5^*A_3^*A_4^*A_2^*A_1^*$$

This suggests a tendency, not quite successful, to establish the regular "mirror-image" pattern, viz.:

$$A_1A_2A_3A_4A_5 \ldots A_5^*A_4^*A_3^*A_2^*A_1^*$$

All these nesting or self-embedding structures can be represented by recursive rules of the following form:

$$B \rightarrow ABA \tag{4}$$

This generates structures *AABAA*, *AAABAAA*, *AAAABAAAA*, . . . by applying the rule again and again to its own output.

The occurrence of such *recursive* rules, viz., rules that generate infinitely many structures by applying and reapplying finite mechanisms (in our case, one single operation) is significant, for it shows that the ritual can be extended indefinitely. The Indian theorists were aware of this. The ritualists constructed rituals of indefinitely increasing complexity, the sattra rituals. These rituals are often purely theoretical, but this does not diminish their significance as both actual and possible rituals exhibit ritual structure. Hillebrandt did not take these theoretical rituals seriously: "Diejenigen Sattra's, welche länger als zwölf Jahre dauern, heissen mahāsattra's . . . und hier versteigt sich Mythus und Phantasie der Yājñika's zu den sechsunddreisigjährigen Opfern der Sāktya's, den hundertjährigen der Sādhya's, den tausendjährigen der Viśvasṛj" (Hillebrandt 1897:158). The Indian grammarian Patañjali, on the other hand, took these rituals quite seriously, because he detected in them the same recursiveness that governs the structure of language. When discussing the infinity of language, which grammar must describe by finite means (cf. page 40), Patañjali refers to these sattra rituals: "There are indeed linguistic expressions which are never used. . . . Even though they are not used, they have of necessity to be laid down by rules, just like protracted *sattras*" (*santi vai śabdā aprayuktāḥ . . . yady apy aprayuktā avasyaṃ dīrghasattravallakṣaṇenānuvidheyāḥ*; *Mahābhāṣya*, Kielhorn, ed., I: 8,23; 9,15).

11

Embedding and Transformation

The indefinite complexity of Vedic ritual is not due solely to the recursive rule (4) we have just reviewed, but primarily to two others. The first of these may be called *inserting* or *embedding*. Structure (4) illustrates the special case of *self-embedding*, as we have seen. The general case of embedding is most easily illustrated when different rituals are compared with each other. We have seen, for example, that the number of Soma sequences in the Atirātra-Agnicayana is twenty-nine, a number that is reached by adding sequences to the original two of the third pressing (Chapter 8, tenth to twelfth day).

I shall discuss three further examples of such embeddings: the first are the kindling verses (*sāmidhenī*), verses from the Rigveda recited by the Hotā when the firewood sticks are placed upon the altar; the second, rituals that are embedded in the Agniṣṭoma and help transform it into the Agnicayana; and the third, the construction of the twenty-ninth or final śastra from the Hotā's morning recital on the tenth day.

11A. The Kindling Verses

During the Full- and New-Moon Ceremonies, sticks of firewood (*samidh*) are placed upon the altar by the Adhvaryu. This act is accompanied by the recitation of kindling verses (*sāmidhenī*) by the Hotā. There are eleven such verses, all from the Rigveda. During the animal sacrifice, two verses are added. During the animal sacrifice for Vāyu on the first day of the Agnicayana (above, Chapter 8), the Śrauta Sūtra of Baudhāyana prescribed 24 verses which are obtained by adding another eleven, some from the Rigveda and some from the Taittirīya

Saṃhitā of the Yajurveda. During the 1975 performance of the Agnicayana, however, only the 13 verses of the ordinary animal sacrifice were recited. This is in accordance with Śānkhāyana Śrauta Sūtra (9.23) but constituted one of the first differences between the 1975 performance and Baudhāyana Śrauta Sūtra.

These differences in number illustrate the structure of *insertion* or *embedding* (from AGNI I:311):

THE SĀMIDHENĪ VERSES

	Full- and new-moon ceremonies	Animal sacrifice and 1975 Vāyavyaṃ Paśu	Vāyavyaṃ Paśu according to Baudhāyana
	RV 3.27.1	RV 3.27.1	RV 3.27.1
	RV 6.16.10–12	RV 6.16.10–12	RV 6.16.10–12
	RV 3.27.13–15	RV 3.27.13–15	RV 3.27.13–15
	RV 1.21.1	RV 1.21.1	RV 1.21.1
	RV 3.27.4	RV 3.27.4–6	RV 3.27.4
			TS 4.1.7.1a–4i
			RV 3.27.5–6
			TS 2.6.11.1a
	RV 5.28.5–6	RV 5.28.5–6	RV 5.28.5–6
			TS 4.1.7.4 k
TOTAL	11	13	24

TABLE 1

11B. From Agniṣṭoma to Agnicayana

Among the rituals that are embedded in the Agniṣṭoma and help transform it into the Agnicayana, the most important ones are: measurement of the Agnikṣetra, the "field of Agni" on which the bird-shaped altar will be constructed; construction of the new domestic altar; and setting up of the Agnikṣetra.

In general, the first two of these rituals take place on the third and fourth day, respectively, prior to the introductory offering or *prāyanīyeṣṭi*. The third ritual is performed on the fourth day after the Pravargya, Upasad, Nihnava and Subrahmaṇyā recitation.

In 1975, the menses of the wife of the Yajamāna began on April 13, scheduled on the second day of the ritual. The rites of the third and fourth ritual day, planned for April 14–15, could not be executed because of the ensuing pollution; expiatory rites were performed instead. Some of the ceremonies of the third and fourth ritual days were combined and performed on April 16. As a result, ceremonies that, in the Agniṣṭoma, are performed consecutively, but that are not consecutive in the Agnicayana, were also performed consecutively on April 16, 1975, but this time as a consequence of the menses of the wife of the Yajamāna. The resulting structures are illustrated in Table 2 (from AGNI I:386):

SEQUENCE OF RITES ON THE THIRD AND FOURTH DAYS

I AGNIṢṬOMA	II AGNICAYANA	III April 16, 1975
	Measurement of Mahāvedi(3)	
	Measurement of Agnikṣetra(3)	
	Construction of New Domestic Altar (4)	*Construction of New Domestic Altar*
Introductory Offering (2)	Introductory Offering (4)	Introductory Offering
Purchase of Soma (2)	Purchase of Soma (4)	Purchase of Soma
Guest Offering (2)	Guest Offering (4)	Guest Offering
Pravargya, Upasad, and Subrahmaṇyā(2)	Pravargya, Upasad, and Subrahmaṇyā(4)	Pravargya, Upasad, and Subrahmaṇyā
Measurement of Mahāvedi (3)		Measurement of Mahāvedi
		Measurement of Agnikṣetra
Preparation of Uttaravedi (3)	*Setting up Agnikṣetra* (4)	*Setting up Agnikṣetra*

TABLE 2

In Table 2, rites specific to the Agnicayana have been italicized and the ritual days are put in parentheses.

These structures exemplify embedding and illustrate in passing that each actual performance of a ritual may be different—an obvious fact that does not affect but exhibits the underlying ritual structure. This confounded Richard Schechner, a Professor of Performance Studies, who argued that the 1975 performance of the Agnicayana was significantly different from all the others that had preceded it (see Schechner 1986, 1987; cf. Staal 1987) instead of recognizing that each performance is a different event and yet exhibits the same ritual competence (Chapter 21).

11C. The Final Śastra for the Aśvin Twins

The twenty-ninth or final śastra recitation of the Agnicayana, dedicated to the Aśvin twins, is recited by the Hotā before sunrise on the final day and consists of a thousand mantras. It is a tour de force not only because of the length of the recital but also because of its complexity. Its demands on the powers of memory are extraordinary and we shall return to this topic (Chapter 27; AGNI I:683–686; Staal 1986b). It is referred to here in order to illustrate that there are cases where *embedding* and *inserting* are supplemented by *omitting*. In general, omitting is merely the reverse of inserting: just as the Agnicayana can be thought of as arising from the Agniṣṭoma by inserting, the Agniṣṭoma can be thought of as arising from the Agnicayana by omitting. However, in the case of the twenty-ninth śastra only the combined operation of inserting and omitting can explain the proceedings.

11D. Conclusions

All the insertions we have discussed operate at different levels, and apply to large as well as small units. Insertions are made into other insertions, and here their recursive character becomes apparent. If we take a closer look at these insertions within insertions, we shall find another type of recursive rule that contributes to the indefinite complexity of the Vedic ritual: transformational rules.

Let us start with the Animal Sacrifice for Vāyu. Call it *B*. It is inserted in the Agnicayana after the Ritual Preparation of the Ukhā Pots (*A*) and before the Election of the Priests (*C*). The ritual rule that effects this insertion may therefore be written as:

$$AC \rightarrow ABC \tag{5}$$

Now let us consider the internal structure of the Animal Sacrifice (*B*). Confining our attention to the Sāmidhenī verses, which I shall call *E*, it consists of various rites preceding these verses, which may be lumped together and referred to as *D*, and various rites following them, together referred to as *F*. Thus the Animal Sacrifice *B* may be represented by *DEF*,

$$B \rightarrow DEF \tag{6}$$

In an Animal Sacrifice, there are thirteen Sāmidhenī verses, as we have seen; the *E* in (6), therefore, consists of thirteen such verses. We also know, however, that the Animal Sacrifice for Vāyu, which occurs in the Agnicayana, should contain (according to Baudhāyana) twenty-four Sāmidihenī verses. This group, which may be called *G*, arises from *E* by inserting another eleven mantras, i.e., by an insertion similar to the insertion represented by (5). It would not be appropriate, however, to express this insertion by a rule of the form:

$$E \rightarrow G \tag{7}$$

This would indicate that in *all* Animal Sacrifices there are twenty-four Sāmidihenī verses. We have to express that *E* is replaced by *G* only in the Animal Sacrifice that is embedded in the Agnicayana. In other words, we must restrict the context, or the configuration in which *E* occurs and which conditions its replacement by *G*. The simplest way to do this is by a rule of the form:

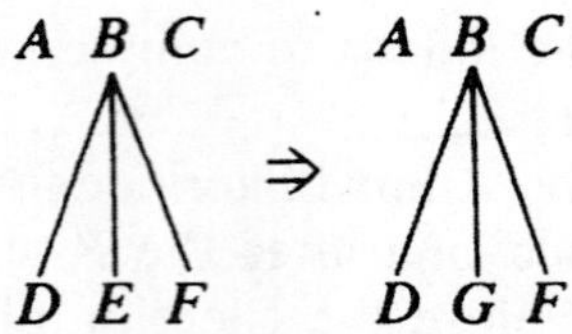

(8)

This rule is formulated with the help of a double arrow to distinguish it from the rules with single arrows such as (5)–(7). Rules of the form (8) are identical with the *transformations* of linguistics (Chapter 6A).

Transformational structures are typical of Vedic ritual, and it is easy to provide other examples. Let *A* denote ceremonies preceding the consecration, *B* the consecration, and *C* ceremonies following the consecration. The prototype of *B* in the Agniṣṭoma consists of a sequence of rites, beginning with the consecration iṣṭi (dīkṣanīyeṣṭi), that will be referred to as *D*. This is followed by the ceremonies with the antelope skin, the mekhalā rope, the turban, and so forth (*F*). In the Agnicayana, between *D* and *F* new rites are inserted relating to the ukhā pot, in which fire originates (*G*). In other words, a rule of the form (9) applies:

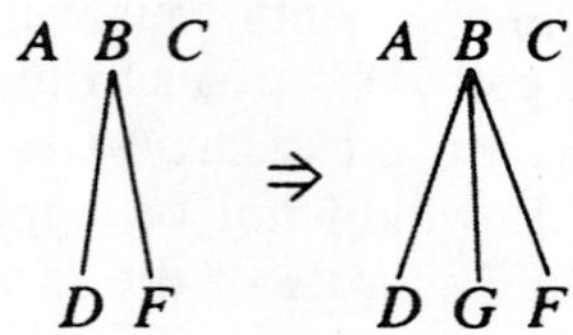

(9)

Actually, *D* itself is also transformed. It is replaced by a new rite called agnidīkṣanīyeṣṭi, or *D**. A transformation must apply that is of the form:

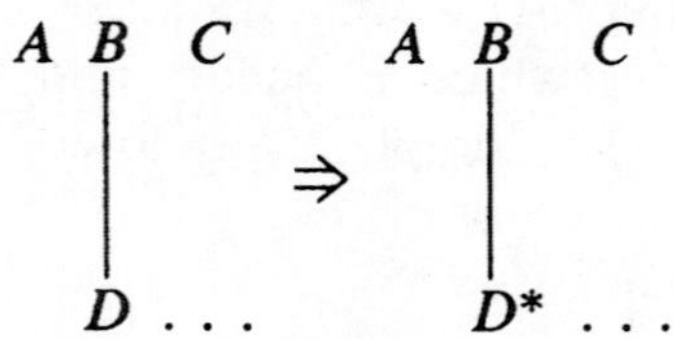

(10)

Another example is the Carrying Forth of Agni (agnipraṇayana; *B*). It follows oblations to Viśvakarman on the domestic altar (*A*) and is followed by Adhvara oblations on the offering altar (*C*). The prototype of the Carrying Forth in the Agniṣṭoma consists of the transportation of the fire by the Adhvaryu, recitations by him and by the Hotā, and chants by the Prastotā (*D*). Afterwards the fire is installed on the altar (*F*). In the Agnicayana, another recital is inserted, viz., the recitation by the Second Hotā or Maitrāvaruṇa of the Song to the Irresistible Warrior. If this is referred to as *G*, the expression (8) expresses the structure again adequately, but it should be understood that *DGF* does not represent a simple sequence of three rites, but a combination in which some of the rites overlap or are simultaneous.

In the Final Bath (avabhṛtha) there is also the insertion of a new rite, characterized by the recitation of Taittirīya Saṃhitā 4.6.2.6 r. This can be described by a structure of the form (9).

In these transformations the context is specified on the left and on the right; in other words, both the following and the preceding ceremonies are specified. Sometimes it is more natural to leave one side unspecified, or to regard it as empty. We might refer to this as the prefixing, suffixing, or mere "adding" of rites. For example, in the Full and New Moon Ceremonies the Formulas of Completion (samiṣṭayajus; *A*) consist of two mantras, Taittirīya Samhitā 1.1.13.3 u-v. In the Animal Sacrifice, *A* follows the final oblations (*C*) and precedes the burying of the heart-spit (*D*). But in this sacrifice the two formulas *A* are replaced by three (A^*), or:

$$C\ A\ D \rightarrow C\ A^*\ D \qquad (11)$$

In the Agniṣṭoma the context is specified differently, as C^* . . . D^*, and another nine formulas (*B*) are added:

$$C^*\ A^*\ D^* \ \Rightarrow\ C^*\ \underset{\overbrace{A^*\ \ B}}{A^*}\ D^* \qquad (12)$$

In the Agnicayana in a context *C*** . . . *D***, another nineteen mantras (*E*) are added:

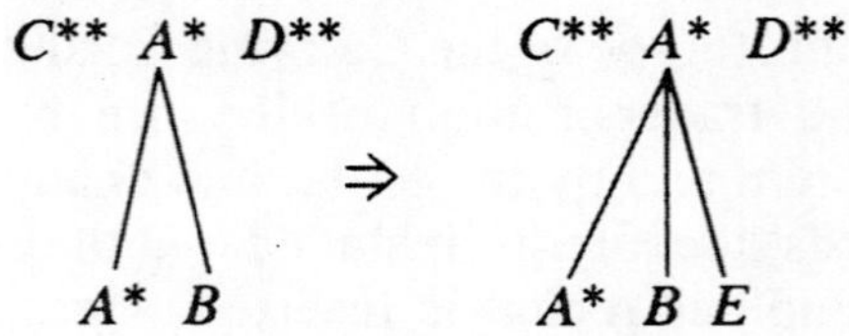

(13)

Such sequences of mantras can be extended indefinitely.

What is the significance of these structures? They show that an apparently empiricist and purely behaviorist description of the sequence of acts of the Agnicayana, *A*, *B*, *C*, *D*, . . . , as if they had a linear structure (14), is inadequate:

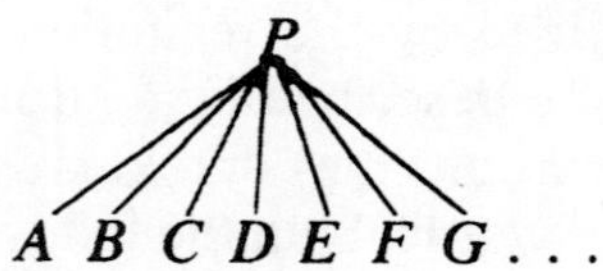

(14)

Underlying the sequence *A*, *B*, *C*, . . . there is in fact a hierarchical structure arrived at through the reiterated operation of embeddings and transformations, viz., something of the form:

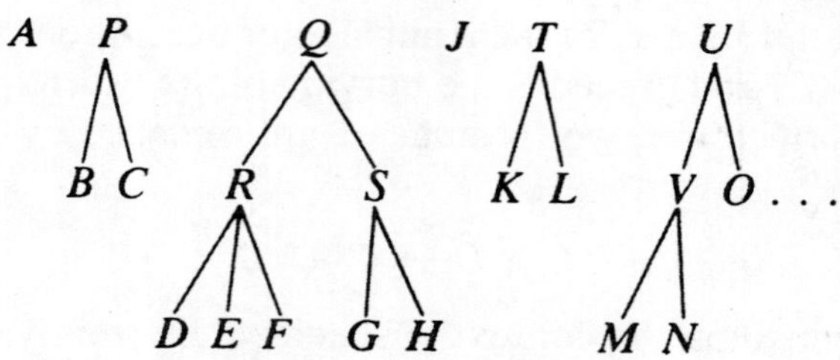

(15)

In the description of the performance in AGNI I we have implicitly accepted that it has a structure of the form (15). This idea underlies the subdivision into episodes and smaller units, described in varying detail, and the references to prototypes of the iṣṭi, the Agniṣṭoma, and other components. For example, we have not described rites such as *B* as merely "following" *A*, which corresponds to the structure expressed by (14). Rather, we have described *B* as the first rite of a ritual *P*, which corresponds to the structure expressed by (15). Thus, the agnidīkṣaṇīyeṣṭi is not described as merely following the rites in the previous chapter of AGNI ("Episode 3": pages 313–317), but as constituting the first rite of the next, the consecration ("Episode 4": pages 317–333).

12

Ritual and Grammar

Indian ritualists have always stressed the hierarchical structure of the ritual, as have Willem Caland and other Western scholars. The Śrauta Sūtras describe the main rituals in a particular order. I have mentioned several of these, but shall now single out four and refer to them by capital letters:

D: Darśapūrṇamāsa
P: Paśubandha
A: Agniṣṭoma
C: Agnicayana.

This sequence is hierarchical. There is increasing complexity. A person is in general only eligible to perform a later ritual in the sequence, if he has already performed the earlier ones. Each later ritual presupposes the former and incorporates one or more occurrences of one or more of the former rituals. Sometimes these embedded rituals are abbreviated. In general, they undergo modification. I shall single out three embeddings:

> In *P*, performances of *D* are embedded when a cake of eight potsherds is offered to Agni and when a cake of eleven potsherds is offered to Agni-Viṣṇu;
>
> In *A*, two performances of *P* (*agnīṣomīyapaśu* and *savanīyapaśu*) and several performances of *D* (e.g., *dīkṣaṇīyeṣṭi*, *prāyaṇīyeṣṭi*, *avabhṛtheṣṭi*, *udayanīyeṣṭi*, *udavasānīyeṣṭi*, not to mention performances of *D* embedded in *P*) are embedded;
>
> In *C*, a performance of *A*, fourteen performances of *P* and numerous performances of *D*, some of which already embedded in *A* and *P*, are embedded.

Chapter 11 has provided an idea of the syntax of these structures. I shall now describe that structure in more general and abstract terms, abstracting from the specific structures we have met before and constructing a *model* of ritual—a formal representation corresponding to what Hubert and Mauss called a "schème abstrait du sacrifice." In order to make this precise, a series of artificial assumptions will be made, redefining *D*, *P* and *A*. The reason for these artificial assumptions and definitions is that they constitute a model which exhibits abstract ritual structures. The model is identical with respect to these structures to the actually existing rituals, but *is less elaborate than the latter*. It may look more complex because it is formal; but it can only be represented in this formalized form because it is, in fact, simpler. Actually existing rituals can be analysed in the same manner as the model with regard to the structures in which I am here interested, but such an analysis would, again, be much more complex.

Such a procedure is common in science but as yet, if we except linguistics, rare in the human sciences. It is also easily misunderstood. Hans Penner (1985), for example, criticized my formalizations of syntactic analysis when they were first published (1979a) by emphasizing that, by my own admission, they "do not correspond to any existing ritual" or "to any actual ritual." I responded (1986a:41): "Rather, they correspond, if they are adequate, to features that are *abstracted* from actually existing rites, just as the laws of physics do not correspond to specific events that take place in my garden, but to features *abstracted* from such events." At the time of writing I had not read Quine's much more succinct answer to similar criticism: "To complain of bare bones is like criticizing the physicist for failing to capture the richness of the rain forest" (Quine 1981: 186).

But enough of mere words. Let us assume that there is an Agniṣṭoma *A* in which three occurrences of *D* and two occurrences of *P* are embedded. In each *P*, furthermore, two occurrences of *D* are embedded. Let us fix the order by assuming that in the performance of *A*, there is first a performance of D_1, then of P_1, then of D_4, then of P_2 and finally of D_7. In P_1, let there be occurrences of D_2 and D_3 and in P_2, of D_5 and D_6, in that order. Next we assume that each *ritual* consists of a sequence of *rites*. We shall adopt the convention, that each ritual marked by a capital letter (such as *A, D, P*) will consist of rites denoted by small letters, indexed with single numerals if the governing ritual is not indexed with a numeral (e.g., $a_1, a_2, \ldots; d_1, d_2, \ldots$), and indexed with double numerals if the governing ritual is already indexed with a numeral (e.g., ritual D_3 will consist of rites d_{31}, $d_{32}, \ldots$; P_2 of $P_{21}, P_{22}, \ldots$). Now we can give a precise description of *A* if we know the exact number and order of these constituent rites. Let us assume that ritual *D* always consists of three rites. Let us assume that *P* always consists of nine rites. Since these include the rites of *D*, a simple assumption would have the rites of *P* which are not rites of *D* at the beginning, in the middle and at the end; and the rites of the two occurrences of *D* in between the beginning and the middle, and the middle and the end. For *A*, we assume a sequence of thirty-three rites including the rites of *P*. A simple assumption would again be that, within *A*, the rituals *P* and *D* are always separated by a single rite *a*.

A *linear* description of Agniṣṭoma model *A* will now look like this:

$$a_1\ d_{11}\ d_{12}\ d_{13}\ a_2\ p_{11}\ d_{21}\ d_{22}\ d_{23}\ p_{12}\ d_{31}\ d_{32}\ d_{33}\ p_{13}\ a_3\ d_{41}\ d_{42}\ d_{43}\ a_4\ p_{21}\ d_{51}\ d_{52}\ d_{53}\ p_{22}\ d_{61}\ d_{62}\ d_{63}\ p_{23}\ a_5\ d_{71}\ d_{72}\ d_{73}\ a_6. \quad (16)$$

It should be apparent that not only the artificial model *A* can be represented by such a sequence of rites, but that the real Agniṣṭoma can also be represented by such a sequence of rites — only a longer sequence. In addition we would need more letters, more indices, and longer indices. What are the advantages of such a representation? The answer is: none. A *linear* representation of this type is not only extremely cumbersome, but it obscures all the elements of structure we have been so eager to detect.

At this stage it should be noted that most of the modern descriptions of Vedic ritual are basically *linear* representations of precisely this type. This verdict is exaggerated, because Caland & Henry refer back to Schwab and Hillebrandt, Schwab refers back to Hillebrandt, etc. The verdict is even less applicable to the *Śrautakośa*, which adopts a type of description which is closer to that of the Śrauta Sūtras. But to the extent that all these works deviate from the Śrauta Sūtras, their deviation is in the direction of linear description. Precisely for this reason these works obscure the structures it has been our aim to make explicit.

How then do we arrive at a representation which reveals these structures? This can only be done by adopting a non-linear method of description. We can arrive at such a description by gradually transforming the representation (16). I shall first replace (16) by a series of expressions in which each ritual is rewritten (which will be symbolized by a single arrow) as a sequence of rites and rituals, as follows:

$$A \rightarrow a_1\ D_1\ a_2\ P_1\ a_3\ D_4\ a_4\ P_2\ a_5\ D_7\ a_6$$
$$P_1 \rightarrow p_{11}\ D_2\ p_{12}\ D_3\ p_{13}$$
$$P_2 \rightarrow p_{21}\ D_5\ p_{22}\ D_6\ p_{23}$$
$$D_1 \rightarrow d_{11}\ d_{12}\ d_{13}$$
$$D_2 \rightarrow d_{21}\ d_{22}\ d_{23}$$
$$D_3 \rightarrow d_{31}\ d_{32}\ d_{33}$$
$$D_4 \rightarrow d_{41}\ d_{42}\ d_{43}$$
$$D_5 \rightarrow d_{51}\ d_{52}\ d_{53}, \text{ etc.}$$

In these expressions there is still a great deal of repetition and redundance. In order to eliminate this, we simply delete all indices of rituals, and omit the first numeral of indices with double numerals. The result is:

$$A \rightarrow a_1\ D\ a_2\ P\ a_3\ D\ a_4\ P\ a_5\ D\ a_6 \tag{17}$$

$$P \rightarrow p_1\ D\ p_2\ D\ p_3 \tag{18}$$

$$D \rightarrow d_1\ d_2\ d_3 \tag{19}$$

At this point we have arrived at a representation of model *A* which clearly exhibits the underlying structure and is as perspicuous as the material allows. The reader can verify that the assumptions we made when constructing A are expressed by (17)–(19).

An equivalent representation of this same information can be given with the help of trees:

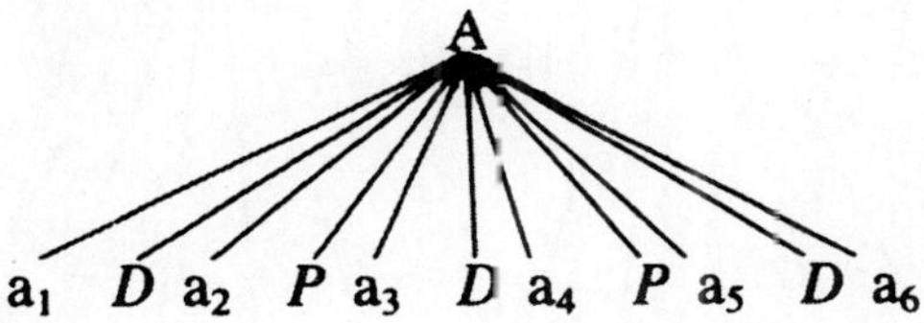

(17′)

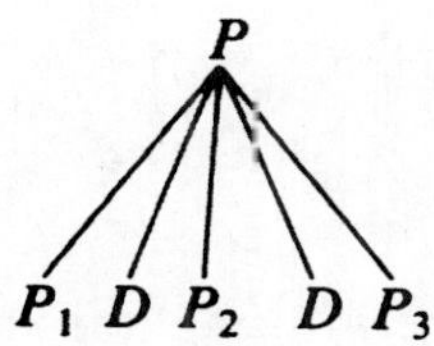

(18′)

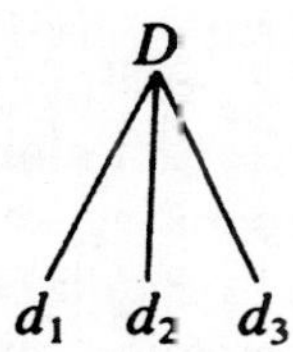

(19′)

The embedding of P and D in A, and of D in P, is represented in (20): see next page.

The structure of (20) can also be expressed by making use of parentheses:

$$A \rightarrow a_1\ (d_1\ d_2\ d_3)a_2\ (p_1\ (d_1\ d_2\ d_3)p_2\ (d_1\ d_2\ d_3\ )p_3)a_3\ (d_1\ d_2\ d_3)$$

$$a_4\ (p_1\ (d_1\ d_2\ d_3)p_2\ (d_1\ d_2\ d_3)p_3)a_5\ (d_1\ d_2\ d_3)a_6. \qquad (20')$$

At this stage it may be noted that representations of the form (17)–(19) are basically equivalent to the organization of the material adopted by the authors of the Śrauta Sūtras. A Śrauta

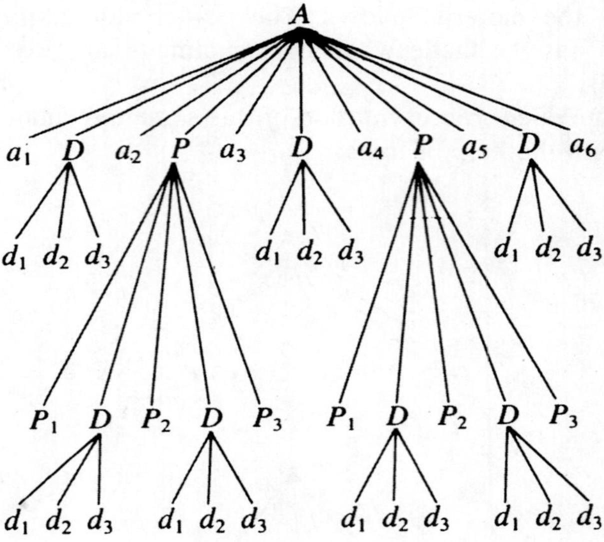

(20)

Sūtra would convey the information as follows. First it would have a section in which D is described as $d_1\ d_2\ d_3$—corresponding to (19). The next section, corresponding to (18), would provide the description of P, referring to D whenever it occurs, but without repeating the information given in the first section. The next section, corresponding to (17), would provide the description of A, referring to P and D whenever they occur, but without repeating the information given in the earlier sections. Only the modifications which the rituals undergo when they are embedded, are always specified.

How can we handle these modifications? Let us try to represent the one example which I gave before. We introduce this into our model by assuming that in ritual D, the first rite, d_1, represents the recitation of *fifteen* samidhenī verses. Let us further assume that in the second occurrence of D in P, rite d_1 has to be replaced by a rite d_1^*, in which *seventeen* samidhenī verses are recited. We cannot simply represent this transformation by adding an expression:

$d_1 \rightarrow d_1^*$ (corresponding to (7) in Chapter 11D, page 95), for the effect of this would be that *all* occurrences of d_1 are replaced by occurrences of d_1^*. What we must do is, replace by d_1^* only the d_1 in the second occurrence of D in P. This can be done by introducing a transformational rule using a different symbol instead of the single arrow $\rightarrow$, for example a double arrow $\Rightarrow$. We have to represent the entire configuration in which d_1 occurs since it is not otherwise possible to single out the d_1 we wish to single out. This can be done as follows:

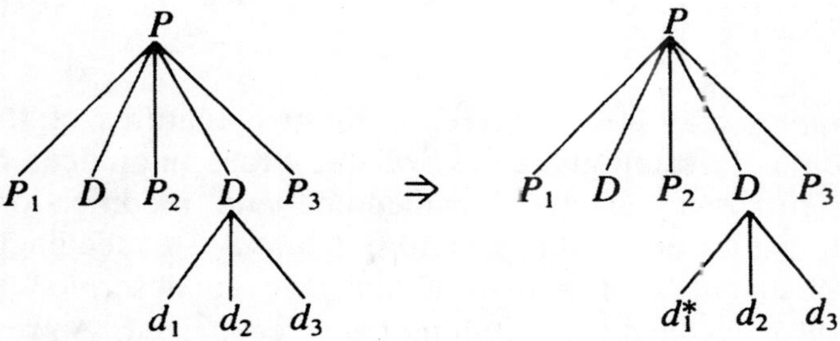

(21)

Another example of this kind of transformation is the following. When I wrote that A and fourteen occurrences of P are embedded in C, I was simplifying. Actually, A and two occurrences of P are embedded in C. Two occurrences of P are embedded in A. But in the occurrence of A which is embedded in C, the second occurrence of P is modified: it involves the sacrifice of eleven goats instead of one.

To represent this, we start with the following two expressions (in which irrelevant rituals and rites are represented by dots):

$$C \rightarrow \ldots P \ldots A \ldots P \ldots$$
$$A \rightarrow \ldots P \ldots P \ldots$$

Here P is the animal sacrifice of one goat. Now let us write P^* for the ritual which involves eleven goats. Then, abstracting from all the other modifications which A undergoes when it is embedded in C, the required transformation can be represented as follows:

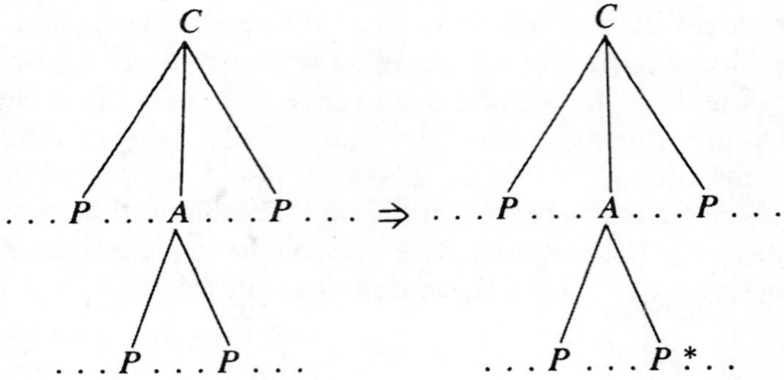
(22)

These examples may suffice to represent two features of the structure of the descriptions of the Śrauta Sūtras, and indeed of the *śrauta* rituals themselves: embedding and modification. What is astonishing about this structure is that it is exceedingly similar to the syntax of a natural language as described in Chomsky 1965. As linguists will long have recognized, expressions of the form (17)–(19) are *phrase structure rules*. (The rites represented by small letters, which I have introduced tentatively, correspond to some extent to lexical items). Expressions of the form (22) are *transformations*. The phrase structure rules are *recursive*, because the same symbols occur to the right and to the left of the single arrows: *P*, which occurs on the right in (17), occurs on the left in (18); and *D*, which occurs on the right in (17) and (18), occurs on the left in (19).

The ritual modifications have another property, which is common in Vedic ritual as Professor Heesterman reminded me (in a letter of January 9, 1976): an embedded ritual may be interrupted, once or several times, by the ritual in which it is embedded, to be continued or completed afterwards. For example, the embedding of *P* in *A* assumes the following form: some rites of *P* are performed, followed by rites belonging to *A*, after which subsequent rites of *P* continue, etc. (in a linear description the sequence has to be interrupted: see, e.g., Caland and Henry 1906:125–8, 186, 188).

For some time it seemed to me that this alternation was a

characteristic of ritual without a linguistic parallel. Several linguists I contacted could not provide a similar structure in a natural language. But when I phoned Professor J. R. Ross, he immediately produced a simple example from English. Let us embed the sentence:

(*S*1) Harry is sad

into another sentence, as follows:

(*S*2) It seems to me that [Harry is sad].
*S*1 *S*1

Applying several transformations we can derive the following sentence, in which constituents of the original sentences alternate:

Harry seems sad to me.
*S*1 *S*2 *S*1 *S*2

The recursive features of the ritual allow the construction of rituals of indefinitely increasing complexity. Such recursiveness is exploited in some of the, partly theoretical, sattra rituals. We have seen that the grammarian Patañjali compared the recursiveness of language to these ritual creations which also have to be described by rules (page 40).

Before discussing possible explanations for the similarities between structures in ritual and language, it should be emphasized that the occurrence of such structures does not imply that the ritualists were any more aware of their precise form than language users are conscious of the syntactic rules which they employ. In linguistics, this has been often misunderstood and Chomsky has repeatedly emphasized that "the structure of particular languages may very well be largely determined by factors over which the individual has no conscious control" (Chomsky 1965:59). The same applies in ritual. It is not invalidated by the fact, that we have based our analysis largely upon descriptions of ritual provided by the ritualists themselves. The structures I have discussed should therefore be distinguished from such structures as Lévi-Strauss found in a native Yoruba theory, about which he says: "But, as theories go, the Yoruba seem to have been able to throw more light than ethnologists on the spirit of institutions and rules which in their society, as in many others, are of an intellectual and deliberate character" (Lévi-Strauss 1966:133). In Vedic ritual, the descriptions by the authors of the Śrauta Sūtras, too, have thrown more light on the subject than any modern author could do without their aid. However, this does not imply that the deeper structures which underlie many ritual constructions have at any time been conceived deliberately.

Despite the specific difference in recursiveness we have found, the occurrence in the syntax of both ritual and language of specific and unobvious rules, viz., *phrase structure rules*, *transformational rules* and *self embedding rules*, is sufficiently striking to demand an explanation. It may be premature to offer such an explanation at this early stage. One reason is that the data upon which these similarities are based are asymmetrical. On the language side, the relevant structures have been shown to be in all likelihood universal. On the ritual side, our data have been confined to Vedic ritual. Though this is most probably the best point of departure, we are only beginning to explore a domain of ritual syntax which appears to be as complex as the syntax of language. Even in the domain of Vedic ritual we have taken into account only a few structures. For example, we have not so far used the fact, that the ritual is executed by combining the contributions of different groups of priests with distinct ritual systems. This is comparable to a language which exhibits the rules of several distinct grammars as do some Creole languages. Also, we have not studied the metarules which are required when different rules, apparently inconsistent with each other, have to be combined (Chapter 26). Similarly, the structure of *saṃpad* 'numerical congruence' (Heesterman 1957:35,53) awaits syntactic treatment. Since there is so much left undone, I can only offer speculation.

The similarities we found may require elaborate explanations. But they might alternatively be explained by one of three simple explanations: either language is the cause, or ritual is the cause, or there is a common cause for both. I shall discount the third which could be almost anything about which we know little—ranging from the 'essence of man' to the structure of his brain. It would seem plausible to opt for the first explanation. In its support it could be argued that it would not be surprising for man, who has a specific structure of language anchored in his brain, to exhibit this same structure in his rituals. I think this is possibly correct, but I wish to point out that it is not the only plausible view. First of all, it smacks of prejudice. It is we who are obsessed by language and who have (despite survivals) lost touch with ritual. Hence it is only natural that the view that language is primary, would appeal to us. But for Early Man, ritual was at least as important as language is for us. Ritual, after all, is much older than language. Unlike language, it can originate on all fours. It is common among animals.

If we adopt an evolutionary perspective, it becomes relevant to consider animal systems of communication or 'animal language.' Evidence for an animal syntax which is at all like the human appears to be meagre or nonexistent. As for monkeys and apes, their communication systems "have little relationship with human language, but much with the ways human beings express emotion through gesture, facial expressions, and tone of voice" (Lancaster 1968:446). In a study which pays some attention to syntactic problems, Reynolds, partly following Altmann, has shown that in the communication among Macaques, "a sequence of displays will determine the probability of the next display" (I quote from Hill 1972:314). But Hill has rightly pointed out that this would precisely be a communication system with the properties of a Markov process model, "which Chomsky (1957) so convincingly demonstrated was not the sort of system represented in human language." Hill has in fact suggested that a basic distinction between animal communication and human language is that the former lacks recursiveness (Hill 1972:313–315; cf. Revzin 1974:25).

To evaluate the problem we also require detailed studies of the syntax of animal ritual. Little seems to be available in the otherwise impressive work of scholars like Crane, Huxley, Lorenz and Tinbergen (see, e.g., Huxley 1966). There is more, but still not enough, in Thorpe 1951 and Barlow 1977. Such information, however, may clench the argument. If there is no recursiveness in the syntax of animal ritual, the issue remains inconclusive. But if there is, and if Hill is right, this suggests that the recursiveness which is the main characteristic of the syntax of human language has a ritual origin.

Another hypothesis is consistent with the view that syntax has a ritual origin: the hypothesis that syntax is older than semantics. This is precisely what I suspect to be the case. The contrary view, that structured systems of meaning developed first, seems to be accepted implicitly by many scholars. It is certainly more logical (hence the original appeal of generative semantics, which denied an independent level of syntax). In addition to the emphasis on synchronistic structure, this view would help to explain the readily accepted taboo which the *Société de linguistique* of Paris imposed upon investigations into the origin of language: for meaning was held to be mysterious and inaccessible to scientific treatment. The question that seems to lurk behind such a view is: why should people wish to establish language if not for the sake of communication? But such an idea rests on flimsy grounds. Language was not deliberately and consciously established, its emergence and growth need not be due to pragmatic or functional needs, and it clearly exhibits a great deal of structure which plays no role in communication. Nature, in brief, is not always logical.

There are many facts that support the view that syntax is older than semantics. Vedic ritual itself provides such evidence. Vedic ritual is replete with recitation and chant. These recitations and chants are comprised of a highly structured mixture of natural language and meaningless sound. But whether or not portions of this mixture are meaningful in other contexts, in their ritual use the only things which matter are the sounds and their configurations. According to the ancient ritualist Kautsa, all *mantras* are meaningless, and this view is indeed applicable to the occurrence of *mantras* throughout Indian culture (page 234). In

Vedic ritual, as in *mantra* meditation, the function of language is phonetic and syntactic, not semantic. We shall return to this curious fact in Part III.

Other facts support our hypothesis in a negative way. During performances of Vedic rituals, the participants are not supposed to communicate with each other through ordinary language. In later times, communication is restricted (and effectively eliminated) by prohibiting the use of any language other than Sanskrit. Linguistic communication of an ordinary sort is also excluded when ritual recitations are prescribed as *anirukta*, 'not enunciated', *upāṃśu*, 'inaudible', or when the rites are executed *tuṣṇīm*, 'in silence' (Renou and Silburn 1954). In the ritual of the chanters, *aniruktagāna* 'unenunciated chant' is a protracted chant of *o* with the same structure and pitch variation as the original *mantra*, which is represented mentally. In meditation, linguistic meaning is also excluded. The meditation *mantras*, which are recited elsewhere, increasingly come to consist of meaningless syllables, which tend to become mental or vanish altogether. Thus phonetic structure disappears and syntactic structure is reduced to mere repetition, expressible by the single syntactic rule $A \rightarrow AA$.

I am inclined to believe that what we witness here is not a curious collection of exotic facts, but a remnant or resurgence of a pre-linguistic stage of development, during which man or his ancestors used sound in a purely syntactic or ritual manner. This would be supported by the generally archaic features of ritual as well as of mysticism, and the claim that there was a golden age when ritual practices and mystical insights were common (cf. Staal 1975a:58). The *locus classicus* is Rigveda 1.164.50 = 10.90.16:

yajñéna yajñám ayajanta devā́s
tā́ni dhármāṇi prathamā́ny āsan

"With the sacrifice the gods performed the sacrifice.
These were the first ordinances"
(transl. Brown 1965:32; 1968:218).

In his presidential address to the 1974 meeting of the *Linguistic Society of America*, Morris Halle expressed a similar view—the conception of language not as a means for communication but as playful activity, a kind of game. He quotes in this connexion from Novalis' *Sprachwissenschaftlicher Monolog* of 1798:

> Das rechte Gespräch ist ein blosses Wortspiel . . . Wenn man den Leuten nur begreiflich machen könnte, dass es mit der Sprache wie mit den mathematischen Formeln sei.—Sie machen eine Welt für sich aus—sie spielen nur mit sich selbst, drücken nichts als ihre wunderbare Natur aus, und eben darum sind sie so ausdrucksvoll—eben darum spiegelt sich in ihnen das seltsame Verhältnisspiel der Dinge . . . so ist es auch mit der Sprache . . ." (Halle 1975:527–528).

The view that syntax has a ritual origin and is older than semantics would explain why there is a syntax in ritual, why there is an independent level of syntax in linguistics, why language is so unlogical and—*pace* Novalis—why language pictures the world in such a roundabout fashion.

13

Interpretations of Ritual

The structural properties of ritual that we have so far considered require not only consummate skill and expertise but also a lot of the priests' attention—not less than is required, say, from the members of an orchestra, a ballet company or a team of engineers set upon the execution of a common task. What then about the *meaning* of the ritual, a dimension we read so much about especially in contemporary works on ritual by anthropologists and scholars of religion? Are the priests also concerned with meaning or is this merely a scholarly pastime?

A widespread assumption about ritual is that it consists in symbolic activities which refer to something else. It is characteristic of a ritual performance, however, that it is self-contained and self-absorbed. The performers are totally immersed in the proper execution of their complex tasks. Isolated in their sacred enclosure, they concentrate on correctness of act, recitation and chant. Their primary concern, if not obsession, is with rules. There are no symbolic meanings going through their minds when they are engaged in performing ritual.

Such absorption by itself, does not show that ritual cannot have a symbolic meaning. However, also when we ask a brahmin explicitly why the rituals are performed, we never receive an answer which refers to symbolic activity. There are numerous different answers, such as: we do it because our ancestors did it; because we are eligible to do it; because it is good for society; because it is good; because it is our duty; because it is said to lead to immortality; because it leads to immortality. A visitor will furthermore observe that a person who has performed a Vedic ritual acquires social and religious status, which involves other benefits, some of them economic. Beyond such generalities one gets involved in individual case histories. Some boys have never been given much of a choice, and have been taught recitations and rites as a matter of fact; by the time they have mastered these, there is little else they are competent or motivated to do. Others are inspired by a spirit of competition. The majority would not be able to come up with an adequate answer to the question why they engage in ritual.

Why ask such personal questions? It might be more proper and fruitful to ask specific questions about the meaning of particular rites. Some such questions do receive specific answers, on which participants and scholars agree. The Yajamāna must keep his hands closed "like a child in the womb of its mother, ready to be reborn." The fire altar has the shape of a bird because fire, as well as Soma, were fetched from heaven by a bird. The priests do not go south if they can help it for the southern direction is inauspicious. Certain bricks of the altar are consecrated so that it may rain (see, however, page 154).

Such simple answers form a small minority. They are given rarely, and only in reply to similarly simple questions. Most questions concerning ritual detail involve numerous complex rules, and no participant could provide an answer or elucidation with which he would himself be satisfied. Outsiders and bystanders may volunteer their ideas about religion and philosophy generally—without reference to any specific question. In most cases such people do not know anything about Vedic ritual. There is only one answer which the best and most reliable among the ritualists themselves give consistently and with more than average frequency: we act according to the rules because this is our tradition (*paramparā*). The effective part of the answer seems to be: look and listen, these are our activities! To performing ritualists, rituals are like dance, of which Isadora Duncan said: "If I could tell you what it meant there would be no point in dancing it."

Ritual, then, is primarily activity. It is an activity governed by explicit rules. The important thing is what you do, not what you think, believe or say. In India this has become a basic feature of all religion, so that we should refer, not to the faithful or orthodox, but to the orthoprax (from Greek *orthos*, "right" and *praxis*, "action"). It is precisely this feature which is least understood by English-writing Indian authors such as V. S. Naipaul and N. C. Chaudhuri, who have recently taken on the role of explaining India to Western intelligentsia.

13A. Indian Interpretations

If we wish to know the meaning or theory of ritual, we should not confine ourselves to practicing ritualists; we have learned, after all, that it does not pay to ask elephants about zoology, or artists about the theory of art. Before asking anyone else, however, let us take a look at what the Indian tradition itself has to offer. Since in India ritual has always been a favorite topic for speculation, there is an abundance of material. Even prior to speculation we find suggestive ideas. In the earliest Vedic literature, rituals, along with metres and chants, are used by gods and demons to fight and conquer each other, and sometimes to create worlds. Even when the aims are not explicit, gods and demons are frequently depicted as engaged in ritual. Commentaries provide rituals with a great variety of interpretations, sometimes inconsistent with each other.

In Vedic literature, a specific class of texts deals with the interpretation of ritual. These are the Brāhmaṇas—the same term that denotes the members of the highest caste who apparently took a special delight in the thinking up of such interpretations. One of the most important of these, the Śatapatha Brāhmaṇa, figures prominently in almost all Western works about Vedic ritual because its translation is widely available and provides such an enormous wealth of interpretations that almost everyone can find something to suit his taste or support her theory.

Julius Eggeling, the translator of the Śatapatha Brāhmaṇa, was not enthusiastic about the work to which he devoted a good part of his life. In the Introduction to the first of his five volume translation, he wrote about the Brāhmaṇas in general: "For wearisome prolixity of exposition, characterized by dogmatic assertion and a flimsy symbolism rather than by serious reasoning, these works are perhaps not equalled anywhere'' (I, 1882: ix). Others have expressed similar views (quoted in AGNI I:62–64). Eggeling wrote during the nineteenth century, when reason was perhaps overrated and irrationalist trends had not yet invaded the humanities. But his view is not a thing of the past. Louis Renou, one of the most distinguished Indologists and Sanskrit scholars of the twentieth century, who wrote extensively on Vedic ritual as well as on literature, philosophy, and all other aspects of Indian culture, expressed in 1953 a more balanced and less extreme view that is not less damaging:

> We must be content with very general theories if we are to avoid arbitrary explanations such as those put forward in the old *Brāhmaṇas*, where we find fabricated accounts of the origin of various details in the liturgical ceremonial. In these stories there is much that deserves attention, but the *nidāna* or *bandhu*, the hidden connection that they try to establish, cannot be accepted; it is too visibly the product of the priestly mind. It is recognized in the texts that comprehension must cease at a certain point: they declare ''*paro'kṣakāmā hi devāḥ*,'' ''the gods love what is out of sight'' (1953:16; with a modification in the translation).

It is exceedingly, indeed embarassingly easy to provide examples from the Brāhmaṇas to illustrate their arbitrariness and inconsistencies. It would be difficult to find the opposite: an interpretation of a rite that convincingly or persuasively explains why it is performed. I shall, for the time being, give a single, simple example of the prevailing *ad hoc* type of interpretation. It concerns the puroruc or ''prior light'' (Chapter 9B, Episode II, Element 1):

> Now, the *puroruc* is he yonder who gives out light (viz., the sun); for he shines in (from the) front. Now, the *puroruc* is the vital breath, the hymn the body (*ātmā*, the person himself). (Or) the *puroruc* is the body, the hymn offspring and cattle (Gonda 1981:63, note 9 = Sreekrishna Sarma in: AGNI II:679).

Anyone who has spent any time with the Brāhmaṇa literature will agree that this passage is quite representative. The fact that such interpretations are arbitrary need not prevent them from constituting a system within themselves. Mylius (1976) has shown that many identifications given in the same Kauṣītaki Brāhmaṇa can in fact be systematically interpreted in social, psychological, or ideological terms. But even if such interpretations refer to reality; they still fail to elucidate rites, or throw light on Vedic ritual.

The three interpretations of the *puroruc* that are provided in this interpretation are neither related nor consistent with each other. The author hands them out without much concern for their apparent validity. Interpreting in the Brāhmaṇas may be an art, a kind of game or entertainment; but it is not an attempt seriously to elucidate or explain. It resembles, in fact, Gadamer's hermeneutics (Chapter 3B) in being empty, arbitrary and ad hoc. This is ironic because Gadamer's oracular judgment of all Oriental thought regards it as utterly alien ("Adapting these things by Western philosophy is out of the question. Only a negative insight can be taken as confirmed: our own philosophic concepts, constituted by the Greeks, change the alien in substance": Editor's Note to Dilthey 1949:18).

Some interpretations of the Brāhmaṇas are predictable. They do not give an acceptable explanation either, but they conform to a general pattern. Some are concerned with the structural properties we have discussed, e.g., the structure "B A B." Although we have noted that this structure is a simple extension of a common feature of human activity, the Brāhmaṇas interpret it in terms of an ascent to heaven. Heesterman (1957:12–13) refers to some of the relevant texts:

> The word *prāyaṇīya-* not only denotes the introduction to a sacrificial session or a festival, but it is also associated with the idea of going to heaven: "through the 'proceeding-day' (*prāyaṇīya-*) the gods proceed (*prāyan*) to the world of heaven: because they proceeded, therefore it is called the proceeding-day" (Pañcaviṃśa Brāhmaṇa 4.2.2, etc.). The counterpart of the prāyaṇīya is generally the udayanīya, the concluding rite . . . . Through the udayanīya the sacrificer is supposed to reach the earth again (Kauṣītaki Brāhmaṇa 7.8, etc.).

In India, too, the interpretations of the Brāhmaṇas were regarded as unsatisfactory. They inspired philosophic or pre-philosophic speculation in the Upaniṣads, but were replaced by systematic and rational analysis in the ritual philosophy of the Mīmāṃsā, which postulated an unseen fruit as the effect of ritual activity. We shall return to this in a moment, but must first note two preceding stages of development, following each other not unlike the sequence of functionalism and structuralism in twentieth century anthropology.

At first, specific rites were thought of as fulfilling specific desires: for health, power, offspring, victory and the like. The list of wishes and desires is not different from that of the majority of our contemporaries. It is neither entirely material, nor exclusively spiritual as some modern visionaries have claimed. But this trend receded again into the background, and a structural point of view came to the fore, which conformed more naturally to the structure of the ritual and joined the efforts of the ritualists to create a science of ritual. This led to the codification of two kinds of rites we have already mentioned: the Gṛhya or "domestic rites," which are *rites de passage*, life-cycle rites or "sacraments," accompanying such events as birth, initiation, marriage and death; and the Śrauta or "traditional rites," which provide the foundation for most of my analysis.

There are several general and formal differences between these two kinds of ritual. For example, the traditional rites require three fire altars and the services of several priests, whereas the domestic rites require only one fire (the domestic fire) and one priest (the domestic priest). While the function of the domestic rites appears to be fairly straightforward, the significance of the traditional rites is not obvious. The traditional ritual, with its myriad ramifications, exhibits the unhampered development of ritual construction and creativity. The domestic rites might seem to be amenable to explanations along the lines of, e.g., Van Gennep's *Rites de passage* (1909) or Victor Turner (Chapter 14B). But since such explanations are clearly inapplicable to the older traditional rites, and domestic and traditional rites are similar in structure, it follows that all such theories are inappropriate. There are, moreover, traditional rituals which last a thousand years, which shows that some rites were purely theoretical. Such theoretical constructs, we have seen, (page 88), are as important for the theory of ritual as are concrete ceremonies. Many rites have in fact an intermediate status. The Agnicayana, which was performed in 1975, is a traditional ritual which seems to have been always "real", though some of its extensions, which the texts describe, smack of theory.

The *Śrauta Sūtras* of the late Vedic period offer several definitions of ritual. One which is often quoted characterizes it as comprising three things: *dravya*, "the substance (which is used in oblations)"; *devatā*, "the deity (to which oblations are offered)"; and *tyāgā*, "renunciation (of the fruits of the ritual acts)". The *tyāgā* is a formula pronounced by the Yajamāna at the culmination of each act of oblation. When the officiating priest makes the oblation into the fire for one of the gods, for example Agni, the Yajamāna says:

> "this is for Agni, not for me" (*agnaye idaṃ na mama*).

At this point a contradiction begins to appear, which becomes increasingly explicit in the ritualistic philosophy of the Mīmāmṣā. The reason for performing a specific ritual is stated to be the desire for a particular fruit or effect. The stock example of the Mīmāmṣā is:

> "he who desires heaven shall sacrifice with the Agniṣṭoma ritual" (*agniṣṭomena svargakāmo yajeta*).

But this fruit is renounced whenever the Yajamāna utters his *tyāga* formula of renunciation. The effect, therefore, is not obtained.

The resulting picture is further complicated by another apparent contradiction. The rites are subdivided into two classes: "obligatory" (*nitya*) and "optional" (*kāmya*). Unlike the Agnicayana, which is *kāmya*, the Agniṣṭoma is a *nitya* rite: every brahman has the duty to perform it. So here is a ritual which appears to be optional, since it is confined to those who desire heaven (nobody's duty); but which is also not optional, because it is a prescribed duty; and which moreover in the final resort does not bear any fruit because its fruits are abandoned. The texts reflect such contradictions. The Mīmāṃsā Sūtra, basic manual of the Mīmāṃsā, lays down that the rites lead to happiness, but the subcommentary "Straight Spotless" (*Ṛjuvimalā*) observes that this does not apply to obligatory acts.

The Mīmāṃsā philosophers faced another difficulty. When a ritual performance is completed, no fruit is seen. The Yajamāna, on whose behalf the rites have been performed, does not raise up and go to heaven. Rather the opposite: he returns home and is, as the texts put it, the same as he was before. In particular, he must continue to perform the morning and evening fire rites (*Agnihotra*) for the rest of his life. The Mīmāṃsā concluded, quite logically, that the fruit of ritual activity is—temporarily—unseen. It will become apparent only later, e.g., after death. An elaborate theory was devised to show that this is in accordance with the mechanism of *karman*, according to which every cause has an effect. A special logical theorem, called *arthāpatti*, was invented in support of this theory. The followers of the Mīmāṃsā were criticized by others (e.g., the philosophers of the Advaita Vedānta) for postulating such unseen effects. For whatever our contemporary fads may suggest—in India, the unseen is resorted to only under duress (see page 190). What the Mīmāṃsā in fact ended up teaching is that the rituals have to be performed for their own sake.

The notion of *tyāga*, "renunciation," has attained an important position in Hinduism through the teachings of the Bhagavad Gītā. Here Śrī Kṛṣṇa advocates as the highest goal of life a mode of activity, in which acts are performed as usual, but the fruit (*phala*) of action (*karman*) is always renounced (*karma-phala-tyāga*).

13B. Western Interpretations

The Indian tradition offers suggestive speculations but it does not come up with a single consistent theory of ritual. The most interesting Indian contribution is perhaps the term *karman* itself: originally and primarily used for ritual and similarly pure or ideal activity, it comes by extension to denote any kind of human activity. So let us see what modern scholars have to offer. For a long time it has been fashionable to believe that rites re-enact myths. This idea was partly inspired by the Babylonian festival of the New Year, which involves a recital of the myth of creation. But this hypothesis is difficult to support and creates an unsolved problem: why should anybody wish to re-enact a myth? The same difficulty applies to several more recent theories, according to which ritual reflects social structure. It is true, again, that there are some parallels which require explanation. But the question remains: why should social structures be represented or enacted ritually, and in a very roundabout manner at that? Such unanswered questions, generated by the theory, suggest that theories of this type are best abandoned.

A related theory, current among anthropologists, is that rituals are used, in preliterate societies, to transmit "cultural and social values" to the younger generation. This would explain the informants' emphasis on tradition. But the assumption is, of course, unnecessary. Not only are rituals not confined to preliterate societies (it is anthropologists who tend to confine themselves to preliterate societies); but such values (e.g., gods, myths, kinship systems) are most readily transmitted by grandmothers and through language, and there is no need for them to be transmitted again by other means. The only cultural values rituals transmit are rituals.

We have seen that "transition" or "liminal" theories of the van Gennep-Turner type do not explain the Śrauta ritual. A subclass of these theories (found, for example, in Mircea Eliade) hypothesizes that ritual effects a transition from the realm of the profane to that of the sacred. (Instead of "transition" we also meet with "communication": a weaker version of the theory). This is very intriguing and unclear. Terms such as "transition" or "communication" do not pose too much of a problem; but "sacred" and "profane" certainly do. One possibility is that the theory expresses a tautology: the distinction between profane and sacred is the distinction between the status of a person or object before and after a relevant ritual is embarked upon; accordingly, if sacred and profane have been defined in terms of ritual, ritual cannot be defined in terms of sacred and profane. This is circular and uninformative.

On another interpretation, this theory would assume that the distinction between sacred and profane is already established and known from elsewhere. For example, in the realm of divinity, "sacred" might have been shown to be the domain of the gods, and "profane" that of men. But a satisfactory distinction of this kind is not easily found, especially outside the realm of ritual. Moreover, the terms do not introduce anything new. The theory would merely claim that ritual effects a transition from the realm of men to that of the gods (or a communication between the two). As a matter of fact, the Vedic ritual offers an immediate contradiction. During the Soma rituals, a transition is effected from the "Old Hall" or small enclosure to the Great Altar space (see above, page 71 and Figure 1). The former is said to be the abode of man, and the latter that of the gods. Thus a transition from the domain of men to that of the gods is effected *within* the ritual, instead of characterizing all of it. The distinction therefore cannot serve as a concept in terms of which the ritual itself may be defined. The distinction between "sacred" and "profane" exhibits a form of dualism that is typically Western. Dualisms are also found in Asia but they are surpassed by monistic and pluralistic perspectives.

Why have Western scholars generally regarded ritual as a symbolic activity? One reason is that the first Westerners who speculated about ritual were Christians who regarded ritual ceremonies as part of their religion and assumed accordingly that it symbolized religious truths and values. In India, this course could not be adopted because interpretations or speculations like those offered by the Brāhmaṇas were never taken literally and rarely seriously outside the particular tradition of their perpetrators. The ritual itself continued to be performed but it was always regarded as more basic than any such speculation, truth, value or religion (cf. Chapter 28).

The sources of the Christian preoccupation with the symbolic interpretation of ritual lie in the Carolingian Renaissance, when the idea was first formulated that the ceremonies of the church express and symbolize the coming of Christ and the history of salvation. With the Protestant emphasis on scripture and faith, ritual receded to the background. In more recent developments within Christianity, Protestant as well as Roman Catholic, the place of ritual or liturgy continues to be a topic of discussion. In India, too, ritual or *karman* has been debated ceaselessly by philosophers and theologians. This goes back as far as the early Upaniṣads and the beginnings of Buddhism in the sixth century B.C.E.

The first Western philosophers and scholars outside the Christian tradition who recognized the importance of ritual continued to place it unquestioningly within the domain of religion. For Hegel, ritual stands at the center of the religious process, where the subject "participates in the absolute and is united with it." E. O. James (1917:215) expressed his views in less pompous but equally vacuous terms: "Generally speaking ritual evolved long before belief, since primitive man is wont to 'dance out his religion' " (both quoted in Cassirer 1925, II:271). The first serious scholar who demonstrated the primacy of ritual over belief was W. Robertson Smith, author of a nineteenth century classic, the *Lectures on the Religion of the Semites* of 1889. This view was incorporated in his philosophy by Ernst Cassirer, who regarded man primarily as a "symbolizing animal" but accepted at the same time that ritual was prior to "dogma," both in a historical and in a psychological sense (Cassirer 1925, II:270–285). For Cassirer, therefore, ritual is to be interpreted in symbolic terms, but since the symbols cannot refer to features of belief, the question arises what do they refer to?

Doubts were cast on the idea that ritual is part of religion and on the symbolic character of ritual by the founders of the "sociology of religion," Emile Durkheim and Max Weber. Durkheim was clearer and more methodical than Weber, his slightly younger contemporary, but he did not go as far. Though he saw clearly that religion is related, through ritual among other things, to social facts and institutions, he did not question the view that ritual is part of religion. On the contrary, he formulated that view with classic succinctness at the outset of his book *Les formes élémentaires de la vie religieuse* of 1912:

> Religious phenomena are naturally arranged in two fundamental categories: beliefs and rites. The first are states of opinion, and consist in representations; the second are determined modes of action. Between these two classes of facts there is all the difference which separates thought from action (Durkheim 1912; English translation of 1915:36).

Following this statement of principle, which he adopted in the organization of his book, Durkheim briefly and tentatively discussed the two categories, but did not question their relationship: "It is possible to define the rite only after we have defined the belief."

We have seen in Chapter 2 that Durkheim, given his empiricist/positivist bias, omitted mystical experience from his classification of religious phenomena. Here we are concerned with another prejudice that underlies his approach.

Durkheim's view of the primacy of belief over ritual, which was a step back from the position that had already been reached by Robertson Smith and others, has remained the preponderant view that underlies Western studies of ritual. One reason for this preponderance is that this view combines more easily with the belief that ritual is symbolic than that it is not: for it can then be simply maintained that ritual is a symbolic representation of what people believe. In his discussions of ritual, Durkheim did not make much use of the category of "symbol," but he referred throughout his book to rites in terms of the human mind, e.g.: "Rites are a manner of acting which take rise in the midst of the assembled groups and which are destined to excite, maintain or recreate certain mental states in these groups" (page 10), or: "At bottom, all these different practices are only variations of one and the same theme: everywhere their basis is the same state of mind, interpreted differently according to the situations, the moments of history and the dispositions of the worshippers" (page 388).

There is a curious consequence of this approach to human ritual. Basing himself upon earlier ethnographic and ethnological investigation, Durkheim paid much attention to the totemic cult. Of his nine chapters on "elementary beliefs," seven deal with "totemic beliefs." Totemic cults involve a close union between men and an animal species. If anthropologists had tried to interpret this phenomenon in the light of the natural relatedness that exists between the human animal and other animals, they would have welcomed the facts about animal ritualization when these became known. But since they emphasized symbols and the human mind, anthropologists have been resistant to the idea that animal ritualization has anything to do with human rituals: for this would then involve the assumption that animals also have human minds and beliefs. To a logician, a different conclusion follows through contraposition: since animals have ritual, but do not have human minds or beliefs, ritual cannot be symbolic.

Durkheim's own analysis of rites throws doubts on his theories about ritual. Discussing data from the Australian tribe of the Arunta made available by Spencer and Gillen, he focussed on a significant feature that the authors themselves did not seem to have noticed. In their first book, these ethnographers had analyzed a ceremony called *intichiuma*, which was "destined exclusively for the assurance of the reproduction of the totemic species, and it seemed as though it ought to lose all meaning, if this unique function were set aside" (Durkheim 1915:383). But in a later work by the same authors, the same ceremony was discussed as part of the initiation ritual, in which function it was called by a different name: *mbatjalkatiuma* (page 384). Durkheim concluded that "according to the circumstances, one and the same ceremony serves two distinct functions" (page 385). He referred to Hubert and Mauss, who had already pointed out a functional ambiguity of the same sort in the "Hindu sacrifice," and then expanded his conclusion as follows:

> This ambiguity shows that the real function of a rite does not consist in the particular and definite effects which it seems to aim at and by which

> it is ordinarily characterized, but rather in a general action which, though always and everywhere the same, is nevertheless capable of taking on different forms according to the circumstances. (page 386)

The idea that a single rite serves different ends would seem to suggest that ritual is to some extent independent of the ends it is supposed to serve; but Durkheim did not draw this conclusion or even consider such a possibility. Neither did van Gennep, who had made the same discovery two years earlier, when he observed that: "the same rite, remaining absolutely the same, can change its meaning depending on the position it is given in a ceremony, or on whether it is part of one ceremony or another. The aspersion rite . . . is a fecundity rite in marriage ceremonies, but an expulsion rite in separation ceremonies" (Van Gennep 1910, in: Waardenburg I, 1973:299).

Van Gennep's observation remained virtually unknown, since it occurred in a lecture delivered at the University of Brussels, which was published in French and Dutch in 1911, and in English translation only in 1973. An English translation of Durkheim's work, on the other hand, was published in 1915, three years after the original had appeared. Durkheim's work was very influential in France, and became widely known in the United States after the Second World War. But Durkheim's observations on the functional ambiguity of rites have not attracted any attention, and nobody has detected their important theoretical implications.

Weber studied religion within the context of society and in a similar spirit as Durkheim had done. However, opposing current theories, he did not take it for granted that symbolization was one of its important features. At the outset of his book on the sociology of religion, he interpreted magic, which is closely related to rites, as a direct manipulation of forces, which *at first* reflects some kind of naturalism, and is *subsequently* transformed into a symbolic activity:

> Various consequences of significance to magical art emerged from the development of a realm of souls, demons, and gods. These beings cannot be grasped or perceived in any concrete sense but manifest a type of

> transcendental being which normally is accessible only through the mediation of symbols and significances, and which consequently is represented as shadowy and even unreal. Since it is assumed that behind real things and events there is something else, distinctive and spiritual, of which real events are only the symptoms or indeed the symbols, an effort must be made to influence, not the concrete things, but the spiritual powers that express themselves through concrete things. This is done through actions that address themselves to a spirit or soul, hence done by instrumentalities that 'mean' something, i.e., symbols. Thereafter, naturalism may be swept away by a flood of symbolic actions. (Weber 1922; English translation, 1963:6–7)

Waardenburg (1973, I:49) has correctly emphasized that Weber's was "a new view of religion which worked against a German tradition stressing the mythological and symbolic aspects of religion." An important implication of this view is that ritual has to be primarily understood without reference to the symbolization which was attached to it afterwards. Weber himself, however, wavered, and did not draw any such conclusion. Both he and Talcott Parsons in his influential *Introduction* to the 1963 American edition of the *Sociology of Religion* were more interested in the later symbolic derivations than in the original "pre-animistic naturalism" somewhat murkily postulated by the theory. Weber had become famous on account of his ideas about the relatedness between Protestantism and Capitalism, welcomed especially in the United States where they were interpreted as an endorsement of both. He came to issue pontifical statements no longer consistent with his original insights, e.g.: "Events are not just there and happen, but they have a meaning and happen because of that meaning." Such statements have become part of the *credo* of anthropology in the United States, where they are highlighted in popular readers on cultural anthropology with sentimental titles such as *Man Makes Sense* (Hammel and Simmons 1970).

The fashionableness of such views should not obscure the fact that they are wholly atavistic and metaphysical. No scholar or scientist has adequate grounds for assuming that the data he seeks to interpret and explain are meaningful to begin with. Nature and culture are governed by chance as much as by necessity. Openmindedness with regard to such questions is required as a matter of course in the natural sciences. In the human sciences, such openmindedness cannot be circumvented by defining man *a priori* and dogmatically as "the animal that makes sense." The unproductiveness of such an approach is particularly clear in biology, where many of the most interesting problems, which also involve the human animal, revolve around the question whether some of the phenomena can be shown to "make sense," or are merely due to chance (see, e.g., Monod 1970). We shall return to this topic (Chapters 24 and 30C).

Durkheim and Weber created the sociology of religion, and it is largely due to them that religion and ritual are nowadays studied not only by scholars of religion and religious scholars, but also by anthropologists and sociologists who should have less of an axe to grind. This development constitutes a significant and valuable widening of perspective. However, Durkheim's return to a view that had already been abandoned by others for good reasons, and Weber's inconsistencies have also created a great deal of confusion. In the study of ritual, in particular, it is not possible to derive much help from their insights. The real issues continue to be obscured by the continuation of symbolic interpretations, due not only to the facts that Durkheim and Weber had wavered, and that the break with the past had not been radical, but also because of the general search for meaning as a substitute for religion that characterizes Western man in the twentieth century.

The only scholars who freed themselves from these overbearing preoccupations of their own culture were fieldworkers who immersed themselves for extended periods of time in a foreign culture without losing their rational outlook and common sense. Malinowski, for example, originally a physicist and accordingly equipped with a good measure of scientific training, spent several years with the Trobriand Islanders and in other parts of the Pacific. He recognized some of the functions of ceremonies in terms that are reminiscent of Durkheim but that are much clearer than anything either Durkheim or Weber had written about ritual:

> We may, therefore, lay down the main function of initiation ceremonies: they are a ritual and dramatic expression of the supreme power and value of tradition in primitive societies; they also serve to impress this power and value upon the minds of each generation, and they are at the same time an extremely efficient means of transmitting tribal lore, of insuring continuity in tradition and of maintaining tribal cohesion. (Malinowski 1948, in Waardenburg 1973, I:555)

This statement rings true, but though it makes use of the notion of "expression," it has nothing to do with symbols or meaning. It is partly applicable to other animals than men, and is moreover not only true of other rites, but applies to many human institutions (universities, for example).

All these different unsuccessful attempts at characterizing ritual teach a lesson already known to philosophers: symbolization requires minds and beliefs. Therefore, to grant that ritual is prior to belief, but to persist in trying to interpret it in terms of symbols is a hopeless task. If ritual is prior to belief, as it happens to be in the scheme of evolution, it must be interpreted in different terms.

13C. The Meaninglessness of Ritual

Why has it proved so difficult to define the meaning, goals and aims of ritual? Why are there so many different answers and theories, not only often contradictory between themselves, but of such disparate character that it is difficult to even compare them with each other? There is one simple hypothesis which would account for all these puzzling facts: the hypothesis that ritual has no meaning, goal or aim.

This is precisely what appears to be the case. Ritual is pure activity, without meaning or goal. Let me briefly digress for a point of terminology. Things are either for their own sake, or for the sake of something else. If I were defending the view that ritual is for something else, it would be necessary to distinguish between such other things as meaning, function, aim or goal. But since my view is that ritual is for its own sake, I shall not bother about these differences. To say that ritual is for its own sake is to say that it is meaningless, without function, aim or goal, or also that it constitutes its own aim or goal. It does not follow that is has no value: but whatever value it has is intrinsic value.

Ritual exhibits its character of pure activity most readily when it is contrasted with the applied activities of our ordinary, everyday life. In ritual activity, the rules count, but not the result. In ordinary activity it is the other way around. In Vedic ritual, for example, an important ceremony is *agnipraṇayana*, "transporting the fire (from the Old to the New Altar) (page 75)". This is sometimes described as a transition from the abode of men to that of the gods. But the priests do not first think of men and then mediate on the gods. They think of neither, at any time. What is essential in the ceremony is the precise and faultless execution, in accordance with rules, of numerous rites and recitations. The result is important, but it has only ritual use and can only be reached in the ritually prescribed manner. I could not come in and assist in the proceedings by picking up the fire from the Old Altar and depositing it on the New. In fact, if I did such a horrible thing, the entire ceremony would be desecrated, interrupted, and expiation rites would have to be performed. Similar disasters would result if anyone used the sacred fire for any but a ritual purpose, e.g., to heat water for tea.

Now contrast this with an ordinary activity. I am about to transport my suitcase from my house to the bus stop, which is about a mile away. There are no rules I have to follow, provided I obtain the desired effect. I may put my suitcase on a skate board. Or my brother may appear on a bicycle, and the two of us use this vehicle to transport my suitcase to its intended destination.

The two kinds of activity, ritual and ordinary, can be juxtaposed without conflict or contradiction. After making fire for the altar in the ritually prescribed manner by rubbing two pieces of wood together, a priest leaves the sacred enclosure and lights a cigarette with a match. Not so different, actually, from Arthur Rubinstein back home after a concert, putting on a gramophone record. But the two domains should not be mixed. If a priest would light a cigarette from the sacrificial fire, it would be bad.

If he would light a cigarette from the fire which he had produced by rubbing two pieces of wood together in the ritual manner, he would be considered mad or very eccentric. The ritual and ordinary ways of making fire are neatly demarcated.

A distinctive feature of ordinary activity is that it runs risks which ritual activity avoids. In ordinary activity, the entire performance may fail to have the desired effect. The bicycle together with its load may fall into a canal, or the suitcase may be seized by armed robbers. In ritual activity, the activity itself is all that counts. Not only have we established the rules ourselves, so that we are completely in control; we are also assured of success. If one rite goes wrong, another takes it place. This goes a long way to explain the curious fact that rituals, so apparently meaningless and useless, are at the same time readily engaged in. *Eo ipso* it explains that ritual activity has a pleasant, soothing effect. If you give up desire, you will be happy. This idea and the notion that ritual is performed for its own sake are closely connected and clearly foreshadowed by the Indian doctrine of *tyāga*, the teachings of the Bhagavad Gītā, and by similar notions in other traditions, e.g., *wu-wei*, "absence of (effective) action" in Taoism, or the categorical imperative in Kant. It also accounts for the similarity between rites and games, which are equally unproductive, as Huizinga (followed by Caillois) pointed out (see below page 427). But ritual is one up on most games because you cannot even lose.

Several anthropologists have detected features of meaningless in ritual, without recognizing that these features express its essence. Lévi-Strauss says that ritual "consists of utterances, gestures and manipulations of objects which are independent of the interpretations which are proper to these modes of activity and which result not from the ritual itself but from implicit mythology" (1971:600). If we remove the word "implicit" from this sentence (which means forsaking the author's ideas about the complementarity of myth and ritual) we approximate what I believe to be the correct theory. Van Gennep came close to the idea that ritual is meaningless. After completing his *Rites de passage*, he noted that marriage ceremonies, in many societies, include an aspersion rite which he interpreted as a fecundity rite. But identical aspersion rites are employed, in the same and in different societies, when a slave is acquired, when a new ambassador arrives in town, to make rain or to expel someone. Like Indian commentators, Van Gennep gave different interpretations to each of these rites. He concluded: "the aspersion rite does not have any personal or basic meaning in the state of isolation, but it is meaningful if seen as a component part of a particular ceremony. The meaning of the rite can, consequently, only be found by determining the relation it has with the other elements of the whole ceremony"(1911:520; above page 128).

Aspersion rites are not confined to humans. In his Sather lectures at Berkeley, Walter Burkert (1979;43) dealt with the ritual pouring of liquids for marking a territory and observed that this is quite common in mammals: "we all know the dog's behavior at the stone."—In the development of our concepts and theories of ritual it is only a small step from "changing meaning" to: "no intrinsic meaning" and "structural meaning," and from there to: "no meaning."

If ritual is useless this does not imply that it may not have useful side-effects. It is obvious, for example, that ritual creates a bond between the participants, reinforces solidarity, boosts morale and constitutes a link with the ancestors. So do many other institutions and customs. Such side-effects cannot be used to explain the origin of ritual, though they may help to explain its preservation. They explain why rituals are preserved though their meaninglessness is recognized, like the Jewish ritual of the Red Heifer which baffled even Solomon and which was considered the classic example of a divine command for which no rational explanation can be adduced.

These side-effects fail to explain the most curious fact about ritual preservation: rituals are always guarded jealously and with extreme conservatism. This is directly explained by the theory that ritual has no meaning. A useful institution is open; it may undergo change, because efforts are made to render it more (or less) useful. A useless institution is closed; it is not understood and therefore can only be abandoned or preserved. There are parallels to this situation from outside the realm of ritual. In India, during the last 3000 years, the Vedic language gave way to classical Sanskrit which was in due course replaced by Middle and Modern Indo-Aryan languages. During all these changes the Vedic mantras were orally transmitted without any change. Why? Because they were meaningless. Languages change because they express meaning, are functional and constantly used. Meaningless sounds do not change; they can only be remembered or forgotten.

Freud has drawn attention to similarities between ritual and neurosis. The obsessiveness which pervades ritual has led several anthropologists to emphasize the emotions and anxiety which sometimes accompany ritual, and which they claim underlie it. In *L'homme nu*, Lévi-Strauss has located such anxiety in the ritualists' fear that reality, which they have cut up ritually, cannot be put together again. But it is apparent that the obsessiveness of ritual is also an immediate consequence of its meaninglessness. Nothing is more conducive to uneasiness than to be entrapped in absurdity. If I detect a mistake in cooking or calculating, I perceive the result and understand the reason. But if I have made a ritual mistake, I don't notice any difference and don't see any reason. I am not even sure whether I made a mistake or not, and there is no way to determine it. It is like being in a foreign culture where strange things happen and it is not clear whether one has made a *faux pas*. The Agnicayana performance of 1975 was followed by a long series of expiation rites, for mistakes that might have been committed. Our anxiety is greatest when we don't know why we are anxious.

The meaninglessness of ritual explains the variety of meanings attached to it. It could not be otherwise. Ideal activity cannot fail to resemble actual activity. Therefore rituals resemble other things, including features of myth and social structure. However, though a ritual activity may resemble a meaningful nonritual activity, this does not imply that it must itself be meaningful. This can be seen in the realm of animal ritualization, as well as in the human domain. Among animals, ritualization often implies that the goal of an activity has changed. Many ritual displays incorporate modes of action which originally had a different function, e.g., fighting. Such ritual displays may acquire a new function: they lead to copulation because they are sexually stimulating, for example. Some of the same ritual displays, however, are post-nuptial or post-reproductive, and therefore not clearly functional. Biologists find them puzzling (e.g., Huxley 1966:254 and below, page 287).

Human ritualization often follows animal ritualization rather closely. Fighting, simulated or real, is still sexually stimulating among humans. But typical human forms of ritualization seem in general to dissolve meaning, not replace it. One of the earliest rituals originated in connection with the use of fire. During most of its existence, mankind did not know how to use it. Subsequently, more than 250,000 years ago, man learned the use of fire; but he could not make it. So fire was collected from natural conflagrations and was carefully kept and carried around. Elaborate techniques were devised for the preservation of fire. Finally, more than 50,000 years ago, man learned how to make fire. At this point ritualization and the cult of fire came into being. For instead of relying on his art of making fire, and producing it whenever he needed it (which is easy at least during a dry season or in a dry climate), man continued to carry fire around. A distinction was made between such "eternal" fire and the "new" fire which could now be made—a distinction we have since abandoned as irrational. To ancient man, and in several existing societies, fires have retained individuality. They should not be mixed. Fires have to be extinguished, or newly made, at set times by ritual experts. Alongside, the continued preservation of "eternal" fire reflects fossilized habits which had lasted some 200,000 years.

A more recent example comes from the Agnicayana (cf. Heesterman 1962:34–36). During the ceremony of *agnipraṇayana*, when fire is transported from the Old to the New Altar, one of the priests engages in a long recitation. The recitation is of an ancient battle hymn, the Apratiratha or "Song to the Irresistible Warrior" (Taittirīya Saṃhitā 4.6.4, cf. Rigveda 10.103 and 6.75). Indra is invoked as a victorious warrior or hero, "fond of slaughter, disturber of peoples", who with the help of his arrows, chariots and troups, destroys the enemies. When the priest recites: "Comrades, follow in Indra's footsteps!", he sounds less like an officiating priest than like a gang leader or a commander-in-chief. And what is the origin of all of this? At an earlier period, the Vedic Aryans fought their way into the Indian subcontinent, moving from west to east and carrying fire. In the *agnipraṇayana* rite, fire is still carried from west to east. But the priests are not celebrating the ancient raids of their ancestors, of which they need not even be aware. The function of the hymn has not changed. It has become ritual, i.e., disappeared.

Can the meaningless of ritual be formulated in terms of development or evolution? Necessarily so, but we must speculate about origins. Originally, ritual was a mere activity performed by animals in accordance with rules. Among humans, when contrasted with ordinary, everyday and purposeful activities, its meaninglessness became patent, and rationalizations and explanations were constructed to account for its persistence. The chief provider of meaning being religion, ritual became involved with religion and through this association, meaningful. Next, rites were attached to important events which thereby acquired religious meaning, too. In the course of time, rituals, instead of remaining useless and pure, became useful and meritorious.

Through the history of man's speculation on ritual we find inklings of this background. Just as the Indians mused about Śrauta rites, the Chinese theorized about *li*, "rites, ceremonies, etiquette; rules of good manners and proper conduct." The Confucian philosopher Hsün Tzŭ (third century B.C.E.) explained the origin of the *li* as follows:

> Man at birth has desires. When these desires are not satisfied, he cannot remain without seeking their satisfaction. When this seeking for satisfaction is without measure or limit, there can only be contention. When there is contention, there will be disorder; when there is disorder, everything will be destroyed. The early kings hated this disorder, and so they established the *li* and standards of justice so as to set limits to this

> confusion, to satisfy men's desires, and give opportunity to this satisfaction, in order that desires should not be stretched to the breaking point by things, nor things be used up by desires; that both these two should mutually support one another and so continue to exist. This is how the *li* originated (Fung Yu-lan 1952, I:297).

We have seen that there are structural similarities as well as dissimilarities between ritual and language. The similarities can be explained by assuming that the origin of syntax is at least partly ritual. We have also seen that syntax is the part of language which stands most in need of explanation. Language relates sounds to meanings, and so it must necessarily comprise a domain of sounds (studied in phonetics and phonology) and a domain of meanings (studied in semantics). If language were rational and adapted to its purpose, sounds and meanings would be related by means of a one-one-correspondance. If this were true of natural languages, assuming semantics to be universal, different natural languages would also stand to each other in a one-one-correspondence, and translation could be effected with the help of dictionaries only. There would be no need for artificial languages, and logicians would be out of business.

What we do find in language is something different. Meanings and sounds are related to each other through a vast and complicated domain of structured rules: syntax. The transition between sound and meaning is unnecessarily complex, roundabout and mathematically absurd. "Nobody in his right mind would attempt to build an artificial language based on phrase structure plus transformations" (J. A. Fodor in: Smith and Miller 1966:270; cf. Chapter 6A).

How are we to explain such apparent redundancies? It is not enough to say, as communication theorists might, that redundancies are necessary for communication because they decrease mistakes in reception. That assumes that language is only for the sake of communication, which it is not. More importantly, such redundancies, to perform their alleged function, merely need be random: which cannot explain syntax, a structured domain of specific rules which in fact makes language unlogical and inefficient. These specific rules, which are without rhyme or reason, must come from elsewhere. They look like a rudiment of something quite different. This supports the idea that the origin of syntax is ritual.

The ritual origin of syntax has implications not only in language but also in religion. I shall mention three. Ritual is replete with language, but it is very often meaningless language. When a small golden image of a man is buried under the fire altar of the Agnicayana, the Priest of the Sāmaveda chants songs which contain such sounds as:

> Kā hvā hvā hvā hvā hvā
> phal phal phal phal phal
> hau hau hau hau hau
> bham bham . . . (eighteen times).

Such structured sounds partake of the syntax of ritual, but do not relate to meaning. This applies to most mantras. The topic of mantras is large and fascinating and we shall return to it in Part III.

A second feature is that mysticism is characterized by the absence of language. It points to a pre-linguistic state which can be induced by ritual, by recitation, by silent meditation on mantras, or by other means, as I have shown in *Exploring Mysticism* (1975). All these methods help to eliminate meaning, sound and (ritual) structure.

Wittgenstein had an inkling of the place which language occupies in religion when he remarked:

> Is speech essential for religion? I can very well imagine a religion in which there are no doctrines, and hence nothing is said. Obviously the essence of religion can have nothing to do with the fact that speech occurs—or rather: if speech does occur, this itself is a component of religious behavior [the German original has: *Handlung*, "activity"] and not a theory. Therefore nothing turns on whether the words are true, false or nonsensical (Waismann 1965:16).

The ritual origin of syntax is connected with another curious fact, which I mentioned in passing (page 117): the Vedic gods fought and created not only with ritual, but also with meters and chants. What an extraordinary thing to do! But no, it is not. Meters and chants are like ritual in that they fail to express meaning, but reflect syntactic structure in its pure form, hence pure activity.

We conclude that the unchanging syntactic structures of ritual are consistent with a great variety of meanings, artificially attached to them. In his studies of the development of Taoist ritual through a succession of historical contexts, Kristofer Schipper has used the expression *accretion of meaning* to refer to this constant search for new significance. This abundance of meanings is tantamount to the nonexistence of a single intrinsic, basic and necessary meaning. Rituals, then, are different from the expressions of a language: for the latter refer to meanings in a manner that has become nonarbitrary, and language can only function because of that fixation. De Saussure rightly emphasized that the sounds of signs are arbitrary. Meanings are attached in haphazard ways. But this refers to origin and etymology, and in the resulting system everything has its fixed place. Language can only be effectively used because it refers to meaning in a systematic manner.

14

Anthropology Without Asia

How, then, is it possible to understand ritual without interpreting it in terms of symbols, meaning, or sense? In order to achieve such an understanding we have to do three things, more or less at the same time: first we must have an open mind with regard to the conceptual question where ritual "belongs." We should detach it in particular from those domains where our culture and history have been predisposed to place it: in the realms of religion and society. Second, we must study ritual in much greater depth than is done by the professional students of religion and society. And third, we should conceive of ritual in more general and abstract perspectives than has ever been attempted. The third requirement remains to a large extent a task for the future. The first two are briefly discussed in the present chapter.

Detaching ritual from religion, anthropology and sociology is not merely a mental exercise, but a methodological prerequisite. Since it amounts to a basic change of perspective, it requires special effort. Fortunately there are two kinds of circumstantial evidence that come to our assistance in attempting to achieve such a turn of mind. The first consists in the realization that the interpretation of particular rites by scholars of religion and anthropologists are often inconsistent with each other, and are sometimes different within each of these fields. This holds also for the Indian Brāhmaṇa literature, as we have seen. The "functional ambiguities" detected by Van Gennep and Durkheim provide more explicit illustrations of these difficulties. Once such inconsistencies of interpretation are met with, we should be prepared to accept that we may be barking up the wrong tree.

The second kind of circumstantial evidence that may help us to detach ritual from religion and anthropology comes from the concept of ritualization that has been adopted in the description of animal behavior. This has led to a new science, ethology, whose roots lie in a nineteenth century classic: Darwin's *Expression of the Emotions in Men and Animals* of 1872. Contemporary zoologists have interpreted ritualization as a change in the function of a pattern of behavior, often serving the purpose of communication. We should be careful, however, that we study the parallels between human ritual and animal ritualization without necessarily adopting the interpretations of the scholars and scientists who provide us with the data. Just as the rites of men may have nothing to do with religion or social structure, the rites of animals may have nothing to do with emotions or communication. What is uncontroversial is only that the detailed formal parallels between human and animal rites and rituals cast doubt on all religious, anthropological and sociological interpretations, since for any of these to be true it would be necessary to assume that animals that perform similar rites as men have similar religious or social characteristics. Such assumptions are, of course, far-fetched outside the realms of mythology and the fairy tale. Animals do have aspersion rites, for example, but these express neither fecundity in marriage ceremonies, nor expulsion in separation ceremonies.

We have argued that Indian and Chinese rituals provide the best data for the general study of ritual (pages 69–70). But when we try to place these data in their proper context, we have to study the large and complex civilizations and societies of India and China that have been made accessible successfully and fruitfully by specialists who have only seen the trees. The neglect of these societies by sociologists and anthropologists, who are trained to see the forest, is largely due to the peculiar way they originally divided up their object of study: sociologists dealt with Western and Westernized (i.e., literary and advanced) societies, and anthropologists with non-Western (i.e., nonliterary and nonadvanced) societies. But the dichotomies do not fit or coincide: India has been throughout most of its recorded history an advanced nonliterary society, and China, though both literary and advanced, is not Western. The main civilizations of Asia thus fell between the stools or were left to philologists who deal only with texts. Weber constitutes a rare exception to this general state of affairs. But it will not do to neglect India and China—the largest societies on the planet, the most important for its future, and the richest in historical depth.

Anthropologists and sociologists have failed to study rituals in depth, both with respect to their historical development and their contemporary richness. Jonathan Smith, who refers in this connection to "snapshot anthropology," makes an exception for Lévi-Strauss, who insisted that a ritual ceremony be "recorded and transcribed in its entirety," which may "fill a whole volume, sometimes a very large one" and take "days" to perform (Smith 1987:193). Lévi-Strauss cannot be criticized for neglecting the complexity of ritual, at least in its contemporary forms, but it is striking that in his voluminous works, which scan the planet from the Amazon to Paris, the civilizations of India or China are hardly mentioned.

I shall illustrate snapshot anthropology outside Asia from the work of two leading anthropologists, one British and one American, whose data are among the best data on ritual in contemporary social science. It is not my aim to criticize these scholars individually, but to illustrate the inherent limitations of the anthropological approach to the study of ritual.

14A. Raymond Firth

Raymond Firth, pupil and successor of Malinowski at the *London School of Economics*, wrote several books and articles on Tikopia, a small Polynesian island with a population of little more than 1,200 and comparatively isolated from Western influence.

Among the ceremonies the people of Tikopia perform for children there is a "fire formula" recited to a new born baby by an elder while an assistant lights a torch so that the light falls on the face of the child. The reciter than addresses the man who holds the child and his principal deity as well:

> Pa Fetauta! Assist me at the fire of Pa Tafua which is being set up.
> Unfold welfare here.

This is followed by a long recitation in which there is some variation, and which Firth has therefore described as a "free formula":

> Thy fire Pa Tafua has been announced to thee
> Unfold welfare
> That the child may sleep well.
> Thy fire Pa Saukirima O!
> Recite hither for welfare for her
> To sleep well.
> My own fire Pa Korokoro
> Light be your eyes
> Unfold welfare for her
> Perfume a thing for her to eat
> That the child may sleep well.
> From its recitation that has been performed
> Clear be its eyes for the work.
> Wake up you for the taro
> To be industrious in the clearing of the taro
> To be healthy for your work.
> Wake you up to go and clear for taro
> The taro which stands overgrown
> To be cleared on the moment and finished
> Wake you up and the seedlings that I filled tie up completely to be carried on your back
> Hasten you and when your parents are hungry go to the woods to gather food for your parents to come and cook it in the oven to be done quickly for your parents who hunger to be filled.
> To go and get food
> To go to the water
> To carry a water-bottle
> For your parents to drink.
> Be fit in your water-carrying
> Stride off, stride back
> We who are thirsty
> Now have become filled.

Climb up there to the mountain standing there
That you may be fit simply to get food.
Cut the leaves of giant taro which stands, to lever it out and proceed hither.
Light the oven
Cook it till it is done
Go and fetch the food-kits of your parents to put it in
Then we are filled.
Go and fetch the water-bottle
Then we have drunk
Then we are filled.
Indeed you are industrious.
Stand at the oven-border to uncover the oven at once to fill the food baskets
Go and give them to your parents
Fill the baskets of the relatives
Clear be your eyes for the fishing
The fish goes to a distance but bar it to dash hither to rest in your net
We have eaten of your netting
The fish that goes to a distance be turned by you to enter the net
When your parents are hungry, go and catch fish
Take your torch, go and take your net to go and fish.
Go and parcel up; parcel up a package for your parents and give them to eat
Parcel up a package for us relatives to carry
Parcel up a package for your brothers
Parcel up a package for your sisters
There they have eaten completely
There have eaten completely the relatives, and I have eaten of the package
Go and roast, there it is cooked
Give to eat, there I am filled
And distribute then to the relatives
There they have eaten completely
Go and give to your grand-parents; go and give to your fathers; go give a package to your mother; go and give a package to your brothers.
Then if there is one left, go and give a package to your brother
There we have eaten of your food-procuring.

(Firth 1967:53–55)

Firth observed these ceremonies in 1928–29. By 1952–53, when he visited Tikopia again, he found that they had been much abbreviated. The question which naturally arises is whether the 1928–29 performances themselves were abbreviations of earlier forms. Firth has not raised this question, but he says in general about the historical depth of his data: "For about two centuries back from the present time the data are fairly clear, but beyond this they become very imperfect and soon can be regarded only as myth" (page 28).

Using data such as these, Firth has formulated his views on ritual in tentative terms in his *Introduction*:

> The notions of ritual and its close analogue ceremonial have been much debated in social anthropology. My own view is that the most convenient way to look at ritual is to consider it as a formal set of procedures of a symbolic kind, involving a code for social communication, and believed to possess a special efficacy in affecting technical and social conditions of the performers or other participants. The formality of these procedures lies in the fact that they are directed not simply to the solution of an immediate technical problem by the most economical means, but are regarded as having in themselves a certain validity irrespective of their technical concomitants. Because of their general validity, apart from the individual situation, they tend to be given a repetitive routinized character which in itself is regarded as strengthening their significance. This significance is basically symbolic in that the physical behaviour of the participants 'stands for' relations of another kind, as between man and an aspect of Nature or man and putative spirits. Many rituals are performed to maintain an existing situation from degeneration; others to change the situation, if only to restore it to an original state of well-being. Ceremonial (ceremony) I regard as a species of ritual in which, however, the emphasis is more upon symbolic acknowledgement and demonstration of a social situation than upon the efficacy of the procedures in modifying that situation. Whereas other ritual procedures are believed to have a validity of their own, ceremonial procedures, while formal in character, are not believed in themselves to sustain the situation or effect a change in it.
>
> (pages 12–13)

In the ancient Indian Vedic ritual several rites and recitations occur that are to some extent similar to the Tikopia ceremonies. When the Agni fire is to be generated by rubbing two pieces of wood together, the Adhvaryu, chief priest of the Yajurveda, says to the Hotā, chief priest of the Rigveda:

Address Agni who is to be churned!

The Hotā now recites three verses from the Rigveda, the first one three times:

We implore you for our share, god Savitr,
owner of all that is worthwhile, always assisting!
(Rigveda 1.24.3)

Great heaven and earth must mix this ritual for us;
assist us with their support!
(RV 1.22.13)

Atharvan churched you, Agni, from the lotus;
priests from the head of the universe.
(RV 6.16.13)

When fire flares up, the Adhvaryu speaks to the Hotā again:

Address Agni who is born!

The Hotā recites:

And people will say: Agni, killer of the demon, has arisen,
who in each fight wins booty
(RV 1.74.3)

When fire is about to be installed on the altar, the Adhvaryu says to the Hotā:

Address Agni who is thrust forward!

and the Hotā recites:

Agni whom they carry like a ring on their hand,
like a new born baby; who performs successfully
rites for the clans!
(RV 6.16.40)

Next the Adhvaryu says to the Hotā:

Address Agni who is kindled!

and the Hotā recites a number of verses while the Adhvaryu puts sticks of firewood on the fire (see Chapter 11A, AGNI I:307–311). The number of verses and sticks of firewood depends on the ritual in which this rite is embedded.

On a later occasion, when fire is about to be transported from the first altar to another, placed further east, the Adhvaryu addresses the Hotā as well as a second Hotā, and all, including the Adhvaryu himself, accompany the fire on its journey east with long recitations from Rigveda and Yajurveda (AGNI I:551–555).

In describing these Vedic rites and recitations I have not specified contexts in the manner in which this was done by Firth with regard to the Tikopia rites. I have not specified, for example, whether these rites are connected with new born babies, initiations, marriages, funerals, or other events. The reason for this omission is that rites such as these may be inserted or embedded in numerous ritual contexts. This corroborates van Gennep's and Durkheim's observations referred to before, and is a significant circumstance to which I shall return. This circumstance is also related to the question whether these Vedic formulas may be regarded as "free formulas" in Firth's sense. These are not, though others are. However, this is a matter too complex to be discussed in the present context (cf. Renou, 1954, s.v. *ūha*; Gonda 1977:565–567; AGNI, I:310–311, 532–533, 683–685, etc.).

I have described these Vedic rites in some detail (omitting many further details, for example those that pertain to the technique of recitation) not because they are so similar to the Tikopia ceremonies recorded by Firth, but in order to illustrate the difference in kind between the data we are dealing with. The anthropologist records what he finds on his island or in his village or tribe; with luck, he is in a position to revisit the area of his earlier fieldwork, and find out whether there have been changes. "Anthropology is basically the process of trying to get a story out of a snapshot, and it usually doesn't work" (Smith 1987:207). The student of Vedic ritual, on the other hand, deals with a very extensive ancient literature on ritual, which includes a complete inventory of all the recitations and chants accompanying rites that have been performed more or less continuously in different parts of the Indian subcontinent for about three millenia. The formulas I quoted with which the Adhvaryu addresses the Hotā are in fact about 2,700 years old, and the recitations by the Hotā are even older.

How can we be certain about such unbelievably remote dates? Because of the structure and continuity of the Indian tradition. These recitations and the rites that they accompany have been the subject of a continuous tradition of commentaries and subcommentaries from shortly after the time of their first composition to the present day. While the works of this tradition have been largely committed to writing, there are also extensive oral traditions that supplement them. The rites themselves continue to be performed as a function of these oral traditions, which have recently become the object of what has been called "Vedic fieldwork" (a term introduced by C. G. Kashikar 1968). A comparison of the oral traditions with each other and with the texts shows that many of the original compositions survive in their pristine form. Cross-references, quotations, and inscriptions, together with their historical, linguistic, philological and literary analysis, enable scholars to check and countercheck the authenticity of texts and traditions, establish their approximate date and origin, and discover what changes they have undergone.

In India, the Vedic rituals have not only been described in painstaking detail, and subjected to careful discussions and commentaries by Indian scholars from about the eighth century B.C.E., but all these ritual texts and their accessories have been studied and made accessible by several generations of modern Sanskritists from about the middle of the nineteenth century. Albrecht (not Max) Weber, Hillebrandt, and Schwab were the founders, and Caland was the grand master of this branch of Sanskrit scholarship. A bibliography of works and publications on Vedic ritual (including surveys, manuals, dictionaries, etc.) by these savants and by contemporary scholars from Europe, America, Japan, and India itself would constitute a sizable volume. The only social scientists who recognized the importance of some of this work were Hubert and Mauss, who published in 1899 in the *Année sociologique* their article "Essai sul la nature et la fonction du sacrifice." This essay, to which I referred several times, over-emphasized animal sacrifice, for which it relied on Schwab's monograph of 1886. It still provides the best starting point from which sophisticated and possibly adequate theories of ritual can be derived. Unfortunately, it has not induced other anthropologists or sociologists to consult the ongoing literature on Vedic ritual. Durkheim referred to Hubert and Mauss' article, as we have seen, in the context of observations that he himself failed to interpret and that were generally ignored elsewhere. The only scholar who has been inspired by the "Essai" is the Indologist J. C. Heesterman, who introduced a sociological perspective into the classical Indological studies on ritual in his book *The Ancient Indian Royal Consecration* of 1957 and in numerous articles, some included in Heesterman 1985.

What is true of India is also true of China, though the ritual tradition is not equally ancient and contemporary scholars are only beginning to tap its resources (see, e.g., Schipper 1975). There is a voluminous literature in Japanese on ritual, Buddhist and Shinto, by ancient ritualists as well as contemporary social scientists. In contrast to the veritable oceans of data and evidence that the classical civilizations of Asia provide and that modern scholars continue to make accessible, the data brought back by contemporary anthropologists, interesting and varied as they are, must strike any unbiased observer as meager. No wonder that the conclusions derived from these data are tentative and unsteady. Firth in his observations on ritual, quoted above (p. 146), refers on the one hand to the symbolic interpretations that reflect the traditional Western perspective reinforced by German philosophers, and recognizes on the other hand that rites and rituals have a certain validity of their own, without however explaining in what this validity consists or where it resides. The cause for such wavering indecision, which is not very different from the inconclusive views espoused by

Durkheim, Weber, and even Malinowski, lies to a large extent in the limited and inadequate nature of the source data. The first conclusion that may be inferred from this state of affairs is that no theory of ritual can be taken seriously unless it comes to terms with the data provided by the classical civilizations of Asia, in particular India and China.

A similar situation as we still find in the social sciences existed not long ago in Western linguistics. At first it was thought that the structure of human language could be studied adequately by collecting data from so-called primitive and exotic languages. Wilhelm von Humboldt in *Über die Verschiedenheit des menschlichen Sprachbaues* of 1836 used Javanese, Burmese, Chinese, Sanskrit, and "Delaware" in this spirit, though he also made some use of concepts that originated with the Sanskrit grammarians. This is reminiscent of those early ethnologists who adopted terms such as *totem* or *mana* from the cultures they had studied, the only difference being that the terms of the Sanskrit grammarians are technical terms with very precise meanings, whereas *totem* and *mana* are hazy notions. The next step of development of Western linguistics is represented by Whitney, who provided in his grammar of Sanskrit a virtually complete inventory of the language, but who still regarded Pāṇini, the greatest Indian grammarian, as an object of Indological investigation, at best an informant, and did not recognize that he was in fact: a deceased colleague of genius. This was not merely an oversight; it went hand in hand with profound misapprehensions that Whitney entertained with regard to the nature of human language (above page 50). The final stage was initiated by Leonard Bloomfield and has culminated in the work of Paul Kiparsky, in which contemporary linguistics comes to terms with the insights and results of the Sanskrit grammarians.

In the West, linguistics is now considerably ahead of the study of ritual, which has not even reached a state of development where it can be regarded as a scientific discipline. If any progress is to be made, these studies will first have to incorporate the ritual evidence from India, China, and Japan. Next they must take account of the Indian science of ritual (Chapter 26). Given further incentives and new creative insights, what has long been a grab-bag of metaphysical and other speculations may then finally turn into a science.

14B. Victor Turner

Some of the comments that were made on the work of Raymond Firth apply to Victor Turner. He reflects on his study of the *Chihamba* ritual in the following terms:

> At one time I employed a method of analysis derived essentially from Durkheim via A. R. Radcliffe-Brown. I considered the social function of *Chihamba* with reference to the structural form of Ndembu society. But this method did not enable me to handle the complexity, asymmetry, and antinomy that characterize real social processes, of which ritual performances may be said to constitute phases or stages. I found that ritual action tended thereby to be reduced to a mere species of social action, and the qualitative distinctions between religious and secular custom and behaviour came to be obliterated. The ritual symbol, I found, had its own formal principle. It could be no more reduced to, or explained by, any particular category of secular behaviour or be regarded as the resultant of many kinds of secular behaviour, than an amino-acid molecular chain could be explained by the properties of the atoms interlinked by it. The symbol, particularly the nuclear symbol, and also the plot of a ritual, had somehow to be grasped in their specific essences. In other words, the central approach to the problem of ritual has to be intuitive, although the initial intuition may then be developed in a logical series of concepts. (Turner 1975:186–187).

Turner, until his recent death the leading and most influential American anthropologist to write on ritual, did not accept the traditional doctrine that rites always have to re-enact myths. He distinguishes, for example, in Ndembu ritual, rites that have a mythological character from others that do not (1975:177). In the passage quoted, he distinguishes two features of ritual: symbol and plot. Both of these, he says, belong to a religious domain and cannot be reduced to, or explained by, secular behaviour. When he says that these features have to be grasped intuitively, before they can be studied logically, he formulates the general characteristic of all scholarly work, whether in the humanities, in the sciences, or in the social sciences to which I referred in Chapter 2 and in the Introductory Note to Part II. The dichotomy religious/secular (or sacred/profane) is another matter: a Western dualistic fetish to which we need not pay serious attention.

From the viewpoint of Vedic ritual, Turner's approach is a step forward from any approach which advocates the derivation of ritual from mythology or social structure. Moreover, Vedic ritual can be described as a "plot", or perhaps more appropriately, as an activity. It is not so easy to see why it should be a symbol. I suspect that this is another category which is imposed upon it from the outside. The main reason for this suspicion is that it is not easy to find anything that Vedic ritual could be a symbol of. So let us look a little more closely.

Earlier, Turner had distinguished three orders of reference for a symbol's use: "(1) its manifest sense(s), of which the subject is fully conscious and which is (are) related to the explicit aims of the ritual (to remove sterility, bring on rain, remove a dead hunter's incisor tooth from the body of his living kinsman, and so on); (2) its latent sense(s), of which the subject is only marginally aware but could have become fully aware and which is (are) related to other ritual and pragmatic contexts of social action; and (3) its hidden sense(s), of which the subject is completely unconscious and which is (are) related to infantile (and possibly pre-natal) experiences shared with most other members of his society, and perhaps with most other human beings" (Turner 1975:176).

As for the third kind of reference, Turner considers that it is outside the scope of anthropology: "It is best left to the various and by no means anonymous schools of depth psychologists". As for the first, it is easily disposed of in the case of the Nambudiri Agnicayana: this Vedic performance is typically self-contained and self-absorbed. There are no symbolic meanings going through their minds when they are engaged in performing the rites (above, page 115).

There are within the Agnicayana single rites which have a symbolic function of which the performers are aware. For example the Yajamāna or ritual patron keeps his fists closed because he is like a child in the womb of its mother, ready to be reborn. Others only appear to have such a function. For example, among the thousand bricks, ten are called "rain-bringing" bricks (above, page 116). Their name is sometimes recognized, but the ceremonies affecting them are not performed when rain is needed; they are performed as part of the Agnicayana when the Agnicayana is performed. Many bricks have names, and some of these evoke associations; but the majority of them, and the accompanying rites and recitations, lack any clear function or meaning. We shall return to this in a different context in chapter 24.

So we are left with the second possibility mentioned by Turner: the latent sense of a symbol. I have nothing against unobservables (Chapter 2) but the burden of proof rests on the shoulders of the person who makes such a claim. A good example to which I shall return (page 453) was provided by Heesterman (1962:18) who drew attention to the peculiar manner in which the victim in the Vedic sacrifice is bound to the stake: the cord is fastened to the right foot, goes round to the left side of the neck and is then wound round the right horn and finally fastened to the stake. Heesterman pointed out that thus room is left for the slaughterer's knife. Since the animal is never killed in this manner, this suggests that it formerly was. One can easily imagine that the performers could be said to be marginally aware of this, or that they would immediately recognize it as true if it were pointed out to them.

Such cases, however, are exceptional. The large majority of rites of the Agnicayana point in a different direction: they are performed for their own sake, and are not symbolic or reminiscent of anything else. Theories which reduce rites to something else are therefore not applicable to this ritual. Even if they are correct in historical terms, namely point to the historical origin of a rite, this origin has nothing to do with the ritual significance of the act. For example, the movement from west to east which characterizes certain ritual activities is connected with the eastward expansion of the Vedic Indians through the plains north of the Ganges. But the ritual is not a celebration of this:

that background has long disappeared. It is as with the etymological explanation of a word: in most cases, this has nothing to do with its function or meaning. It falls entirely within the scholar's domain.

In India this is well-known: usage prevails over etymology (*yogād rūḍhir balīyaḥ*) (page 23). The Mīmāmsā philosophers apply a similar argument to ritual: the ritual is to be performed for its own sake. Ritual is not for the sake of gods, but gods are for the sake of ritual. Ritual is not for wish fulfilment, since rites have to be performed by those who are eligible. I suspect that the stress on symbol and meaning is largely due to the preoccupations of scholars. It is they who connect rites with myths and with sense. It is they who want to understand, namely, explain in words and language what is basically activity. The irreducibility of ritual shows that action constitutes a category in its own right. To the Vedic ritualist, it is the action which counts, not verbal elucidation or interpretation. Of course, in India there have also been scholars, such as the authors of the Brāhmanas. But practising ritualists pay no attention to their theories.

It is possible that there is a further reason for this state of affairs that is historical. Western religions stress "right opinion", or *orthodoxy*. Indian religions stress "right action", or *orthopraxy*. To Western scholars, Indian religions only make sense if they express ideas. To Indian practitioners, ideas are optional. A practising Hindu ritualist can be a democrat, a communist, an atheist, a magician, or a rationalist. What counts and makes him a Hindu is primarily what he does. This topic, too, has ramifications to which we return in Chapter 28.

15

Syntax, Semantics and Performatives

The argument to show that Pravargya and Upasad form a single unit within which the two parts occur in the given order (Chapter 10) paid no attention to meaning and was a purely syntactic argument. Many of the observations made in the previous Chapters amount to saying that in the study of ritual, a syntactic approach is more fruitful and promising than the semantic approach that is customary. We shall expand this observation later, but it is high time to form a more precise conception of the distinction between syntax and semantics before we go any further and contemplate ramifications. The definitions are simple: syntax is concerned with relations between (logical, mathematical, linguistic, or other) expressions; and semantics is concerned with the relations between such expressions and their meanings.

The clearest examples of syntax and semantics are found in elementary mathematics. One difficulty that schoolchildren often experience when they are introduced to algebra is that its letter symbols are devoid of specific meaning. They are "abstract." This applies not only to the *x*, which stands for the unknown answer of a problem, and to other so-called "variables," but also to "constants," such as *a* and *b*, in terms of which the problems themselves are formulated. For example, the expression:

$$(a + b)^2 = a^2 + 2 \cdot a \cdot b + b^2 \qquad (23)$$

applies to many values and interpretations given to *a* and *b*, and to operators other than "=," "+," and " · ". The constants may be interpreted as integers, e.g.:

$$(2 + 3)^2 = 2^2 + 2 \cdot 2 \cdot 3 + 3^2$$

or also:

$$(29 + 37)^2 = 29^2 + 2 \cdot 29 \cdot 37 + 37^2;$$

but the expression (23) also applies to real numbers, imaginary numbers, or even geometrical configurations, as in:

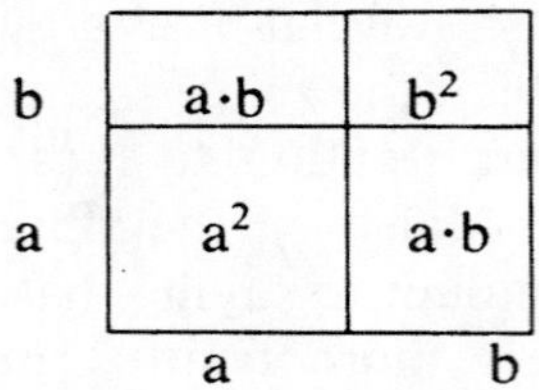

In this figure, the total area of the square is $(a + b)^2$, which consists, as mere visual inspection shows, of four areas: a^2, b^2, and twice $a \cdot b$. Such wide and flexible applications of the symbols of algebra are characteristic of all of mathematics, and explain why it is at the same time abstract and powerful.

The importance of the syntactic approach is that it studies expressions such as (23) without paying attention to any of the interpretations or meanings that might be assigned to them. The identity or equality that (23) expresses applies to all readings assigned to "*a*" or "*b*" without distinction. So we are in a position to do many things at the same time, and more things than we can possibly imagine, by restricting ourselves to the syntactic manipulation of such expressions. Moreover, we will not be swayed or influenced by particular interpretations and arrive at slanted or biased views that have nothing to do with intrinsic structure.

I shall now illustrate the semantic and syntactic approaches with respect to an even simpler symbolic expression:

$$\text{A B C B A.} \tag{24}$$

In the semantic approach, the symbols A, B, and C are interpreted as meaning something or referring to something. In the syntactic approach we pay no attention to such possible meanings or interpretations, but study the configurations of the letter symbols only.

Adopting first the semantic approach, (24) may be understood in many different ways, for example:

I. referring to numbers, e.g.: 3 8 7 8 3.
II. referring to segments, e.g.:

III. referring to algebraic symbols, e.g.: (a + a).
IV. referring to words, e.g.: found sleepy on sleepy found.
V. referring to tones, e.g.:

VI. referring to movements, e.g.: three steps up a staircase and then down again; or: making a pirouette, jumping up, kneeling, jumping up, making a pirouette again.
VII. referring to activities, e.g.: unlocking a box, opening it, putting something inside, closing it, locking it.
VIII. referring to rites, e.g.: making fire, pouring Soma, chanting a hymn, pouring Soma, making fire.

There is literally no end to the possible interpretations of (24).

Adopting a syntactic approach, there are also indefinitely many possibilities. For example, (24) is part of:

I. M N A B C B A N M, but also of:
II. M N A B C B A M N.
III. it is a mirror image of itself.
IV. it consists of five units, just as: P Q R S T.

V. it has specific instances, such as:
A B B C C C B B A, but also:
VI. A B C B A – B C B – C – B C B – A B C B A.
VII. it is interspersed through: P A Q B R C R B Q A P, but also through:
VIII. P A B Q R S C T B U V W A.

And so on. The expression (24) may be looked upon as a specific instance of a more general expression, viz.:

$$A_1 \ldots A_{n-1}\, A_n\, A_{n-1} \ldots A_1 \qquad (25)$$

where "n" is a natural number. In the case of (24), n = 3, for (24) can be rewritten as:

$$A_1\, A_2\, A_3\, A_2\, A_1$$

It is relevant in the present context that the elementary units of mathematical theories, and anything that can be stated in terms of such units, may be of any size or kind: these structures operate on many levels. Mathematics applies accordingly to the inside of the atom as well as to the universe.

The semantic approach often seems richer than the syntactic, but that is based upon the idea that syntax studies nothing but sequences of symbols that follow each other in linear order. Chapter 12 made it clear that syntacticians are not behaviorists who are only concerned with sequences of events. In the simple sentence:

I gave Peter his book back,

the underlying syntactic structure explains that "his book" is a unit and "book back" is not. This may be expressed by "trees" or by simple parentheses, e.g.:

I gave Peter (his book) back.

We have studied the syntactic structures of ritual from Chapter 8 onward and have not yet paid any systematic attention to semantics. We shall do so in Chapter 25, but will first approach semantics through one of its sub-disciplines: the study of performatives. The first scholar who explored the idea that performatives may be relevant to the study of ritual was the anthropologist S. J. Tambiah in his Radcliffe-Brown Lecture of 1979 entitled "A Performative Approach to Ritual."

Tambiah's lecture is rich in facts and ideas, and I cannot do it full justice in the present context. Moreover, it develops results from an earlier study, Tambiah 1968b, and the reader is urged to consult both. Tambiah's 1979 lecture also discusses ideas from other disciplines that may fruitfully contribute to the anthropological study of ritual. Unfortunately, this richness is sometimes misleading and some concepts are probably incompatible with each other. For example, Tambiah's emphasis on rule-governed activity in which the rules are *constitutive* contradicts his continuing emphasis on "symbolic communication"—the prevailing anthropological doctrine that is probably wrong on both counts (for ritual is neither symbolic nor communication). Let me try to disentangle some of these ideas.

When Tambiah refers to Austin's performatives he invokes Searle's distinction between *regulative* and *constitutive*. Regulative rules regulate a pre-existing activity, an activity whose existence is logically independent of the rules, as for instance when dinner-table manners regulate the eating of food. Constitutive rules constitute (and also regulate) an activity the existence of which is logically dependent on the rules, as in the rules of football or chess (Searle 1969:34–35). One of Tambiah's chief theses is that many rites are constitutive acts:

> To Austin's classical examples of constitutive acts such as greeting, baptizing, naming a ship and marriage vows—all of which are created and understood within the bounds of the conventions themselves—to these we can add several anthropological examples: the installation of a Tallensi chief, Ndembu circumcision rites, Lodagaa mortuary rites, a Japanese tea ceremony, a Catholic mass, and a multitude of cosmic rites and festivals which are self-constituting events and of which we have several classic descriptions (Tambiah 1979:128).

Tambiah derives interesting conclusions from this important insight but these are somewhat obscured because he also inserts a long section entitled "Application of Information Theory to Ritual" which would be relevant if we were dealing with the transmission of messages between a sender and a receiver. Tambiah uses the latter idiom when criticizing Egan's contrary contention that the Sinhalese *edura* healer "can be compared to an individual stranded on a desert island with only a radio transmitter, but no receiver" (Tambiah: 150). The idea is, apparently, that healing and ritual are communicative acts in which there *are* transmitters and receivers between whom there is communication of information. I am in no position to comment on Egan's comments on healing, but such criticism, whatever its force, does not throw light on ritual, especially if we have agreed that ritual consists of rules that constitute it, that is, on whose forms it logically depends. Tambiah alludes to this insight later, for example, when he observes that the Thai tonsure rites, whenever and for whomever performed, "followed certain obligatory sequences" (Tambiah: 157). But in contexts where communication or information theories are invoked (as in Geertz: see Chapter 25C), one feels that Tambiah has not fully exploited the implications of his insights which may incidentally explain why he has not made use of them in some of his later work (Chapter 25A). The inapplicability of communication and information theories to the study of ritual follows *a fortiori* from the fact that such theories have been singularly unhelpful even in explaining language, where meaning, communication and information play a larger and more obvious role than they do in ritual.

The anthropological examples Tambiah added to Austin's are constitutive but they are not performatives for the simple reason that they are not utterances of language. Austin dealt only with those: he was concerned with linguistic utterances that not only say but also do something, or, more precisely: that in saying, do something (above, page 22). Austin drew attention to the fact that some utterances of language are *acts*. Searle's distinction between regulative and constitutive has a wider application: it applies to rules and rule-governed activities, language as well as ritual. But to say that rites are performative. i.e., that they *do* something, is nothing special or remarkable: they are acts to begin with. To call an utterance performative is interesting because it calls attention to a special class of utterances; to call an act performative is trivial because most acts are performative.

To say that a rite is constitutive means that its existence and meaning depend on rules. If the rite *only* depends on rules (the condition implicit in Searle's use of the term) it cannot also be explained because of its alleged symbolic or semantic reference or value; it may possess such features, but they cannot, in that case, be constitutive; they must be added. This is remarkably often the case, as we have seen: all the symbolic explanations of Vedic ritual in the Brāhmaṇa literature are ad hoc, arbitrary or rationalizations, i.e., after-thoughts. If this holds true of the rites Tambiah refers to, their existing explanations in semantic terms (for example, Turner's explanations of Ndembu rites) must be wrong. Tambiah has not drawn this conclusion for otherwise he would have been led to the analysis in syntactic terms that I am advocating. In that case he would have discovered that syntactic structures can be explained by postulating rules, some of which are constitutive of the rites themselves.

I have mentioned that I cannot do justice to Tambiah's important study; the above remarks should be taken with a grain of salt. They mainly intend to demonstrate that Tambiah, by advocating a rule-oriented approach, somewhat misleadingly called performative, went significantly beyond the semantic approach that is characteristic of almost all anthropological work on ritual. Lévi-Strauss in his "structuralism" took a similar step but it was still inextricably connected with semantics.

By walking with a more vigorous stride than he himself realized, Tambiah showed that explanations in terms of meaning are inadequate. He thereby paved the way for a syntactic approach that may ultimately lead to the scientific study of ritual.

16

Music and Ritual

When looked at from a syntactic perspective there are numerous similarities between music and ritual. I shall discuss seven examples from Music in 16A, and seven examples from ritual in 16B.

16A. Seven Musical Structures

The examples of musical structures are taken from Western classical music but include some references to classical Indian music. The units range over a wide area, from single tones, motives and phrases ("approximating to what one could sing in a single breath": Schoenberg 1970:3) to Sonatas and Symphonies.

I. REFRAIN. In poetry as well as music, it is common to end each of a sequence of structures with the same form, as in:

$$A\,R - B\,R - C\,R - D\,R - \ldots \qquad (26)$$

Music differs from poetry in that the refrain frequently occurs at the beginning as well as at the end. In Gregorian chant, the variable elements A, B, C, . . . are often sung as a solo, and the refrain R by a chorus. In church music, the refrain may be *Amen* or *Alleluia*, the latter closing with the *jubilus*, a long vocalization on the final *–a*. Medieval and Renaissance music is known for its *formes fixes* such as *rondeau, ballatta*, and *virelai*. In the *virelai*, the refrain occurs at the beginning and serves each time as the opening of the next unit, as in:

$$R\,A\,R\,B\,R\,C\,R. \qquad (27)$$

In all these forms, the refrains are each time exactly the same. After the Renaissance, refrains tend to be varied in many ways, making them musically more interesting. I shall express a variation of a form "R" as: "R′". In the following example, the second Nocturne for Piano by Erik Satie, the refrain consists of

four measures. It occurs at the beginning, and recurs twice in a varied form (where the score says: "Reprendre"):
The structure is:

$$\text{R A R}' \text{ B R}''. \qquad (28)$$

II. CYCLE. I shall use this term, which is very general, to refer to a structural property that is equally general, viz., one that begins and ends with the same element, as:

$$A\ B\ C\ D\ \ldots\ A. \qquad (29)$$

In musical phrases, it is extremely common to begin and end with the same note, e.g., in Mozart's *Nozze di Figaro*, No. 3 ("Se vuol ballare"):

Larger compositions often begin and end in the same key. For compositions to begin and end with exactly the same phrase is actually rather rare: the *Harvard Dictionary of Music* refers to two seventeenth century examples, from Giovanni Maria Trabaci and Steffano Landi (Apel 1970:218a referring to Davison and Apel, 1974, Nos. 191 and 208).

It is nearly universal, on the other hand, for musical compositions to return to their point of departure at the end by means of a variation of the opening theme, viz., adopting a structure of the form:

$$A\ B\ C\ D\ \ldots\ A'. \qquad (30)$$

A very well known example is the first movement of Beethoven's Symphony No. 5, which begins as follows:

and ends:

A particularly important simple form of (30) is:

$$A\ B\ A'. \tag{31}$$

This is the basic form of many types of composition, including the Sonata and the Symphony to which I shall return. The musical term for "A′" in such cases is recapitulation or restatement.

III. PALYNDROME. I shall use this term for a special type of cycle, also referred to as *retrograde* or *mirror*. It is a musical illustration of the structure discussed in the previous section:

$$A\ B\ C\ B\ A, \tag{24}$$

or its generalization:

$$A_1 \ldots A_{n-1}\ A_n\ A_{n-1} \ldots A_1. \tag{25}$$

The simplest example is ascending and descending a scale (or the other way round). In a musical composition there is generally some kind of variation. In classical Indian music, when the scale is introduced by an ascent (*ārohaṇa*) followed by a descent (*āvarohaṇa*), the latter often uses different notes and is therefore not a mirror of the former. An identical retrograde movement occurs in Debussy's *Prelude* No. 10 ("The Engulfed Cathedral"):

Retrograde structures are used in most canonical, fugal, and 12-tone compositions. In the *cancrizans* (crab canon), the melody is accompanied by itself played backwards, as in the following example from Bach's *Musical Offering*:

The palindrome occurs with variations in larger structures. The structure of Fugue No. 16 in Book I of Bach's *Wohltemperiertes Clavier* can be expressed by the following scheme of expositions (referred to by A's) and episodes (referred to by B's and C's): (cf. Green 1965:265–267)

$$A\ B\ A\ C - A'\ B'\ A'' - C'\ A'''\ B''\ A'''' \quad (32)$$

Bach's motet *Jesu, meine Freude* consists of eleven parts: the music of No. 11 (a 4-part *Chorale*) is identical with that of No. 1, and No. 10 (a 5-part *Chorus*) is a shortened version of No. 2 (Steinitz 1978, 34), so that the structure is:

A B . . . . . . B′ A. (33)

A similar pattern, ranging over longer stretches and closer to a full-fledged palindrome, occurs in Bach's *Johannes Passion* (Steinitz, *ibid.*). If we omit the Evangelist recitatives from the section consisting of parts Nos. 27 through 52, and regard Nos. 31 and 32 as parallel interpolations with No. 48, the structure may be described as follows (the numbers of the parts are written below the corresponding structural elements):

A	B			C	D	E	D′	C′	B′			A′	
27	29,	31-2,	34	36	38	40	42	44	46,	48,	50	52.	(34)

IV. OVERLAPPING. This feature of structure applies only to simultaneous occurrences, i.e., two (or more) tones, motives, phrases or melodies played or sung at the same time. It cannot therefore be represented by linear sequences of symbols, such as I have used so far. Here is a simple example of overlapping motives from Mozart's *Sonata for Violin and Piano*, K.402:

Overlapping occurs frequently in counterpoint and polyphonic music, especially in fugues, canons, etc.

V. THREESOMES. Triple repetitions are common on many levels, from simple triplets to the threesomes that were universal in church music because of their symbolism (viz., the trinity). For compositions to begin or end with a triple repetition of a motive or theme is very common in Indian music and occurs, e.g., in Mozart's *Sonata for Violin and Piano*, K.377–II:

or in Schubert's *String Quartet*, Op. 29-III:

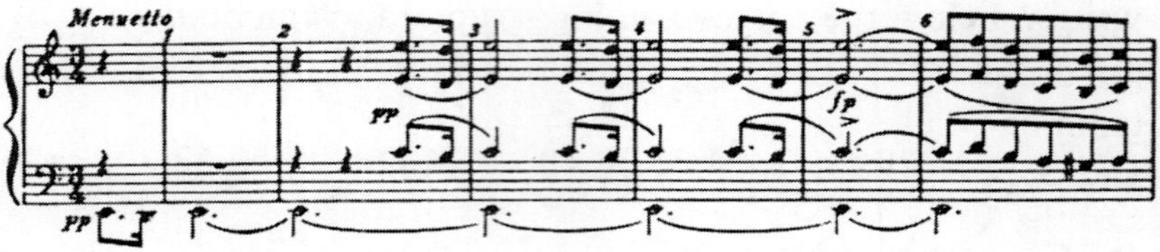

Throughout classical western music, the chief function of the number "three" is that it is the most common number of subdivisions of many larger units. It is characteristic of the two following structures, Sonata and Symphony.

VI. SONATA. This form is characteristic of classical Western music since Haydn and Mozart. It has the following structure:

$$A\ B\ A', \tag{31}$$

which originated from the simpler form:

$$A\ B\ A, \tag{35}$$

which is found in the Rondo and Minuet. Often the elements themselves are again of the same form. In the paradigm, A is called the exposition, B the development (German: *Durchführung* which is better translated as "elaboration": Schoenberg 1970:200, note), and A′ the recapitulation. A and A′ are usually in the same key, while B uses various keys and therefore modulation.

The prehistory and history of the Sonata form exhibit extraordinary variety. Sometimes the structure is influenced by the use of various instruments, or varying numbers of players. At first the parts were numerous and brief, and followed each other without a break. Later they became fewer, longer, and more separate from each other. The solo parts were played by violins, flutes, oboes, etc.; the accompaniment was often on the harpsichord. Before the eighteenth century, the principle was simple: if someone was around who was able to play the part on his instrument, he was welcome to do it.

VII. SYMPHONY. The symphony started tripartite, in the Sonata form, with more instruments and performers: a Sonata for orchestra. Soon a fourth part was added, chiefly for entertainment: the Scherzo. The two middle movements, Andante and Scherzo, are frequently of the form (35), whereas the first and the last movement are more often of the form (31). The form was perfected by Haydn and Mozart, and enlarged and extended by Beethoven. Beethoven lengthened the *coda*, a final piece following A′, and the development, introduced numerous variations and added introductions to the various pieces. The increasing complexity of symphonies after Beethoven has from time to time been counterbalanced by simplification of the thematic structure. In Berlioz' first two symphonies, for example, a single theme (the "idée fixe") appears in each movement. The opening theme of the first movement returns in the final movement in Brahms' *Third Symphony* (the same return is found in his *Clarinet Quintet*). The finale of Bruckner's *Eighth Symphony* includes a simultaneous statement of the principal themes of the three preceding movements (Green 1965:176). (Some recurrences are incidental, or have the character of reminiscences or quotations, as in Beethoven's *Fifth* and *Ninth Symphonies*, and in his *Piano Sonata*, Op. 101.)

To express these structures adequately more complex mathematical expressions than the linear are required (for other formalizations see Ruwet 1966, reprinted in Ruwet 1972:100–134). Although the expression ABA (35) is linear, the expression ABA′ (31) is only apparently so: it has an inner or underlying structure that is not linear. The variation A′ depends on the original statement A, and therefore on the context. However, it does not depend on the immediately preceding context, in which case it would have been possible to express it with the help of a *context-sensitive rule* of the form:

$$\mathrm{B\ A} \rightarrow \mathrm{B\ A'}. \qquad (36)$$

The variation depends on a context that is further away, which can be expressed by using *transformational rules*—the kind of rules that are characteristic of human language (Chapter 6). With the help of such rules, the variation A′ can be introduced by rule structures like the following:

(37)

This expresses at the same time that the variation is a variation of the first movement, and that it occurs in the finale.

I have purposely provided a medley of musical forms in order to illustrate the variety of musical structures. Whenever such a structure is given, it is possible to define a notion of "structural meaning" that depends entirely on structure. The "structural meaning" of the entire structure is that structure itself, and the "structural meaning" of an element within the structure is defined in terms of the position the element occupies in that structure. For example, part of the structural meaning of a phrase may be that it is a refrain because it occurs as a refrain. The notion of structural meaning adds nothing to the existing structures themselves.

Another type of structural meaning that is typical of classical Western music may be defined in terms of the notions of consonant and dissonant intervals. Consonant intervals are intervals such as the fourth and fifth that "sound stable and complete" (Piston 1962:6). Dissonant intervals deviate from these and require a resolution into consonant intervals. Such resolutions operate on the harmonic as well as on the melodic level. The musicologist Schenker and the composer Hindemith have used the terms "tension" and "release" to characterize this fundamental opposition between the formation of dissonance and its resolution into consonance.

The resolution is only rarely introduced by a single move. It is more often reached through intermediate steps that introduce new dissonances and resolutions. An example occurs at the end of the first *Prelude* of *Das Wohltemperierte Clavier*:

Consonance and dissonance are to some extent relative concepts: their perception changes with history because ears get used to dissonances. This was pointed out by the devil to the composer Adrian Leverkühn in Thomas Mann's *Dr. Faustus* (English translation, 1949:239):

> The diminished seventh is right and full of expression at the beginning of Op. 111. It corresponds to Beethoven's whole technical niveau, doesn't it?—the tension between consonance and the harshest dissonance known to him. The principle of tonality and its dynamics lend to the chord its specific weight. It has lost it—by a historical process which nobody reverses. . . . Every sound carries the whole, carries also the entire history in itself.

Notes possess structural meaning when their occurrence can be explained because it contributes to the formation of dissonances or their resolution into consonances. Since some dissonant intervals have different resolutions, notes may have multiple meaning. In other words, there is functional ambiguity. The diminished seventh cord, for example, may be interpreted in four different ways, each expecting a different resolution. The four interpretations can be distinguished by sounding different notes (in the left hand) against the chord (in the right hand) in the following example constructed by Piston (1962:193):

Philosophers and musicologists have not been satisfied with structural meaning alone, even with functional ambiguity added. They have mused and written extensively on the meaning of music in general. In simplified terms, there can be said to be two schools. According to the first, music is allegorical and expresses nonmusical elements, e.g., features of the universe or of man, such as emotions, passions, or moods. According to the second, music is to be understood on its own terms. This somewhat academic distinction corresponds to a distinction made by some composers, musicians and music critics between "program music" and "absolute music." Program music is inspired by a nonmusical program, for example, a poem or picture, usually indicated in its title (like Debussy's "Engulfed Cathedral" actually placed at the end of the music between parentheses.). Absolute music is not characterized in nonmusical terms. The *Harvard Dictionary* (s.v. "program music") elaborates instructively:

> Although examples of program music are found in nearly all periods from at least the 14th century, it was not until the 19th century that it became a serious rival of absolute music, to the point of ousting the latter—at least temporarily—from its dominating position. About 1900, many persons, particularly writers on music, believed that in order to be understandable music must 'express something' or 'tell a story.' . . . Today such views are a thing of the past . . ." (Apel 1970:696a).

Sometimes music actually imitates the sounds of nature or culture. Schoenberg (1970:95–97) quotes examples from Beethoven and Smetana (the sound of a brook or river), Wagner (flickering flames), Schubert (the weathervane) and Bach (the tearing of the temple veil). The *Harvard Dictionary* refers to

Beethoven's renderings of the cries of the nightingale, cuckoo and quail, Wagner's imitations of the toad and serpent, and Richard Strauss' of a flock of sheep. "The climax of this trend (and, in a sense, the *reductio ad absurdum* of program music) is Respighi's *The Pines of Rome*, where the problem of imitating the nightingale is solved by simply using a recording of an actual nightingale's song" (Apel 1970:697a).

It is obvious that all such imitations are anecdotal and have little or nothing to do with "the meaning of music." Musical compositions may be inspired or occasioned by nonmusical things such as a cathedral, but no music conveys the meaning *cathedral* in the systematic manner in which the word "cathedral" of a natural language such as English refers to a cathedral. What such titles indicate is that music may be composed or played on almost any occasion. These titles are mere names, and therefore arbitrary. Architectural monuments may also be referred to by names (e.g., "The Parthenon," "The White House"), but such names convey no architectural meaning. Similarly, Sonatas may be referred to by names such as "Spring," "Waldstein," "Moonlight," or "Appasionata," but these convey no musical meaning. They give radio announcers something to talk about for the benefit of listeners in need of nonmusical entertainment. If the expression "the meaning of music" *must* be used, it can only refer to the *structure* of music, that is, to syntactic structures like the ones I have exemplified under the headings I-VII, and expressed by formulas such as (24)–(37).

What is characteristic of music, viz., formal structures, is not equally characteristic of other arts. Schopenhauer expressed this insight in the following terms:

> *Die Musik ist . . . darin von allen andern Kunsten verschieden, dass sie nicht Abbild der Erscheinung, oder richtiger, der adäquaten Objektivität des Willens, sondern unmittelbar Abbild des Willens selbst ist und also zum allen physischen der Welt das Metaphysische, zu aller Erscheinung das Ding an sich darstellt* ("Music differs from all the other arts in that it is not representation of appearance, or rather, of the adequate objectivity of the Will, but a direct representation of the Will itself, and

therefore manifests the metaphysical in all that is physical in the world, and the thing-in-itself in all appearance").

The idea is buried in metaphysical notions such as Kant's "thing-in-itself" and Schopenhauer's "Will". However, *des Pudels Kern* is straightforward: "music differs from all other arts in that it represents no appearance of anything else, but only itself." This passage occurs in Schopenhauer's *Welt als Wille und Vorstellung* of 1818 and is quoted by Nietzsche in *Die Geburt der Tragödie aus dem Geiste der Musik* of 1872. Schopenhauer clarified his view later by adapting traditional scholastic terms: concepts are the *universalia post rem*, music provides the *universalia ante rem*, and reality the *universalia in re*.

16B. Seven Ritual Structures

I shall again begin with seven examples described in syntactic terms, this time of ritual structures. The first five correspond to the first five musical examples discussed in 16A. The latter two structures are the Iṣṭi and the Soma Sequence (discussed in Chapters 9A and 9B). Here the correspondence is more roundabout, but not less significant. The structural elements range again over units of different size, from small elements of single rites that take less than a minute to perform, to larger rituals that take several days or more to execute.

Most of these ritual structures involve recitations or chants. In the discussion of Tikopia ceremonies (Chapter 14A) we have had occasion to observe that recitations are often an important feature of ritual. To the extent that the ritual recitations and chants exhibit musical features, the similarity between ritual and music is unsurprising. It will be found, however, that even if we disregard musical features of rituals, the similarities remain. Those interested in the purely musical structures that are also features of Vedic ritual should turn to the chants of the Sāmaveda. Their internal structure is taken into account elsewhere (see Staal 1961:chapter VII; Howard 1977; below, Chapters 19 and 23).

I. REFRAIN. There are several reasons for the frequency of ritual refrains. The ritual acts often culminate in an offering or oblation made by the Adhvaryu priest into the fire. These offerings and oblations are of several kinds, but they naturally come at the end of acts which exhibit great variety themselves. The refrains consist of two parts: an exclamation by the Adhvaryu (either *svāhā*! or *vauṣaṭ*!) and the "renunciation" (*tyāga*) recited by the Yajamāna or patron of the ritual, for example: "This is for Agni, not for me!" (above, pages 80, 121). The general structure is therefore of the form:

$$A\,P\,Q - B\,P\,Q - C\,P\,Q - D\,P\,Q - \ldots \qquad (26')$$

In long recitations from the Rigveda, such as the *śastra* recitations to which I shall return, the verses are recited uninterruptedly, without taking breath at the end of each verse. Breath is taken at the caesura between the second and third quarter of each verse. At each caesura, the final vowel or nasal is lengthened. Each verse ends in a lengthened *OM*—the famous mantra of later Hindu mysticism.

The bird shaped altar that is characteristic of the Agnicayana is constructed from a thousand bricks, each consecrated with three mantras. Of these, the first is generally specific and described for each brick or group of bricks, but the second and third are always the same, so that the structure is again the same as (26′) (see AGNI I:399).

The mantras recited before the final exclamations that accompany offerings, have often a similar internal structure. Here are two examples. After the altar has been completed, there are six oblations of curds mixed with honey. The accompanying mantras differ in their first lines, but all end with:

> Him whom we hate and who hates us
> I place in your jaws!

which is followed by: *sváhá*! (AGNI I:104, 381, 544–545).

Not long after this rite, which takes place on the ninth day of the Agnicayana performance, there is a long recitation called *camakam* after *ca me*, "and for me!" recited by the Adhvaryu after each word (AGNI I:563–574). This is immediately followed by seven butter oblations, made through a copper pipe attached to a small toy cart. Each mantra ends with the same refrain:

> May he protect brahman, kṣatram,
> may they protect brahman, kṣatram!

followed by: *svāhā*! (AGNI I: 574–575). Both rites have the same structure, expressed by (26′).

II. CYCLE. I shall use this term again for a structure of the form (29) (above, page 168). This is relatively rare in Vedic ritual, but an interesting variant occurs in the Agnicayana just before the *camakam* recitation. Seven oblations of cooked rice are made on potsherds for the Maruts, storm gods and companions of Indra. Seven recitations are involved that will be referred to a $A_1, \ldots, A_7$. These mantras are recited in low voice, cyclically, and in overlapping pairs, the first mantra always ending in the long vocalic insertion *–o*, and the oblation made with the last, as follows:

A_1 - A_2 – *svāhā!*
A_2 - A_3 – *svāhā!*
A_3 - A_4 – *svāhā!*
A_4 - A_5 – *svāhā!*
A_5 - A_6 – *svāhā!*
A_6 - A_7 – *svāhā!*
A_7 - A_1 – *svāhā!*

(AGNI I:562–563). This kind of pairwise overlapping, but without the cycle, is also found in the *kramapātha* mode of Veda recitation, used in the traditional transmission of Rig- and Yajurveda (see Staal 1961:24, 44; below, page 372).

III. PALINDROME. This is a very basic structure in Vedic ritual. It ranges, generally with variations, over small as well as large units. The Agniṣṭoma, a ritual performance that lasts five days, has such a structure, which is also found in the Darśapūrṇamāsa, or "Full and New Moon Ceremonies." Many *śastra* recitals and *stotra* chants are embedded in similar portmanteau patterns. I shall not describe these structures in greater detail, since I discussed them in Chapter 10.

IV. OVERLAPPING. A variety of this structure was described in the cycle discussed in II. The basic structure is very common and reflects a general principle that is metaphysical as well as structural: *horror vacui*. There should be no gaps; accordingly, everything has to be performed continuously (*saṃtatam*). The next rite is therefore begun before the previous one is over, and the same holds for recitations, chants, and their similar units (e.g., *bhakti*, to be chanted with one breath, from which the chants are constructed). The practice extends to forms of transmission of the ritual material. For example, some recitations are "prompted" by a helper, line for line, "before" they are recited by the ritually chosen and qualified officiating priest: but this priest starts each time before the prompting is over. It might be felt that this kind of "overlapping" is a practical matter and not the outcome of a structural principle. However, it is widespread and based upon principles. I have included it precisely in order to show that we are not in a position to pass such kinds of judgment when we are only beginning to subject the data to a structural analysis.

V. THREESOMES. Triplets are everywhere. All longer recitations from the Rigveda are subject to the rule: "Recite the first thrice, recite the last thrice," resulting in the structure:

$$A_1\ A_1\ A_1\ A_2\ A_3\ \ldots\ A_{n-2}\ A_{n-1}\ A_n\ A_n\ A_n. \qquad (38)$$

The Yajamāna and some of the priests frequently begin their recitations with the so-called *vyāhṛti*: *BHŪR-BHUVAḤ-SVAR* ("Earth-Sky-Heaven!"). Many larger units are subdivided into three, though four is also met with. We have already found such triplets in the Iṣṭi and the Soma Sequence. Each of the bricks of the bird-shaped altar is also consecrated with three mantras. All these are structural threesomes and are different from unstructured groups such as the three fires or altars, the three assistants of each chief priest, the three *stotra* chanters, the three Vedas, etc.

VI. The Iṣṭi has already been described (Chapter 9A).

VII. The Soma Sequence has already been described (Chapter 9B).

Some of the variations of Soma sequences exhibit dependencies that may be described as *thematic*. In many Soma sequences, the chant of the first episode is composed by putting to music three verses from the Ṛgveda. The recitation of the second episode begins with the same three verses, the first repeated three times. In the nocturnal rounds of the Atirātra, there is an additional refinement: in the *first* nocturnal round, the *first* quarter verse of each of these three verses (that occur both in the chant and in the recitation) is repeated; in the *second* nocturnal round, the *second* quarter verse of each of these three verses is repeated; and in the *third* nocturnal round, the *third* quarter verse is similarly repeated (see AGNI I:663–680).

16C. Conclusions

Now let us return to our old question: what do music or ritual mean? I hope it has become clear by this time that this question, with respect to the structures we have discussed, does not make sense. These structures do not mean anything apart from and beyond the structural complexity they display. They do not "refer" to specific aims, and although their names (insofar as they have names) may seem to hint at their longforgotten origins, these names do not evoke anything. The complexities inherent in these structures have to be learned and practised, and can be expressed with the help of precise rules—but they are not symbolizations of anything else and do not point to a realm beyond themselves.

In all these respects, there is considerable similarity between the musical and ritual categories we have considered. The similarities are not only structural, but also circumstantial. Just like Sonatas and Symphonies, iṣṭis are performed on different occasions (providing ample evidence in support of van Gennep's and Durkheim's observations, quoted in Chapter 13B) and have different names (like the *intichiuma* and *mbatjalkatiuma* rites referred to by Durkheim). Even the fact that a Soma sequence ends with drinking Soma is reminiscent of what may happen to music. Smoking and drinking of coffee and beer was quite common during musical performances throughout the nineteenth century. In Amsterdam it took strong conductors like Willem Kes and Willem Mengelberg to get rid of the cups, glasses and ashtrays, and introduce the musical puritanism that assimilated concert performances further to church services.

To dissociate rituals from religious services and group them together with music performances is only a small part of a general reclassification of the ritual phenomena. This becomes clear only at a level of abstraction sufficiently high to enable us to abstract from, or disregard, certain dissimilarities in order to detect certain similarities. Of course, there are dissimilarities as well as similarities between Sonatas, Symphonies, iṣṭis, and Soma sequences. But all four structures are also different from many other things, e.g., poems, epics, laws, theories, stories, cults, commercial transactions, educational projects, etc.—and similar to many others, e.g., dances, games, and certain sports.

Ritual is more rigid than music although this is partly due to the nature of our evidence, as we shall see in a moment. Western music is more rigid than Indian music although some cadenzas in concertos are improvised. A parallel occurs in the Soma rituals where a lecture in the local language (Malayalam), originally largely improvised, is addressed to the Yajamāna after his consecration by a senior member of the community (AGNI I: 329–333, 698–702). It is noteworthy that this address is concerned with the *meaning* (*artha*) of a command (*praiṣa*), which explains the use of the vernacular and underscores that the uses of Vedic Sanskrit elsewhere in the ritual are devoid of meaning.

The structural similarities between music and ritual discussed under the heading I through V are more than mere similarities: they are identities. However, the structures discussed under VI and VII are not sufficiently similar for one to say more than: Iṣṭi and Soma Sequence are to some extent to Vedic ritual what Sonata and Symphony are to classical Western music. Why then compare them with each other? The true significance of the comparison is this. Sonata and Symphony exhibit structural categories that characterize classical Western music, and do not refer to anything nonmusical. Similarly, Iṣṭi and Soma Sequence exhibit structural categories that characterize Vedic ritual, and do not refer to anything nonritual. Not even the defenders of program music have ever claimed that the Sonata form or the Symphony as such (as distinct from particular Sonatas and Symphonies) exhibit nonmusical features of the world—unless these are themselves syntactic or mathematical structures. Sonata and Symphony are obvious features of "absolute music." In the realm of ritual, Iṣṭi and Soma Sequences are equally obvious features of "absolute ritual." It has been assumed without question that every ritual structure must have meaning; in other words, that all ritual must be "program ritual." However, it should be obvious from the structures I have discussed that these can only be described as features of what may be called "absolute ritual." This is especially clear in the cases of the Iṣṭi and the Soma sequence.

There are important differences between data on music from roughly the second millenium C.E. in Europe and data on ritual from roughly the second millenium B.C.E. in India. The European data, for example, are much more complete in historical terms. We can trace the development of classical Western music step by step. The Indian data are relatively exhaustive only for the period during which the classical ritual was codified, i.e., approximately from the 8th to the 6th century B.C.E., when the Śrauta Sūtras were composed. There is much less information on the pre-classical ritual, though there are hints in the Rigveda and scholars like Heesterman have been able to reconstruct some of its general features. About the post-classical development of Vedic ritual we are informed to some extent, but unevenly. These later developments show mainly that the structures of the rites have not changed; but some ritual substances have been abandoned (e.g., the original Soma; some of the sacrificial animals; an occasional human head), and there have been new flurries of interpretation, from time to time. All this supports the thesis, that the most important feature of ritual is structure, and not substance or interpretation. Finally, the facts that we know Vedic ritual in a relatively codified form, and Western music throughout a period of dynamic and often revolutionary development explain in part that our ritual data appear to be more rigid than our musical data.

The structural similarities between Indian ritual of the second millenium B.C.E. and Western music of the second millenium C.E. are surprising, and certainly more interesting and significant than would be such similarities found between Indian ritual and music at different periods, or between European music and ritual at different periods of time. The similarities we have discussed are obviously not due to influences and are independent of historical relationships. The relations are purely structural, exhibit intrinsic similarities, and entitle us therefore to use the kind of synchronic treatment that the syntactic approach presupposes and demands. At the same time, it remains desirable to compare these findings with other similar specific data on music and ritual from other civilizations and periods of history.

It is possible that the high level of abstraction and formalization that characterizes both Vedic ritual and classical Western music is not widespread in terms of space or time. One thing seems certain: there was no highly developed music unconnected with ritual in India, and no highly developed ritual unconnected with music in Europe during the periods we have considered. What we know of classical music in India during the Vedic period is confined to the chants of the Sāmaveda, which are closely related to ritual. In Europe, the example of J. S. Bach is instructive. During 1717–1723, when he was employed at Köthen at a Calvinist court where music and ritual were not encouraged, he composed mainly secular music, adopting the same styles he had earlier used and was to use subsequently, when he spent much of his time composing music for the church.

All the evidence we have considered points in one direction: ritual and music have no meaning or content, and can be provided accordingly with any number of different meanings or interpretations. The preponderant and enduring characteristics of music and ritual are that they consist of formal structures of sounds and acts that can be studied most effectively and fruitfully by adopting a syntactic approach. These sounds and acts are like the letter symbols of mathematics in that they are abstract and can therefore be interpreted in any way we like.

There is additional evidence from Vedic ritual that leads to the same conclusion. The rites are traditionally transmitted from each generation to the next with the help of methods and techniques that pay exclusive attention only to their form. Meaning is not mentioned, and interpretations are not given. Of course, interpretations, or rather: speculations, exist, but they are no part of the ritual tradition. Such interpretations are found elsewhere, for example, in religious and philosophical texts. The recitations and chants that accompany ritual are also handed down without paying attention to their meaning (in as far as they possess meaning: for many chants and some recitations consist of meaningless syllables). Whereas all recitations and many of the chants are handed down in schools or houses, independent of their ritual applications and uses (see Staal 1961), ritual knowledge is primarily transmitted during ritual performances and their rehearsals. This applies to a limited extent to ritual recitations, as illustrated by my earlier reference to "prompting" (above page 181).

The transmission of ritual is illustrated on the Frontispiece, where an experienced ritualist, Cherumukku Vaidikan Vasudevan Akkitiripad, instructs his son Vallabhan, during the 1975 performance of the Agnicayana, how to perform the *nihnava* rite (see page xi; AGNI I:359; MacFarland-Staal 1988; and cf. Brough 1950). The son, C. V. Vallabhan Nambudiri, was the youngest among the seventeen officiating priests (he assumed the office of Neṣṭā). He was already an excellent reciter, and had witnessed numerous rites and ritual performances, but at the time of the Agnicayana he had never performed *nihnava* himself. His father appeared at the right time, and showed him precisely *how to do it*. No words were used. Neither father nor son would pause to think of the outsider's question, what the *nihnava* rite is supposed to mean. This is how ritual is transmitted—successfully, one might add, since it has gone on in India for about three thousand years. What is remarkable about this case of ritual transmission is that it disregards not only meaning, but does not even use language.

The most important contemporary anthropologist to pay attention to music is Lévi-Strauss. According to Lévi-Strauss (1964), there exist close links between myth and music, which are both "machines or instruments for the obliteration of time." Music is also, according to him, "the supreme mystery of the sciences of man" (*la suprême mystère des sciences de l'homme*). It is remarkable, however, how a synchronistic approach, valuable not only in its own right, but necessary for the understanding of structure, may obscure simple diachronic facts. In the scheme of evolution, music is obviously much older than myth. If there is a link between the two, it can only be that myth has adopted structures inherent in music. Since ritual displays similar structures, this explains the parallelisms between myth and ritual that have often been mentioned but that do not signify anything.

Lévi-Strauss sees music embodied in "that God, Richard Wagner," who has always exercised a morbid spell in French intellectual circles. But this is mere fashion, like Lévi-Strauss' own presentation of *Le cru et le cuit* as a musical composition, subdivided into Overture, Theme and Variations, Sonata, Fugue, Three-part invention, Rustic symphony in three movements. "The conceit is not new," says George Steiner, "one finds it in Baudelaire's theory of *correspondence* (to which Lévi-Strauss implicitly refers), in Mallarmé, and in Broch's *Death of Virgil*, a novel ordered in analogy with the changes of mood and rhythm in a string quartet. Lévi-Strauss does little, moreover, to enforce the musical mimesis. It remains a labored *jeu d'esprit*." The passage that contains the phrase referring to music as "the supreme mystery of the sciences of man," says:

> But since music is a language with some meaning at least for the immense majority of mankind, although only a tiny minority of people are capable of formulating a meaning in it, and since it is the only language with the contradictory attributes of being at once intelligible and untranslatable,

> the musical creator is a being comparable to the gods, and music itself the supreme mystery of the sciences of man, a mystery that all the various disciplines come up against and which holds the key to their progress (Lévi-Strauss 1964:26; English translation 1969:18).

Lévi-Strauss often uses concepts taken from linguistics or communication theory. A distinctive feature of human language is that it possesses, in addition to phonological and syntactic components, a third component which is semantic and which enables language to convey meaning or "transmit messages" (Chapter 6). This semantic component is linked in a precise and intricate manner to the other two components, so that meaning is systematically expressed by the speaker and understood by the hearer when structured sounds are transmitted through the air. Misunderstandings between users of a language occur, of course, but on account of this system, combined with redundancy and other communicative devices, these are kept to a minimum. Otherwise language could not function.

Music and ritual are not languages precisely because they lack the corresponding third component. Music can convey so many different things because it has no intrinsic meaning: there is no systematic relationship between its structured sounds and these many things. Systems of music differ not only between cultures (which is true of language); it is also patent within a culture that music means different things to different people who are equally familiar with it (which is not true of language). The only features of music that can be universally perceived are either the purely structural and physical (corresponding to syntax and phonology in language), or nonmusical accessories such as names or titles, provided of course they are explicitly attached. For this reason, Debussy's piece called after a cathedral does not convey the meaning *cathedral* in the systematic manner in which the word "cathedral" of a natural language such as English refers to a cathedral (see above, page 177).

Music, then, conveys no message. It is intelligible only in two respects: objectively with reference to its structure and physical properties, including labels arbitrarily attached to it; and subjectively with reference to everything else it may or may not convey to various individuals, depending not only on their imagination, but also on their individual past experience ("La musique est un fait de mémoire" as the French proverb says). Music is untranslatable because there is nothing to translate (for *translation* of a sentence A in one language into a sentence B in another language is, roughly, detaching the *meaning* expressed by the form of A from A, and providing it with a new form, B). That the alleged messages are sent out by a few and understood by many is not only false (because there are no messages to understand) but also irrelevant: with reference to language the same can be said and would be tautologically true of prophets, but this throws no light on the nature of language.

That in music, form is more important than content has been expressed by musicians and musicologists in different ways. I shall confine myself to two examples from Igor Stravinski:

> I regard music essentially as incapable of *expressing* anything whatsoever: a sentiment, an attitude, a state of mind, a natural scene, etc. *Expression* has never been an immanent property of music . . .
>
> The phenomenon of music has been given to us only for the sake of ordering things. It requires for its realization, necessarily and uniquely, a construction. When the construction is complete, when order has been established, everything is said and done. It would be useless to seek or expect anything else (quoted in Boulez 1966: 9–10).

Should we, then, abandon meaning altogether? It is difficult to say, at this stage. On methodological grounds we should pursue the syntactic approach that has been totally neglected in the study of ritual in spite of the fact that it obviously works. In order to do this, we cannot operate on a level of generalities. Our data must be specific, exact, and as exhaustive as possible. We have seen that such data are available in India and other parts of Asia, and can be studied through literature as well as through fieldwork. Other ritual traditions of mankind insofar as they are still accessible should be studied exhaustively and with the same concern for detail that the Indian and Chinese ritualists themselves already displayed, but that is rarely employed by contemporary Western anthropologists, sociologists, or scholars of religion. The resulting structural descriptions should be compared with the structural descriptions of animal rituals, and will then yield unbiased results with regard to the relationships between humans and other animals. When we have done all that and still feel that something is lacking, we are entitled, by all means, to search for meaning. Even then it recommends itself, again on methodological grounds, to adopt the Talmudic saying that is the motto of the *Harvard Dictionary of Music* although it is more appropriate to ritual (which is not only audible but also visible):

> If you want to understand the invisible,
> look carefully at the visible.

The Mīmāmsā philosophy of ritual supplements this:

> *dṛṣṭe sambhavaty adṛṣṭakalpanā 'yogāt*
> "for when a visible result is possible, it is improper to postulate an invisible one" (Mīmāṃsā Paribhāṣā, ed. Mādhavānanda, 1948:73–74).

Part III

Mantras

Introductory Note

We have seen that Vedic ritual consists of rites and *mantras*, a term used for recitations and chants that accompany rites and that are derived from sentences or bits and pieces of the Vedas. The term *mantra* is derived from a verbal root *man-* which means "think" and the suffix *-tra* which often expresses instrumentality. The etymology, therefore, suggests the meaning: "instrument to think." However, this meaning fits only occasionally, which is not surprising since meaning is determined by usage, not etymology (above, page 155). Cognate words in other Indo-European languages, which include English "mind" and "meaning," are suggestive but this fact is also without much significance. If one wants a brief, approximate and practical translation of the term *mantra* into English, "sacred formula" or "spell" is often appropriate. But such translations do not explain: they are soothing, at best. The question remains: what *are* "sacred formulas" and "spells"? Modern associations are unlikely to be helpful and it is more appropriate, therefore, to inquire what the Indian tradition has to offer. This we shall do in the next four chapters. That an interpretation like "spell," apart from being vague, is not enough follows, for example, from the fact that mantras are not only believed to conjure up deities which is what a spell may be expected to do; in Tantrism, they *are* deities. In other words, there must be more afoot.

The poets of the Vedas were fascinated by the power of inspiration on which their poetic activity depended and to which they referred with a variety of terms, including those derived from the root *dhī-* such as *dhīḥ* and *dhītiḥ* (see Gonda 1963a).

From this root, or its close relative *dhyā-*, derives the later *dhyāna*, the "meditation" which Buddhism introduced into China (as *ch'an*) and Japan (as *zen*). Vedic poets knew that inspiration is not enough unless it is manifest in language. These manifestations were also referred to by several terms, one of which is mantra. At an early period, the term accordingly denoted the versified portions of the Vedas (including the Rigveda in its entirety) as distinguished from their prose passages, called *brāhmaṇa*, not considered similarly inspired and consisting of comments and explanations of the poems given either by the bards themselves or, more likely and increasingly, by thinkers of a more speculative bend of mind: interpreters, scholars and philosophers.

During the middle Vedic period—approximately, from 1,000 B.C.E. to 500 B.C.E.—ritual became the most prominent expression of Vedic culture and civilization. The ritual meaning of mantra already referred to—a recitation or chant accompanying a rite—was now established and became widespread. Mantras were derived from all Vedic compositions, and may therefore include *ṛc*, "verse (from the Rigveda)," *sāman*, "chant (from the Sāmaveda)," *yajus*, "formula (from the Yajurveda; generally muttered)," and *nigada*, "formula (also from the Yajurveda, but generally spoken loud)." Mantras are always the elements that are recited or chanted; they are neither the ritual acts themselves, nor their glosses or meanings, nor Vedic expressions that prompt such acts. In the later systematization of ritual, for example in the ritual philosophy of the Mīmāṃsā, mantras are distinguished not only from brāhmaṇas but also from the *vidhis* or "injunctions" that enjoin ritual acts.

I shall primarily study mantras in this second, ritualistic, sense and in their Vedic contexts, but refer to the later Tantric (Buddhist and "Hindu") uses as well. With reference to these latter traditions, I shall use the term "mantra" in the more general but as yet unspecified sense in which it is generally employed in the study of Indian religion. We shall see that mantras or similar entities occur in other Asian traditions as well. In India, the emphasis is always on oral elements and transmission; elsewhere in Asia, "mantras" need not be recitations or chants but may be "written," like the pseudo-Sanskritic "cosmic writing" or "celestial script" of Taoism (Bokenkamp 1983:463; Schipper and Hsiu-huei 1986:193).

Many ritual structures consist largely of mantra recitation. The Iṣṭi (Chapter 9A) consists, prior to the final act of oblation, of mantras (Wheelock 1985:180, for this reason, calls it a "mantra cluster"). Other rites—for example, the Soma sequence (Chapter 9B)—consists of mantras (chants and recitations) as well as acts. According to some Śrauta Sūtras there is a one-one-correspondence between mantras and acts, expressed as follows in Āpastamba Śrauta Sūtra 24.1.38:

> *ekamantrāṇi karmāṇi*, "each act is accompanied by one mantra."

There are exceptions (as the examples cited demonstrate) but according to the sūtra, they should always be marked:

> *vacanād ekam karma bahumantram*, "when it is explicitly stated, one act corresponds to several mantras." (Āpastamba Śrauta Sūtra 24.1.44).

In actual practice, exceptions are numerous, including many not explicitly referred to in the sūtras. Among the former, some exhibit regular features and are formulated by rules. It is common in Śrauta ritual to repeat rites four times, three times with a mantra, and the last time without. That is, if we refer to ritual acts as "A" and to mantras as "M", the resulting structure may be represented by:

$$A\,M\;/\;A\,M\;/\;A\,M\;/\;A \tag{1}$$

This is often mentioned when such a sequence occurs, e.g., in Baudhāyana Śrauta Sūtra 10.23:21.14:

> *trir yajuṣā tūṣṇīṃ caturtham*, "thrice with a *yajus*, the fourth time silently" (cf. AGNI II:524–525).

The corresponding practice in the domestic, Gṛhya ritual is a triple repetition of the ritual act of which only the first is accompanied by a mantra. The rule, which I have not found in a text, is: *sakṛñ mantreṇa dvis tuṣṇīm* (C. R. Swaminathan, personal communication). Gonda (1980b:362), who provides similar references, adds that we also find rites repeated thrice, "twice with different mantras and once silently." Thus we find two structures:

$$A\ M\ /\ A\ /\ A \quad (2)$$

and:

$$A\ M\ /\ A\ N\ /\ A \quad (3)$$

(cf. Staal 1988d).

As these examples indicate, deviation from the norm of one-one-correspondence arises more easily through acts being performed without mantras, than through mantras being recited without acts. Exceptions are mentioned (Mīmāṃsā Sūtra 12.4.1 refers to mantras that do not accompany acts as *akarmasaṃyuktaḥ*) but they are rare. In general, mantras are more important than acts. Baudhāyana illustrates this and demonstrates in addition that acts may owe their existence to mantras. In a case where the number of mantras is greater than that of acts, new acts are introduced to make up the difference and save the principle of one-one-correspondence. Fully described in AGNI (I:493–503), it is of sufficient interest to be briefly explained here.

Almost all the mantras with which the bricks of the Agnicayana altar are consecrated are taken from specific sections of the Taittirīya Saṃhitā of the Black Yajurveda. However, these sections contain 118 more mantras than the fixed number of 1,000 bricks, made up of five layers of 200 each (actually, there are five more since ten bricks are half as thick as the others: see AGNI I:202–203, 482–485). Such a discrepancy could be resolved in one of three ways: either the principle of one-one-correspondence is violated or abandoned; or the extra mantras are not recited; or new acts are introduced to make up the required number. The last alternative is adopted by Baudhāyana: 118 *pebbles* (called *śarkara* in Sanskrit and *kōlipparan*, "chicken-fish," in Malayalam) are inserted between the bricks, like mortar or cement. Each pebble is treated like a brick, that is, consecrated with three mantras, the first two always the same (as in the case of the other bricks), the third mantra specific to each pebble and taken from the 118 extra mantras. Thus the number of mantras and the principle of one-one-correspondence are both preserved. (The term *śarkara*, incidentally, is pre-Indo-European: it is cognate with Latin *calculus* and, via Arabic, with English *sugar*.) Another important rule about the relationship between mantras and acts states:

> *mantrāntaiḥ karmādīn saṃnipatayet*
> "one should let the beginning of the acts coincide with the end of the mantras"

(Āpastamba Śrauta Sūtra 24.2.1; this topic is further discussed in Mīmāṃsā Sūtra 12.3.25 and following). An example occurs in the Iṣṭi rite where the offering is made when the Hotā shouts -*ṣaṭ*!, the last syllable of *vauṣaṭ*, "may (Agni) lead the offerings to the gods."

It is likely that the idea that mantras are succeeded by acts is related to the practice we find elsewhere of "magical rites" being succeeded by "technical operations." Tambiah has drawn attention to Malinowski's analysis of the relation between Trobriand magic and practical activity, which shows that "the whole cycle of gardening or of canoe building must be seen as one long series of activities which form a regular pattern of M → T, M → T, M → T, M → T: where M stands for the magical rite and T for the technical operation that succeeds it" (Tambiah 1968:198, followed by detailed examples).

To what extent do mantras *refer* to the acts they accompany? It is important to hear what this question asks. It is clear that brāhmaṇas refer to mantras: they were composed to interpret them. That mantras are suitable companions to rites and that they two belong together is also not open to doubt. The question is, do mantras *express* rites, or express what rites express, or refer to rites in the manner in which linguistic expressions refer to their meanings? In the past, many scholars have thrown doubt on the nature of this relationship. Gonda has dealt with this problem in a series of publications (1981, 1982, 1985), including a thorough examination of the mantras of the Agnyupasthāna and the Sautrāmaṇī (Gonda 1980a). Gonda has emphasized that the scholarly literature on Vedic ritual generally refers to mantras without ever quoting them in full (S. Einoo, in an unpublished review of Gonda 1980a, shows that Gonda himself continues to do the same in the majority of cases). It is clear from Gonda's work that many connections between mantras and acts exist. However, most of these are historical connections: they throw light on the original associations that may have existed between mantras and rites. But this is not the same as the ritual function of mantras or their function in the ritual system.

If we adopt the synchronistic perspective of the Śrauta Sūtras, and look at the system of mantras and acts as a "système où tout se tient" (as did de Saussure with respect to language) we find, in general, that mantras do *not* refer to the acts they accompany. Absence of reference is what linguists call the "unmarked" case; there is no general term to refer to it. But a technical term exists for those *ṛks* of the Rigveda that refer to, or "address" (*abhivad-*) the accompanying act. They are called *rūpasaṃṛddha*, "perfect in form." The existence of such a technical term shows that these mantras were regarded as special and exceptional. The majority of mantras, by implication, do not "refer" or "address."

"Perfection of form" means no more than that the mantra contains a particular word. Aitareya Brāhmaṇa 1.16 (3.5) applies the term to the mantra Rigveda 1.74.3, which contains the word *ajani*, "is born," and is recited when Soma "is born." It refers to such cases in the following terms:

> *etad vai yajñasya saṃṛddhaṃ yad rūpasaṃṛddhaṃ yat karma kriyamāṇam ṛg abhivadati*, "the perfection of ritual is when it is perfect in form, viz., when the ṛk addresses the act that is being performed" (cf. Kane V.II,1962:1097).

We shall study the relationships between ritual acts and mantras in greater detail, but it is important that the reader develop—*pace* Gadamer—a *feel* for mantras first. Mantra is not exactly what is sometimes defined as such or what it is felt to be in subcultures of the counterculture. I shall therefore first list six representative examples of Vedic mantras. They will be given in Sanskrit, together with a translation into English. I have omitted the accents for the sake of simplicity even though they are considered important (we shall return to them in Chapter 24). Afterwards the six mantras will be placed in their ritual context and we shall return to their general discussion.

17

Six Vedic Mantras

(1) *agnīn* . . .

agnīn jyotiṣmataḥ kuruta / dīkṣita vācaṃ yaccha / patni vācaṃ yaccha /
"Kindle the fires! Consecrated one, control your speech!
Wife, control your speech!"

(*Baudhāyana Śrauta Sūtra* 6.6)

(2) *mitro na ehi* . . .

mitro na ehi sumitradhā / indrasyorum ā viśa dakṣiṇam / uśann uśantaṃ śyonaḥ śyonam /
"Come to us as a friend, making good friends. Enter the right thigh of Indra; you willing, it willing, you gracious, it gracious"

(*Taittirīya Saṃhitā* 1.2.7.1 f)

(3) *yo'sman dveṣṭi* . . .

yo'sman dveṣti yaṃ ca vayaṃ dviṣma / idam asya grīvā api kṛntāmi /
"He who hates us and whom we hate, here I cut off his neck!"

(*Taittirīya Saṃhitā* 1.3.1.1 c)

(4) *devasya tvā savitaḥ* . . .

devasya tvā savituḥ prasave'śvinor bāhubhyām pūṣṇo hastābhyām agnaye juṣṭaṃ nirvapāmi /
"On the impulse of the God Savitṛ, with the arms of the two Aśvins, with the hands of Pūṣan, I offer you dear to Agni."

(*Taittirīya Saṃhitā* 1.1.4.2 m)

(5) *indra juṣasva* . . .

indra juṣasva pra vahā yāhi śūra haribhyām / pibā sutasya mater iha madhoś cakānaś cārur madāya / / indra jaṭaraṃ navyo na pṛṇasva madhor divo na / asya sutasya svarṇopa tvā madāḥ suvāco aguḥ / /indras turāṣāṇ mitro vṛtraṃ yo jaghāna yatīr na / bibheda valaṃ bhṛgur na sasahe śatrūn made somasya / /

"Indra enjoy—drive on,
come, hero—with your two steeds,
drink of Soma—like a sage,
loving the sweet, pleased with inebriation!
Indra, your belly—like one to be praised,
fill it with sweet—like heavens,
with pressed Soma—like paradise,
well-spoken inebriants have gone to you!
Indra fast conquering—like a friend,
killing the demon—like ascetics,
he split the cave—like Bhṛgu,
he conquers his enemies inebriated with Soma!"

(*Atharvaveda* 2.5.1-3)

(6) *hā bu hā bu hā bu . . .*

hā bu hā bu hā bu bhā bhaṃ bhaṃ bhaṃ bhaṃ bhaṃ bhā bhaṃ bhaṃ bhaṃ bhaṃ bhaṃ bhā bhaṃ bhaṃ bhaṃ bhaṃ bhaṃ / hā bu hā bu hā bu brahma jajñānaṃ prathamaṃ purāstāt / vi sīmatas suruco vena ā vāt / sa budhniyā upamā asya vā yi sṭhāḥ / sataś ca yonim asataś ca vā yi vaḥ / hā bu hā bu hā bu bhā bhaṃ bhaṃ bhaṃ bhaṃ bhaṃ bhā bhaṃ bhaṃ bhaṃ bhaṃ bhaṃ bhā bhaṃ bhaṃ bhaṃ bhaṃ bhaṃ / hā bu hā bu hā vu vā / brahma devānāṃ bhāti parame vyoman brahma devānāṃ bhāti parame vyoman brahma devānāṃ bhāti parame vyomān / /

Here translation becomes more difficult even than in the previous case; but it may be attempted, in free fashion, as follows:

"Hey hey hey! BANG bang bang bang bang bang BANG bang bang bang bang bang BANG bang bang bang bang ! Hey hey hey! Born as brahman first in the ea-east, Vena has shone out of the glimmering horizon. He has revealed its highest and lowest positionemes, the womb of being and of non-be-beying. Hey hey hey! BANG bang bang bang bang bang BANG bang bang bang bang bang BANG bang bang bang bang bang! Hey hey, hey man! Brahman shines in the highest heaven of the gods brahman shines in the highest heaven of the gods brahman shines in the highest heaven of the gogodeses!"

(*Jaiminīya Araṇyageyagāna* 12.9)

18

Ritual Context

The six expressions which we have listed are either mantras or consist of mantras. I have listed them in a sequence in which the formal elements gradually increase and the semantic elements decrease: that is, they increasingly exhibit "mantra" characteristics. Let us now review these mantras again, and place them in the ritual context which conveys their "ritual meaning." We shall find that in the simple cases listed first, the relationship between mantras and acts is simple. In the first case, the mantra may be said to "refer" to the act. In the later cases, that relationship becomes increasingly complex and indirect until it virtually disappears.

(1) *agnīñ* . . .

This mantra is a command and belongs to the category of *nigada*. It is addressed by the Adhvaryu priest, shouting in a loud voice, to the other priests, the Yajamāna, and the Yajamāna's wife, after the Yajamāna's consecration has taken place. Following the mantra, fuel is added to the fires, and the Yajamāna and his wife "control their speech" (i.e., they pronounce only what is prescribed, but do not chatter: see AGNI, I:333). It stands to reason to assume that this mantra is an ordinary command, that has been understood as such by those to whom it was addressed. This implies, among other things, that the Adhvaryu priest is the kind of person who has the authority to issue such commands.

(2) *mitro ṅa ehi* . . .

This mantra is a *yajus*, muttered by the Yajamāna after the Soma plant has been purchased by the Adhvaryu from a merchant. The Yajamāna mutters the first part of the mantra (through . . . *sumitradhā*) when the Adhvaryu approaches him with the Soma bundle. He then uncovers his right thigh, places the bundle on it, and recites the remainder of the mantra (Caland-Henry 1906, I:46; *Śrautakośa*, Sanskrit Section, II, I:50). Here no command is given or followed. The mantras accompany an act or acts, and may be interpreted as comments on that act or on those acts.

(3) *yo'smān dveṣṭi* . . .

This mantra has a purely ritual use: it is recited when the soil within a ritual enclosure is prepared with the help of the *sphya*, a wooden knife. One of the brāhmaṇas associated with this mantra provides it with an interpretation which is, as is usual, a rationalization: the enemy has to be excluded from the altar, for making the altar is a cruel act. "Let him think of anyone he hates; he does truly inflict trouble upon him!" (*Taittirīya Saṃhitā* 2.6.4.4). Another brāhmaṇa comments: "There are two persons: one whom he hates, and one who hates him. Surely, he should cut off the necks of both, successively" (*Taittirīya Saṃhitā* 6.1.8.4; cf. AGNI I:104).

When I call such interpretations rationalizations, I do not intend to deny that there were real enemies in Vedic times, whose necks could be and actually were cut off. There is ample evidence for battles, sometimes intruding on ritual (see, e.g., Heesterman 1962). Such a background is reflected in the mantra, and points to one of its possible origins. However, the "meaning" of the mantra is its ritual use, that is, the act it accompanies; in ritual terms, the mantra means that the soil is scratched with the *sphya*.

(4) *devasya tvā savituḥ* . . .

This mantra, recited frequently, accompanies and indicates the measuring out of the material for an offering (*nirvāpa*). The first three phrases (through *hastābhyām*) occur at the beginning of many other mantras (see Bloomfield 1906:492–94). Characteristically, the *brāhmaṇas* are unhelpful, e.g.:

> He says "On the impulse of the God Savitṛ," in order to give impulse (to his action). "With the arms of the two Aśvins," (for) the two Aśvins were the Adhvaryus of the Gods. "With the hands of Pūṣan," for the guidance (of his action). "I offer you dear to Agni," he offers it indeed dear to Agni (*Taittirīya Brāhmaṇa* 3.2.4; Dumont 1957:227–28).

That the ritual meaning is only "measuring out for an offering" is obvious from a discussion in the Mīmāṃsā Sūtra (2.1.46). The purpose of this discussion is to establish that mantras always consist of a single sentence because they express a single meaning (*arthaikatvād ekaṃ vākyam*). The commentator Śabara elucidated this as follows: "The sūtra is explained because mantras fulfill a single purpose. *Devasya tvā* . . . , for example, indicates 'measuring out for an offering'. The words that comprise the mantra express precisely this, and therefore consist of a single sentence" (*ekaprayojanatvād upapannam / yathā tāvad devasya tveti nirvāpaprakāśanam / tasya viśiṣṭasya vācaka etāvān padasamūhas tadvākyam*).

(5) *indra juṣasva* . . .

These verses are mantras in the original sense: they are inspired compositions and may, in fact, have been composed under the influence of Soma. This is rare, if not exceptional. In the Rigveda, there is only one hymn (10.119) which describes the effects of drinking Soma in detail. Even with respect to this hymn, Brough (1971:341) judges: "Such a hymn cannot have been composed by a poet under the influence of *soma*: the artifice of its structure excludes this."

I don't know whether this verdict is true, but there are good reasons to doubt it. I knew at least one mathematician who could only do mathematics when he was drunk, not on account of the auspicious inebriation (*sumada*) of Soma, but on account of the evil intoxication (*durmada*) of alcohol. It is therefore not unreasonable to suppose that the mantras *indra juṣasva . . .* might have been composed under the influence of Soma, even though they consist of *svarāj* meters—relatively uncommon meters consisting of 34 syllables each.

These verses are the point of departure for modifications that turn them into mantras, fit for ritual use. They constitute the source from which ritualists have constructed the beginning of the sixteenth Soma sequence called the "sixteenth" (*ṣoḍaśī*). There is a good arithmetical reason for the number sixteen (Chapter 9B), but it is also a favorite, auspicious number (see, e.g., Gonda 1965:115–130). The *Ṣoḍaśī* śastra consists of *anuṣṭubh* verses, their meter defined by a sequence of four octosyllabic verses, each consisting of 8 syllables. An *anuṣṭubh*, therefore, consists of 32 syllables, that is twice sixteen.

Since the mantras *indra juṣasva . . .* consist of three verses in the *svarāj* meter, and the first verse of a *śastra* recitation is always recited thrice, we have 5 × 34 = 170 syllables at our disposal. If we disregard the syntax and meaning of these verses, and concentrate on the counting of syllables only, we can make use of 160 = 5 × 32 syllables to obtain 5 *anuṣṭubh* verses, leaving an excess of 10 syllables. Such a procedure is in accordance with the stress on formal features such as meter that characterizes Vedic mantras. In terms of syntax or meaning, the resulting *anuṣṭubh* verses do not make sense, for they are arrived at by cutting off the last *two* syllables of the first verse and adding them to the beginning of the second (which is a repetition of the first); cutting off the last *four* of the second and adding them to the beginning of the third (another repetition of the first); cutting off the last *six* of the third and adding them to the beginning of the fourth; cutting off the last *eight* of the fourth and adding them to the beginning of the fifth; and cutting off the last *ten* of the fifth and putting them in storage, so to speak.

The entire procedure may be pictured as follows:

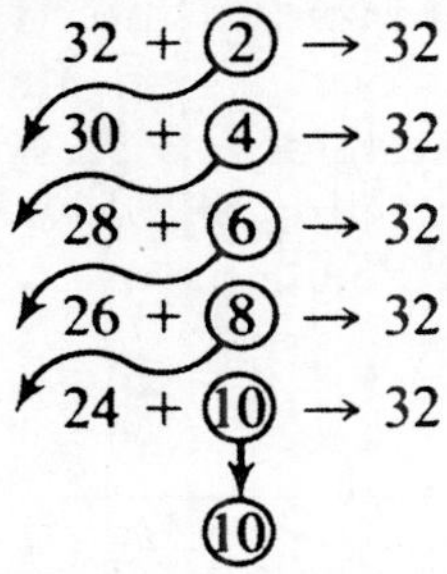

To provide a translation is hazardous, but an idea may be gained from the following:

1. "Indra enjoy—drive on,
   come hero—with your two steeds,
   drink of Soma—like a sage,
   loving the sweet, pleased with!

2. Inebriation, Indra enjoy,
   drive on, come, hero, with
   your two steeds, drink of Soma,
   like a sage, loving the sweet!

3. Pleased with inebriation—Indra,
   enjoy, drive on, come, hero,
   with your two steeds, drink of
   Soma like a sage, loving!

4. The sweet, pleased with inebriation, Indra,
   your belly, like one to be praised, fill,
   it with sweet—like heavens with,
   pressed Soma, like paradise well-spoken!

5. Inebriants have gone to you, Indra,
   fast conquering like a friend killing,
   the demon like ascetics he split,
   the cave like Bhṛgu he conquers!"

The remainder—"His enemies inebriated with Soma!"—is used for the beginning of the next part of the *ṣoḍaśi śastra*, which I shall not write out in full, because it results in the same kind of meters, and the same kind of absurdities in terms of syntax and semantics.

Later in the *śastra* (which is very long) use is made of a technique called *viharaṇam*, "intertwining," or "transposition." Its first occurrence is in the construction of two *anuṣṭubh* verses (consisting of 2 × 32 syllables) from intertwining a *gāyatrī* verse (consisting of 3 × 8 syllables) with a *paṅkti* verse (consisting of 5 × 8 syllables):

$$\begin{array}{r} 3 \times 8 = 24 \\ 5 \times 8 = 40 \\ \hline 2 \times 32 = 64. \end{array} +$$

The *gāyatrī* verse is Rigveda 1.16.1:

> *ā tvā vahantu harayo vṛṣaṇaṃ somapītaye / indra tvā sūracakṣasaḥ / /*
> "The tawny horses take you bull to the Soma drinking,
> You, Indra, with your sunny eyes!"

The *paṅkti* verse is Rigveda 1.84.10:

> *svādor itthā viṣūvato madhvaḥ pibanti gauryaḥ / yā indreṇa sayāvarīr vṛṣṇā madanti sobhase vasvīr anu svarājyam / /*
> "The gaurī cows drink from the sweet liquid, basic to the ritual, enjoying themselves with their companion, Indra the bull, to look beautiful; beneficient to his supremacy."

The intertwining of these two is as follows:

> *ā tvā vahantu harayas* svādor itthā viṣūvataḥ / *vṛṣaṇaṃ somapītaye* madhvaḥ pibanti gauryo / / *indra tvā sūracakṣaso* yā indreṇa sayāvarīḥ / vṛṣṇā madanti sobhase vasvīr anu svarājyo / /

In this construction, the portions from the underlying *gāyatrī* verse are in italics, and the portions from the underlying *paṅkti* verse are in Roman. (The *-o* ending is another feature of *śastra* recitation, to which I shall return.)

The meaning can only be guessed at, but the following may convey some of its flavor:

> "The tawny horses take from the sweet, basic to the ritual. You bull to the Soma drinking, the gaurī cows drink from the liquid. You, Indra, with

your sunny eyes—enjoying themselves with their companion, Indra the bull, to look beautiful; beneficient to his supremacy."

An intoxicated Sanskrit scholar might interpret this as a poetic rendering of a Soma orgy; however, it merely results from the metrical arithmetic of the *viharaṇam* technique. In terms of syntax or semantics, none of these mantras make sense; their ritual meaning, on the other hand, is straightforward and uncontroversial: they constitute the first portion of the sixteenth *śastra*.

In the sequel there are further cases of *viharaṇam*, and also instances where mantras, though recited in regular sequence, are re-analyzed into *anuṣṭubh* meters by counting the syllables of their original meters differently. The reader interested in these exercises can find them in AGNI, I:661–663, and can listen to them on the accompanying cassette. The examples given should be sufficient to illustrate the ritual use and meaning of such mantras.

(6) *hā bu hā bu hā bu . . .*

These mantras are chanted by the Udgātā priest of the Sāmaveda after the Adhvaryu has placed a small image of a golden man (*hiraṇ-mayapuruṣa*) above the lotus leaf that was earlier deposited and buried at the center of the Agni field; later the large bird-shaped altar of the Agnicayana will be constructed there. These chants (see AGNI, I:414–417 and the accompanying cassette), which continue through some of the following rites, consist of four parts, and the mantras we are considering constitute the last chant of the third part. In this third part, many chants are similar in structure. They start with: *hā bu hā bu hā bu . . .*, followed by a triple repetition of six syllables, five of them identical, and the first a variation, e.g.:

phāt phat phat phat phat phat
hā bu hau hau hau hau hau
kā hvā hvā hvā hvā hvā.

This is followed, in each case, by a verse, generally from the Rigveda, set to music in accordance with a melody (*sāman*), after which there is another round of meaningless syllables and finally a "coda" (*nidhana*), also meaningless.

Such meaningless syllables from the Sāmaveda are called *stobha*. If Vedic mantras are called bits and pieces, it is the *stobhas* that are the bits. *Stobhas* are very similar to the *bīja*-mantras of later Tantrism, to which we shall return (Chapter 20).

The six mantras we have reviewed suggest that the ritual use of mantras has little or nothing to do with their meaning. This is independent of the fact whether or not these mantras had meaning to begin with. What is important for their ritual use is the formal characteristics they possess. The stobhas of the Sāmaveda are particularly rich in repetitions, inversions, interpolations, and other specific structures. This is the topic of the next Chapter.

19

The Syntax of Stobhas

The stobha chants of the Sāmaveda may be analysed from different points of view. I shall not be concerned with either textual or musical analysis, but with the structure and distribution of some of these chants. The material, based upon the 1975 performance described in AGNI, is in several respects different from the Śrauta texts, as a comparison of the following notes with Parpola 1983 shows.

When referring to the unpublished chants of the Jaiminīya Sāmaveda, I adopt the system of reference used in the manuscripts put at the disposal of Asko Parpola by Itti Ravi Nambudiri, the foremost *sāmaga* of Kerala. In these manuscripts—written down in the Malayalam script, without sound notation, and largely from memory (that of Itti Ravi, his elders, and his pupils)—the Jaiminīya Ārcika is divided into 112, the Grāmageyagāna into 59, and the Araṇyegeyagāna into 25 *ōttus* or "songs". I shall chiefly refer to the chants of the Araṇyegeyagāna, which the Nambudiris call *candrasāmāni*, "moon chants". A reference such as AG 25.7 would thus denote the seventh sāman of the 25th *ōttu* of the Jaiminīya Araṇyegeyagāna . For the terminology, see below, page 297.

The first Agnicayana chants (AGNI I:410–411) are sung immediately after the Adhvaryu has placed a lotus leaf at the centre of the Field of Agni (*agnikṣetra*) over which the bird-shaped altar will subsequently be constructed. The Udgātā enters, and takes up his position to the west of what will be the tail of the bird, against the northern post of the eastern door of what will later become the Havirdhāna shed. From this position, he sings most of the Jaiminīya chants that characterize the Nambudiri Agnicayana. The first chant is based upon a cryptic mantra of the Taittirīyasaṃhitā (4.2.8.2d), which also occurs in the Atharvasaṃhitā (4.1.1), but not in the Ṛksaṃhitā. The Adhvaryu recites it at the same time, while he places the golden breastplate (*rukma*) which the Yajamāna wore at his consecration to the north of the lotus leaf:

brahma jajñānam prathamam purastād
vi sīmataḥ suruco vena āvaḥ
sa budhniyā upamā asya viṣṭhāḥ
sataś ca yonim asataś ca vivaḥ

"Born as brahman first in the east,
Vena has shone out of the glimmering horizon.
He has revealed its highest and lowest positions,
the womb of being and non-being."

This verse (above, page 200) is turned into a chant consisting of the five customary parts (1: *prastāva*; 2: *udgītha*; 3: *pratihāra*; 4: *upadrava*; and 5: *nidhana*; see page 299) by prefixing and affixing *stobha* elements that will be referred to with the help of capital letters, in the following manner:

A: *huve hā yi*
B: *heṣāyā*
C: *au ho vā*
D: *e ṛtam amṛtam.*

I shall refer to the four lines of the verse of TS 4.2.8.2d with the help of lower case letters: a, b, c, and d, respectively. Then the chant can be represented as follows:

prastāva:	A A B a /	
udgītha:	b /	
pratihāra:	c /	(4)
upadrava:	d A A B C /	
nidhana:	D D D /	

We need to adopt one more convention to interpret this correctly: whenever there is a triple occurrence of a *stobha*, viz., an expression of the form X X X, the final syllable of the third occurrence is lengthened. For example, in D D D, the third occurrence ends in *amṛtām*, and not in *amṛtam*.

Written out in full, the above expressions represent the following chant, which is Jaiminīya Grāmageyagāna 33.9.2:

prastāva:	*huve hā yī huve hā yi heṣāyā/brahma jājñānām prāthāmām purāstāt/*
udgītha:	*vi sīmatās suruco vena ā vāt/*
pratihāra:	*sa budhnyā upamā asya vāyīṣṭhāḥ/*
upadrava:	*sataś ca yonim āsātāś ca vīvaḥ huve hā yī huve hā yī heṣāyā au ho vā/*
nidhana:	*e ṛtam amṛtam e ṛtam amṛtam e ṛtam amṛtām/*

The only feature that is not represented in the formula (4) is the lengthening of certain vowels within the lines a, b, c, and d of the mantra. Of course, further abbreviations of this representation are possible. For example, the sequence "A A B" may be replaced by "W". In that case, the chant becomes:

1. W a /
2. b /
3. c / (5)
4. d W C /
5. D D D /

The advantage of these representations is that they picture the structure of the chant clearly, and enable us to compare the structures of different chants with each other. Such representations also enable us to express in a simple form differences between different traditions and schools. For example, the corresponding Kauthuma-Rāṇāyanīya chant differs from the above Jaiminīya variety only in that two of the *stobha* elements have different forms: A has to be replaced by:

A*: *huve hā ī*

and B has to be replaced by:

B*: *hi ṣā yā.*

If these substitutions are made in (5), the result is Kauthuma-Rāṇāyanīya Grāmageyagāna 321.2 (in the edition of R. Nārāyaṇasvāmī Dīkṣita).

From now on, I shall not write out the texts in full, but only represent them by symbolic representations such as (4) or (5).

The second chant of the Udgātā that accompanies the Adhvaryu's rite with the golden breastplate is a musical composition on a single word: *satya*, "truth". The *stobhas* may be referred to by:

E: *ho yi*
F: *hā ā vu vā*
G: *e suvar jyotiḥ*

The chant may then be written as:

AG 25.24: *satyom* / *satya* E *satya* E *satya* F / G. (6)

How much more abbreviation or simplification should be resorted to, in a case like this, depends entirely on the occurrence or nonoccurrence of other chants of a similar form: if there are no others, there is no point in abbreviating any further, but if there are, it depends on the degree of similarity between them to what extent further abstraction may be helpful in expressing the structure.

After these relatively modest beginnings, the Udgātā bursts into a much longer sequence of songs. These accompany the deposition by the Adhvaryu of the golden man (*hiraṇmayapuruṣa*) upon the lotus leaf, and continue through several subsequent rites. This sequence consists of four parts (AGNI I:414–417). The first is called the Great Chant (*mahāsāman*: AG 25.7), and the second consists of seven songs (AG 9. 1–7), based upon verses of the Puruṣa hymn of the Rigveda (10.90), with changes in the text and in the order of these verses. I shall not analyze these two parts here, because it is not easy to extract or abstract a general structure from them.

The third part begins to exhibit marked regularities, partly obscured by irregularities. It is quite possible that the latter have crept in over the centuries, for these chants have been sung for almost three millenia. This third part consists of nine Moon Chants, AG 12. 1–9. Four of these, AG 12. 3–6, consist entirely of *stobhas* and are relatively short. Of the remaining five, three (AG 12. 7–9) exhibit the same structure, and two (AG 12. 1–2) a very similar pattern. I shall confine myself here to the structure that is the most obvious, and that can be represented in a simple manner with the help of our notation if we adopt one further convention, viz., express repetition of elements by superscripts. For example, instead of writing "R R R R R" for a five-fold repetition of the element "R", I shall write: "R^5".

The structure of each of AG 12. 3–6 may now be represented by:

$$\begin{array}{c} P^3\ (QR^5)^3 P^3 \\ X \\ P^3\ (QR^5)^3\ P^2P^* \\ Y \end{array} \qquad (7)$$

The use of parentheses is self-explanatory: everything within parentheses should be repeated as many times as is indicated by the superscript following the closing parenthesis. Thus, "$(QR^5)^3$" stands for: "QR^5 QR^5 QR^5", or: "QRRRRR QRRRRRQRRRRR". "X" represents an underlying mantra, different for each of the three songs, and "Y" represents the *nidhana* which consists of the final portion of this mantra and/or a *stobha*. The *stobhas* which exhibit the invariant structure are "P", "Q", and "R". Of these, "P" is the same in the three songs:

P: *hā bu.*

"P*" is a modification of "P" which is used in the final round when "P" is repeated only once and its third occurrence (like the *amṛtam/amṛtām* we considered before) is replaced by:

P*: *hā vu vā.*

While the structure of the three chants is the same, the remaining *stobhas*, "Q" and "R", are different, in the following manner:

AG 12.7 has Q: *phāt*
R: *phat*
AG 12.8 has Q: *hā bu*
R: *hau*
AG 12.9 has Q: *bhā*
R: *bham.*

Written out as far as its *stobhas* are concerned, the last chant, for example, becomes:

hā bu (3 ×) *bhā bhaṃ bhaṃ bhaṃ bhaṃ bhaṃ* (3 ×) *hā bu* (3 ×)
X
hā bu (3 ×) *bhā bhaṃ bhaṃ bhaṃ bhaṃ bhaṃ* (3 ×) *hā bu* (2 ×) *hā vu vā*
Y

In this chant, X happens to be the same mantra TS 4.2.8.2d we have met with before. The structure of AG 12.1–2 deviates to some extent from this pattern (7), but it also possesses the characteristic feature "$(QR^5)^3$", in the following manner:

AG 12.1 has Q: *u*
R: *ha*
AG 12.2 has Q: *kā*
R: *hvā*

The fourth and last part of this sequence consists of a single chant, similar to the chant for the golden breastplate (6), but with *puruṣa* as the main *stobha*:

AG 25.25: *puruṣom* / *puruṣa* E *puruṣa* E *puruṣa* F / G (8)

After the *agnikṣetra* has been prepared, the ritual continues with the piling up of the five layers of the altar. The bricks are consecrated by the Adhvaryu on behalf of the Yajamāna, and the Udgātā contributes songs to some of these rites. I shall here consider the sequence of chants that is sung when the "Space Filler Bricks" are consecrated. Most of the bricks are consecrated in a specific order, and are therefore numbered, at least conceptually (cf. Staal 1982, Lecture III). The only exceptions are certain bricks, occurring especially in the intermediate layers (i.e. the 2nd, 3rd, and 4th), that are consecrated without an individual mantra and in any order. These bricks are not consecrated without mantras, but the mantras are the same for each brick. There are three: the first two are called *tayādevatā* and *sūdadohasa*. These are used for the consecration of every brick of the altar. The third is the specific "Space Filler" (*lokampṛṇa*) mantra (Taittirīya Saṃhitā 4.2.4.4n):

lokam pṛṇa chidram pṛṇā 'tho sīda śivā tvam
indrāgnī tvā bṛhaspatir asmin yonāv asīṣadan

"Fill the space! Fill the hole!
Then sit down in a friendly manner.
Indra, Agni, and Bṛhaspati
have placed you in this womb."

While the Adhvaryu recites these mantras over the Space Filler Bricks, the Udgātā intones eight Space Filler Chants: AG 24.5–6 and AG 25.32–37. The latter six are of the same form as (6) and (8), but other *stobhas* are substituted in the place of *satya* or *puruṣa*:

§3. AG 25.32: *agna* for Agni
§4. AG 25.33: *vāya* for Vāyu, "wind"
§5. AG 25.34: *sūrya*, "sun"
§6. AG 25.35: *candra*, "moon"
§7. AG 25.36: *nāka*, "vault"
§8. AG 25.37: *śukra* "glow" or "Venus."

The *nidhana* portions are not always the same. At this point it has become obvious that it would be helpful to express the structure of these chants by representing them by means of a general functional expression, e.g., Ψ (X), defined as follows:

Ψ(X) = "X-*oṃ* / X *ho yi* X *ho yi* X *hā ā vu vā* /"

In this expression, "X-*oṃ*" is obtained from "X" by replacing the final "*-a*" of X by "*-oṃ*". An example is:

Ψ(*satya*) = "*satyoṃ / satya ho yi satya ho yi satya hā ā vu vā* /"

The different *nidhana* portions may now be substituted, and all the chants of this form that we have so far considered may be represented as follows:

AG 25.24 Ψ(*satya*) G
AG 25.25 Ψ(*puruṣa*) G
AG 25.32 Ψ(*agna*) *e jyotiḥ*
AG 25.33 Ψ(*vāya*) *e rājā*
AG 25.34 Ψ(*sūrya*) *e bhrājā*
AG 25.35 Ψ(*candra*) *e ā bhrājā*
AG 25.36 Ψ(*nāka*) *e pṛṣṭham*
AG 25.37 Ψ(*śukra*) *e bhrāḷā bhrājā*.

Other chants of this form are sung by the Udgātā on the three occasions (on the first, third, and fifth layers of the altar) when the "perforated pebbles" (*svayamātṛṇṇā*) are deposited at the centre by the Adhvaryu in collaboration with the "Ignorant Brahmin" (AGNI I:419, 461, 505; cf. Staal 1978a and 1982a:42–53). Using our notation, these three chants may be represented as follows:

on the first layer: AG 25.21 Ψ(*bhūr*)G (for *bhū*, "earth")
on the second layer: AG 25.22 Ψ(*bhuva*)G (for "sky")
on the third layer: AG 25.23 Ψ(*suva*)G (for "heaven")

In each of these three cases, "G" represents again: *e suvar jyotiḥ*.

The last sequence of songs I shall consider is chanted after the bird altar has been completed and fully consecrated. It is now vibrating with power, ferocious (*krūra*) and dreadful (*ghora*), and has to be pacified and brought under control. To this end the Adhvaryu, assisted by the Pratiprasthāta, pours a continuous libation of goat milk over the furthest western brick of the northern wing. This brick is chosen because it is eccentric, i.e., far from the centre of power, and also because it can be easily approached from different sides (AGNI I:509 sq.). While performing this oblation, the Adhvaryu recites the famous *Śatarudriya* or *Rudram* (Taittirīya Saṃhitā 4.5), which derives its popularity partly from the fact that it was later interpreted within the perspective of Śaiva theism (Gonda 1979). During this oblation and recitation, the Udgātā chants a sequence of 57 sāmans, together called Flow of Milk (*kṣīradhārā*). These chants last very long and continue after the Rudra ceremonies have been completed. Their complete structural analysis would take up more space than is available here, but I wish to draw attention to two of their most striking features.

I shall first take up the one that appears last. The final seventeen of these 57 Flow of Milk chants have the structure of (6) and (8) we have just considered, and incorporate again the chants we have already mentioned. The others can be represented in a straight-forward manner with the help of our notation in terms of Ψ and G:

§41. AG 25.21 (see above page 216)
§42. AG 25.22 (see above page 216)
§43. AG 25.23 (see above page 216)
§44. AG 25.24 (see above pages 212, 216)
§45. AG 25.25 (see above pages 214, 216)
§46. AG 25.26: Ψ (*gaur*) G
§47. AG 25.27: Ψ (*ḷoka*) G
§48. AG 25.28: Ψ (*agner hṛdaya*) G
§49. AG 25.29: Ψ (*dyaur*) G
§50. AG 25.30: Ψ (*antarikṣa*) G
§51. AG 25.31: Ψ (*pṛthivī*) G
§52. AG 25.32 (see above pages 215, 216)

§53. AG 25.33 (see above pages 215, 216)
§54. AG 25.34 (see above pages 215, 216)
§55. AG 25.35 (see above pages 215, 216)
§56. AG 25.36 (see above pages 215, 216)
§57. AG 25.37 (see above pages 215, 216)

In this list, I have only incorporated the representation of the "new" sāmans, viz., sāmans we have not yet met with. The other representations have already been provided. Thus far, the survey of these structures conveys an idea of the distribution of a specific chant structure or melody throughout many sections of the Agnicayana ritual. This structure is like a musical theme that appears and reappears, with variations, at many important junctures of the ceremony.

The second structural feature I wish to discuss occurs earlier in the Flow of Milk chants: in the ten chants §18–§27(AG 11.1–10). I shall write out the first of these in full, to clearly exhibit its structure:

§18. *hā bu* (3 ×) *aham annam* (3 ×) *aham annādo* (3 ×) *ahaṃ vidhārayo* (2 ×) *ahaṃ vidhārayaḥ* / *hā bu* (3 ×) *yad varco hiraṇyasya* / *yad vā varco gavām uta* / *satyasya brahmaṇo varcaḥ* / *tenamāsaṃ sṛjāmasā yi* / *hā bu* (3 ×) *aham annam* (3 ×) . . . *vidhārayaḥ* (as at the beginning) / *hā bu hā bu hā vu vā* / *e aham annam aham annādo ahaṃ vidhārayaḥ* (3 ×) *e ahaṃ suvar jyotiḥ* /

This chant incorporates a mantra, *yad varco* . . . , from the Jaiminīya Árcika (107.34) which also occurs in the Kauthuma-Rāṇāyanīya tradition, but is neither found in the Rigveda nor in the Yajurveda. The structure of the chant exhibits a special feature that may be represented in a simple fashion if we make use of indexed lower case letters to express elements, as follows:

a_1: *aham annam*
a_2: *aham annādaḥ*
a_3: *ahaṃ vidhārayaḥ*.

The special feature of these chants is that the mantra *yad varco* . . . , which I shall refer to as "Y", is *preceded* by the structure:

$$a_1^3 \quad a_2^3 \quad a_3^3$$

and *followed* by the structure:

$$(a_1 \quad a_2 \quad a_3)^3.$$

This feature occurs in all the ten sāmans, but the number of elements need not always be three. Using the following abbreviations:

P: *hā bu*
P*: *hā vu vā*
T: *e ahaṃ suvar jyotiḥ*,

the general structure of the ten sāmans is expressed by:

$$P^3 \; a_1{}^3 \; . \; . \; . \; a_i^3 P^3 \; Y \; P^3 \; a_1^3 \; . \; . \; . \; a_i^3 \; P \; P \; P^* \; e(a_1 \; . \; . \; . \; a_i)^3 \; T.$$

We are now in a position to specify the number of elements ("i"), and the elements themselves, for each of the ten sāmans, as follows:

§18. $i = 3$ a_1: *aham annam*
a_2: *aham annādaḥ*
a_3: *ahaṃ vidhārayaḥ*

§19. $i = 3$ a_1: *ahaṃ sahaḥ*
a_2: *ahaṃ sāsahiḥ*
a_3: *ahaṃ sāsahānaḥ*

§20. $i = 1$ a_1: *ahaṃ varcaḥ*

§21. $i = 1$ a_1: *ahaṃ tejaḥ*

§22. $i = 4$ a_1: *manojait*
a_2: *hṛdayamajait*
a_3: *indrojait*
a_4: *aham ajaiṣam*

§23. $i = 4$ a_1: *diśanduhe*
a_2: *diśauduhe*

a_3: *diśoduhe*
a_4: *sarvāduhe*

§24. i = 1 a_1: *vayo vayo vayaḥ*

This could alternatively be expressed as:

i = 3 a_1: *vayaḥ*
a_2: *vayaḥ*
a_3: *vayaḥ*

§25. Same as §24, but with *rūpam* instead of *vayaḥ*

§26. i = 4 a_1: *udapaptam*
a_2: *ūrddhonabhāṃ svakṛṣi*
a_3: *vyadyaukṣam*
a_4: *atatanam*

An irregularity here is that P is: *hi hi yā au*.

§27. i = 2 a_1: *prathe*
a_2: *pratyaṣṭhām*

This chapter has dealt with only a few of the structures of the stobhas of the Sāmaveda. There are many more types and none of them have been studied. I have three concluding remarks. The first is the most obvious: these chants exhibit structures that are sometimes similar to musical structures, but almost always totally different from anything found in the syntax of natural languages.

My second remark relates to the psychology of the chanters. All these chants are transmitted orally and learned by heart, together with their order, distribution, interrelationships, and ritual applications and uses. Such an astonishing feat of memorization can only be accounted for by assuming that such abstract structures as we have postulated and expressed by symbolic formulas are actually represented, in some form or other, in the minds or brains of the chanters. This reflects the obvious fact that it is possible to remember such vast amounts of material only because of implicit, underlying regularities.

My third concluding remark relates to the significance of these chants. We have witnessed, even in this relatively small sample, many strange forms, strange from a linguistic point of view, and also strange for anyone who is looking for meaning, especially "religious meaning." It should be obvious that language or religion are not proper categories within which to evaluate the significance of these ritual chants. Rather, their significance lies in the structure and composition of the resulting edifice, and the abstract structural qualities that we have represented by formulas. If there are anywhere structures similar to these ritual features, it is in the realm of music. This is not so merely because the Sāmaveda may be described as "mantras set to music." What is more significant is that the structure of these chants, both internally and in relation to each other, corresponds to musical structure. Close parallels to these structures are found, for example, in the complex expressions of polyphonic music in Europe during the eighteenth century. The ritual chants of the Agnicayana resemble in this respect the arias of Bach's oratorios, and are similar in character: their language is uninteresting, their poetry mediocre, and their meaning trite; but the sounds, with their themes and variations, inversions, interpolations, and counterpoint, and the particular distributions of their elements is what makes them remarkable. To those who have grown up in such a tradition, and who have learned to perceive and appreciate it in its traditional perspective, it is the structure of these chants that reveals to a large extent what is felt to be their beauty.

20

Vedic and Tantric Mantras

Having gained some idea of Vedic mantras, we are now in a position to discuss other types of mantras. The first that require attention are the mantras of Tantrism: for although mantras are important throughout the history of the Indian tradition, with Tantric ritual they move once again to the center stage. I shall primarily discuss Tantric mantras from Hinduism, and occasionally refer to their Buddhist counterparts. As for Jaina mantras, the most important is a set of seven that developed from ritual salutations and refuge seeking formulas (see Jaini 1979:296–297).

Several scholars have attempted to characterize the difference between Vedic and Tantric mantras. One difficulty is that the latter have not been studied as well as the former and are only now beginning to receive scholarly attention. However, some of these comparisons have failed because even Vedic mantras have been inappropriately described. Wheelock (1988:118), for example, has written that "the Vedic mantra truthfully *describes* and thereby actualizes a bandhu between ritual object and cosmic entity," and that the Vedic mantra "stands as a *means* to the ends of the sacrifice. The Tantric mantra, on the other hand, as the essence of the ritual procedure, is an object of value *in itself* . . .".

It is clear that these expressions are not applicable to any of the mantras we have considered. Wheelock's terms are obviously inspired by the *Brāhmaṇa* literature and not products of his own fancy. However, that does not make them any more relevant. Brāhmaṇa interpretations are more fanciful than anything contemporary scholars have yet come up with. Most mantras, for example, do not describe, nor do they refer to cosmic entities. The further we proceed along the six entries of our list, the more obvious it becomes that mantras are ends in themselves. The Udgātā continues to chant long after the golden man has been laid down. There are no specific ritual acts with which any of these mantras are individually associated, and which could explain their occurrence—just as there are no events in the life of Christ that explain any bars or themes in the C Major Aria "*Geduld!*" for Tenor and Cello from Bach's *St. Matthew Passion*. Vedic and Tantric mantras, therefore, are not different in terms of the characteristics attributed to them by Wheelock.

According to Padoux (1963: 296), Śaivite mantras are different from Vedic mantras because a Vedic mantra is essentially a verse or a group of verses: "un verset ou un groupe de versets." However, as we have seen, this is applicable only to the textual sources of some Vedic mantras. It does not apply to prose mantras, to *stobhas*, or to any of the numerous sounds and noises that pervade the other ritual uses of the Vedas. Moreover, even if a Vedic mantra seems to be a verse, in its ritual use it is not treated like a verse at all. It is treated in the same manner as other sound sequences that never were verses to begin with. The counting of syllables that features in the ritual use of *indra juṣasva* . . . (Chapters 17 and 18) is not similar to the counting of syllables that we find in true versification; it is similar to the counting of syllables that is applied to *stobhas*, and is typical of their ritual use. Even if stobhas are interpreted, as in *Chāndogya Upaniṣad* 1.13.1-4, the interpretations should not be taken symbolically (as was done by the philosopher Śaṅkara in his commentary on this passage), but should themselves be explained in terms of syllable counting (see Faddegon 1927, and Gren-Eklund 1978–1979). In other words, in all these mantras, language, whether versified or not, is not treated in the manner ordinary language ever is. Vedic and Tantric mantras can therefore not be different on account of the fact that Vedic mantras are "in verse."

A functional difference between Vedic and Tantric mantras may seem to be that the latter are used not only in ritual, but also in meditation. But meditation is not so different from ritual as is sometimes assumed. It is also alluded to in the Vedas (see, e.g., Staal 1975:79). Moreover, a characteristic of meditation, namely, that it is silent, is also applicable to the ritual use of mantras. Both Padoux and Wheelock have emphasized the silent use of mantras in Tantric ritual. But silence plays a very important role in Vedic mantras also. Many Vedic mantras are *anirukta*, "not enunciated," *upāṃśu*, "inaudible," or are recited *manasā*, "mentally." The *brahman* priest is in principle always silent. Though all the deities "love what is out of sight" (*parokṣapriyā devāh*), Prajāpati is the one who has a special preference for silent mantras and silence (perhaps because he was not an Aryan deity, and most mantras are Aryan imports). True, Rigveda 10.95.1 says (see Findly 1988:26):

> "If these mantras of ours remain unspoken
> they will bring no joy, even on the most distant day."

But in their ritual use, Vedic mantras are often silent, that is, objects of meditation, just as they are in Tantrism.

In terms of the characterizations so far mentioned, it is not easy to make a clear distinction between Vedic and Tantric mantras. Actually, some of the latter *are* Vedic, and it is likely that, with further study, more Vedic sources for Tantric mantras will be found. Varenne (1962) discovered that in the Tantric rite of *kālanyāsa*, "touching the body (of the deity or the officiant who has become the deity)," Vedic mantras from a relatively late Vedic text, the Taittirīya Āraṇyaka, are used. The Vedic mantras are:

> *īśānaḥ sarvavidyānām īśvaraḥ sarvabhūtānām brahmādhipatir brahmaṇo'dhipatir brahmā śivo me astu sadāśivoḥ*
> "Ruler of all knowledges, lord of all beings, brahman master, master of brahman, Brahma, be favorable to me, the Always-Favorable!"

In the Tantric rite, various elements have been inserted and "mantricization" has increased as follows:

> *oṃ hoṃ / īśānaḥ sarvavidyānām śaśinyai namaḥ / ūrdhvamūrdhni /*
> *oṃ hoṃ / īśvaraḥ sarvabhūtānām aṅgadāyai namaḥ / pūrvamūrdhni /*

oṃ hoṃ / brahmādhipatir brahmaṇo'dhipatir brahmā / iṣṭāyai namaḥ / dakṣiṇamūrdhni /
oṃ hoṃ / śivo me astu marīcyai namaḥ / uttaramūrdhni /
oṃ hoṃ / sadāśivom / jvālinyai namaḥ / paścimūrdhni /

The resulting sequence is again difficult to translate, that is, to make sense of in terms of its lexical meaning. In terms of structure, however, it is clear. Obviously, the original mantra has been cut in five pieces, each of them introduced by the same bīja mantra or stobha: *oṃ hoṃ*. Then, five items are inserted and saluted (. . . *namaḥ*), and each piece ends with a direction which specifies how the head is to be touched:

To Śaśinī—on top of the head;
to Aṅgadā (?)—on the east (front) of the head;
to Iṣṭā (?)—on the south (right) of the head;
to Marīcī—on the north (left) of the head;
to Jvālinī—on the west (back) of the head.

It is not uncommon for "stage directions" to become parts of mantras. An example is the mantra *suśravaḥ*, "renown," which accompanies the giving of a staff to a brahmin boy during his Upanayana or initiation. The sūtra text specifies this:

suśravaḥ . . . iti daṇḍaṃ dadhyāt
"with (the recitation of) 'suśravaḥ . . .' he should give the staff."

When I filmed this ritual in Madras in the early sixties, the priest recited the entire text *suśṛavaḥ . . . iti daṇḍaṃ dadhyāt* as if it were a mantra. On another occasion, when the text specified other mantras that had to accompany a rite, the priest recited the mantras immediately followed by the "stage direction" formulated by the text: *iti mantrābhyām*, "with these mantras."

The subdivision of the mantra into five pieces that accompany the touching of five parts of the body is reminiscent of the five layers of the Agnicayana altar which Ikari (1975) has shown to be equivalent to the five *kośas* or "sheaths" of the Taittirīya Upaniṣad and which recur in other quintuples. Touching parts of the body is not uncommon in Vedic ritual: parts of the body of the boy who receives the Upanayana initiation just mentioned are also touched by the priest.

One type of Tantric mantras is best known in the West or at least its counterculture: the *bīja* or "seed" mantras which often consist of single syllables, frequently vowels or diphthongs followed by a nasal. We have already met with *oṃ* and *hoṃ*, two syllables that answer this description. There are striking similarities between these seed mantras and the Vedic stobhas exemplified in the sixth example of Chapter 17 and in Chapter 19. Whether these similarities exist throughout the Tantric domain is difficult to determine because so few Tantric mantras have been studied. On the Vedic side the documentation is good. Apart from Maurice Bloomfield's monumental *Vedic Concordance* of 1906 (reprinted in India in 1964), we have in the domain of stobhas a collection called *Stobhānusaṃhāra*, published by Satyavrata Sāmāśramin in the *Bibliotheca Indica* (Volume II, 1874, pages 519–542) and made accessible by van der Hoogt (1929). This collection contains such stobhas as:

ā	*(e)re*	*hā-u*	*iṣ*	*phat*
as	*hā*	*hṃ*	*iṭ*	*pnya*
auhovā	*hahas*	*ho-i*	*kāhvau*	*um*
bhā	*hai*	*hum*	*kit*	*up*
dada	*hā-i*	*hup*	*mṛs*	*vava*
(e)bṛ	*ham*	*hvau*	*nam*	*vo-i*
(e)rā	*has*	*ihi*	*om*	

The stobha *dada* inspired Faddegon to coin the felicitous expression "Ritualistic Dadaism" (Faddegon 1927; cf. Gren-Eklund 1978–1979).

In Tantric seed mantras we find similar or identical forms. They often occur in groups of five, a number we meet everywhere: the Danish missionary Ziegenbalg recorded them in South India in the early eighteenth century (Caland 1926:108–109) and the "Five Syllable Mantra" (*pañcākṣara*) *Namaś Śivāya* is found throughout Asia (for Bali, for example, see Goris 1926:62–63).

These seed mantras often reflect phonological discoveries of the Indian grammarians. The following quintuple illustrates the five semi-vowels of Sanskrit phonology disguised as mantras and incorporated in a mystic diagram, the Śrī Cakra (see Michael 1986: 134):

haṃ
yaṃ
vaṃ
raṃ
laṃ

Elsewhere, we find the vowels and diphthongs of Sanskrit developed into a system of mantras, e.g. (Brunner 1986a:102):

haṃ	*hāṃ*
hiṃ	*hīṃ*
huṃ	*hūṃ*
heṃ	*haiṃ*
hoṃ	*hauṃ*

Such "phonological" systems of mantras are neither rare nor confined to India. Similar mantras occur in the 1986 volume on Maṇḍalas and Mantras, edited by Padoux, in which the Michael article just quoted is published. The entire Sanskrit alphabet becomes a system of mantras and is found on representations of deities such as Hanumān, whose limbs they cover. Outside India, similar systems occur throughout Asia wherever Tantric influences have gone: Central Asia, China, Korea and Japan, and the countries of Southeast Asia. Numerous examples are found, for example, in Hooykaas' monographs on Balinese ritual and in Payne's dissertation on the Japanese *goma* ceremony (1986).

In Tantrism, mantras are placed in diagrams and circles, maṇḍalas or yantras, like those studied in the 1986 collection edited by Padoux, in *Understanding Mantras* (Alper 1988), and in earlier publications such as Zimmer 1926 and Pott 1966. I have referred to them elsewhere in a cosmological context (see Staal 1988d). For the distinction between maṇḍala and yantra in the Śaiva tradition, see Brunner 1986a. For illustrations of yantras in Bali in the form of simple drawings of the human figure with the mantras added, see Hooykaas 1983:541–548.

A characteristically Tantric doctrine is that mantras and deities are identical. This is referred to in passing by Goudriaan (1981:130), but emphasized by Hélène Brunner (1986b:129) who has advanced the hypothesis that the point of departure for this idea lies in the *āhāvana* or invocation rite. The argument runs, in rough approximation, thus. The Tantric ritualists generally assume that the deity is present as soon as the mantra that invokes it has been recited; the two thus being co-extensive, the notion arose that the deity was already present in the mantra. These ideas are not confined to Tantrism, except the strict identity of mantras and deities. The notion that deities are called down by mantras, songs or invocations, and that they heed those calls, is a common interpretation of Vedic rites and is frequently expressed in the Vedas themselves. For example, Rigveda 1.6.9:

> *ataḥ parijmann ā gahi divo vā rocanād adhi*
> *sam asminn ṛñjate giraḥ*
> "Come down, you who are always going around, from there or from the divine realm of light! The songs propitiate you around!"

or Rigveda 8.1.18:

> *adha jmo adha vā divo bṛhato rocanād adhi*
> *ayā vardhasva tanvā girā mama 'jātā sukrato pṛṇa*
> "Come here from earth or from the large divine realm of light!
> Grow your body by these songs of mine, complete your descendents, you skillful one!"

or Sāmaveda 1.1.1:

> *agna ā yāhi vītaye gṛṇāno havyadātaye*
> "Come here, Agni, to the feast, after being extolled, come to the gift of offerings!"

The connection between these invocations and the making of oblations or offerings (expressed by two identical verbal roots *hu-*), led Thieme to the hypothesis that Vedic ritual originated in a *Gastmahl*, a feast offered to a guest. I shall return to this theory which has been defended with ingenuity but does not account for the ritualization that characterizes ritual (page 438).

The Vedas come tantalizingly close to the further step, that the invocatory mantras *are* deities. The Mīmāṃsā philosophers assert that the deities are entities postulated in order to give a semblance of existence to what is referred to in a mantra by a name. According to Mīmāṃsā Sūtra 9.1.9, ritual is the principal factor (*pradhāna*) and the deity a subordinate factor (*guṇa*). The commentary by Śabara on this passage shows, however, that the idea of deity in Vedic ritual is in some respects different from what it became in Tantrism. Ganganatha Jha, who translated this commentary (Jha 1936,III:1432–1437), has summarized it in the following terms (Jha 1942:336–337):

> The deity and the offering material are both accomplished entities, while the act of ritual is what is to be accomplished. The deity, therefore, cannot be the prompter . . . The view of the opponent makes it necessary to admit of deities having material bodies and actually eating and drinking the substances offered; and this idea is utterly repugnant to the Veda, which does not lend support to any such idea regarding deities. The text quoted by the opponent regarding the right hand of Indra ("we have taken hold of what is Indra's right hand") [Cf. the thighs of Indra, the arms of the Aśvins, the hands of Pūṣan in examples (2) and (4) of Chapter 17] does not mean that Indra possesses a right hand. Moreover, even if he did, it would be impossible for any human being to "take hold" of it. . . . The texts that speak of the "arms" of Indra being *hairy* or his "eyes" as *tawny*—all these are purely eulogistic. Nor is there actual *feeding* or *eating* at rituals; in fact, the deity never eats. . . .

Hélène Brunner made a special study of the limbs of Śiva that are touched in the Tantric *kālanyāsa* rite. Touching the deity is equivalent to touching one's body in accordance with a principle frequently invoked in Tantric texts:

> *yathā deve tathā dehe cintayet tu vicakṣaṇaḥ*
> "the intelligent person must realize in his own body (*dehe*) what he realizes in the divine (image) (*deve*)"

(Brunner 1986a:100). There also exists a close correspondence between the limbs of the divine body and the *mūlamantra* or "root mantra" which invokes the deity. This mantra is divided into parts that are called limbs (*aṅga*). Brunner has referred to a passage of a late Vedic text, attached to the Āśvalāyana Gṛhya Sūtra, which refers to *nyāsa* and invokes the famous Gāyatrī mantra, taught at Upanayana and recited daily by almost every brahman:

> *tat savitur vareṇyam*
> *bhargo devasya dhīmahi*
> *dhiyo yo naḥ pracodayāt*
> "May we receive this desirable
> light of the god Savitṛ,
> who shall impell our thoughts"

(Rigveda 3.62.10). The Āśvalāyana text subdivides the mantra into pieces called *aṅga*, each of four syllables and connected with parts of the body. For other subdivisions and insertions see Varenne 1962:186, who refers to Bṛhad Áraṇyaka Upaniṣad 6.3.6.

Brunner has quoted several Tantric texts that support the conclusion that the limbs of the deity are set up following the division of the mantra and not the other way round. This suggests that the Tantric deities themselves originated at least in part from mantras. Such a hypothesis would explain the notion, often met with in popular books, that there are millions of gods in Hinduism. For enormous quantities of mantras are imagined to exist in superior worlds (70.000.000, for example: Brunner 1986a:91 and note 9). That gods come from language is a variant of the Wittgensteinian doctrine adumbrated by Max Müller, that mythology and philosophy are diseases of language. We have watered down Western versions in personified allegories, for example, Victory, Melancholy or the Muses, sometimes solidified as in the Statue of Liberty, an idol as welcome in Tantrism as it would be unwelcome in Islam.

The Tantric rite of *nyāsa*, "imposing a mantra" (on the body: Padoux 1963, Index) expresses primarily a *system* of mantras so that it is misleading to characterize it as a "ritual projection of divinities into various parts of the body" (Eliade 1958:210–211). The idea is connected with the more spectacular aspects of Tantrism dealt with in popular literature, especially its emphasis on sex, which is not absent from the Vedas either (see, e.g., Bṛhad Āraṇyaka Upaniṣad 6.4).

In Vedic, meaningless syllables such as the Tantric "seed" mantras are not confined to the Sāmaveda but occur also elsewhere. In the śastra recitations of the Rigveda, for example, there are lengthened "*o*" 's (see Chapter 9B: Episode I, Element 3). They often end in a nasal which results in the famous mantra OṂ.There are also insertions of *śoṃsāvo* which means "Let us both recite!" but is treated as a similarly meaningless element with various forms (e.g., *śośoṃsāvo*.) The Adhvaryu responds with *othāmo daiva, āthāmo daiva, othāmo daiva made, modāmo daivotho*, and other "bizarres contortions liturgiques," as Caland and Henry (1906, I:232, note 8) called them. In the *Āśvalāyana* tradition of the Rigveda, the Hotā priest murmurs before the beginning of his first *śastra*:

su mat pad vag de

(Caland-Henry, I:231). Each *śastra* recitation moreover, has its own syntactic structures which have nothing to do with semantics. During the noctural rounds in the more advanced Soma rituals, for example, the first quarter verse is repeated in the first round, the second in the second, and the third in the third (see AGNI, I:663–680, II:750–752, and above page 182).

The Sāmaveda is different only in the sense that the choreography of mantras becomes richer and more varied. Most of the ritual chants consist of elaborate structures, generally preceded by: *ō hiṃ*, and certain sequences by: *hiṃ*. The patterns become so complex that the priests keep track of them by constructing figures, called *viṣṭuti*, with the help of sticks on a piece of cloth (for illustrations see AGNI, I:Figures 48–51). In many melodies (called *gāyatra*) the *udgītha* or second portion of the chant, sung by the Udgātā, is:

ō vā ō vā ō vā hiṃ bhā ō vā.

In musical chants, the occurrence of such sounds is of course not surprising. Their function is simply to fill out the melody when there is no text. The same holds for insertions such as *o* or *śoṃsāvo*. This is found all over the world. The Kosi of Cameroun insert whistling in their chants (Dammann 1963:117), but this is exceptional. In general, melodic insertions are induced by the phonological structure of the language in which they are inserted. For example, *heisa hopsasa* would not fit in a Vedic or Sanskrit context, but fits in German when sung by Papageno in Mozart's *Zauberflöte*:

> Der Vogelfänger bin ich ja,
> stets lustig, heisa hopsasa!

Heisa hopsasa is reminiscent of the kind of sounds one would use, in German, when addressing a horse or a pack animal. It would be helpful to know what sounds the Vedic Indians used in everyday life in similar circumstances. Such information would not assist in explaining the ritual meaning or use of mantras, but it would throw light on their origins and on the associations they may have evoked in ancient India.

Before closing this section I should make brief references to non-Tantric forms of Hinduism and to Buddhism. It is often assumed that Tantric mantras are different from the other mantras of medieval Hinduism. However, there are similarities. The so-called Purāṇic mantras, or mantras prescribed in the Purāṇas, are a case in point. Whereas they are literally meaningful, unlike the Tantric *bīja*-mantras, they are treated as if they were devoid of meaning. This is shown by the fact that the mantras

> *namaḥ śivāya*, "homage to Śiva"
> *oṃ namaḥ śivāya*, "OṂ! Homage to Śiva"
> *oṃ namo nārāyaṇāya*, "OṂ! Homage to Nārāyaṇa"
> *oṃ namo bhagavate vāsudevāya*, "OṂ! Homage to Lord Vāsudeva"
> *śrīrāmajayarāmajayajayarāma*, "(long) live Śrī Rāma, live Rāma, Rāma live!"

are *not* distinguished from each other (as scholars are likely to assume) by the different deities to which they refer, or by their meanings, but by the fact that these mantras are, respectively, five-syllabic (*pañcākṣara*), six-syllabic (*ṣaḍakṣara*), eight-syllabic, twelve-syllabic, thirteen-syllabic, etc. (Kane V, 1958, 1962, notes 219 and 1775). Just like Vedic and Tantric mantras, these Purāṇic mantras are treated not like utterance of language but as if their main characteristic were the number of their syllables. This is both characteristically Indian and characteristically "mantra."

In Buddhism, the term most frequently used for mantra is *dhāraṇī*. The theoretical distinctions made by the Yogācāra philosophers are especially reminiscent of Vedic notions. They distinguish *artha-dhāraṇī*, "meaning(ful)-memorizations," which consist of words and phonemes, not yet formulated or even expressed mentally, from *mantra-dhāraṇī*, which are similar but more effective: Bodhisattvas use the latter to alleviate the afflictions of beings. This distinction is related to that between *dhāraṇī* and *samādhi* or "concentration": whereas the latter is always associated with thinking (*cittasamprayukta*), the former, according to these theorists, may be associated with thinking or dissociated from it (*cittaviprayukta*). In other words, some *dhāraṇī* are meaningful, others meaningless; but all are treated similarly and belong to the same category (Lamotte IV, 1976:1857–1859). This speculation is compatible with the Vedic and Tantric uses of mantras which is also characterized by the fact that they are independent of the distinction between meaningful and meaningless.

The idea that mantras are meaningless goes back to the Vedic ritualist Kautsa. Both the *Nirukta* (1.15), an early work on etymology from the Vedic period, and the *Mīmāṃsā Sūtra* (1.2.31–39), refer to his doctrine that "mantras are meaningless" (*anarthakā mantrāḥ*: see below page 373 and Staal 1967: 24–26, 45–47). This view has always remained the view of a minority, for most Indian commentators and philosophers have tried to provide mantras with meaning even if it meant invoking the improbable or the impossible. In the Brāhmaṇas we have found *ad hoc* interpretations, contradictions and rationalizations. In the later literatures of Hinduism and Buddhism such rationalizations develop, and tend to become more systematic. In Buddhist philosophy, a distinction is made between "explicit meaning" (*nītārtha*, Tibetan: *ṅes don*) and "implicit meaning" (*neyārtha*, Tibetan: *draṅ don*; see, e.g., Murti 1954:254; Ruegg 1969:56; 1973:58). In Buddhist Tantrism this developed into full-fledged systems of "hermeneutics."

Such systems and concepts derive from metaphysics and are not directly concerned with the practice of mantras. Steinkellner (1978) studied one such system, due perhaps to Candrakīrti, which distinguishes one literal and three "Tantric" meanings. This system formed the basis for the Guhyasamāja school and was adopted by Indian and Tibetan exegetes from the eighth century onward. It should be noted that, as in the case of the Brāhmaṇas, nothing is authoritative about such interpretations. They are the predictable professional views of philosophers, theologians, and exegetes all over the world. They need not be taken seriously as possible explanations because they themselves stand in need of an explanation. They do not throw light on the nature of mantras.

There are more important kinds of evidence that have to be taken into account before we can conceptualize, explain or even picture the history of the Indian mantra from Veda to Tantra, Hindu as well as Buddhist. Foremost among these are techniques of chanting and recitation in the context of which many mantras developed. The relevance of such evidence is clear in the case of the Sāmavedic *stobhas*, which can only be understood within the context of the chants and melodies (*sāman*) of the Sāmaveda (see, e.g., Staal 1961, Chapter VIII). For Buddhist chants, Paul Demiéville has collected the relevant facts in two articles, published with an interval of half a century between them (Demiéville 1930 and 1980). The evidence from chant and recitation (or "hymnology", in the words of Demiéville) is far too rich and varied to be taken into account in the present context; but it demonstrates, among other things, the importance of musical categories for explaining some of the characteristics that distinguish mantras from language. The close relationship between mantras and music reflects the general relationship between ritual and music (see Chapter 16). All we can do in the present context is emphasize that mantras cannot be understood unless their musical character is taken into account. This constitutes one reason why mantras cannot be explained in terms of language.

It remains a curious fact that monosyllabic mantras of the *stobha* type reemerged in Tantrism after apparently lying dormant for more than a millenium. Their popularity stands in need of an explanation, not their occurrence somewhere on the subcontinent. For traditions of Sāmaveda chanting have been handed down without interruption from Vedic times, and continue to the present day. Knowledgeable Sāmavedins have always been rare, secluded, orthodox, and reluctant to divulge their art; but we need only assume that one became a Tantric or Buddhist and chanted *stobhas* for the edification or entertainment of his fellow *sādhakas* or monks. Though controversial, this would not be unheard of. The Buddha himself had on several occasions asked a young novice with a beautiful voice to come to his cell at night and chant (Demiéville 1930:93). An opportunity for transmission in centers of Vedic and Buddhist culture, such as Banaras or Kanchipuram, was always available. That such mantras found their way into meditation is not surprising, especially in Buddhist monasteries. Their subsequent diffusion is known as the spread of Tantrism in India and over large parts of Asia.

21

Performatives, Pragmatics and Performance

In Sanskrit, the performative force of an entity is called its *siddhi*. This is one of those formations that exemplify the productivity of Sanskrit morphology. The root *sidh-*, the weak form of *sādh-*, means "establish, accomplish." Therefore, *siddha* means "established" and *siddhānta* the finally established view in philosophy and in the traditional sciences in general. *Sādhana* is the means by which a result is established: for example, ritual practice interpreted as a means. *Sādhaka* is the practitioner or follower, sometimes wrongly translated into English (because of the similarity in sound?) as "Seeker": erroneous, because the Indian *sādhaka* does not *seek* but *follow*. Another related term is *sādhya*, the thing-to-be-established, that is, in logic, the conclusion. Finally, *siddhi* becomes the supreme performance: the Siddhas are the happy few who have obtained it and become Members of the Spiritual Establishment.

21A. Performatives Again

What I propose to do in this chapter has nothing to do with Siddhas but deals with the Western categories of "performatives" and "performance," and the discipline of "pragmatics" which has a similar intermediate status. We have seen (Chapter 3) that Austin introduced performative utterances in an attempt to go beyond the customary logical categorization of utterances as statements that are either true or false. This is not quite correct, as Quine pointed out, but these utterances of language are in any case utterances that in saying something also establish something.

Tambiah made the most important contribution to the theory of ritual in the seventies by giving grounds for abandoning the semantic approach and advocating an analysis in terms of rules (Chapter 15). Tambiah looked upon rites as things that do not *mean* but *do* something. This is different from Austin in two respects: Tambiah did not claim that rites *do* something *by meaning* something; and he did not state that for rites to *do* something is not surprising *unless* it is by saying or meaning something. Rites, after all, are acts. In India, they have always been called *karmāṇi*, which means "acts." The ancient Greeks also called them *δρώμενα* (*dromena*), "activities," which corresponds to Latin *acta*. Negatively, the view that Tambiah defended was salutary as a corrective to the over-emphasis on symbols and meaning that had begun to invade the study of ritual, in anthropology as well as the study of religion. Positively, it constituted a return to earlier views and common sense on the one hand, and made an important innovation on the other. The scholars who defended the *do ut des* doctrine, for example, had always interpreted ritual as consisting of *acts* and not of *utterances*. But Tambiah was the first to establish that the exclusive emphasis on meaning had become an obstacle to an adequate understanding of ritual, and that ritual acts had to be understood in terms of *rules*.

In dealing with mantras, Wheelock (1982, 1987) defended views that are in some respects similar to Tambiah's because he also took his inspiration from the performatives explored by Austin and further analysed by Searle. The view he espoused, that mantras are speech acts, was more radical than the view that rites are performative acts. For although it was generally agreed—albeit tacitly—that mantras belong to the realm of speech, it had not been claimed before that they could be looked upon as acts. It is to be noted, however, that this view is not supported by the Indian tradition which had made a basic and clear distinction between acts and mantras, as we have seen in the Introductory Note to Part III. In Sanskrit, a mantra is *never* called an act (i.e., *karman* or *kriyā*). The two are distinguished in order that a one-one-correspondence between them can be established.

Wheelock began his discussion with Austin's distinction between locutionary, illocutionary and perlocutionary acts, and concentrated on Searle's taxonomy of illocutionary acts as "perhaps the most significant advance over Austin's primitive classification" (Wheelock 1982:54). In order to clarify this we shall slightly modify Austin's original formulation into saying that speech acts have three kinds of force, the locutionary, the illocutionary, and the perlocutionary. The illocutionary force of a speech act is concerned with the effect the speaker intends to produce in the hearer. This was developed by Paul Grice—subsequently by S. Y. Kuroda—and led to Searle's classifications of speech acts based on the assumption that all speech acts are concerned with such effects. viz., with *intention*.

Adopting Searle's classification, Wheelock pointed out that there are several basic differences between "ritual speech acts" and "ordinary speech acts." For example, "the very basic requirement that an ordinary speech event involves a speaker and a hearer is one that is often lacking in ritual speech acts" (Wheelock 1982:58). Also, "the most essential distinguishing feature of ritual utterances is that they are speech acts that convey little or no information" (ibid.). Wheelock referred, with apparent approval, to Tambiah's view that "in ritual, language appears to be used in ways that violate the communication function" (page 57).

Wheelock and Tambiah 1968 are undoubtedly right that mantras do not always require a speaker and a hearer, are not always communicative and do not necessarily convey information. In fact, they rarely or never do any of these things. However, that mantras cannot be speech acts follows directly from Searle's view, because on his view, all speech acts involve intention and it is obvious from the six representative mantras illustrated in Chapter 17, that most mantras do not involve intention. The theory according to which they are performatives depends, moreover, on the assumption that mantras are linguistic utterances. We have already seen that rites are not performatives because they are not linguistic utterances. We shall see that mantras are not linguistic utterances either and hence are neither speech acts nor performatives.

The confusion to which Tambiah and Wheelock fell prey may be summed up in the following terms: both adopted a philosophical distinction which was applicable to the area which logicians and philosophers had long been discussing, that is, the area of language and linguistic utterances. But since it had not been established that rites and mantras are utterances of language, the distinction failed to apply to these categories. Applying it to rites did not make sense since it was already agreed that rites were acts; and applying it to mantras was unpersuasive because the Indian tradition consistently distinguished between mantras and acts throughout the long period of its development.

We should be grateful that Indologists, anthropologists and scholars of religion look beyond the boundaries of their disciplines and attempt to make use of concepts developed by philosophers. It has not been my intention to criticize Tambiah or Wheelock for misunderstanding or misapplying such concepts, but merely to disentangle some of the confusions that easily result. It is not uncommon for philosophers themselves to misunderstand these concepts. Searle criticized Foucault for claiming that statements were not speech acts, and Foucault replied in a letter to Searle of May 15, 1979: "As to the analysis of speech acts, I am in complete agreement with your remarks. I was wrong in saying that statements were not speech acts, but in doing so I wanted to underline the fact that I saw them under a different angle than yours" (Dreyfus and Rabinow 1983:46, note 1).

Though mantras are not speech acts, Austin's ideas may throw light on mantras in another respect. Austin was originally interested in performatives, which he contrasted with constative utterances. Later he arrived at the conclusion that all speech acts exhibit both features or forces. Performatives are speech acts that perform acts in saying something (e.g., promising or baptizing). They cannot be false, but they can go wrong, or be "unhappy." Austin formulated six conditions for the *felicity* of performatives. The first four are:

(A.1) There must exist an accepted conventional procedure having a certain conventional effect, that procedure to include the uttering of certain words by certain persons in certain circumstances, and further,
(A.2) the particular persons and circumstances in a given case must be appropriate for the invocation of the particular procedure invoked.
(B.1) The procedure must be executed by all participants both correctly and
(B.2) completely (Austin 1962:14–15).

It is clear from what has been said before that mantras are not performatives: they do not perform acts, and need not say anything. However, their use is governed by conditions that are similar to Austin's four conditions. The chief differences are that mantras need not have an effect, or a visible effect (the Mimāṃsā thinkers devoted much discussion to their *adṛṣṭa*, "invisible", effects); what is uttered need not be words; and there need not be more than one person uttering a mantra. It is certainly a necessary condition for the use of mantras, on the other hand, that only the appropriate person can properly use them (e.g., the Adhvaryu priest: see above page 72). In general, only brahmins can utter or hear Vedic mantras. Within a given ritual performance, only the appropriate priest can use the prescribed mantras at the proper place and time. In order to be able to discharge this priestly function, a person has to be eligible, and elected beforehand. The election of priests constitutes a special ceremony (*ṛtvigvaraṇa*) that takes place at the beginning of a ritual performance (AGNI, I:313–316).

While Austin emphasized, in his illustrations, the appropriateness of the speaker (e.g., a bridegroom saying "Yes, I will," or a person naming a ship), Indian theorists have been equally concerned about persons hearing or receiving mantras as about those who recite or give them. The restrictions in Veda and

Tantra are similar. No mantras may be learned from books. They can only be learned, at the appropriate time, by eligible students from eligible teachers. Members of low castes, or people beyond the pale of caste (such as outcastes or foreigners) may be punished (e.g., by having molten lead poured into their ears) for hearing Vedic mantras even inadvertently. Among Vedic brahmins, other restrictions obtain. The few Sāmavedins of Kerala, for example, will not teach their mantras to Rigvedins, thereby further endangering the continued existence of their own Veda. In Tantrism (as in Maharishi's "Transcendental Meditation"), a person is given his own mantra, and is not supposed to divulge it at any time.

All such conditions are similar to those formulated by Austin—only they go further. Mantras should be pronounced correctly and completely; but they should in addition be recited with the correct degree of loudness, at the correct pitch, and at the correct pace (*Āpastamba Śrautasūtra* 24.1.8–15: below, page 355). Moreover they, or their specifically prescribed portions (e.g., *bhakti* in the Sāmaveda), should be recited in a single breath (see AGNI, I:311, 602, 622). All such requirements that govern the use of mantras resemble the conditions formulated by Austin, but they are more extensive and more stringent than anything that applies to the normal use of a natural language such as English or Sanskrit.

21B. Pragmatics

Performatives are a category of linguistic utterances that are acts that perform something. Their analysis is therefore part of semantics, the discipline that studies the relations between the expressions of a language and their meanings—which may include sense, reference, and whatever other category of meaning philosophers, logicians, linguists or others have convincingly postulated. Performatives do more than connect with "reality" through referring; they make an impact upon it. In so doing, performatives may be said to go beyond semantics. There is another area of studies that is also closely related to semantics without it being quite clear whether it should, or should not be regarded as part of it: pragmatics. Although this field of studies has never turned into a broadly recognized discipline, it addresses real problems. In such sentences as: "You were here yesterday," the truth of the sentence depends on who is "you,", where is "here," and when was "yesterday." When these variables vary, the truth value of the sentence may change. For example, if I say "You were here yesterday" to Peter it may be true while if I say the same to Kazuo it may be false. Saying it in different places at different times increases this variability. Variables such as "you," "here" or "yesterday" have been called "indexical terms," "egocentric particulars," or "token-reflexives" (in the words of Peirce, Bertrand Russell, and Hans Reichenbach, respectively). Carnap initially considered pragmatics an empirical field of investigation (Carnap 1936–1937) but subsequently dealt with its theoretical foundations (Carnap 1947), following which the field was developed as a formal system by logicians such as H. Kamp, D. Lewis, R. M. Martin, D. Scott, R. Stalnaker and especially Richard Montague (1968, 1970: reprinted in Thomason 1974). I related pragmatics to Austin's performatives and attempted a linguistic analysis of one of its characteristic features (Staal 1970a).

Pragmatic notions were current in classical antiquity as well as in ancient India; they are undoubtedly here to stay. At the same time, the status of pragmatics as a science has so far remained undetermined; in fact, it may be argued that, outside the domain of formal logic, pragmatics died in Jerusalem (Staal 1971).

Pragmatics is generally defined, following Morris and Montague, as the discipline that is not only concerned with the relations between expressions (as is syntax), or between expressions and their meanings (as is semantics), but with the relations between expressions, their meanings, and their users or contexts of use. Pragmatics may be relevant to the study of ritual and mantras provided we extend the notion of "expressions" beyond language so as to include rites as well as mantras. This is what Tambiah and Wheelock did unsuccessfully, for mantras or rites are not like linguistic expressions in possessing meaning or reference. It is appropriate in the present context, however, because they are similar to linguistic expressions in that they are *being used*. They involve, therefore, the specific features that are the subject matter of pragmatics, namely, users and contexts of use.

In the Vedic area pragmatic relationships are straightforward since the users, executors or performers of rites and mantras are invariably the same in almost all ritual contexts. Like the ritual acts themselves, most ritual recitations are executed by the Adhvaryu on behalf of the Yajamāna, although on specific occasions other priests recite particular pieces. In Soma ceremonies, the *śastra* recitations are always executed by the Hotā, Maitrāvaruṇa, Brāhmaṇācchamsin or Acchāvāka priests in accordance with specific rules. The ritual songs are always chanted by the Udgātā, with a few exceptions, well-known from the tradition (e.g., the Subrahmaṇyāhvāna: AGNI I:369, 386, 596), while the *stuti* or *stotra* chants of the Soma ritual are always executed in the same fashion by the trio of Prastotā, Udgātā and Pratihartā. Were we to add a list of exceptions and special cases, the information contained in the present paragraph, suitably formulated, would therefore take care of pragmatic problems as far as the users are concerned.

As for "contexts of use," the ritual context determines throughout what is to be recited or chanted, as well as when and on what occasion. The knowledge of these contexts of use is an important part of what constitutes a knowledge of the ritual—the knowledge that distinguishes a ritual specialist from a nonritualist. But such "pragmatic" information depends on the structure of the ritual itself, and cannot replace the latter.

A pragmatic analysis of the function of the users of the mantras, i.e., of the priestly functions, may throw light on their position in society *outside* the ritual enclosure. Such an analysis pertains to historical reconstruction and is therefore a diachronic enterprise, unlike the synchronic analysis that seeks to understand the ritual as a system. One contemporary scholar who has studied these historical problems fruitfully is the German Sanskritist Klaus Mylius. Mylius has, for example, analysed the offices of two Rigvedic priests who take part in the Soma ceremonies, the Potā and the Acchāvāka (Mylius 1977; 1982; 1986). His analysis led him to conclude that both these priests had a lower status than the majority of the other officiants, but that the Acchāvāka occupied the lower status of the two; he is in fact related to the *vaiśya* class. The Potā is referred to in the Rigveda, where he is assigned menial jobs; the Acchāvāka is of later origin and he is not "elected" but "called." Yet his office cannot have been created long after the Rigveda, as was, for example, the office of the Grāvastut.

It is clear from these examples that a pragmatic analysis may be relevant to historical reconstruction. However, pragmatics does not have the same function here as it has in linguistics or philosophy, because it does not apply to individuals who determine the truth value of a statement, but to priestly functions which are stereotypical roles.

21C. Performance and Competence

Turning now to "performance" we are faced with another concept taken from the confines of contemporary linguistics and philosophy. "Performative Studies" have been applied to the study of ritual and are also applicable to mantras. So far, this has not shed much light, as we have seen (Chapters 15 and 21A). Applying pragmatics makes more sense and yet, the results do not contribute to the study of ritual systems (21B). Applying performance studies (which has nothing to do with "performatives") has not shed much light either but this is not to say that the concept of "performance" is not applicable to ritual. Rituals, after all, are performed, and it is their manner of performance in which students of performance are interested. The lack of success of these studies is due to the fact that they have adopted a behavioristic or phenomenological perspective and confined their attention to a feature of "appearance" that cannot be understood without paying attention to its underlying reasons, causes, or "reality." For "performance" is based upon "competence," and may be described, but cannot be understood or explained, without taking competence into account.

Without using these neologisms and in only slightly misleading but simpler terms, we say that what people *do* is based upon what they *know*. This knowledge need not be conscious, let alone consciously formulated knowledge, but there must be an internal structure that explains overt behavior, *unless* it is a product of chance. It has accordingly become clear, especially in linguistics, that the investigation of performance will proceed only so far as the understanding of underlying competence permits (see, e.g., Chomsky 1965:10–15). According to Chomsky, any investigation of an activity such as language or ritual

> necessarily deals with performance, with what someone does under specific circumstances . . . To the extent that we have an explicit theory of competence, we can attempt to devise performance models to show how this knowledge is put to use. If we knew only that language consists of words, our performance models would necessarily be very primitive and of restricted interest; we could study the sequence of linguistic signs and their formal and semantic properties but nothing else. With a richer theory of competence that incorporates structures of greater depth and intricacy, we can proceed to more interesting performance models. Study of performance relies essentially on advances in understanding of competence. But since a competence theory must be incorporated in a performance model, evidence about the actual organization of behavior may prove crucial to advancing the theory of underlying competence (Chomsky 1980:225–226).

The study of generative grammar as universal grammar has proved so fruitful precisely because of this:

> We saw that the study of generative grammar shifted the focus of attention from actual or potential behavior and the products of behavior to the system of knowledge that underlies the use and understanding of language, and more deeply, to the innate endowment that makes it possible for humans to attain such knowledge. The shift was from the study of language regarded as an externalized object to the study of the system of knowledge of language attained and internally represented in the mind/brain. A generative grammar is not a set of statements about externalized objects constructed in some manner. Rather, it purports to

> depict exactly what one knows when one knows a language: that is, what has been learned, as supplemented by innate principles. Universal grammar is a characterization of these innate, biologically determined principles, which constitute one component of the human mind—the language faculty (Chomsky 1986:24).

Performance Theory, at the time of writing an American favorite, exhibits all the faults of the empiricist caricature of scientific method we have studied in Chapter 2. At present it is another, not interestingly different, form of behaviorism. It is applicable to the study of ritual but only insofar as the understanding of ritual competence permits.

In linguistics, or psycholinguistics, performance studies have reached results that are nontrivial and even surprising. This is due to two facts: (1) they have been undertaken in the context of studies of competence; and (2) performance, which is by nature finite, exhibits, in linguistics as in the study of ritual, a capacity that is infinite. This explains why the inherent limitations of a performative approach are especially clear in linguistics. A simple example may serve as an illustration.

Imagine we wish to study the verbal forms of English from a performance that exhibits English usage. Assume we have collected a small corpus of data which includes the following six forms:

he goes	he went
he sees	
he goes to see her	he went to see her
	he used to see her.

The pattern in which these forms have been printed exhibits a structure which suggests that there should be two more forms to complete it:

	he saw
(*?) he uses to see her.	

Considerations of symmetry, however, are not decisive, for no one has demonstrated that language must be in some sense, "symmetrical." The question arises: is the form that is marked (*?) grammatical?—We may find the answer only by going beyond this finite corpus of data, study other finite corpora of data, and then go beyond *all* of them and postulate rules that account for the formation of the past tense. It is likely that there will be limiting conditions under which these rules operate, for the rules of language are of a restrictive sort. This can not be done, however, by restricting oneself to a theory of performance. For such a theory adopts a behavioristic methodology which refuses to go beyond the immediate data or admit that performances may be different from each other and yet reflect the same competence that is in people's minds.

We learn from data beyond our small corpus that "he saw" is English; but we never come across "he uses to see her." The rule system must exhibit patterns of structure that explain this and relate it to other structures. They may come under syntax, semantics, phonology, or some other domain. It is conceivable that we cannot find any explanations among these theories of competence, and that the theory of performance offers an explanation. Chomsky and Miller have found restraints of a performative nature that prevent sentences that are perfectly grammatical according to the model of linguistic competence from being actually produced. Miller (1964:36) has discussed three examples:

(R) Remarkable is the rapidity of the motion of the wing of the hummingbird.
(L) The hummingbird's wing's motion's rapidity is remarkable.
(E) The rapidity that the motion that the wing that the hummingbird has has has is remarkable.

Miller comments:

> When you parse these sentences you find that the phrase structure of (R) dangles off to the right; each prepositional phrase hangs to the noun in

> the prepositional phrase preceding it. In (R), therefore, we see a type of recurring construction that has been called right-branching. Sentence (L), on the other hand, is left-branching; each possessive modifies the possessive immediately following. Finally, (E) is an onion; it grows by embedding sentences within sentences. Inside "The rapidity is remarkable" we first insert "the motion is rapid" by a syntactic transformation that permits us to construct relative clauses, and so we obtain "The rapidity that the motion has is remarkable." Then we repeat the transformation, this time inserting "the wing has motion" to obtain "The rapidity that the motion that the wing has has is remarkable." Repeating the transformation once more gives (E).
>
> It is intuitively obvious that, of these three type of recursive operations, self-embedding (E) is psychologically the most difficult. Although they seem grammatical by any reasonable standard of grammar, such sentences never occur in ordinary usage because they exceed our cognitive capacities (Miller 1964:36).

Generative grammar explains that and why (R), (L) and (E) are all grammatical because it provides a theory of competence. Psychology has shown that the measure of complexity of (E) exceeds our cognitive capacities. As a theory of performance based upon a theory of competence, the psychology of language can therefore explain what linguistics cannot, namely, that (E) is unintelligible and never uttered.

Miller reports on an experiment he and Stephen Isard carried out with Harvard undergraduates. They were asked to memorize sentences that differed in their degree of self-embedding. They found that everybody can manage one embedding, some people two, but everybody has trouble with three or more (Miller 1964: 37).

When we study mantras or ritual, we are primarily interested in competence—in what the ritualists *know* and not only in what they *do*. That is why we include information that the Śrauta Sūtras and other sources provide—for example, that certain mantras are not uttered or "uttered mentally." Neither a tape-recorder nor a behaviorist can accept this; but then neither is in a position to arrive at a general and explanatory model or theory. The same holds for a performance theorist. He can describe and enumerate, but not account for anything. Of course, performance cannot be ignored. In the present book, we are primarily concerned with a theory of competence but such a theory cannot be evaluated without the kind of evidence that was presented in AGNI, and that consists largely of performance. The account of the 1975 Agnicayana that was the subject of AGNI provided both the "thick description" of performance and the "grand theory" of competence. Some features of its methodology were explained in the book itself in the following terms:

> The 1975 Agnicayana was a traditional Nambudiri performance, though we were partly responsible for its occurrence and indirectly contributed to the nonsacrifice of goats, which was in some sense a deviation from the tradition. In the social sciences there is much interest in modernization and other changes that influence people's behavior and societies as a whole. The traditional philologist confines himself to texts and to what they can teach us about the past. In the humanities we are not only interested in people's behavior and in their past, but also in what is in their minds—for example, in what they know. Unfortunately, minds and knowledge are invisible, and therefore have to be made manifest, something that can be done in many ways, including outside prompting. This would cause no surprise to the scientist working in his laboratory, where he studies reactions he has himself induced. Naturally, we need not be surprised that, in any situation, the observer may influence what he observes. The philosopher muses on the boundaries of objectivity, the romantic may wish to limit such influence, and the moralist to direct it. The scholar or scientist is content to describe, analyze, and explain its occurrence and extent (AGNI II:475).

Patañjali was perhaps the first to state that the enumeration of forms of performance lead nowhere unless they are accounted for by a system of rules that exhibits competence (page 40). AGNI posed the question: what insight can be gained from a single performance of a known tradition about ritual performance as well as competence? Schechner (see Schechner 1986, 1987; Staal 1987 and above page 93) noted that the 1975 performance of the Agnicayana must have been different from other, earlier performances. That fact was taken into account in AGNI; it is a dead issue. Schechner presented his case with flair. As the Sanskrit says, "even a crow assumes the demeanour of an eagle when it comes upon a dead lizard" (*mṛtaṃ duṇḍubham āsādya kāko'pi garuḍāyate*).

A sociologist or political scientist may explain why in the seventies and eighties, many American social scientists have been fascinated by the study of performance. It may not be accidental that these scholars belong to the society that re-elected a President noted for performance, not competence.

22

Mantras and Language

One assumption underlies all accounts of mantras that I am familiar with: the assumption that mantras are a kind of language. Since many mantras are expressions of Vedic or Sanskrit, they obviously often *consist of* language. However, it does not follow that they *are* language. Nor does this follow from the fact that linguistic methods appear to be fruitful in their study.

Since language has been studied well, and mantras have been studied only rarely, one way to determine their relationship is by trying to find out to what extent linguistic methods are applicable to the study of mantras. We have seen that the syntactic approach is promising as distinct from both the semantic, which has run into problems, and the pragmatic, which has limited significance. What about a phonological approach?

Mantras that consist of sentences of a language are always constructed in accordance with the phonology of that language. We should therefore look at those cases where mantras do not consist of language, e.g., at stobhas and bīja mantras. But here we reach the same conclusion: even if they are not words of Sanskrit, these mantras are constructed in accordance with the phonological rules of Sanskrit. I have found two apparent exceptions to this rule, one in the *Stobhānusaṃhāra* (referred to on page 227), and one discussed by Padoux. The first is *pnya*. I do not believe that *pna-* occurs in Sanskrit in initial position, and neither does *pnya-*. In middle position both are available, e.g., *svapna*, "sleep, dream," and *svapnya*, "a vision in a dream" (the latter occurs in the Atharvaveda, and is rare). Perhaps *pnya* was constructed by a Sāmavedin who heard *svapnya* and mistakenly made the assumption that this form consisted of the familiar reflexive pronoun *sva-* and a hypothetical *-pnya*.

The unphonological mantra studied by Padoux is certainly not pronouncable: *rkhkṣem*. However, its analysis (Padoux 1963: 356–358) is both pronouncable and clear in Tantric terms: *ra-kha-kṣem*. I therefore believe that we are entitled to retain the general conclusion that Indian mantras are constructed in accordance with the phonological rules of Sanskrit.

This conclusion is further supported by the fact that, when mantras are exported from India to other countries, their phonological structure generally adapts itself to their new environment. In Tamil, for example, the term mantra itself becomes *mantira* both as a word of the language and inside mantras in which it occurs (Diehl 1956:290). For Chinese, numerous illustrations of a similar nature may be found in van Gulik 1980. For Japanese, Payne (1986:400–412) has listed ninety-three mantras used in the Japanese Buddhist fire ritual called *goma* (from Sanskrit *homa*) in their Sanskrit forms and Japanese equivalents that are not translations but transliterations. I shall quote a few, adding a translation if it makes sense:

1. Sanskrit: *oṃ sarva-tathāgata-pāda-vandanaṃ karomi*, 'OM. I salute all the Tathāgatas''
   Japanese: *on saraba tatagyata hana mana nay kyaromi*
2. Sanskrit: *oṃ tathāgatodbhavāya svāhā*, ''OṂ. For the production of Tathāgata—Svāhā!''
   Japanese: *on tatagyata dohanbaya sowaka*
3. Sanskrit: *oṃ padmodbhavāya svāhā*, ''OṂ. For the production of the Lotus—Svāhā!''
   Japanese: *on handobo do hanbaya sowaka*
4. Sanskrit: *oṃ vajra karma kaṃ*, ''OṂ. Thunderbolt rite—Kaṃ!''
   Japanese: *on bazara kyarama ken*
5. Sanskrit: *oṃ bhūḥ khaṃ*, ''OṂ. Earth—Space!''
   Japanese: *on boku ken*
6. Sanskrit: *oṃ agnaye gaccha gaccha bhūḥ*, ''OṂ. Go, go to Agni!''
   Japanese: *on agyanau ei gessya gessya boku*.

Anthropologists have paid much attention to ritual, and to a lesser extent, mantras. Scholars of religion have studied both topics. All have assumed that mantras are some kind of linguistic utterances. This assumption on the part of anthropologists is in line with the high regard some have had for linguistics as an example or paradigm of scientific methodology. Such an explanation hardly applies to scholars of religion who, in general, have stayed away from scientific methodology (an exception is Hans Penner to whom we will return). Anthropology has been repeatedly inspired by developments in linguistics, and these waves of inspiration have flowed along channels cut by the subdisciplines of phonology, syntax, and semantics. Thus Lévi-Strauss has been inspired by the phonology of Jakobson, Singer (e.g., Singer 1984) by Peirce's semiotics which is a kind of semantics, and Tambiah by Austin's performatives, as we have seen. Oddly enough, what appears to be missing is *syntax*—the most basic of these disciplines, at least according to many linguists, logicians and mathematicians.

Syntax is not really missing in anthropology. We find it in the famous 1899 article by Hubert and Mauss already referred to: "Essai sur la nature et la fonction du sacrifice." Hubert and Mauss offered a "schème abstrait du sacrifice" which is primarily syntactic in nature: for example, they made, for the first time, the elementary but fundamental syntactic observation that rites have a beginning, a middle and an end. Their analysis is to a large extent derived from the syntactic analysis of Vedic ritual found in the *Śrauta Sūtras*. Mauss had been introduced to these texts by Sylvain Lévi who taught during 1896–1897 at the *Collège de France*, specifically for Mauss (Mauss 1969, III:538) a course on Vedic ritual which was subsequently revised and published in 1898 as "La doctrine du sacrifice dans les Brāhmaṇas." Hubert and Mauss also referred in their article to published sources based upon the Vedic *Śrauta Sūtras*, such as Schwab's 1886 monograph on the Vedic animal sacrifice entitled "Das altindische Thieropfer." Durkheim (1915:386) concluded from Hubert and Mauss, as well as from other anthropological data, that a rite can serve different ends; but he did not draw the further conclusion that ritual is therefore independent of the ends it is supposed to serve. Accordingly, he did not pay much attention to syntax, which is a pity for anthropology (cf. above, pages 125–130).

Why are we justified in characterizing the analysis of Vedic ritual given in the *Śrauta Sūtras* as *syntactic*? To provide an adequate answer to this question would necessitate a lengthy excursus into Vedic literature, but in the present context it should suffice to state that the *syntactic* analysis of ritual in the *Śrauta Sūtras* supplements and is to some extent supplemented by its *semantic* interpretation in the *Brāhmaṇas*. Just as the *Brāhmaṇas* stand at the source of much of Indian mythology, the syntactic analysis of the *Śrauta Sūtras* is closely related to the origins of grammar. We shall see in Chapter 26 that (1) the ancient Indians possessed a *science of ritual* which used primarily syntactic methods, and that (2) linguistics originated in India in close association with this syntactic analysis of ritual.

European phonology has been profoundly inspired by the Indian grammarians, and Jakobson's concept of "distinctive features" still bears the stamp of their influence. The study of syntax entered Western linguistics much later, with Zellig Harris and more definitively with Noam Chomsky (Chapter 6A). Thus, if we had to picture the influence exerted by linguistics (and by logic and philosophy via linguistics) on anthropology in tabular form, and in terms of the three subdisciplines to which we have referred, adding "performatives" as a fourth, we should properly include these ancient Indian forerunners, as follows:

	Linguistics	*Anthropology*
phonology	Prātiśākhya, Pāṇini, Jakobson	Lévi-Strauss
syntax	Pāṇini, Chomsky	Śrauta-sūtras, Hubert & Mauss
semantics	Frege, Peirce, Saussure	Singer
performatives	Austin, Grice, Searle	Tambiah

In most of these relationships, the influence has been in the direction from linguistics (including logic and philosophy) to anthropology; the only exception is the ritual science of the *Śrauta Sūtras*, which I have listed in the table under "anthropology" for lack of a better heading and which influenced Pāṇini and the other Indian grammarians.

What, then, is the relation between these various disciplines and the science of religion? Before we address this question we must make several observations. First of all, it is not really anthropology as a whole that has undergone the influence of syntax and pragmatics; it is rather the anthropological study of ritual. In the case of phonology, the case is different, and the consequences have been baffling: for Lévi-Strauss introduced into anthropology a form of analysis that stressed binary oppositions and that was based upon distinctive features, though all linguists know that distinctive features had been postulated successfully only in phonology, and play no role in syntax or semantics. Lévi-Strauss, in other words, introduced into anthropology a linguistic method he regarded as a universal panacea, while it is applicable only to a subdiscipline of linguistics. One might even go further and reason that it is *a priori* unlikely that a method that can be used in phonology but not in syntax or semantics could be useful in anthropology. Moreover, why should *two* suffice for man when so many other natural numbers exist and are found elsewhere in nature? In his 1957 article "In Defense of the Number Two," Halle has shown that the system of distinctive features due to Jakobson can make do with much less conceptual machinery than is usually employed by assuming that the structure of features is *binary*. In other words, specific empirical restrictions and conceptual sophistication combine to show that, in phonology, *two* is the number we need. But Lévi-Strauss has not given a similar demonstration for anthropology. If Lévi-Strauss had studied linguistics later, or Chomsky developed syntax earlier, Lévi-Strauss, instead of paying attention to binary opposition, might have introduced the syntactic methods that had been adumbrated by Hubert and Mauss in their study of ritual, but that were not fully developed in linguistics until Chomsky.

Since ritual is one of the main areas of research common to anthropology and the science of religion, one might expect that the latter science would have been inspired by linguistics or logic as well. In fact, the scene for such an influence had long been set. As early as 1867, Max Müller predicted: "It was supposed at one time that a comparative analysis of the languages of mankind must transcend the powers of man: and yet, by the combined and well directed efforts of many scholars, great results have been obtained, and the principles that must guide the student of the Science of Language are now firmly established. It will be the same with the Science of Religion" (in: Waardenburg 1973, I:86). What happened, in fact, was that the comparative study of religions developed as Müller had predicted; but when the "Science of Language" made a methodological transition from comparative and diachronic philology to a synchronic science of linguistics, the "Science of Religion" lagged behind. Instead of developing a syntactic method of analysis appropriate to its object, it fell prey to phenomenology, existentialism, and hermeneutics. It was left to anthropologists such as Mauss to study religious phenomena like ritual in the manner in which de Saussure had studied language, as a "système où tout se tient." Thus the science of religion failed to make the transition which would have turned it, like linguistics, from a respectable branch of scholarship into a contemporary scientific discipline as well.

Belatedly, scholars of religion have expressed an awareness of the need for such a transition. In a reaction to my article "The Meaninglessness of Ritual" (Staal 1979b), Hans H. Penner has stated that "the study of linguistics is the necessary foundation for explanations in religion" and that "language as we all know is composed of signs, and all linguistic signs have phonological, syntactic and semantic components" (Penner 1985). Yet, in the same article, Penner has asserted that my syntactic analysis of ritual is "irrelevant." He has supported this by emphasizing that, by my own admission, these pieces of analysis "do not correspond to any existing ritual" or "to any actual ritual."

Disentangling some of the misconceptions that are at the root of these assertions should help us to understand more precisely the relationships between the methodology of science and the science of ritual—or *any* empirical science, for that matter. It would be correct to say that anthropology has been influenced by linguistics; but this does not mean that specific pieces of linguistic analysis have been of great use to anthropology. For example, some of Lévi-Strauss' work serves to warn us that an uncritical acceptance of distinctive features is artificial and unproductive within anthropology. In my study of Vedic ritual I found something different, viz., that some ritual structures can be generated by rules that are similar to the rules that linguists call transformations, while others are unlike any structures found in natural languages or with which linguists are familiar (Chapters 11, 19 and 23). From a methodological standpoint, the most basic issue is not whether ritual or anthropological structures are similar to linguistic structures. Of importance is that all such structures are *postulated* and never correspond exactly to actual facts such as rites. They correspond, if they are adequate, to features that are *abstracted* from actually existing rites (cf. page 102).

Lévi-Strauss may have been wrong with regard to the specific binary oppositions, or other specific phonological or syntactic structures, that he postulated; but he is right with respect to method. What is basic to his method, and to all scientific method, is that structures are postulated entities that are not empirically given—that are, in fact, invisible—but that enable us, provided they are adequate, to account for what is empirically given and visible. Lévi-Strauss has in fact told us where he came upon this idea, which was novel and startling to him, a French philosopher by training, and which remained the main insight that separated him from existentialists such as Sartre (see Sartre 1960 and Lévi-Strauss 1962, Chapter 9): he took from geology, from Marx and from Freud the idea that is basic to all science, viz., that reality is different from what it appears to be

(Lévi-Strauss 1968:61–62). This is obvious to scientists, as indeed it is to most ordinary people; the only persons who have failed to understand it are certain types of philosophers *bien étonnés de se trouver ensemble*, such as behaviorists, phenomenologists, practitioners of hermeneutics and ordinary language philosophers such as Wittgenstein (Chapter 2). What anthropology has taken from linguistics is therefore, in the final analysis, nothing peculiarly linguistic but rather an insight into the characteristic features of science.

These general considerations at the same time help to explain the importance of logic and mathematics. These latter disciplines study structures in general, including the most general structures that can be imagined. The abstract, underlying structures that are postulated in order to account for empirical facts and events can generally be expressed in a mathematical or logical form. This is the common insight and methodology shared by anthropologists such as Singer, Tambiah and Lévi-Strauss (whatever their differences), but that empiricists such as Edmund Leach (e.g., in his 1985 review of Singer 1984), and many scholars of religion, fail to appreciate and understand.

We are now in a position to see that the influence of linguistics on anthropology and on the science of religion does not necessarily imply that the objects of the latter two sciences are *languages* or even "systems of meanings and symbols." What I have attempted to demonstrate is that ritual is not a language, but is, like language, a *rule-governed activity*. Since it is an activity that is governed by rules, it becomes important to discover what actual rules, and what kind of rules, govern it. In pursuing such questions, I found that ritual structures can be analysed in syntactic terms not by methods specific to linguistics, but by mathematical and logical methods that have also influenced linguistics. I cannot say whether other traditional object areas of anthropological or religious study are also rule-governed systems; but mythology, for example, does not appear to be such a system, at least insofar as Vedic mythology is concerned. Vedic ritual and Vedic mythology are in fact remarkably separate developments, that rarely correspond with each other and that are accordingly distinguished from each other by the relevant experts (e.g., Tsuji 1952:187; Renou 1953: 16—above page 65—29; Dandekar 1982:77). This continues to apply to later Indian rituals: Hindu or Tantric rites do not attempt to reproduce any story, legend or myth (Renou 1953:59).

We are now in a position to extend the hypothesis on ritual and grammar to the origin of language from syntax (above, page 112). It seems likely that human language is not as old as was once believed: perhaps around one hundred thousand years (Burkert 1987:152 suggests about forty thousand). Ritual is much older; Neanderthaler man had elaborate rituals (Burkert, ibid.). This is supported by the facts of animal ritualization which are similar to human rituals especially with regard to their structure (see, e.g., Barlow 1977). It is likely that the same holds for mantras, for mantras occupy a domain that is situated between ritual and language. To mantras or mantra-like sound structures among animals we shall turn in Chapter 23.

An important fact that supports the idea that mantras are older than language, is the following. Mantras are generally transmitted within linguistic contexts, but when the language of the context is translated, the mantra is not: it remains invariant. Thus we find the same or similar mantras in India, southeast Asia, China, Korea and Japan. The only difference between such mantras is, as we have just seen, that their form is adapted to their new phonological environment, just as Sanskrit *homa* or *dhyāna* becomes Japanese *goma* or *zen*. Such transformations are akin not to translation but to transliteration. This applies equally to apparently "meaningless" mantras such as *oṃ* or *huṃ phaṭ* and to apparently "meaningful" mantras such as *namo buddhāya* or *śivāya namaḥ*. The evidence for the untranslatability of mantras is plentiful all over Asia (see e.g., Hooykaas, Skorupski and Strickmann in AGNI II). Among the "Bauddha Brahmans" of Bali, for example, *namo buddhāya* or *śivāya namaḥ* are not translated as "Hail to Buddha!" or "Hail to Śiva!," but remain in their original form (see Hooykaas 1973, passim). We meet not only with such clear-cut cases but also with mixtures of translated and untranslated (because untranslatable) forms. This is not confined to "Greater India," but occurs on the subcontinent itself as in the following example "translated" from the Tamil: "Kan̲ Kan̲ Kal Kal Cun̲atin̲ Pin̲ Pin̲ Kalai Kalai Separate Separate Tuva Tuva Tūma Mantirakāḷi Lord of the Smoke Svāhā!" (Diehl 1956:290).

There are additional reasons which support the idea that mantras are older than language. Mantras may or may not consist of language; but they are treated, in either case, in a manner which is totally different from the way we use language. The situation is similar to a common occurrence in biology when a part of the body that is used for a specific purpose is also used for something quite different; for example, when legs, which are used for walking or running, and perhaps kicking, are also used for swimming. Legs are used, in that case, as if they were fins. If we assume that language was preceded by mantras in the course of biological evolution, but that the "original" mantras are no longer there, it follows that all we have access to at present is mantras-couched-in-language. These vestigal mantras are not used for the expression of meaning, like the other forms of language, but they are used differently, like the original mantras. In other words, we have an analogy: language is to mantras what legs are to fins.

We may formulate this conclusion in slightly different terms by distinguishing between apparently meaningless mantras such as *oṃ* and apparently meaningful mantras such as *śivāya namaḥ*. Let us assume that *oṃ* was an "original" mantra; that is, we assume it existed before language was born. Suppose that Pithecanthropus, for example, was humming *oṃ* but could not talk. Let us further assume that this *oṃ* re-appeared in Sanskrit where it is now used in the manner mantras are used, e.g., preceding, following, or interspersed between chants and recitations, accompanying rites, meditation, etc. This *oṃ* is not used in the manner in which other words are used: it is not declined like a noun, for example, but it may be quoted like other words (e.g., with *iti*). Now contrast this with *śivāya namaḥ*, apparently a Sanskrit expression: this can be construed as a sentence consisting of two nouns with an implicit verb, there is a *kāraka* relation between the two nouns which is expressed through case endings, etc. This expression, then, is a mantra, like *oṃ*, but it is couched in language: it belongs to language in the sense that it is governed by the rules of language; but it is also used in the context of ritual recitation, meditation, etc. Though an expression of language, it may be used in the manner of *oṃ*, just as legs, though ordinary human limbs and not piscine accretions, may be used in the manner of fins.

The hypothesis that mantras are in some respects unlike language, and are remnants of something that preceded language, may explain certain curious and hitherto baffling facts about mantras: for example that they are repeated endlessly, but also that they have a proclivity to reduce to nothing (via *japa* "mutterings" and *upāṃśu* "murmurs" to *manasā* "in thought": Renou 1949; Renou and Silburn 1954); that they consist of "poussière védique," as Renou called it; or that they result from "le découpage des vieux hymnes en formules ou même en fragments devenus des corps inertes dans la trame liturgique" (Renou 1960:76; quoted in Malamoud 1983:33).

While form, in a natural language, is at most as important as meaning, the form of mantras is more important than their meaning. In this respect, mantras are a typical product of Indian civilisation—a civilisation where form is all-important, where, as in Malamoud's summary of Renou's formulations, "c'est l'arrangement des formes et la spéculation sur les formes qui revèlent le plus clairement le contenu, qui sont, en fin de compte, le contenu" (Renou 1978:3). Mantras are not confined to India, but this insistence on form may explain why India has produced more mantras than any other civilization.

That mantras are different from language is supported by their being cut and broken into pieces, and subjected to strange insertions and musical or other sound transformations. But this hypothesis does not seem to derive support from the fact that some mantras consist of language: for such mantras cannot be older than language *at least in their present form*. In order to address this problem in appropriate terms we should take account of an important difference: that between historical origin and current function. We have already met with a special case of that difference: the difference between etymology and usage. The general distinction is deeper and wider, especially in a biological perspective.

Illustrations of this distinction are discussed in a recent review on the relations between culture and biology and the origin of the human mind by S. J. Gould (1983). In the course of evolution, our ancestors first began to walk upright, and subsequently developed a large brain. The humanoid creatures that lived in Africa some three or four million years ago did already walk upright, but their brain remained at an ape's characteristic size. It took a long time before the brain began to develop to its present dimensions. Whatever the complex reasons for these developments, the outcome enabled men to perform all manner of operations bearing no direct relation to their original impetus or motivation. Walking upright, for example, enabled them to develop gestures (e. g., *mudrā*) and to make fire, but may also be related to the origin of speech, since hands were now free to do certain things that previously had to be done by mouth (e. g., carrying food). Similarly, the brain came to be used to perform many tasks that are unlikely to be related to the original reasons for its biological growth. Such a state of affairs is not confined to biology: "I may put a computer in my factory only to issue paychecks and keep accounts," writes Gould, "but the device can (as a consequence of its structure) also calculate *pi* to 10,000 places."

Now let us return to mantras. These have, by and large, been studied by Sanskrit scholars and therefore primarily within a diachronic perspective. But once we adopt a synchronic point of view, it is apparent that the Sanskrit that occurs in mantras is often used in an unintelligible fashion and not in the manner in which any natural language is normally used. Even those mantras that say something or have meaning are not used like linguistic utterances when they are ritually used. From the point of view of their ritual use, there is no difference in treatment between mantras we would regard as meaningful and mantras we would regard as meaningless. In the context of a natural language such a state of affairs is inexplicable—nay, unthinkable; the distinction between meaningful and meaningless is fundamental to human language in all its normal uses. Though specific mantras may derive from sentences of a specific language, their use indicates a different background which has nothing to do with language. The synchronic study of this usage has therefore diachronic implications: it points to a more distant origin, preceding the succession of stages or periods in the development of any particular language.

We have already met with many illustrations of uses of mantras that are different from any use of language. Here is another example. The original meters of many mantras, that were accorded great importance during the period of Rigveda, are lost in the ritual application (*prayoga*). In the transmission of mantras (*adhyāya*), the *names* of the metres are sometimes preserved, but in actual recitation the characteristics of the metres have disappeared and are replaced by special renderings, often musical, of the Vedic accents (*udātta*, *anudātta* and *svarita*). This treatment is characteristic of Veda recitation and is given not only to poetry, but also to prose (provided the originals were accented), and not only to meaningful but also to meaningless mantras. The entire development has nothing to do with the normal preservation, continuation, development or change of language, but is rather a musicalization of language.

Let me summarize. Many mantras are constructed from language, but in their ritual use, which is their proper use, they do not conform to any of the normal uses of language. Though many specific mantras are derived from language, the species of mantra need not therefore be derived from the species of language. On the contrary, in order to explain these various anomalies, we must assume the opposite, viz., that language derived from mantras in the course of evolution. In that case, the origin of language marks an entirely new use of mantras, unrelated to their original function—just as the many functions of walking upright or of a large brain mark new uses that are unrelated to their original uses.

Can we set up a more detailed hypothesis about the development from mantras to language? We may guess, provided we do it in such a way that our speculation can be discussed rationally. My present guess is that meaning was introduced last into an evolution that consists of three stages:

I. *Earliest Stage*	MANTRAS of TYPE 1 These are sounds subject to phonological constraints, e.g., *bíja* mantras such as *him*, or *stobhas* such as *bham*.
II. *Intermediate Stage*	MANTRAS of TYPE 2 These are sequences, two-dimensional arrangements, or elaborate constructions of mantras of type 1, sometimes subject to syntactic constraints, e.g.: *hā bu hā bu hā bu bhā bham bham bham . . .* or: *huvā yi vācam / vācaṃ huvā yi / . . .* (*Jaiminíya Araṇyageyagāna* 1.2: AGNI, I:525).
III. *Final Stage*	LANGUAGE These are mantras of type 2 subject to semantic, further syntactic and different syntactic constraints, e.g.: *vācaṃ yaccha*, "Control your speech!"

I must leave it to specialists to provide chronological estimates for the duration of the first two stages in this scheme of evolution. The earliest stage represents features that are found among vertebrates, and are certainly pre-human. (The term "phonological" in this context refers to any rules that put constraints on the combinations of sounds.) The intermediate stage may be anthropoid or characteristic of early man, but is probably much older. This is at any rate suggested by the bird songs discussed in the next Chapter. The final stage corresponds to the last fifty to hundred thousand years of the development of *homo sapiens*.

I regard the evidence in support of the hypothesis that mantras are older than language as strong enough to be subject to rational discussion. The evidence for the priority of monosyllabic mantras over polysyllabic mantras, that is, for the priority of Stage I to Stage II, is less compelling and stands in greater need of empirical data on bird song and on growling, miauling, singing, barking and chirping by many other animal species, from whales to grasshoppers. To think that monosyllabics are earlier than polysyllabics may be an instance of what may be called the fallacy of "atomistic reductionism." On the other hand, there may be serious grounds for such a priority. Apart from the evidence from babbling babies, there is one kind of aphasia, in which the patient is in a position to produce and recognize phonemes, but not words; in another kind, he can produce and recognized words, but not sentences (see Jakobson in: Jakobson and Halle 1960, 1964). Such facts suggest the priority of Stage I to Stage II. That language itself developed from monosyllabic forms is an old speculation. Von Humboldt discussed it in the last chapter of his famous monograph (Humboldt 1836:373–414).

Let us take another look at the form of our hypothesis. Since mantras are used in a manner that is different from the manner language is used, we postulate that their use reflects the function of something else that preceded them and that is more properly "mantra". In other words, we postulate "original" mantras, now lost, and "later" mantras which survive and sometimes resemble language, but language used in a pre-language fashion. In other words, I assume that there has been a development of B (human language) from A (mantras), followed by the occasional emergence of functions in B that are more easily explained in terms of its predecessor A than in terms of its successor, B.

Such a situation, we have seen, is not rare in biology. The earliest vertebrates were fish, and the wings of birds, as well as the limbs of reptiles and mammals, developed from fins. The present functions of these body parts are clear: fins are for swimming, wings for flying, and legs for running. Of course, these limbs did not originate for the sake of performing these functions. They arose by chance and were selected in accordance with the demands of the environment. The variation we find is, in fact, extraordinary. Crocodiles no longer have fins, but use their legs for swimming. The earliest crocodiles, such as *Pelagosaurus*, lived in the open seas. Since their legs and tail did not enable them to swim well, they began to live in and around rivers. So here we have a case of the development of B (crocodiles' legs) from A (fishes' fins), followed by the emergence of functions in B (swimming) that are more easily explained in terms of A (fins) than in terms of their successors B (legs).

Another interesting case is penguins. These are birds, but they cannot fly. Their wings have developed into flippers which enable them to swim extremely well (20 miles per hour). Walking is difficult for penguins, but they can glide on their bellies on ice over long distances with the help of their flippers. So here we have a development from fins (A) into wings (B), but the wings are mostly used in the manner in which fins are used, and to some extent in the manner of ski poles. This becomes more like humans using language in the manner of mantras. Men use their arms and legs as they use their language: the former are generally used for walking, running, grasping, catching, gesticulating, etc., and sometimes, archaically, for swimming; the latter is generally used for speaking or thinking and sometimes, archaically, in the manner of mantras. Numerous parallel developments in other animals, and countless more distantly related cases, therefore support the hypothesis that human language developed from mantras, and still preserves rudiments of this mantric background.

There are cases outside religion where man uses language entirely or almost entirely in the manner in which mantras are used. This resembles the penguins' use of wings as if they were fins, but in the case of man, it either is considered regressive and pathological, or is confined to babies. Leopold von Schroeder observed in 1887 that there are striking similarities between mantras and the utterances of mental patients. Such similarities have been noted and commented on by Eggeling, Keith, and others, but mostly in rhetorical fashion. Von Schroeder (1887:

112–114) was more straightforward and serious. He began his discussion with an illustration of mantras, quoting those that are recited by the Adhvaryu priest when the *ukhā* pot, chief vessel of the Agnicayana, is manufactured. Von Schroeder translated from *Maitrāyaṇi Saṃhitā* 2.7.6, but I shall provide here the parallel passages from *Taittirīya Saṃhitā* 4.1.5 1-q and 6 a-d (see AGNI, I:297–299 and cf. Ikari in: AGNI, II:168–177):

l. You are the head of Makha

m. You are the two feet of the ritual.

n. May the Vasus prepare you
with the gāyatrī meter
in the fashion of the Aṅgirases!
You are the earth.

May the Rudras prepare you
with the triṣṭubh meter
in the fashion of the Aṅgirases!
You are the sky.

May the Adityas prepare you
with the jagatī meter
in the fashion of the Aṅgirases!
You are heaven.

May the Viśvedevas, common to all men
prepare you with the anuṣṭubh meter
in the fashion of the Aṅgirases!
You are the directions.

You are the unchanging direction.
Make unchanging in me children,
abundance of wealth,
abundance of cattle, heroism,
and similar things for the Yajamāna.

o. You are the waist band of Aditi.

p. May Aditi grasp your hole
with the paṅkti meter
in the fashion of the Aṅgirases!

q. Having fashioned the great ukhā
made of clay as a womb for Agni,
Aditi gave it to her sons saying, "Fire it!"

a. May the Vāyus smoke you with the gāyatrī meter
in the fashion of the Aṅgirases!
May the Rudras make you smoke with the jagatī meter
in the fashion of the Aṅgirases!
May the Viśvedevas, common to all men,
make you smoke with the anuṣṭubh meter
in the fashion of the Aṅgirases!
May Indra smoke you in the fashion of the Aṅgirases!
May Viṣṇu smoke you in the fashion of the Aṅgirases!
May Varuṇa smoke you in the fashion of the Aṅgirases!

b. May Aditi, the goddess,
in union with the All-gods,
dig you, trench, in the realm of the earth
in the fashion of the Aṅgirases!

c. May the wives of the gods, the goddesses,
united with the Viśvedevas,
put you, ukhā, in the realm of earth
in the fashion of the Aṅgirases!

d. May the Dhīṣaṇās, the goddesses,
united with the Viśvedevas,
fire you, ukhā, in the realm of earth
in the fashion of the Aṅgirases!
May the wives, the goddesses,
united with the Viśvedevas,
fire you, ukhā, in the realm of the earth
in the fashion of the Aṅgirases!

Von Schroeder compared these mantras with the following piece written by a patient and quoted from Th. Güntz (1861; I translate from the German):

First Prayer:

Schiller save his soul and consciousness
Jesus save his soul and consciousness
My mother save her soul and consciousness
van der Velde save his soul and consciousness
Trommlitz save his soul and consciousness
Gerstäcker save his soul and consciousness
Voss save his soul and consciousness
Seume save his soul and consciousness
Körner save his soul and consciousness
Arndt save his soul and consciousness
and save the soul and consciousness of all poets of the book of songs.

Second Prayer:

for all the names that are in Schiller's work.

Third Prayer:

for the soul of my family.

Fourth Prayer:

to destroy my consciousness and my ego.

Von Schroeder also quoted a prose passage from a patient at the hospital Rothenberg near Riga (I translate from the German):

> With humility and affection walk the streets, the indicated, with full knowledge go the streets, which favor going the road with humility, and with deep devotion go the streets, which favor to build the church and keep the peace, which indicated the way which is necessary and desirable for that, build the road with God's desire, buy the peace, and then with good spirit build the church, which is favored, and with good intention gain the stage of learning, which could be desirable for that, with devoted endeavor give roses to the institution, build God's church and show his submission with much humility, with much submission and humility try to reach that goal, with much submission try to gain that, and with humility walk the way which is required, make use of God's love, with good intentions lead a good life, with right decision take the road which is required, with good intention go the road which is required, use God's love, with progress go the way, of God's love, build the church, God's love, build the church, God's love, build the church and with good intention, God's love, build the church and with good intent, God's love, build the church (the last two phrases are repeated about 80 times, and it goes on like that for several pages).

When the psychiatrist asked why he wrote the same thing all the time, the patient answered that he did not know anything else.

Though these writings are pervaded by religious notions, no one would regard them as religiously inspired writing. It is likely that we have here a case of regression to an earlier stage of development: language is used here in the manner of mantras—type II mantras, to be precise, for it is mainly semantics that is affected. *Stobha*-like mantras are used by other kinds of patients, and in cases of aphasia, to which I shall return.

Mantra-like uses of language are also found among babies, and here the recapitulation of phylogeny by ontogeny provides even more striking support for the thesis that language has developed from mantras. Nancy Budwig drew my attention to Ruth Weir's study on the babblings and pre-sleep monologues of a two-and-a-half year old child, alone in his crib, talking to himself. Here is an example of what he uttered a few minutes before the onset of sleep:

like like
one like
two like
three four like
monkey's like
up up
light light
turn the light
light
all gone all gone
it's all gone it's all gone
it's not all gone
it's not all
stop it stop it
there (squealing)
yayaya wau wau gigouboubou gigouboubou
now it's all gone
all gone (falsetto)
go go go go
all gone all gone all gone all gone
good luck
that's one
two

go go go go (falsetto)
close the door
gee gee gee gee gee gee

(Weir 1970:128). The following sequence immediately preceeded sleep, and contains more *stobha*-like elements (I have replaced the phonetic transcriptions by approximate spellings):

yiii (squealing)
I I I
did
gi gi gi gi
the baby the baby the baby
(Baby is crying in the adjoining room)
baby the baby baby (6 times)
iii
baby baby baby
bay
baby
bay
happy baby
that's the baby
bay
baby
that's the baby
baby
yaa
aa (squealing)
SLEEP

(Weir 1970:197).

Mental patients and children often display features that are reminiscent of earlier stages of evolution, and that may be referred to as archaic. Religion is generally conservative and characterized by archaic features. It is probable that there are other features of religion that may be interpreted as regressive. Glossolalia or speaking-in-tongues is a related form of regression (see May 1956). Mantras are always archaic. They are often attributed to ancestors or primeval sages (such as the Vedic ṛṣis), or are regarded as eternal or as having originated in a golden age (*kṛtayuga* or *satyayuga*). In Sri Lanka, where demons are apparently primeval, mantras are referred to as the "language of the demons" (*yaksā bāsāva*: Tambiah 1968:177).

The archaic nature of mantras is related to the fact that many mystical phenomena are archaic (cf. Staal 1975). The mystical state is a state of awareness that can be reached or produced with the aid of mantras, a state of consciousness that is "beyond language" or "ineffable." Mantras give access to this ineffable state. To say with Renou, Padoux, and Wheelock (in *Understanding Mantras*:Alper 1988) that mantras are beyond the boundary of language, at the highest level of speech "situated beyond language and eventually right to the zone of silence," or to say that mantras "point backwards to the source of language, which is the source of all creation itself" (pages 98, 120) is not merely a matter of phenomenological, religious or spiritual metaphor, also found in the Indian texts; such expressions may be taken literally as asserting that mantras are the predecessor of language in the process of human evolution.

All natural languages share certain phonological properties that are regarded as universal (see, e.g., Chomsky and Halle 1968, Part IV). Are there also universal mantras? It may seem premature to ask such a question since mantras, outside the Vedic realm, have been studied so haphazardly. Moreover, we should exclude historical influences, borrowing and exports: for example, mantras exported from Sanskrit into Chinese, Korean, Japanese, or Tibetan, and adapted to the phonological structure of the recipient languages. All of these illustrate, incidentally, T. R. V. Murti's statement that "Buddhism is Hinduism for export." However, Vedic and Sanskrit have no monopoly in the export of mantras. There are purely Chinese mantras in Taoism and, according to Parpola, the famous mantra *oṃ* may have been imported into Vedic and Sanskrit from the Dravidian (Parpola 1981).

Actually, as far as *om* is concerned, we are on firmer ground. According to Jakobson (1962:541), "the most natural order of sound production is an opening of the mouth followed by its closure." This is a very apt description of the mantra *om*. As for ontogeny, Jakobson informs us that the child first passes through a babbling stage in which precisely such sounds are produced, and then arrives at the "first acquisition of conventional speech" in which it clings to the model "consonant plus vowel." Then *repetitiveness* comes into operation—the most basic element of ritual syntax—resulting in what in linguistics is called *reduplication*. Consonants formed by a complete oral closure predominate, and this leads first to *mama*, which does not, however, refer to the mother but is a general expression of affection. Language comes into being only when purely referential mechanisms begin to operate, when there is, in Jakobson's words, "the transition from affective expression to designative language." Thus *papa* arrives on the scene—"the first distant, merely deictic, rudimentary cognitive attitude in the child's verbal behavior" (page 543).

The importance of *oṃ* and its priority to language is inherent in this scenario, which depicts how *oṃ* comes before *mama*, and *mama* before *papa* who introduces language. Variations of *oṃ*, with repetition, survive in Western Asia: *am-en*. Another universal mantra answers the general description of "opening the mouth followed by its closure" equally well: the mantra *hiṃ* with its variant *huṃ*, both common in Vedic and Tantric contexts. Intoned at the beginning of many chants, it is not confined to India or even Asia. In Mozart's *Zauberflöte* Papageno sings:

Hm hm hm hm – – – –
– – – – – – – – – !

Hum is no longer confined to the old world since the American composer Ruth Crawford-Seeger composed in 1930, as Paul Attinello informs me, *Chant 1930* which begins:

Hum Hum Hum.

The occurrence of "h" in these mantras may be due to their onomatopoeic representation of breathing. This is much clearer than in the case of *ong* and *ang*, about which the Danish missionary Bartholomaus Ziegenbalg wrote around 1711: "The heathens say that breath, when it is inhaled, produces the sound *ong*, and when exhaled, the sound *ang*" (Caland 1926:109). *Oṃ* itself is also related to breathing: it figures prominently in *prāṇāyāma* recitations (see AGNI I:283, 380, Plate 62). Or perhaps, the author of the *Taittirīya Saṃhita* explained it correctly when referring to the wind:

> *vāyur hiṃkartā*
> "The maker of the sound HIṂ is Vāyu"
> (*Taittirīya Saṃhitā* 3.3.2.1 a).

Other candidates for universal mantrahood are *hi* and *ha*. Compare for example the German jingle:

> Unter einen Apfelbaum
> hi ha Apfelbaum
> hatt' ich einen schönen Traum
> hi ha schönen Traum.

Hi and *hay* are common in Peyote songs, which consist in general of meaningless syllables, especially among the Arapaho (see Nettl 1953). *Ha* is also found on Tierra de Fuego: when Waldon and Drayton landed there in 1838 from H. M. S. *Beagle*, "a group of natives took their arms and jumped with them in time to the following song:

> "Ha ma la ha ma la ha ma la ha ma la
> O la la la la   la la la la" (Bowra 1966:388).

Throughout our investigation, I have mainly used data from Asia. Similar phenomena occur all over the world under different names, and should be studied within a similar perspective. Anthropologists are familiar with Peyote songs and related phenomena (e.g., McAllester 1949 and Nettl 1953, just quoted). Classical scholars are familiar with the Greek magical papyri, mostly from Egypt, that abound in meaningless sounds and syllables. Edited first by Preisendanz, they have now been revised and republished by Henrichs (Leipzig 1973–1974). Biblical scholars are familiar with the description in the New

Testament (*Acts* 2) of the Holy Ghost descending on Jesus' disciples, taking the form of tongues of fire and making them "speak with other tongues." Glossolalia, already referred to, is especially common in contemporary America as a recent survey depicts:

> Tongue speaking, or glossolalia, almost vanished after the apostolic age except for a brief revival by Montanus in the second century. Saint Augustine set the pattern for the Catholic Church and the Reformers by asserting that God withdrew the gift after it served its purpose. This was also the view of Thomas Aquinas. There is no evidence that Luther or Calvin spoke in tongues, but early Methodists revived the gift, and it was soon flourishing among the Quakers, Shakers, Irvingites, Mormons, and other fringe sects. After 1900 a variety of churches sprang up in the United States, on fire with tongues and faith healing, to become the denominations now called Pentecostal. Today there are about thirty-five of them. They are the fastest growing segment of Christianity, not only here but throughout the world.
>
> Charismatics, sometimes called neo-pentecostals, are evangelicals, not necessarily fundamentalist, who accept the gifts of faith healing and tongues. The term applies of course to the old or "classical" Pentecostals, but also to Catholics, Episcopalians, and members of mainline Protestant churches where there has been since 1960 an astonishing inrush of Pentecostal fervor.
>
> Non-Christian glossolalia is a problem for charismatics. Ancient soothsayers, and devotees of Greek and Roman mystery cults, often gurgled meaningless sentences. In the *Aeneid* (Book 6) Virgil describes tongue speaking by a Roman sybil. Some Moslem sects and primitive cultures practise glossolalia. In *The Great Dictator*, Charlie Chaplin's Hitler gives a rousing speech in German double talk. None of this, charismatics maintain, is the real thing. Non-Pentecostal fundamentalists think the babbling of their Pentecostal brothers isn't the real thing either, and may even be inspired by Satan (Gardner 1987:18).

23

Mantras and Bird Songs

If mantras are older than language in the course of biological evolution it would seem likely that similar sounds exist and are used in a similar manner by other animal species. This expectation can only be properly explored by biologists, but even a cursory look at bird songs shows that it is fulfilled at least to some extent. Let me begin with a specific example.

When the "extra" pebbles of the Agnicayana we have already discussed (above page 194) are being consecrated by the Adhvaryu on behalf of his patron the Yajamāna, the Udgātā sings his pebble songs. The first of these is Jaiminīya Grāmageyagāna 45.2.1:

> *yo no hā bu / idam idam purā hā bu / pra vā pra*
> *vasya yā hā yi / ninā nināya tam u vo hā bu / stūṣā yi*
> *sakhāya yā hā yi / dramūtāyāyi / ō yi ḻā / /*

We can represent the structure of this chant by introducing capital letters to stand for its units, which are either bits of mantras or stobhas, as follows:

"A" for *yo no*
"B" for *hā bu*
"C" for *idam idam purā*
"D" for *pra vā pra vasya*
"E" for *yā hā yi*
"F" for *ninā nināya tam u vo*
"G" for *stūṣā yi sakhāya*
"H" for *dramūtāyāyi*
"J" for *ō yi ḻā.*

The structure of JGG 45.2.1 may now be represented by:

AB / CB / DE / FB / GE / H / J / / (9)

How do we arrive at an analysis of this type? How arbitrary are the units we have selected to be represented by capitals? The answer to these questions is that we can only arrive at a nonarbitrary analysis provided we analyse a number of similar forms. First of all we make use of the subdivision of the sāmans into smaller units, called *bhakti*, that are preserved by the tradition (because a new breath has to be taken at the beginning of each *bhakti*) and that are represented in printed texts, and in the version given here, by slanted bars ("/"). In addition we have to take into account that *hā bu*, *yā hā yi*, and *ō yi ḷā* are stobhas that function as units in many other songs. The correctness of (9) therefore depends on the correctness of other forms. When the same sort of analysis is applied to other recitations it yields the following structures:

A A B / . . . / A A B C / D D D / / (10)

(the first chant of the Udgātā, sung during the foundation ceremonies of the altar: AGNI I:410);

A A A B B B C C C / . . . /A A A B B B C C C′ /D D′ D′ / / (11)

(the first space-filler chant during the consecration of the first layer: AGNI I:443; note that we use the convention that C and C′ are similar, or have identical beginnings, and the same holds for D and D′);

A A A / . . . / A A A′ / / (12)

(*agner vrata* sung at the northern hip of the altar after the five layers have been consecrated: AGNI I:539);

A A A B / . . / A A A C B′ / / (13)

(*agner arka* sung at the head of the altar on the same occasion); and so forth.

Now let us look at a bird song: four stanzas sung by the Black Flycatcher *Ficedula hypoleuca* published by J. C. Roche

("L'oiseau musicien" no. 6) and analysed by François-Bernard Mâche (1983:93) in the following form:

A B C B C B D E /

B′ C B C B C B F E′ /

A B C B C D /

B′ C B C B C B F E′ // (14)

Here the capital letters stand for small phrases, motifs or figures that each consist of a few tones, and are therefore comparable to the units of mantras that each consist of a few syllables. I have used the slanted bar "/" where Mâche begins a new line or "strophe." Here too the selection of units on which the analysis is based derives from a study of other songs that consist of similar units, for example:

A B B C / A A A A B / A B C B / A A A B C B / A
A B C / A A A A C B / A A A C B / A A B / A A B
C B / A A A B / A A B / A A B B / A A // (15)

(song of *Acrocephalus schoenobaenus*: Mâche 77);

A A A B / A A C / A A C B / A A C B / A A A C
B / A A A C / A B / A A C B / A A C // (16)

(song of *Acrocephalus dumetorum*: Mâche 78);

A B A B C A′ B B′ A″ B′ B (17)

(song of *Sylvia communis*, Mâche 97; note that A′ and A″ are again similar, hence A and A″ are similar, but less similar than either A and A′ or A′ and A″). And so forth.

If we compare these structures of mantras and bird songs with each other we find a certain similarity (e.g., the doublets, triplets, and refrains discussed in Chapter 16 occur in all) but no strict identity. However, all we are interested in is structural similarity. If the structures happened to be strictly identical, it might prove that JGG 45.2.1 was caused, influenced or inspired by the songs of *Ficedula hypoleuca*, perhaps because that bird occurred in a part of India where the composers of the sāman might have heard it. Mâche (page 82) has argued that a certain structural pattern in Stravinsky which also is found in a bird song was copied "plus ou moins consciemment" because the bird is common on the banks of the river Bug in Ustilug where Stravinsky used to work. Such a causal explanation would be interesting if we could establish it in the realm of the Sāmaveda, and might demonstrate that there is a similarity in structure which makes such causal links possible. Actually, *Acrocephalus dumetorum Blyth* or "Blyth's Reed Warbler" of example (16), which breeds in Baluchistan, is a winter visitor to the entire subcontinent, and *Sylvia communis Latham*, the "Whitethroat" of example (17) is an autumn migrant to Pakistan and northwest India (Ripley 1982:424). However, similarities in the realm of biological evolution only rarely express specific causal links; what they do express is similar responses to the pressure of selection—a feature of biological theory to which I shall return.

So far we have chiefly looked at structural patterns. The structural similarity between mantras and bird songs is certainly striking, but it would only be significant if it were not also to occur in language, the domain to which mantras have been generally—albeit unwittingly—assigned by the authors of the Brāhmaṇas as well as by contemporary scholars. What we find in this respect is unexpected, and therefore intriguing. Repetitions such as AA, AAA, AAAA, ABBB, etc., and refrain-like structures that seem to be common to both mantras and bird songs, are entirely absent from the syntax of ordinary language. In fact, any linguist who is familiar with syntactic structures cannot fail to be struck by the absence in almost all such structures of the typical repetitive features of both mantras and bird songs. There is an area of overlap: the domain of poetry. However, poetry seems in several respects to constitute an intermediary area between mantras and ordinary language. Excluding poetry (which would deserve separate treatment) and confining ourselves to mantras and bird songs, their similarity in structure and dissimilarity from the structures of language are curious and suggestive. But are we not barking up the wrong tree because we are confining ourselves to structures at the neglect of meaning and function, categories in terms of which mantras and bird songs seem to be vastly different?

I have argued in Chapter 13 that many mantras and rites do not possess a clear meaning or function. Many mantras, as well as stobhas or bīja mantras, consist of meaningless sound; but even those that are sentences of Vedic or Sanskrit are often unrelated to the rites they accompany. As for rites, the rites of the śrauta ritual are especially devoid of meaning or function. Rites of the gṛhya or "domestic" ritual, on the other hand, seem often quite meaningful and functional. But how can there be such a difference in meaning or function if the actual forms of śrauta and gṛhya rites, together with the accompanying mantras, are so often similar or even identical?

We shall approach this problem by first taking a closer look at the meaning and function of the gṛhya rites, or, more generally, of the general category of non-śrauta rites. This would be too vast a task to undertake within the compass of the present chapter had not Gonda fortunately come to our aid by publishing a manual in the *Handbuch der Orientalistik*, which assembles precisely the data we need under the title: "Vedic Ritual: the non-solemn rites" (Gonda 1980). Here we witness rites performed not only in connexion with the traditional *saṃskāra* ceremonies which correspond in part to the "rites de passage" familiar to anthropologists following Van Gennep, but also on a great number of other occasions, e.g.: making rain, warding off dangerous or annoying animals, averting dangers such as fires and robbers, curing illness and preserving health, going on and returning from a journey, entering a house, conquering enemies, inheriting property, a variety of occupations connected with cattle, anniversaries, attaining great age, austerities, prayers, vows, magic, witchcraft, exorcism, divination, purity and impurity, auspiciousness and inauspiciousness, learning and concentration, not to mention seasonal ceremonies of many kinds. "Thus occasions were few," concludes Gonda, "when Vedic man did not seek the aid of rites and mantras to promote in some way or other his welfare or to avert the ills, real or imaginary, which might invest him'' (page 410).

In Tantrism, which develops the domestic rites in several respects, mantras are similarly ubiquitous. A tenth or eleventh century Tantric text, the Prapañcasāra declares (8.15):

> Therefore this famous string of letters, which attaches itself to the world, with devotion assign to your body, mutter with soft voice, sacrifice and worship,
> in order to obtain incomparable poetic power, longevity, fame, loveliness and fortune; for the sake of the destruction of all calamities and sorrows, and for release from existence
> (translation by Goudriaan 1981:134).

In all these cases, rites and mantras seem to have a meaning or function. Our startling earlier conclusion that rites have *no* meaning seems to turn into the opposite which is not less startling: there is no meaning or function rites can *not* possess. But this has always been a problem with regard to rites and rituals. Jack Goody drew attention to this problem as we saw at the onset of our discussion of ritual (Introductory Note of Part II). Kristofer Schipper introduced the expression *accretion* to capture another dimension of the same phenomenon.

We shall revert to this problem but only after having paid attention to the corresponding problem in the realm of birds and bird songs, which seem to have a much clearer function. Or do they? To begin with, ornithologists were satisfied with a general characterization, stressing first that bird song ''probably always serves in one way or another to distinguish the sexes'' (because bird songs are mostly found in males), and second that ''there must be a need to communicate. The need may be to show the signaler's location (contact notes), his awareness of danger (alarm calls), or his readiness to mate (courtship songs) or defend a breeding or foraging territory (territorial song)'' (summarized in Hartshorne 1973:15).

Another account of the functions of bird song runs as follows: ''The singer, more usually a male than a female, has two primary reasons for which to sing, the one to defend its territory against other males, and the other, to attract females. The same song or call (which is shorter and simpler than a song) may have different meanings, depending on its context—the call that in the mating season both defends territory and attracts females functions, after the mating season is over, to defend territory alone. As against such general signals, there may be specific ones, and these specific ones may be graded in structure, length, and other characteristics, by which I mean that different intensities may call forth different intensities of response. The occasions that have been said to elicit distinctive songs or song-variants are many. They include the search for a nest-site; the building of the nest; the incubation of the eggs; the spelling of the female in her incubation duties; the leaving of the nest by the young; migration; and autumn and winter. Calls, too, have many varieties and functions. One classification includes those for pleasure, territorial defense, flight, feeding, nesting, flocking, aggression, general alarm and specialized alarm (to distinguish flying from non-flying predators)'' (Scharfstein, forthcoming).

That the same song or call may have different meanings depending on the context accords with our earlier observation that rites have all kinds of functions. A similar observation was made by van Gennep in 1911 (''the same rite . . . can change its meaning depending on the position it is given in a ceremony'') and by Durkheim in 1915 (''according to the circumstances, one and the same ceremony serves two distinct functions''): see above, page 127. Later in his essay Scharfstein specifies this context dependence in the case of a blackbird song as follows: ''Toward the end of the season, when the song has lost its overt sexual function, it reaches its most highly organized, in the human sense: most musical, form.''

In more specialized studies, ornithologists have felt the need to use the ethologists' concept of ritualization. This concept is invoked when the original function of a behavioral pattern is no longer visible or known. Let us start with an example not involving song. In a general study of the behavior and songs of a species of finch (*Estrildida*), Güttinger (1970) has tried to explain a pattern of inflexion (''Verbeugung'') during which the male bird bends its head either to the right or to the left, independent of the position of the female even if she is close by. Güttinger says (1970:1054): "Aus dem Bewegungselement der bisher besprochenen Arten kann infolge des hohen Grades der Ritualisierung die ursprüngliche Bedeutung der Verhaltensweise nicht mehr ermittelt werden."

German ornithologists use "ritualization" in contrast to "Ableitungsmöglichkeit," or "possibility to deduce": the latter term is used when it is possible to explain a pattern of behavior, including a song, in functional terms. Applying the distinction to the realm of Vedic ritual we could say that there exists an "Ableitungsmöglichkeit" for the gṛhya rites, but not for the śrauta rites. As in the Vedic realm, such a distinction requires a great deal of analysis in specific cases. Some young finches of the species *Spermestes*, for example, when in the nest and about to be fed by the parents, raise their wings in a special manner. Immelmann (1962) explained this as a kind of contest between siblings; moreover, the wings can be raised in such a way that the neighbor is partly hidden, so that the young bird who performs the act is more likely to be fed first. But the theory does not hold, as Güttinger (1970:1063) has pointed out, because the parents take great care to feed all their young equally, including not only those that do not raise their wings, but also those that are sick. In such cases, there seemed at first to be an "Ableitungsmöglichkeit," which on further analysis turned out to be spurious.

Detailed examples of the ritualization of songs have been studied by Thielcke (1964) in the European tree creeper (*Certhia brachydactyla* Brehm and *Certhia familiaris* L.). The sounds from which these songs are constructed are primarily three, which Thielcke, using German phonology, represents as *tür*, *tüt* and *srih*. Though the functions of some of the songs are clear, the functions of others are not, and ritualization is accordingly postulated. Tree-creepers exhibit all the characteristics of ritualization that Lorenz (1951) and Morris (1957) have enumerated: the primary sounds are rhythmically repeated; the sequences are changed in such a way that "eine urspünglich weitgehend veränderliche und aus verschiedenen Gliedern bestehende Folge von Verhaltensweisen zu einem einzigen, in sich starren Bewegungsablauf zusammengeschweisst wird" (Thielcke 1964:405, after Lorenz 1951); and there are "typical intensities." The latter concept, introduced by Desmond Morris, indicates, for example, that a bird in the course of a courtship dance may *repeatedly* twist its body *four* times (Morris 1957:4–5). Since the order of elements, the sequence of pitches, the intervals between the elements, and the number of elements are much more constant in songs than in sounds, Thielcke has argued that the phylogenetic development of the song of the European treecreeper has taken place in the direction from sounds to song.

I am not an ornithologist and I am not in a position to provide a detailed and exhaustive discussion of the vast amount of information on bird song that is nowadays available. However, a general trend in these studies seems to be the following. Whereas originally, most ornithologists stressed functional explanations, and were convinced that there were good pragmatic or utilitarian reasons for the execution of songs by birds, it has increasingly been found that there are no such reasons, and that birds often seem to sing simply because they like to. This is expressed in the more specific context of the "ontogeny" of bird song, for example by Nottebohm (1970:951) when he writes: "One is forced to conclude that the achievement of a relatively stable and predictable song does not imply the existence of a preconceived or acquired goal." Or it is expressed in more general and theoretical terms, for example by Lorenz (1967:75): "there are mechanisms in existence which reinforce economical perfection in motor skills independently of the attainment of the ultimate biological goal in whose pursuit the learned movement is developed." Lorenz mentions as examples the swimming of a shark, the gallop of an antelope, and the gymnastics of a gibbon. Here the singing of birds may be plausibly added: in fact, we have already seen that "pleasure" is listed as one of its possible reasons (Scharfstein quoted above). Lorenz adds: "The most convincing argument in favor of my speculative assumption lies in the fact that acquired motor skills of this type, more than any other types of movements, are forever being performed for their own sake in the obvious absence of any other motivating or reinforcing factors. Indeed, the very concept of play is based on this fact to a large extent." All of this does of course apply to the human animal: "we know that when we skate, ski, or dance, we perform these activities for their own sake, for the enjoyment they give us" (ibid.). To add music, mantras and ritual is but a natural extension of this list.

Two of the books and one of the articles from which I have quoted are concerned with a similar problem: the relation between bird songs and music. The first book, Charles Hartshorne's *Born to Sing* (1973), is by an ornithologist who is also a philosopher; the second, François-Bernard Mâche's *Musique, Mythe, Nature* (1983) is by an ornithologist who is also a musicologist and composer; the essay by Scharfstein, a chapter from a forthcoming book on the nature of art, is by a philosopher and esthetician interested in birds. All are concerned to show that it is impossible to define "human" music in such a way that it will not also encompass bird song. All stress that birds must accordingly be assumed to possess something like an aesthetic sense. (Scharfstein has in fact cast doubt on the functionalist bias of some of the professional ornithologists: "They tend to assume that every nuance of song or display has survival value or disvalue, and they try, often with conspicuous cleverness, to turn each apparent exception into further evidence for the truth of their theses.") In the present context I need only the least controversial feature of the conclusion of these three authors: I don't need the hypothesis that birds have an aesthetic sense (though it may be correct) but accept that these authors have demonstrated beyond reasonable doubt that bird songs cannot be explained in functionalist, utilitarian, or pragmatic terms.

We may now return to mantras, only to find that we are in a position to make an important observation. The idea that birds can talk, and that bird songs are a kind of language, belongs to the realm of myth and has never been taken seriously by ornithologists. But the idea that mantras express meaning, and are a kind of language, has generally been taken for granted by

Sanskritists. Of course, there are good reasons for this silent assumption. It is due not merely to the circumstance that Sanskritists tend to confine themselves to Sanskrit, but to the much more important fact that man, the animal that speaks (*ζῶον λόγον ἔχον*), is obsessed by language so that we tend to assume that any articulate sound is "language" in its usual sense. This is exactly what happened in human history and prehistory. It has generally been fancied that birds could really talk even though the evidence has never been telling. No wonder that mantras, which are often indistinguishable from it, continue to be regarded as language.

Conceptual issues involving cross-overs between nature and culture tend to be complex. Functionalist explanations in the realm of mantras are always closely connected with problems of semantics, whereas functionalist explanations in the realm of bird song are not connected with semantics. However, in both areas, emphasizing syntax combines in a natural manner with de-emphasizing semantics. Thus there is a close association between Chapters 10, 11, 12 and 13. Similarly, when ornithologists found that it was difficult or impossible to provide functionalist explanations, their interest in syntax increased. Thus we find, since roughly 1965, syntax mentioned in the studies of bird songs by Thielcke, Güttinger, Baptista, Nicolai, Payne, Beer, Nottebohm, Johnson, and Bertram. The work of these scholars is discussed in an unpublished paper by Luis Baptista, "On Parallels between Bird Song and Speech Development." However, the first systematic use of syntactic methods and representations on a large scale is found in Mâche's book of 1983. The author is aware of the novelty of his approach, "abandonnant le point de vue phonétique qui est celui des zoologistes pour un point de vue syntaxique" (Mâche 1983:64).

The contrast between functionalist and non-functionalist explanations in biology is closely related to the continuing debates on the theoretical foundations of Darwinian natural selection—a problem that can not be adequately discussed in the present context, but to which a brief reference should be made. The notion of "survival of the fittest," in particular, can be easily misinterpreted in such a manner that it becomes tautologous and empty. Eldredge exposes such views in the following terms: "Only (God, natural selection) could have fashioned such a marvellous organic machine! There *is* a difference, of course: God, as a supernatural being, does not belong in science, whereas natural selection patently does. But used in this inappropriate fashion, natural selection becomes a mere substitute for the Creator. It tells us nothing, really, about tribolite eyes or anything specific or meaningful about how they came into existence" (Eldredge 1982: 508–509; quoted by Koster 1983: 4).

Such interpretations were actually given by Tom Bethell (1976), according to whom "survival of the fittest" involves no more than "differential reproductive success," viz., the production of more surviving offspring than other competing members of the population. This formulation, however, defines fitness in terms of survival only and is therefore empty because survival of what survives is a tautology. Such interpretations are similar to the functionalist bias of some ornithologists who seem to be "straining to accomodate awkward facts" (Scharfstein).

Gould (1977:40–45), from whom the quote from Bethell has been taken, has convincingly shown that Darwin did not make such a basic logical mistake. Biologists define the fittest beforehand, not only by their subsequent survival. Natural selection is a theory of *local* adaptation to immediate but changing environments; it does not preach *general* progress in the cosmic sense as inherent in the workings of evolution, which explains the Victorian unpopularity of the idea. In fact, the theory of natural selection did not triumph until the 1940s. Voltaire's Dr. Pangloss asserted that the nose was fashioned to bear spectacles, but we can now see clearly that our world is not, as Candide thought, "the best of all possible worlds." We know, as François Jacob formulated it in *Le jeu des possibles* (1981:33), that "le monde vivant aujourd 'hui, tel que nous le voyons autour de nous, n'est qu'un parmis de nombreux possibles."

How then are mantras and bird songs related within the perspective of biological evolution? Their similarity is not what biologists call "homologous," but what they call "analogous."

The difference is explained by Gould (1977:254): "Similar features due to common genetic ancestry are 'homologous'; similarities due to common function, but with different evolutionary histories, are 'analogous': the wings of birds and insects, for example—the common ancestor of both groups lacked wings." To apply this definition, we have to broaden it in a curious fashion: for the similarity between mantras and bird songs is due not to common function, but to common non-functionality. Mantras and bird songs share not only certain structural properties, but also lack of an inherent or absolute purpose. It is precisely these features that express the common characteristic of both as essentially satisfying, pleasurable and playful—features that, in the case of mantras, have remained even though language has intervened.

I shall briefly deal with a final objection to the thesis that mantras and bird songs are analogous: are not mantras and language *learned*, whereas bird songs are instinctive and *inborn*? The first reply to any such objection should be that the difference between these two modes of acquisition may be large from the point of view of the individual, but is less important in terms of biological evolution, and need not prevent certain phenomena from being analogous to each other. However, this first reply is not relevant in the present case, for the distinction between learned and innate does not obtain in any straightforward fashion. Language, first of all, unlike languages, is partly inborn. One's first or mother language is learnt in a realtively short period and through a process that is different from the learning of any subsequent language because "universals of language" are characteristic structures of the human mind. This much, if anything, has been established conclusively by Noam Chomsky. It is entirely likely that the same holds true of rites and mantras: though specific cases have to be learnt, their general underlying structures are innate.

Bird songs, on the other hand, are partly learnt. Kroodsma (1978) provides a comprehensive recent survey on "Aspects of Learning in the Ontogeny of Bird Song: Where, From Whom, When, How Many, Which, and How Accurately?" Kroodsma (1974) had already shown that juvenile males of the species Bewick's wren (*Thryomanes bewickii*) "are probably capable of learning from their father . . . but a premium is placed on matching the song types of neighboring males with whom interactions will occur throughout life; thus, song types of the father may be modified or new ones learned in order to match more closely the songs of neighboring males.'' Many birds learn songs only within a ''critical period,'' for example, within the first 10 months of a potential lifespan of 5 or more years. ''After the end of this sensitive period further acoustic stimuli do not alter the bird's repertoire'' (Nottebohm 1970:952). However, in the indigo bird (*Vidua chalybeata*), ''flexibility to change song types in the repertoire of the individual is apparently maintained throughout life'' (Kroodsma 1978:216). Since so many songs are learnt, ''variation in song repertoire sizes among different populations of a given species may be striking. Long-billed marsh wrens near Seattle, Washington, may have 150 song types, while an Illinois male may have as few as 30'' (Kroodsma 1978:221).

That mantras are similar to bird songs may seem far-fetched to Western Sanskritists, but it would not cause surprise to the sāman chanters, other composers of mantras, or Indians generally. Following *Genesis*, the Western tradition has generally stressed the difference between man and the other animals (see Staal 1979c:2–3). But in India, the names of many sāmans are in fact inspired by birds. The *krauñca* melody evokes a kind of curlew. We also have sāmans called *tṛtīyakrauñca* and even *vāṅnidhanakrauñca*, a *krauñca* melody ''ending in speech.'' Other sāmans are called *plava* after an aquatic bird, *bhāsa* after a bird of prey, and *vāśa* after a croaking bird. The well known chant *śyena* is called after a vulture (see AGNI I:88–90), and *sauparṇa* derives from *suparṇa* which is not only a lotus leaf, but also a large bird of prey. Vedic schools have been called after birds, e.g., the Kauśika after the owl and the Taittirīya after *tittiri*, the partridge (a totemic bird according to Kosambi (1950) who concluded that the Taittirīya was a totemic clan—a hypothesis criticized by Brough (1953)). No wonder that *vāc* was used, already in the Rigveda, not only of men, but also of other animals and especially of birds.

Geese informed Janaśruti Pautrāyaṇa about the great master

Raikva-with-the-chariot (Chāndogya Upaniṣad 4.1–3). A goose and a diving bird taught Satyakāma Jābāla each a quarter of *brahman* (Chāndogya Upaniṣad 4.7–8). Indian sages have always been eager to gain knowledge and insight from birds. So why shouldn't we?

The similarity between mantras and bird songs, which is greater than that between mantras and ordinary language, may have to be studied in the wider perspective of "animal language," a topic that goes far beyond the confines of the present investigation. Let me only note that many claims made ealier on behalf of language-like communication among chimpanzees, gorillas and even dolphins, have been largely retracted. It is now widely recognized that there is a difference between communication and human language. It is obvious that animals communicate with each other; but these communications, even if they are systematic, do not resemble the system of human language. This is not to say that human language is something incomparably grand: we have seen something different, namely, that it is illogical and roundabout. These puzzling features are precisely the features that call for an explanation and that have led to confusion (see Chapters 28–30).

To suggest explanations for human data within a biological perspective implies acceptance of a form of Darwinism. Although many features of biological evolution in terms of Darwin's original theory have been abandoned or at least questioned during recent decades (e.g., the gradual nature of evolution), one tenet remains central: the importance played by *chance*. Variations arise *by chance* and some are selected subsequently in accordance with the demands of the environment. A theory that explains human data in terms of "meaning" tries to make sense of everything and minimizes chance or rejects it altogether. It becomes important, therefore, to inquire whether chance plays any role in the domain of mantras. We have seen that mantras and acts are generally associated with each other but that the association is unlike that between linguistic utterances and their meanings. How then is a specific mantra selected to accompany a specific rite or *vice versa*? This is the topic of our next chapter.

24

Mantras by Chance

The verse that is our point of departure is the first of the ninth book, the only book of the Rigveda that deals in its entirety with Soma and its ritual purification and preparation. It is the first verse of a hymn (RV 9.1) that belongs to a group of hymns all written in the same meter, called *gāyatrī*. The text of this *gāyatrī*-verse is:

svā́diṣṭhayā mádiṣṭhayā
pávasva soma dhā́rayā (18)
índrāya pā́tave sutáḥ (RV 9.1.1)

The translation is straightforward and uncontroversial:

"With most delicious and inebriating flow.
Soma, purify yourself,
Pressed for Indra to drink."

The *gāyatrī* meter consists of three octosyllabic meters which have the scheme:

x x x x ∪ — ∪ — (19)

where *x* may be occupied by a syllable of any kind, ∪ by a verse-medial short syllable and — by a long syllable or by a verse-final short syllable. In the case of RV 9.1.1, the distribution is as follows:

— — ∪ — ∪ — ∪ —

∪ — ∪ — ∪ — ∪ — (20)

— — ∪ — ∪ — ∪ —

The accent "´" which has been printed over certain syllables of the text in (18) is called *udātta*, "raised," and it is possible that it was originally spoken with raised pitch (but see Gray 1959a and b for a dissenting view). Whatever its original pronunciation, it was later marked by reciting the previous syllable at a lower pitch, and the following at a higher pitch. A few more rules have to be taken into account before we can properly pronounce this verse, but we shall not trouble ourselves with them. The lower accent is called *anudātta*, "not raised," and is written in the manuscripts (that are all of later date) with a horizontal bar below the syllable; the higher, *svarita*, "(re)sounding," is written with a vertical bar above it. The result is as follows:

svadıṣṭhayā̱ madıṣṭhayā̱

pavasva soma̱ dhārayā (21)

indrāya pātave su̱taḥ

This mode of recitation, which is called *svādhyāya*, only serves the purpose of transmission, from teacher to pupil or from father to son. Mantras are never recited in this manner in the ritual itself: to be fit for ritual use, the traditional recitations have to undergo certain modifications. In many cases, verse have to be turned into songs which are then incorporated in the Sāmaveda. In the above case, the first step of that process of incorporation is extremely simple. The *udātta*, *svarita* and *anudātta* are chanted at three different pitches, each at an interval of about a second from each other, the first (*udātta*). the highest, the last (*anudātta*) the lowest, and the *svarita* at an intermediate pitch. The manuscripts refer to these tones with the help of numerals:

"1" for *udātta*
"2" for *svarita* (22)
"3" for *anudātta*.

These numerals are written above the syllables, as follows:

```
1 2      3   1   2   3
svādiṣṭhayā madiṣṭhayā

1 2        3     1 2
pavasva soma dhārayā        (23)

1    2 3 1 2    3  2
indrāya pātave sutah
```

(23) is closer to (18) than it is to (21), which shows that the Sāmaveda is earlier and closer to the original Rigveda than the Rigveda system of horizontal and vertical strokes used in the manuscripts. This is in accordance with the chronology proposed by Kiparsky (1982, Lecture II) for the development of the Vedic accent system, provided we insert the Sāmaveda *after* the Rigveda as it was known to Pāṇini, but *before* the Rigveda recension with which we are familiar.

Before we can sing (23), we have to know at which pitch the syllables not marked with a numeral have to be sung. The rule is again simple: these are sung at the pitch of the preceding syllable. The basic chants of the Sāmaveda, thus provided with a pattern of song that derives from the accentuation of the original, are listed in the first part of the Sāmaveda, which is referred to as Saṃhitā—as in the case of the other Vedas—and also, more appropriately, as *arcikā*, "list of verses," from *ṛk* "verse" from which the appellation *ṛgveda*, "Veda of Verse," is also derived.

The next portion of the Sāmaveda lists the melodies to which these verses are sung. It consists of the more common *grāmageyagāna*, "songs to be sung in the village," and the more esoteric *araṇyageyagāna* (or *araṇyegeyagāna*), "songs to be sung in the forest." Both these *gāna*-books correspond to the *svādhyāya* of the other Vedas: they mainly serve the purpose of transmitting the tradition to the following generations; they are sometimes ritually used in their *gāna* form, but more often this form undergoes further modification for the sake of "ritual application'' (*prayoga*). This application is the actual purpose of these songs and of the Sāmaveda itself.

There are numerous melodies in these *gāna* collections because one verse is generally sung to different melodies. But we also meet with the opposite: different verses are sung to the same melody. In that case, the melody needs to be listed only once; and this has led to some confusion among students of the Sāmaveda.

The Vedic tradition is celebrated for the care with which it has been handed down; despite the vicissitudes of Indian history during the last three thousand years, there are in the Rigveda no variant forms or ''readings'' (a term based upon the Western assumption that these compositions are ''texts'' which are ''read''). This applies to the place of the accents as well: it never varies. In the case of the transmission of melodies, greater variation is expected; and this may well account for the belief that there were originally a thousand schools in the Sāmaveda (Renou 1947:88) as against two in the case of the Rigveda and Yajurveda each. When one hears contemporary traditions of the Sāmaveda, the musical renderings vary greatly. Yet, two traditions can be clearly distinguished: the Kauthuma-Rāṇāyanīya, which is still found in many parts of India (chiefly Tamilnad, Andhra, Karnataka and Maharashtra); and the Jaiminīya which is confined to Kerala and a few villages in Tamilnad.

The Jaiminīya is almost extinct; its manuscripts are rare and have, with few exceptions, remained unpublished. The Kauthuma-Rāṇāyanīya tradition of two closely connected schools, which I shall refer to as K-R, is still relatively strong, and its texts have been published in their entirety. In these latter texts, a simple notation for the pitch of tones of the songs has been adopted in the manuscripts, most of which are of recent date (i.e., no more than a few centuries old). The printed texts have adopted this notation in which the notes are referred to with the help of the numerals 1, . . . ,7 which designate pitches in their descending order, again with intervals of roughly a second. There are seven notes in the Sāmaveda according to these manuscript notations, which is consistent with some musicological accounts (e.g., that of the Nāradaśikṣā).

In the *grāmageyagāna* of the K-R school, our verse is listed as item 468, and it is provided with nine melodies to which it is sung. The first of these, referred to as "GG 468.1", is the following:

```
 1 r         2  1          2   1       2 r    1  2          2
svādāiṣṭhāyā/ madāiṣṭhāyā / / pavasvaso / mādhā'1 rā 23 yā / /
1         2        1         2        1
indrāyāpā / / tavāisū'23 tā'343ḥ / o'2345 i / / ḍā / /           (24)
```

In order to know how this actually sounds, a few more conventions must be explained: "r" denotes lengthening; the numerals in the line sound the same as those written above the syllables, each lasting one beat or time unit (*mātrā*); they also induce lengthening of the preceding syllable. The song consists of *five* portions that are separated by double bars ("/ /"), further subdivided into smaller portions separated by single bars ("/"). The number of these latter, smaller subdivisions varies, but the former subdivision into five is constant in an important class of rituals: these five portions, called *bhakti*, are of fundamental importance in the Soma rituals, where they are chanted by different priests facing different directions, sitting in a particular fashion and following a pattern that is always the same (see AGNI I:608–609). The five portions, which should each be sung with a single breath, are called: (1) *prastāva* ("prelude"), (2) *udgītha* ("chant"), (3) *pratihāra* ("response"), (4) *upadrava* ("accessory") and (5) *nidhana* ("finale"). Three of the four Sāmaveda priests participate in such a chant, viz., Prastotā, Udgātā, and Pratihartā. The assignment of *bhakti* portions to them is as follows:

1) *prastāva* by Prastotā;
2) *udgītha* by Udgātā;
3) *pratihāra* by Pratihartā;
4) *upadrava* by Udgātā; and
5) *nidhana* by all three.

When we compare (24) with the original verse (18), we observe that certain syllables have been expanded, or otherwise modified. For example, many of the short *a*'s are lengthened into long *ā*'s, and *i* and *e* have become *āi*. The latter modification is well known to linguists: it is the famous *vṛddhi* ("lengthening") discovered by the Sanskrit grammarians that is referred to in the first sūtra of Pāṇini's grammar. At the same time, the notion of *vṛddhi* is one of the cornerstones of Indo-European comparative phonology, as well as the basis of our notion of "sound law." This illustrates in passing that the derivation of the ritual chants of the Sāmaveda from the Rigveda (and not only the formation of the Padapāṭha from the Rigveda, as V. N. Jha has shown) has contributed to the origin of the Sanskrit grammatical tradition.

These phonetic or sound modifications are often determined, or partly determined, by the formal nature of the syllables of the original, in particular their length; the structure of the song is therefore related to the original meter which is also based upon the distinction between short and long syllables. These relationships are dealt with in texts such as the (K-R) Puṣpasūtra, which makes use of grammatical technical terms such as *vṛddhi* and a great many others. Song (24) is also called a *gāyatrī* song—a circumstance to which we shall return.

We finally observe that in (24) new syllables have been added, in particular the termination of the *upadrava* and all of the *nidhana*:

1
o'2345 i. / / ḍā //

This is a stobha of the familiar type, but properly expressed together with its musical structure.

In order to study the ritual significance of our song we need to be familiar with the structure of the entire system of its derivatives in the corpus of the Sāmaveda. Instead of pursuing this by numerical references to the published texts of the K-R Sāmaveda, which would be intelligible only to specialists, it will be more interesting and worthwhile to publish songs from the corpus of the Jaiminīya. Since these songs have never been published, I have made use of recordings and of a copy of a manuscript in the Malayalam script prepared by my collaborator Itti Ravi Nambudiri. The original (see page 209) is in the possession of Asko Parpola (University of Helsinki). Two other manuscripts of the Jaiminīya songs are known: they are B 497 and B 61–62 of the India Office Library, both discovered by A. C. Burnell in the 1870's in the Tamil region and both written in the Grantha script. I have mentioned the most important variant "readings" (referred to as "C") that occur in a handwritten copy completed by Willem Caland in 1906, which was based upon B 497 and collated with B 61 and B 62. (For the Araṇyageyagāna, Caland did not note the stobhas or the muscial syllable notation given in B 62). A photograph of Caland's manuscript was in the possession of Dr. A. A. Bake at the School of Oriental and African Studies, and was given to me by Mrs. Bake. The original is in the University Library of Utrecht. As the reader will see, some of the variants help to establish the boundaries between the *bhakti* portions. There are still instances where these remain unclear in the manuscript tradition, and therefore must be determined from oral tradition. This is easy to do because of the rule that one *bhakti* has to be chanted with one breath (page 280). If the number of *bhakti* portions is different from five, the method of chanting has to be further specified.

Here follow the nine songs based upon the gāyatrī verse from the Grāmageyagāna:

Jaiminīya Grāmageyagāna 49.2.1–9

(1) svādāyiṣṭhāyā madāyiṣṭhāyā / pavasva somādhārāyā / indrāyāpā / tavāyi sūtāḥ / oyiḷā / /

(2) svādiṣṭhayā iyā iyā madiṣṭhāyā /pāvasva so iyā iyā madhārāyā / indrāyapā iyā iyā /tavāyi sūtāḥ / oyiḷā / /

(3) svādiṣṭhayau ho vā iyā madiṣṭhāyā / pavasva sau ho vā iyā madhārāyā / indrāya pau ho vā iyā / tavāyi sūtāḥ / oyiḷā / /
C: poho

(4) oyi svādi / ṣṭhayā mādīṣṭhāyā vuvovā / pavasva somā dhārāyā o indrā / yā pā au ho vā / tave sūtāḥ / /

(5) uhuvāyi svādī / ṣṭhayā mādīṣṭhāyā au ho vā / pavasva soma dhārāyā uhuvā indrāyāpā / tāvā au ho vā / sūtāḥ / /

(6) svādāyiṣṭhayā madiṣṭhayā pāvāsvā somadhārayā āyindrāyā pā hā bu / tavā yi sutā bu / vā / /
C: madiṣṭhayā / somadhārayā /

(7) svādiṣṭhayā madiṣṭhayā / pavasva somadhārayā / indrāyapā / tavā ū tavā ū tavā vu vā au ho vā / sūtāh / /
C: somadhārayā /

(8) au ho hṃ bhā e hiyā hā hāyi svādāyiṣṭhayā mādī o yi mādī / au ho hṃ bhā e hiyā hā hāyi ṣṭhayā pavāsvā so o svā so / au ho hṃ bhā e hiyā hā hāyi ma dhāraya indrā o indrā /au ho hṃ bhā e hiyā hā hāyi ya pā tavāyi sūtā oyi sūtaḥ / au ho hṃ bhā e hiyā hā hā au ho vā / ī / /

(9) svādiṣṭhayā madāyiṣṭhayā / pavāsvā soma dhārāyā / ā yindrāyā pātavā hā vu vā / sūtaḥ / /

A few observations may be made. First of all, the Jaiminīya does not use a numerical notation to refer to the pitch of the tonal pattern which characterizes the melodies. There exists a Jaiminīya musical notation by means of syllables from the Grantha script, of which we noted that Caland copied it from B 497 but not from B 61–62. It is not marked in the Malayalam manuscript.

Secondly we observe that the differences between the Jaiminīya and the K-R version (above (24)) are phonetic: K-R often has "āi" where the Malayalam manuscript of the Jaiminīya version has "āyi", although Caland's manuscript also has "āi." This is not due to differences between the Malayalam and Grantha scripts, because both of these can express "āi" as well as "āyi." These minor phonetic differences are determined not by differences of affiliation but by geography (Tamilnad versus Kerala). Important differences, however, are due to the Vedic school. For example, the K-R has often "o" where the Jaiminīya has "ā"; and the well known K-R stobha "o iḍā" appears in the Jaiminīya tradition always as "o iḷā," using the Dravidian sound "ḷ", pronounced like *r* in American English, but further back (see Renou 1947:99; Staal 1961:69). The occurrence of this sound may indicate that the Jaiminīya tradition originated in South

India or in an area of the North at a time when a Dravidian language was still spoken there.

The third observation was made in AGNI, from which I quote (I:278):

> When dealing with these songs and chants it should be remembered that the Sāmaveda is replete with what, from a textual point of view, are unexpected variations and varieties. These features are characteristic of the Sāmaveda, Kauthuma-Rāṇāyanīya as well as Jaiminīya. Whenever regular patterns seem to emerge, there are new deviations that break the pattern. To treat the text as if it were corrupt would be to miss its very raison d'être. But even if we accept its playful deviations, we find that the rules of this game often escape us. Many forms that may seem to be printing mistakes or mistakes of the manuscripts are therefore in fact what they should be.

The seventh of this sequence of nine songs is used in its Grāmageyagāna form in the Agnicayana ritual. We have studied other chants from the same ritual context (page 217). After the bird altar has been consecrated, it has to be brought under control and pacified. The Adhvaryu, assisted by the Pratiprasthātā, pours a continuous libation of goat milk over the western brick of the northern wing. This brick is chosen because it is relatively soft and tender, far away from the center of the altar which is a center of power, and also because it can be easily approached from different sides (AGNI I:509 sq.). During this oblation, the Adhvaryu recites the famous *Śatarudriya* or *Rudram* (Taittirīya Saṃhitā 4.5), which derives its popularity partly from the fact that it was subsequently interpreted within the perspective of Śaiva theism (Gonda 1979; Arnold, forthcoming). During this oblation and recitation, the Udgātā sings a sequence of 57 sāmans, together called Flow of Milk (*kṣīradhārā*). The fourth of these is our GG 49.2.7.

Why was this song chosen to perform this function? It fits with the others only to some extent: it shares with most a triple repetition (of "tavā ū"), and with many the stobha "au ho vā." Both these features, however, are quite common in the Sāmaveda. The more complex features that distinguish a series of later songs in the Flow of Milk sequence (Chapter 19) are not found in it. One is tempted to believe that there is no answer to the question of why this particular song was selected for use at this particular point of the ritual. It came from the collection like a seed that falls from a blossom and is carried through the wind until it settles down somewhere.

What about the stobha "tavā ū" itself? Again, we observe a phonological, and therefore linguistic correspondence—or is it pseudo-linguistic? "Tavā ū" comes from "-tave," which should yield, in linguistic terms, "tavāi" or "tavāyi," as indeed it does in many other songs of the sequence GG 49.2. What we find, therefore, is a variation of a linguistic relationship. This is quite common in these songs, and it supports the idea that the derivation of songs from verses is closely connected with the origination of linguistics in India.

In Sanskrit, "tava" also has a meaning: it means "yours." The stobha can be taken to mean "yours U," which is almost as good as "yours truly." But this meaning correspondence is adventitious and without significance, which does not imply, however, that it could not evoke semantic associations among some users. "Tava," moreover, occurs in other stobhas (see Puṣpasūtra, ed. Simon, 1909: 770 s.v. *tava tyad*), and "ū" is quite famous in later Tantrism (see, for example, Padoux 1963: 203–206). Historical connexions between Vedic stobhas and Tantric bījamantras are likely to exist (Chapter 20): a good example is the famous Tantric *phaṭ* which occurred already in the Sāmaveda (see van der Hoogt 1929:99; cf. *phāt phat phat phat phat phat*: AGNI I:416).

Next we shall consider some of the more esoteric "songs to be sung in the forest." Jaiminīya Araṇyageyagāna 15.7 (corresponding to K-R AG 16.1) includes the following song based upon our verse:

ayāmāyām ayāmāyām ayāmāyāṃ svādiṣṭhayā madāyiṣṭhāyā / pavasva somadhārāyā / indrāyapā tavāyi sūtaḥ / ayāmāyām ayāmāyām ayāmāyā au ho vā / ī / /

C: ayāmāyāmayāmāyā (2×). ayāmāyāmayāmāyāmayāmāyāmauhovā

Again, there is triple repetition, and "ayam" also happens to *mean* something, viz., "this one," without carrying any deeper significance. It is a well known Vedic stobha (see van der Hoogt 1929:11: *ayaṃ yaḥ*, 91: *ayam ayāyam*, 99: *ayaṃ vāyau*, 111: *ayam*) and is perhaps the source of the equally well-known Tantric stobha "aiṃ" (see, for example, Bharati 1970:119).

This song is ritually used in the construction of the Agnicayana altar. When the bricks of the first layer are laid down the Udgātā chants whenever it is the turn of a ritually significant brick to be deposited and consecrated. At the consecration of the seventh brick, called Dūrvā after the grass of that name, the Adhvaryu recites Taittirīya Saṃhitā 4.2.9.2 c-d (see AGNI I:423):

> "Rising up from every stem, from every joint, dūrvā, extend to us a thousandfold, a hundredfold.
> You who extend with a hundred, arise with a thousand!
> To you, goddess brick, may we offer with oblation."

At the beginning of this recitation the Adhvaryu looks at the Udgātā, to alert him, and the Udgātā intones his song, AG 15.7. Why this song is chanted here at this time is not known. There is no specific phonetic, phonological, syntactic, semantic or pragmatic similarity between recitation and chant, apart from the fact that the recitation is again in the gāyatrī meter and the chant is a gāyatrī chant—both varieties that are exceedingly common.

No specific semantic connexion appears to exist between the ritual applications of these two derivatives from our Rigvedic verse that occur in the two basic *gāna* books of the Sāmaveda. Other ritual uses of chants that are derived from these songs pertain to the Soma ritual and are listed in the Ūha and Ūhya (or Rahasya) Gāna collections of the Sāmaveda. In these two collections, the songs are ordered in the same sequence in which they are used in the Soma rituals, and they are given in the actual forms in which they are sung.

The ritual context of the Soma ceremonies has been treated in Chapter 8. In the Agniṣṭoma, there are three pressings of Soma;

at the third pressing, there are two sequences of chants and recitations; the first of these, which is the eleventh sequence of the entire pressing day, consists of a series of seventeen songs, of which the first and the fourth are based upon our verse. These songs are listed in Ūhagāna 3.2–6 (see AGNI I:646–648), but there are several difficulties, notably one remarked upon by Caland (Caland-Henry 1907:180): the first three songs are *not* listed there (though their textual form, without melody, occurs in the corresponding passages of the Saṃhitā). So how should they be sung?

The answer is that these are to be sung in the Gāyatra melody, which is explained somewhere else, once and for all, but not in the corpus of the Sāmaveda. The same holds for other verses in the *gāyatrī* meter, in particular the famous Gāyatrī verse of the Rigveda (3.62.10: see above, page 231) that is not listed in the Sāmaveda either. It is often quoted in Vedic literature, sometimes in the context of a wish for inspiration (see, for example, Gonda 1980a:45, 104); and is recited during many rites and on many occasions (see Gonda 1980b, s.v. "Sāvitrī"). According to the Śatapatha Brāhmaṇa (2.3.4.39), all wishes of the ritualist will be fulfilled by this mantra because they are impelled by Savitṛ, who is the "impeller" (*prasavitṛ*) of the gods. This is a typical comment of that Brāhmaṇa—vacuous and ad hoc.

Why was this mantra picked to play such an important and auspicious role? There are hundreds of mantras in the Rigveda that say something similar. The answer to such questions is always the same: there is no answer. It fell from the heap like the windblown seed we have already encountered. For some arbitrary reason, supreme significance is attached to it. It occurs everywhere, with one exception: it does not occur in the Sāmaveda. Or rather, it is placed at the beginning in some collections (in some manuscripts and in most of the printed editions), remaining outside the systematically numbered sequences and all classifications, while in other collections it is simply not found.

The reason for this special treatment, once the mantra had acquired its special function, is not difficult to find: this mantra had too much meaning. A prayer for inspiration that is daily recited, that defines a brahmin and distinguishes him from others, is not the kind of mantra that provides the auspicious but meaningless sounds that make up the melodies that accompany ritual activity. The Sāvitrī, in fact, is so important to a brahmin that it has spilled over to other twice-born castes, albeit in a different form: Kṣatriyas have a Sāvitrī in the *triṣṭubh* meter, and Vaiśyas have one in the *jagatī* meter (see Malamoud 1977:89). The Gāyatrī thus has meaning as well as social significance—unlike most mantras and other ritual chants—although this significance is partly theoretical, like much that concerns the ancient *varṇa* system (the theory of four castes, set up in the law books, as distinct from the reality of thousands of *jāti* units of caste which characterizes Indian society). The Gāyatrī, therefore, remains significant and *eo ipso* isolated.

The Gāyatrī melody occupies a similar position in the ceremonies of the Soma ritual. Many of the *stuti* or *stotra* chants, whose sequences define a Soma ritual, are set to this melody. They all receive the same treatment, a treatment which in fact obliterates almost all the meaningful characteristics of the originals, replacing them by stobhas and other meaningless sounds, particularly long *ō*'s. Since only the *prastāva* retains the original text, it is only that portion that is explicitly noted in the tradition. The other *bhakti* portions are always sung in the same manner. The *udgītha* is always (see above, page 232):

ō vā ō vā ō vā hiṃ bhā ō vā

with very long *ō*'s (note that South Indian scripts, unlike Nāgarī, distinguish between short *o* and long *ō*). The remaining *bhakti* portions are collectively treated as follows. The Pratihartā always sings "hiṃ" together with the Udgātā, breathes in, and chants "vāk" (which comes from nowhere) while he holds his breath—therefore almost inaudibly. The Yajamāna and some other priests, in accordance with complex rules, should also chant "ō" (see AGNI I:603).

We are now in a position to return to the ritual uses of our verse, Rigveda 9.1.1, in the Soma ceremonies. We can now understand why, for the first song of the third pressing sequence of chants, only the *prastāva* needs to be known. It is listed in the Saṃhitā as follows:

svādiṣṭhayā madiṣṭhayōm (Jaiminīya Ārcika 64.1).

The fourth chant is listed in Ūha Gāna 3.2. It preserves more of the original text although the *udgītha* has also disappeared:

svādiṣṭhayā ma dā yiṣṭhayā / svā sō ō /ā yindrā / ō pā tavā hāvu vā /sū taḥ / / (see AGNI I:646).

In all the cases of ritual application of mantras we have so far studied, nothing remains of the rich literature of the Vedas but a collection of sounds and syllables. Entire passages that originally were pregnant with meaning are reduced to long *ō*'s. This is precisely what distinguishes *mantras* from the original verse: to be made into a mantra, and thus fit for ritual consumption, a verse has to be subjected to *formal* transformations, operations that apply to form but not to meaning. This is why Renou referred to mantras as "poussière védique," and why he mentioned "le découpage des vieux hymnes en formules ou même fragments devenus des corps inertes dans la trame liturgique" (1960:76–77 quoted by Malamoud 1983:33).

Ritual traditions have obvious social significance in that they identify groups and distinguish them from each other. They give people, in that hackneyed contemporary phrase, "a sense of identity." That identity, however, is often due to distinctions that rest upon meaningless phonetic variations. Thus the Jaiminīya and Kauthuma-Rāṇāyanīya schools differ from each other by such characteristics as vowel length, or because the former uses "ā" where the latter uses "o." Up to the present time, the Vedic schools themselves are distinguished from each other by such variations of sound that can be more easily explained in grammatical than in religious terms. The Gāyatrī mantra itself is pronounced differently by Nambudiri brahmans belonging to the Yajurveda or Sāmaveda and Nambudiris belonging to the Rigveda: the former pronounce the *visarga* "ḥ" at the end of "naḥ" (p. 231) as an "f," a sound that is generally believed not to occur in Sanskrit.

Actually, the bilabial spirant "f" is an optional variant prescribed by a grammatical rule which also introduces another sound, the velar "kh", which is believed to be absent from Sanskrit. Special symbols are needed to add these sounds to the alphabet, as in the manuscripts or printed editions of Pāṇini's rule 8.3.37: kupvoḥ ᳵ kᳶpau ca, " ᳵ and ᳶ may be substituted in the place of the visarga when a voiceless velar or a voiceless labial, respectively, follow."

In this symbolism, "ᳵk" refers to the velar "kh", and "ᳶp" to the bilabial spirant "f". The interpretation of this rule depends on conventions that have been established elsewhere in the grammar. Thus we have to supply *padasya*, "in the place of a word," from 8.1.16; *saṃhitāyām*, "in continuous pronunciation," from 8.2.108; and *vā*, "optionally," from 8.3.36. That the rules are to be understood in this order follows from 8.2.1, and that the optional *vā* means "preferable" has been shown by Kiparsky (1979). That the Yajurveda and Sāmaveda have adopted the preferred form is in accordance with the central place they occupy in the ritual tradition.

In the Gāyatrī, the voiceless labial which follows the visarga "ḥ" is the initial "p" of "pracodayāt." Thus the variation between Vedic schools and between the Vedas themselves is reduced to the optionality of grammatical rules. This is not a modern phenomenon; it goes back to the origin of the tradition. The bilabial spirant "f" occurs not only in the grammar of Pāṇini, but in two phonetic treatises (Prātiśākhya) of the Yajurveda, namely, the Taittirīya of the Black and the Vājasaneyi of the White Yajurveda. (It is lacking again in the Mādhyandina, another school of the White Yajurveda: Renou 1942, 1957:396).

Throughout this section we have observed that considerations of form and formal derivations and transformations are foremost in the minds of the ritualists. In some cases these forms appear to be purely arbitrary, since they do not correspond to any type of formal relationship that is known or seems to make sense. In other cases the rules of grammar, especially those that introduce options, are used and lead to further ritual developments and proliferation. In both cases, we can give a syntactic but not a semantic account of the relationships between mantras and acts. We shall formulate such an account for Rigveda 9.1.1 by means of a syntactic structure that represents the knowledge of the ritualist. We have to make some distinctions to begin with.

The ritualist, first of all, *knows* this verse. That is, he knows how to recite it, for this is what he learned when he learned the Rigveda by heart as a boy—a knowledge he shares with many other brahmins who also belong (by birth) to the Rigveda but are not ritualists. But there is no traditional transmission of the *meaning* of the verse, and so he does not necessarily know its meaning. If he does, he must be a Sanskrit scholar to whom meaning has become a matter of personal interest. A practising ritualist who is asked for the meaning of a recitation or song invariably replies: go to a scholar of language or philosophy.

A brahmin who belongs to the Sāmaveda knows more: he knows how the verses of the Rigveda have been transformed into songs. He will probably know various chants derived from that verse, depending on his expertise, and if he is really good, he will know where these occur in the collections of the Sāmavedic corpus—which is large and complicated, as we have seen. He shares such knowledge, however, with other Sāmavedins and it still does not qualify him as a ritualist.

Only the ritual expert or *vaidika* knows, unlike an ordinary Rigvedin or Sāmavedin (or Yajurvedin, for that matter), the association between mantras and acts, and when and where in the ritual these have to be inserted and executed. He knows something like the following structure (I say "something like," for he uses, as we shall see in Chapter 27, a system of reference rooted in oral tradition and in some respects different from the system used by Western scholars, which presupposes the availability of printed texts):

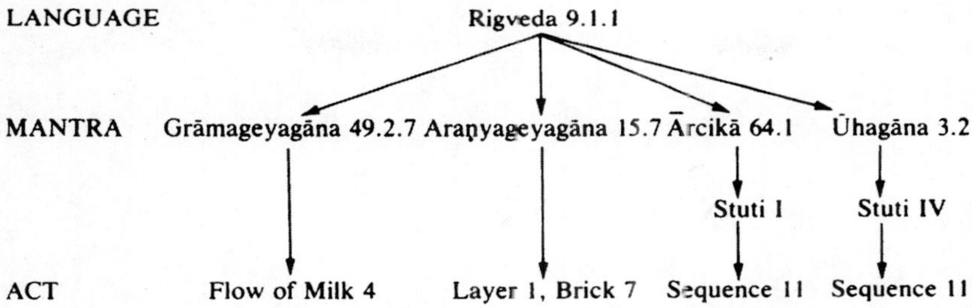

Such a structure makes sense only within the larger pattern of hundreds of similar structures, which together constitute the edifice of the ritual. Vedic ritual makes sense, but it is structural sense. An exhaustive synchronic analysis of the ritual can be given in terms of the structural relationships between such forms, without reference to meaning or external function. Such an analysis will refer to the rules that relate structures to each other, and is therefore syntactic in nature. If and when the system changes (which may be due to a variety of causes, semantic as well as nonsemantic), the rules or the relations between them change, and this can again be studied in syntactic terms. The syntactic approach can therefore completely account for the ritual facts. It also shows that many cases of association between a mantra and an act are accidental and due to chance. I shall refer to this structural feature as *inner chance*.

There are other developments in the domain of ritual that illustrate the workings of chance. Many of these are connected with the origins of ritual systems. The study of such systems has been undertaken by anthropologists, who have paid insufficient attention to mantras and history and whose orientation has been predominantly semantic. We have to study such semantic accounts, however, because they often provide the only information that is available, and also in order to find out whether the case of Vedic ritual is perhaps unique (see below, Chapter 30C). I shall discuss three anthropological studies in the next Chapter and return to the question of chance afterwards.

25

Anthropology Without Mantras

The three anthropological studies we will study in this chapter are concerned with Southeast Asia and all have links with India. The three geographical areas are Thailand (studied by Stanley Tambiah), Sri Lanka (studied by Gananath Obeyesekere) and Bali (studied by Clifford Geertz). These three authors differ in the degree of their semantic involvement: Tambiah possesses the least (not surprising in view of his earlier studies) and Geertz the most. Tambiah and Obeyesekere pay attention to mantras which Geertz hardly mentions. I was tempted to characterize the three approaches as "Weak Semantics," "Medium Semantics," and "Strong Semantics;" but this could be taken as a criticism, especially of the weak, which is not what I had in mind. I have therefore accepted the lead of these authors themselves and called their approaches, respectively: "Object Semantics," "Psycho-semantics," and "Thick Semantics."

In each of these case studies I shall attempt to approximate, at least in principle, that (practically as well as philosophically) impossible ideal demanded by Franz Boas: complete the data before embarking upon theory. Of course, I cannot be exhaustive; I am only interested in illustrations. However, in the case of Tambiah and Obeyesekere, this procedure can to some extent be realized because their data are presented independently of theory, and are, moreover, similar in kind. I shall therefore start with the data of these two authors. The theories of Tambiah and Obeyesekere, on the other hand, are very different, and so I shall save them for last. In the case of Geertz it is almost impossible to draw the line between facts and interpretations. This will require special attention and since Geertz has also written the most, his section will be the longest.

25A. OBJECT SEMANTICS: Stanley Tambiah

Popular prejudice would expect Tambiah's book *The Buddhist Saints of the Forest and the Cult of Amulets* (1984) to contain no mantras and little on ritual. For did the Buddha not condemn both?

Popular prejudice, of course, is not a good guide, even though, by definition, many people follow it. Both Buddhism and Jainism rejected Vedic ritual, but neither rejected ritual (see Heesterman 1964:29; reprinted 1985:42). We know, moreover, that Mahāyāna Buddhism, which is not simply "later" Buddhism (as a previous generation, reared on Rhys Davids, imagined) but which is in many respects as close to the lost "original" Buddhism as the Theravāda, is replete with ritual (for references, see pages 399–400, 411–412). The same holds for the Theravāda itself, even in its contemporary forms. Spiro (1972; 1982:191) observes: "Indeed, for those who conceive of the latter form of Buddhism as a precursor of modern humanism (or even of analytical philosophy!), its rich ritual system comes rather as a shock, or is viewed as a late degeneration of ritualless purity."

Spiro's observations derive in part from his fieldwork in Burma. Roughly a fifth of his book is in fact concerned with Burmese Buddhism as a ritual system. Tambiah's book is partly based upon his fieldwork in Thailand, and although his treatment is more specific and sophisticated than Spiro's, it confirms the latter's impressions as formulated in the above quote. Neither work is confined to what is labelled "Buddhist," and they include local Burmese and Thai traditions, sometimes referred to as "animist." Spiro has tried to keep these two trends apart, but Tambiah has convincingly shown that this cannot be done. As for the term "saints of the forest," which occurs in Tambiah's title, it is not a product of the author's imagination, nor is it Thai or "animist:" it derives from the Pali *āraññavāsī* or *vanavāsī*, "forest dweller," which contrasts with *gāmavāsī*, "village dweller" or *nagaravāsī*, "town dweller" (Tambiah 1984:53). We recognize here the same distinction encountered in the previous chapter (page 297) between *grāmageyagāna*, "songs to be sung in the village," and *araṇyageyagāna*, "songs to be sung in the forest," a distinction that is quite common in Vedic tradition (see, for example, the Āraṇyakas or "forest books," a class of works to which the classical Upaniṣads are generally attached as a kind of appendix; cf. also Malamoud 1967). Buddhist tradition has preserved the terminology, although *nagara*, "town," has been added, reflecting the progress of history and increasing urbanization. The latter development was more important for the growing Buddhist order than for the successors to the Vedic tradition. Even so, though the label is "Buddhist," we are dealing with an Indian tradition.

The distinction between "forest" and "village" is, of course, related to the distinction introduced by Louis Dumont (1959, 1966) between the renouncer and the man-in-the-world or man-of-caste (cf. also Heesterman 1964, reprinted 1985:26–44). One might expect that the renouncer of village, family and caste has also renounced ritual; but this is refuted by many facts, including two that we have encountered: the "songs to be sung in the forest" are also ritual songs; and Buddhist monks, who are renouncers, also perform rituals. In Buddhism, the exemplary outcome of a renouncer's experience, we find Dumont's distinction not only obtaining between monks and laymen, but also, within the community of monks themselves, between the "forest" and "village/town" monks. It might be supposed that the former operate on a level that is beyond ritual. But the forest monks are in fact given to "practice" (*patipatti*) which includes ritual as well as meditation, and meditation itself is closely related to both recitation and ritual, as we shall see in a moment. Since the "village/town" monks also perform rituals—albeit different ones—we have come full circle.

Thai Buddhism is replete with mantras, and they have left their traces in Tambiah's book. For example, Achar Man, the saint whose life in the forest is graphically described by Tambiah in a long and fascinating chapter, used a system of mantra meditation that was adopted by Acharn Fun and other leading disciples (Tambiah 1984:139). The amulets, which play a very important role in Tambiah's book, derive their power from the fact that they have been consecrated, which is also done in the time-honored manner by ritual and mantras. The consecration ceremony, attended by the supreme patriarch of the Buddhist *saṅgha* and by representatives of the government (the deputy prime minister and the minister of defense, no less), begins with offerings made to the shrine deities with the chief court brahmin presiding. (I cannot expatiate on these Thai brahmins who are marginal to Tambiah's subject; but they add another Indian element to the amalgam of Buddhist and Thai traditions; cf. Filliozat 1965 and Sarma 1972.) "Thereafter, the most important sequence was staged. While 4 monks at the time, sitting on the side, chanted *paritta* chants continuously, 72 senior monks, divided into three batches of 24, sat for four hours at a time meditating silently and transferring virtue to the pile of amulets by means of a cord that passed through their hands and was attached to the pile . . . The monks sit cross-legged, close their eyes, practice concentration, and say words mentally and silently" (pages 244–245).

Transfer of power by means of a cord predates the invention of electrical wiring. It is a common ritual theme that we find, for example, in the Agnicayana consecration where a string made of hemp links the Yajamāna to the ukhā pot (AGNI I:323–324; Plate 46). What is of interest in the present context, however, are *paritta* chants and silent meditation. The former term, which means "protection," refers to the chanting of Buddhist scriptures as charms and for the sake of exorcism. This was introduced to Sri Lanka in the fourth century C.E. (Lamotte 1976:1860) and is still extremely popular. As for meditation, it might be supposed that it is something rather different from recitation or chanting—something more "spiritual" than "ritual." The answer is provided by Tambiah in the above passage: meditation is not some sort of idling in emptiness, but "saying words mentally and silently." Read "mantras" for "words," and the situation becomes indistinguishable from that of Vedic ritual where silent recitation plays a very important role (see, e.g., Renou 1949; Renou and Silburn 1954; above, page 263).

The details of these meditations are not described by Tambiah, and it is unlikely that considerations of form play as important a part in them as they do in Vedic ritual. Yet they deserve much closer study for they are at the core of the consecration that gives life to the amulets.

The consecration of amulets is a special case of the consecration of a Buddha statue, or *Buddhābhiṣeka*, which Tambiah describes on pages 248–257: "The climactic sequence is the chanting by the four monks of the *gāthā buddhābhiṣeka* (verses of consecration) . . . The four monks recite a particular cycle of verses, and each recitation takes about thirty-five minutes . . ." (Tambiah 1984:249).

I submit that these "particular" ritual recitations, which constitute the core of the consecration, which itself is the essential step in providing the amulets and Buddha statues with the powers that are the subject of Tambiah's book, have a complex structure that can be exhaustively described in syntactic terms. Moreover, I would suggest that such recitations are the heart of the matter, not only in the eyes of the participants, but also for any scientific analysis that succeeds in making sense of such cults.

Before we turn to theory *pur sang* I must refer to a controversy that raged in the pages of *The Times Literary Supplement* and to which my attention was drawn by Michel Strickmann. The controversy is not only entertaining, but relevant in the present context because it is concerned with the relationship between philology and anthropology, and the study of ritual requires the assistance of both these disciplines. We often find classical scholars and historians complaining when anthropologists and other social scientists ignore or neglect the historical background of the society in which they are working. Tambiah cannot be faulted for doing this; on the contrary, he has taken pains to inform himself about the historical and doctrinal background of Buddhism, a subject that he rightly regarded as indispensable for the understanding of his Buddhist monks, but with which he was not professionally familiar. Now, Buddhism is an enormously complex subject; even if one confines oneself to the Theravāda (a confinement that is definitely unnatural), it requires sustained and concentrated study for a goodly number of years. We should respect Tambiah for his efforts to go beyond his professional field of expertise, where his fieldwork appeared to demand it; and one should not be surprised or upset when, occasionally, he errs.

Not so Richard Gombrich, an Oxford Sanskritist who has himself done fieldwork in Sri Lanka and written a book about Sinhalese Buddhism (Gombrich 1971). In a savage review (Gombrich 1985) he pins on Tambiah a long list of errors, mostly pertaining to spelling, languages and history. Tambiah has replied to this charge, and turns out to be right in many cases (though least often in matters of history where he or his proofreader has incurred Gombrich's wrath by twice replacing "A.D." by "B.C."). Most of the items on this laundry list of errors and alleged errors are marginal to the chief concerns of Tambiah's book. Some are of general interest, however, and are also related to our present context. Among these is a discussion on the traditional class of extraordinary powers (*siddhi*, *iddhi*, *abhijñā*) found in the Yoga, Hindu as well as Buddhist (cf. above, page 237). One of the most colorful of these is levitation, and Tambiah has a story to tell about a pilot of the Royal Thai Air Force, who, on a practice flight over the Mae Pang mountain:

> saw a monk sitting in meditation upon a cloud, and (he) had to practice much skill in swerving away to avoid hitting the apparition. Having grounded the plane, the pilot with his flight map in hand went scouting on the mountain, and there he recognized Luang Pu Waen as the monk he had seen in the clouds. The news of Luang Pu Waen's power of levitation and flying spread quickly—it was broadcast on the radio and splashed in the newspapers. And the public's demand for his medallions soared (Tambiah 1984:272).

Gombrich accused Tambiah of attributing to the Buddha the view that such powers are commendable, to which Tambiah replied that he had only followed the descriptions of Buddhaghosa's *Visuddhimagga* which Gombrich himself had acclaimed in his book as "the unitary standard of doctrinal orthodoxy for all Theravāda Buddhists." The *Visuddhimagga* belongs, as a matter of fact, to the fifth century C.E., and since the earliest accounts of the Buddha describe him "only as a man, not as a super-human being" (Nakamura 1980:83), we don't know anything about what his opinion might have been with regard to such special powers. What we do know is that in the Yoga system these powers were not frowned upon. Gombrich's opinion is therefore based upon Western prejudice—the same prejudice we find in Mircea Eliade (1964:223,401 and 1969:338) whose pertinent statements were refuted by Wasson (1968:331) followed by myself (1975:97). This is ironic, for Gombrich himself has demonstrated that Eliade's statements on Buddhism are riddled with errors of fact and interpretation (Gombrich 1974). What is instructive in the present context is that prejudice is more pernicious than ignorance—a circumstance which is strikingly relevant to the understanding of ritual and to which we shall return.

The last part of Tambiah's book deals with "Conceptual and Theoretical Clarifications" (pages 291–347). Tambiah does not make much use of the ideas on performative analysis developed in his 1979 lecture. True, he uses the term "indexical," but it does not make much of a theoretical contribution. The idea that is most interesting in the present context is the "objectification of *charisma* in objects and fetishes" which the cult of amulets illustrates. Though Weber's theory allowed for the "routinization of charisma" in social institutions and social positions, Tambiah notes that "he was blind to the symbolism of objectification of charisma in objects and fetishes" (page 339).

Given such a process, semantic analysis is clearly applicable and appropriate. It is these features that suggested my caption "object semantics." For if the introduction of semantics is justified by anything, it is the use of objects that refer to something else; and if amulets are not that, nothing is. Thus we have ample justification for semantics, albeit outside the domain of ritual.

Tambiah also uses the expression "semiotic code," but it is not clear what it can do that plain English cannot. More striking is the description in his last chapter (entitled: "The objectification of charisma and the fetishism of objects") of the relative scarcity and ensuing commercial value of the Thai amulets. They become "private possessions of laymen who expect to use the amulet's potency to manipulate, overpower, seduce, and control their fellow men and women in an ongoing drama of social transactions." Tambiah applies to his amulets Mauss' expression of a "magico-religious guarantee of rank and prosperity" (page 342). Actually, if one replaces in many of these passages "amulets" by "dollars" one obtains an interesting theory of the origination of capitalism. In this respect, Tambiah's work supplements what we now know of the development of Buddhist monasteries on the trade routes between India, Central Asia and China into fortified constructions that served not only as motels but also as banks (see Staal 1988b).

Tambiah's conclusions suggest a clarification of my own position on questions of semantics. I do not reject semantics or the use of symbols in anthropology or the study of culture. I only reject the idea that these notions are helpful tools in the analysis of ritual. The home of semantics is language, and semantic analysis applies in the first place in contexts of language; then, via language, it may also apply to mathematics, philosophy, art, mythology and many other domains of experience. To say that semantics does not apply to ritual is tantamount to saying that ritual is not a language. To claim that *all* of culture consists of symbols and meanings, and is in that respect language-like, would simply entail that ritual cannot be part of culture.

25B. PSYCHO-SEMANTICS: Gananath Obeyesekere

Gananath Obeyesekere's *Cult of the Goddess Pattini* (1984) provides a detailed description of a cult that still thrives in Sri Lanka and South India and that has close connexions with

Buddhism, Jainism, Hinduism and Sinhala tradition. The textual traditions of this cult are embodied in a compendium of thirty-five ritual texts or songbooks. Obeyesekere has translated most of these texts, although the number 35 is an idealization that is artificially maintained by emendations, splitting, addition and elimination (page 32). He has in fact provided translations of 58 different ritual texts that together occupy more than 150 pages of his book. Many of these texts are sung and enacted in the course of rituals. It is obvious that we are dealing with a very rich tradition of rituals and songs, and that Obeyesekere has done pioneering work in making it accessible. His interests in this tradition is clearly semantic, and this is not surprising when one places it in the various contexts in which he himself has placed it with consummate skill.

Obeyesekere's book consists of 629 pages packed with information and it would be impossible to do it any justice within a short compass. In fact, the author says in his Preface (page xvii): "My Pattini research spans the whole of my anthropological career." I recall how I accompanied Obeyesekere once to one of those beautiful isolated villages where he had already done a great deal of fieldwork. That was in 1965, when I was recording mantras, ranging from Buddhist *upasampadā* ordinations to Sinhalese charms against snakes and cattle's foot disease. A half day walk across a hill and through scattered jungle patches led to a lush green valley of rice-fields, cocoa-nut palms and rubber trees, with a river flowing at the bottom—a paradise not for the people who live there, unfortunately, and not for the inquiring mind, but certainly for the senses of any intrepid visitor who has not yet lost them. And yet, despite abundant meaning and social context, the semantic analysis of the Pattini cult may not be all there is to it. There are definite indications that another approach could contribute something that is still missing.

Some of the texts are never sung or enacted, and Obeyesekere has omitted most of these. But there are also cases where a text is omitted because it does not seem to fit semantically. For example, when the *kapurāla*'s white robe is consecrated, Obeyesekere says about the accompanying song (text 11): "it is not an important one in content, and I shall only quote excerpts from it'' (page 111). Instead, he concentrates on the semantically relevant contrast between the whiteness of the *kapurāla*'s robe, which has to be pure because he interacts with gods who are pure, and the patched yellow robe of the Buddhist monk, which in theory should be made of rags and which relates to "his involvement in processes of death and decay (polluting activities)."

There are other similar cases where a song is omitted because its content does not fit its ritual context, and where Obeyesekere makes comments such as "this text is of little significance" (page 240). The reader wonders why, in many such cases, the songs are nevertheless sung. There are also examples that display some degree of formal complexity. A text that was first recited by the chief *kapurāla* continues to be recited by him and another senior priest, while an assistant dances to the beat of drums (page 189). The rhyme structure can be quite complex, so that Obeyesekere comments: "This kind of complexity is a function of greater specialization, literacy and book learning and closeness to Buddhist civilizing influences" (page 190). Elsewhere the audience intersperses the song with shouts (page 191; cf. AGNI I:642, and the *pratigara* interjections of the Adhvaryu: above page 232 and AGNI I:623, 640, 650, etc.). We also come across "high-sounding combinations of Pali or Sanskrit, or both, and Sinhala" (page 202). In all these cases, formal considerations play a role, and a syntactic analysis might be able to account for structures that the semantic approach fails to explain.

There are numerous instances where the content of a song is not clear or intelligible to the participants (e.g., page 239). The identity of particular gods is often unclear or controversial (e.g., page 87). There is a mystery of twelve "missing deities," which the author interprets as a survival of a gradually disappearing cult (pages 285–293). Elsewhere, songs that are meant for a particular occasion are sung on other occasions as well (e.g., page 221). Some songs are "not intrinsic to the ritual" (page 231); others (e.g., the "head-to-foot verse") are "standard" and appear in various sections of the ceremony (page 96). Many chants incorporate intricate numerical and metrical structures (e.g., "twenty-one short stanzas and sixteen long stanzas:" page 101). All these are cases of ritualization which can probably be explained along syntactic lines. Phonological analysis would be in order when studying the various modes of chanting, about which Obeyesekere does not provide much detail although he sometimes refers to style or mentions particular songs that are sung at a faster or slower pace. In one context, an *a* is deleted, because "it would introduce an extra syllable and upset the rhyme scheme and rhythm" (page 89: "hence *sura* is used instead of *asura*"—a fact that should delight Sanskritists, as the author hints).

It is likely that the songs of the Pattini cult are often more closely related to the acts they accompany than is the case in Vedic ritual. Some acts are very similar to Vedic rites. The cutting of the *milla* tree, for example (pages 141–143), which provides firewood for the fire-trampling rituals, is very similar to such Agnicayana rites as the fetching of mud for the ukhā pots (AGNI I:288–296) or the cutting of the *bilba* tree from which the sacrificial pole will be made (AGNI I:590–591 and Plate 96). The extent of such similarities would further depend on the structural relationships that obtain in the Pattini cult between the songs and the acts, a topic that Obeyesekere has not enlarged upon. It is clear that there are, in this instance, semantic similarities, and likely that there are syntactic similarities as well.

The importance of form and formal structures is obvious to anyone who reads between the lines, and it sometimes comes to the surface. The most telling example is a rite that asks permission from the gods and forgiveness for accidental faults, which is necessary because, as the *kapurāla* says, "the hand may go wrong and the mouth may go wrong" (page 112). Rarely do we find a more straightforward indication of the continuing emphasis not on meaning, but on act and recitation as the two main vehicles of ritual activity.

What, then, has Obeyesekere to say on meaning, and what are the theoretical observations he makes? It would be foolhardy to deal with a topic so large in the context of a book so rich in information that is entirely new. However, I shall try to give at least an idea of the author's two chief contributions in this area. We should first of all note that Obeyesekere includes much information and speculation on the historical background of rites, and in so doing goes beyond the synchronic analysis of the ritual system. About this he has some remarkable things to say—remarkable not least because they apply to ritual as well as to myth:

> Any mythological tradition comes from historically diverse sources. A tradition of myth is a composite of preexisting beliefs, beliefs that are newly invented, and those incorporated from other belief systems. An analysis of the sources of a given mythic tradition may help us unravel the processes by which a religious tradition came to be constituted. Anthropologists have been averse to a historical study of myth ever since Radcliffe-Brown castigated the diachronic study of oral tradition as 'pseudohistory.' However, in a literate culture like Sri Lanka, with historical records going back about two thousand years, it may be possible to relate the tradition of myth and ritual to historical periods or events and thereby to 'verify' hypotheses or propositions regarding the former. It may therefore be possible to construct a "speculative history" of a mythic tradition, grounded on historical data (page 283).

As a matter of fact, these historical reconstructions are not so different from what professional historians are often engaged in doing. What is interesting is what Radcliffe-Brown did not say: namely, that insofar as anthropology deals with the study of ritual, such historical reconstructions are "pseudo-anthropology." For although these reconstructions may be of interest by themselves, they may not be relevant to an understanding of the ritual per se—just as the etymology of a word may not be relevant to its meaning or use. Obeyesekere is, of course, conscious of this. His readers should be similarly aware that these explanations do not explain the ritual system. They only add to the impression that, in historical terms, it is a hodge-podge—just like the systems Tambiah studied and like the Vedic "Great Tradition" itself (Staal 1963, 1972^2)—a topic to which we shall return in Chapter 28A. In the meantime—and before another Gombrich comes along—one should be grateful to the author for his historical reconstructions which do not merely connect Sri Lanka with South India, but point at more distant origins for certain features (in particular, the ritual drama of the resurrection of Pattini's consort) in Western Asia and in the Mediterranean. Although such connexions remain unproven they do not conflict with what is presently known about early Indian history. Moreover, although Obeyesekere is not frightened of speculation, he knows when to stop—unlike S. B. Steever, the author of a perfunctory review in the *Journal of American Oriental Studies* who wishes that Obeyesekere had gone further and included theology and existentialist metaphysics (Steever 1985:187).

There is perhaps a reason for Steever's unreasonable expectations: for Obeyesekere uses similarly alien kinds of semantic interpretation by adopting the Freudian psycho-analytical reductions that he had earlier used, for example, in *Medusa's Hair* (1981). This is the second area of "semantic interpretation" offered to elucidate the cult. I am not competent to judge these psycho-analytical attempts at explanation, but it strikes me that they may only be helpful when we are dealing with neurotic individuals about whose personal life and childhood a great deal is known. In *Medusa's Hair* we were provided with seven case studies of people who Obeyesekere had not actually put on the couch, but with whom he had lengthy personal conversations. In the Pattini book, however, we are dealing with cults that are much less personal. Even though the author asserts in his Preface that he "got to know intimately" the *kapurālas* from a number of villages and towns, a psycho-analytical treatment is accordingly less convincing. I shall not belabor this point but give one illustration of a psycho-analytical interpretation that is simply out-of-date.

Although Obeyesekere's book is primarily devoted to the Pattini cult, many other closely or less closely related ritual developments are also provided with a detailed description and analysis. More than a hundred pages are devoted to the *Aṅkeḷiya* rituals that have nothing to do with ankles but a great deal with anal intercourse. This is regarded by the participants with both fascination and abhorrence. According to Obeyesekere, however, the homosexual theme is not as important as the "key emotions" of "castration and impotence anxieties" (page 487). (It is only on these pages (486–487) that I found two Freudian slips: "heterosexual" for "homosexual," and "superordinate male" for "subordinate male.") But when he tells us that an important part of the ceremonies, in which only adult males participate, consists in two teams pulling ropes that are attached to two interlocked horns (either horns of the sambar deer, or wooden hooks or tree roots representing such horns) until one of them snaps, and that these horns stand for penises, while in a closely related rite a male demon shaves the body hair of another man, one wonders. One also wonders whether these reductions of homosexual activities to castration fears, so outmoded and yet so tediously familiar, could not be straightened out by some measure of Gay Liberation. As it is, they are no more than stains on a book that in every other respect is vibrant with new facts, new ideas, and new insights.

The historical reconstructions add much to the value of this book and the psycho-analytical suggestions, although of limited relevance, do not interfere with the presentation of the materials and hence do not detract from its value. I shall revert to the former which exhibit *outer chance* (pages 344–346). However, neither type of analysis throws light on the ritual systems as such. Given the nature and abundance of the data, a syntactic analysis should therefore be rewarding.

25C. THICK SEMANTICS: Clifford Geertz

Clifford Geertz' monograph *Negara: The Theatre State in Nineteenth-Century Bali* (1980) takes us further away from India but not from Hinduism and Buddhism. Geertz doesn't only write about cults; he has become a cult figure himself. One thinks of expressions such as "deep play" (Geertz 1972) or "thick description" (Geertz 1973), that have not only become slogans (from Sanskrit *śloka*, a verse in a popular meter) but that can hold their own even with mantras such as *om* in suggesting profound and hidden significance.

Early in his career, Geertz put Dutch scholars of Indonesia to shame by writing a brilliant book entitled *The Religion of Java* (1960). Using purely anthropological and synchronic methods of fieldwork, he showed that Javanese religion on the village or "small town" level consists of three strata, corresponding to the three levels that historians had distinguished as having originated in Islam, (Buddhism-) Hinduism and what had been vaguely referred to as "animistic beliefs." One of the results of this work was that it became clear that traditional characterizations of Hinduism and Islam along the lines of the Christian concept of religion, implying exclusiveness and incompatibility with other religions, are inappropriate, at least in Java. Geertz is aware of some of the conceptual problems inherent in the Western concept of religion, but being interested less in what "the religion of Java" is *not* than in what it *is*, he concentrates on features of a different sort, for example (Geertz 1960:238):

> The three major foci of *prijaji* "religious" life are etiquette, art, and mystical practice. I admit to using "religion" in a somewhat broader sense than may be typical, but there is nothing else to do when these factors are so fused as to make their separate consideration nearly meaningless.

This usage of the concept of religion is not only *broader*, but also *narrower* than the typical sense; it excludes, for example, considerations of doctrine or belief—a significant fact to which we shall return.

If we compare Geertz' work with the monographs on Indonesian Islam by earlier Dutch authors (e.g., Drewes 1925, Kraemer 1921, van Nieuwenhuijze 1945, Rinkes 1909, Schrieke 1916—none of them referred to by Geertz) we find, not surprisingly, that the picture based upon contemporary anthropological observation shows a much greater degree of integration of historically distinct features than the picture based upon the philological study of texts. Most of the books mentioned deal with Sufi texts from Java and Sumatra that closely resemble the Islamic mysticism of Gujarat on the west coast of India from which they derive. Islam took root in Gujarat soon after the Muslim conquest of Sind, viz., within a century after Muhammad's death (the campaign started in year 92 of the Hijra, i.e., 711 C.E.); and it began also, almost immediately, to undergo Indianization. Thus we find, for example, the followers of Shāh Madār, a Sufi born in Aleppo in 1051 C.E. who spent much of his life in India, smoke *bhang* with Indian ascetics (there are stories in their writings about Muhammad using it in paradise: Husain 1929:29). Under such circumstances, it is not surprising that Hindu and Muslim currents merged; according to Husain, the Madāri cult was "très répandu parmi les paysans sans distinction de religion." Combining philology, history, and anthropology we thus find that the situation in Java as observed by Geertz, in respect of emerging syncretism, may not have been so very different from what it had been in India several centuries earlier. After settling in Java, Indian Sufism, already a mixture, was further enriched and modified by local elements, some of them also of Indian provenance, others purely Indonesian.

Another of Geertz' books, *Islam Observed* (1968), provided an account which implied that the types of Islam met with in Indonesia and in Morocco, i.e., at the geographical extremities of the Muslim world, have been so thoroughly moulded by local culture and history, and have accordingly so little in common, that the appropriateness of applying a single religious label such as "Islam" again becomes questionable. This book also illustrates that certain features of civilization are stronger and more permanent than religion. This was already evident from India, as we have just seen; applies especially to caste (a feature that is often preserved, for example, when an Indian converts to Islam or Christianity); and was later confirmed with specific reference to ritual ("the invariance of ritual under religious transformation," or "the invariance of ritual across religious boundaries:" see pages 261, 390–394; Schipper and Staal 1988).

The Bali book dates from 1980, and followed a series of more specialized studies on Bali (1964, 1972, 1973, etc.). The term *negara*, which in Bali and Indonesia generally means "state," is none other than the Sanskrit *nagara*, or "town," which Buddhist monks added to "village" so as to form a pair in opposition to the tradition of "forest." In Bali (as in India), *negara* contrasts with *desa* as "state" or "town" does with "countryside."

Geertz' book deals primarily with politics, but since in Bali political theory is hard to come by, he has sought it in the ritual performances that are the subject of his final chapter, entitled: "Political Statement: Spectacle and Ceremony." In this chapter, ritual ceremonies are interpreted as symbolic expressions of power. Geertz concentrates on the more spectacular and popular "outstanding features" of these ceremonies—e.g., in the case of cremation, "a social one, the procession; an aesthetic one, the tower; and a natural one, the fire" (page 118). A categorization in terms of "social," "aesthetic," and "natural" is Western, which does not mean that it must be inapplicable—unless, of course, it *is*. The available evidence suggests precisely that. For much is indeed known about the ritual structure of these ceremonies from other sources, some of which are quoted by Geertz himself, especially a series of monographs by C. Hooykaas on Balinese Hindu and Buddhist rituals which are almost as detailed and precise as our monographs on Vedic ritual because they are based not merely upon Hooykaas' observation of performance but also upon *competence*, that is, the knowledge and traditions of the officiating priests. (Hooykaas was not familiar with Vedic ritual until a few years before his death in 1979; he was much impressed by Diehl's 1956 book on South Indian agamic rituals: see Hooykaas 1964:17).

Hooykaas' oeuvre (which is a culmination of earlier investigations by Dutch scholars such as Goris, Grader, Swellengrebel and others) has established that Balinese culture is in one respect very similar to Indian, and especially Vedic, culture: what we tend to label as "religion" consists there almost entirely of complexes of mantras and rites. While processions, towers and fires are among their more spectacular manifestations, these complexes themselves are elaborate constructions that are in many specific respects similar to the Vedic ceremonies. They may also be of equally ample proportions. For example, an extended ceremony called *Ekādaśarudra* ("The Eleven Rudras"), reputedly celebrated only once in a century, was performed in April 1963 in Besakih on the slope of Gunung Agung (cf. Hooykaas 1973:167–249). Allegedly Buddhist, it refers to the same Rudra who is addressed on the eighth day of the Agnicayana by the Adhvaryu when the Udgātā sings his Flow of Milk (above, page 303). (Such cultural diffusion or Indianization is familiar to Indologists. Another ceremony from the Agnicayana, "Flow of Wealth" [*vasor dhārā*: above, page 75], turns up in Nepal, centuries later, as a popular Buddhist goddess.) These ritual complexes are celebrated on all kinds of occasions and may be used to express all kinds of things: myths, history, ideologies, power relationships, status, political and personal ambitions, etc.; but in no case is there an intrinsic and necessary relation between the rites or mantras and what they are called upon to express. That Geertz had an inkling of this may be inferred from two paragraphs of the Bali monograph that are of particular methodological interest and deserve to be quoted in full (Geertz 1980:103).

> The Balinese, not only in court rituals but generally, cast their most comprehensive ideas of the way things ultimately are, and the way that men therefore should act, into immediately apprehended sensuous symbols—into a lexicon of carvings, flowers, dances, melodies, gestures, chants, ornaments, temples, postures, and masks—rather than into a discursively apprehended, ordered set of explicit 'beliefs.' This means of expression makes any attempt to summarize those ideas a dubious business. As with poetry, which in the broad, *poiesis* ('making') sense is what is involved, the message here is so deeply sunk in the medium that to transform it into a network of propositions is to risk at once both of the characteristic crimes of exegesis: seeing more in things than is really there, and reducing a richness of particular meaning to a drab parade of generalities.
>
> But whatever the difficulties and dangers, the exegetical task must be undertaken if one wants to be left with more than the mere fascinated wonderment—like a cow looking at a gamelan orchestra, as the Balinese put it—that Helms, for all his responsiveness and powers of description, displays. Balinese ritual, and most especially Balinese state ritual, does embody doctrine in the literal sense of "teachings," however concretely

> they are symbolized, however unreflectively they are apprehended. Digging them out for presentation in explicit form is not a task for which the Balinese, aside from a few modernists nowadays, have ever had any interest. Nor would they feel, any more than a translated poet ever feels, that any such presentation really gets to the heart of the matter, gets it really right. Glosses on experience, and most especially on other people's experience, are not replacements for it. At the very best they are paths, twisted enough, toward understanding it.

But has Geertz proved his point? Are there teachings, is there a metaphysics ("most comprehensive ideas of the way things ultimately are") or a system of ethics ("the way that men should therefore act") underlying this "lexicon" of carvings, flowers, dances, and so on? Do the ritual ceremonies to which Geertz refers (and rather synoptically characterizes) express teachings about power? And is to deny this facile assumption equivalent to being a cow, or being like that nineteenth century British globe-trotter and sightseer L. V. Helms who authored a travelogue entitled *Pioneering in the Far East and Journeys to California in 1849 and to the White Sea in 1848*? One rather doubts it.

Let us take a closer look at that proverbial cow. What do the Balinese mean when they refer to a cow looking at a gamelan orchestra? That she misses its metaphysics, ethics, teachings or meaning? Well, so do most people, because a gamelan orchestra possesses none of these. What the cow misses and what the connoisseurs appreciate is the structure of the music (its "syntax") and the tonal qualities of its melodies (its "phonetics"). That music expresses meaning like language is a nineteenth century Western belief, inspired by program music, that certainly does not apply to gamelan—a belief about which the *Harvard Dictionary of Music* (1970:696a, quoted above page 176) stated: "About 1900, many persons, particularly writers on music, believed that in order to be understandable music must 'express something' or 'tell a story' . . . Today such views are things of the past . . . " Why, then, should we return to such superstitions when interpreting gamelan, or ritual, for that matter?

I do not deny that what Geertz says about power and politics may be relevant to Balinese culture; but that it constitutes *the* implicit teaching or *the* implicit meaning of the ceremonies he refers to is at least far-fetched. In any case, it would need to be demonstrated. The Balinese are intelligent enough to express their political notions explicitly and in direct terms. They are not cows; they have language and can express their ideas without having to sing or dance them. True, there are all kinds of connexions and relationships, but these hold between all the phenomena that Geertz has enumerated—the rites, the flowers, the chants, the ornaments, the temples, and the political ideas as well. The relationships between all these entities constitute a rich and intricate structure that will undoubtedly be difficult to unravel. That would be a task worthy of an anthropologist, and Geertz himself hinted at the desirability of such an investigative analysis when he claimed that the Balinese cockfight is a "cultural document," "at least as important a revelation of what being a Balinese 'is really like' " as Balinese art and social organization (I quote after Jonathan Lieberson's 1984 review of Geertz' *Local Knowledge* to which I shall return). However, in the *Negara* book, Geertz does the opposite: he isolates and concentrates upon one term as the key that must unlock all the others. Such a move can serve no purpose other than to reveal one's own particular interests and prejudices. Any author is free, of course, to write about whatever he likes. Geertz' book is about politics; but that does not imply that Balinese ritual is about politics. Moreover, to collect ideas and meaning on one side and relegate all concrete entities to the other, and then to postulate one-to-one-correspondences between these two collections, smacks of the kind of naive dualism that Western philosophers are trying so hard to overcome. (Note that this is different from Tambiah, who started with concrete entities [amulets] and postulated an interpretation; Geertz starts with [religious or political] meanings and offers them as interpretations for a variety of concrete entities.)

After having first (in *Cockfights*) claimed that everything hangs together, without demonstrating it, Geertz now (in *Negara*) claims the opposite, viz., that one thing holds the key to everything, or at least much else, again without demonstrating it. The question is not only whether this theory is true; the question is, does it even make sense? How could people be so obsessed by politics and yet so collectively inarticulate as to express it entirely through ceremonies without being able to refer to it in words? Where is the "hermeneutic circle" (referred to on the same page, 103)? Why can we not simply recognize that these ceremonies are rule-governed activities, which we may begin to understand only when we know the rules? Geertz himself suggests this implicity (on the next page) when he compares them, rather more aptly, to a baseball game. Must a baseball game necessarily also teach a lesson, have a meaning, a metaphysics, and an ethic? We all know better: if we wish to know and understand baseball, we must know what the rules are. Subsequently we can discuss its relationships to art, literature, religion and politics. And of course, we may learn about its psychology or anthropology by including spectators' responses and much else. Alan Dundes has done it brilliantly for American football (Dundes 1978).

Long before *Negara*, Geertz had a much better idea about "the religion of Bali." In a 1964 article, reprinted in 1973, he wrote:

> In Java, where the pressure of external influences has been relentless, and where traditional social structure has lost much of its resilience, not just one but several relatively well-rationalized systems of belief and worship have developed, giving a conscious sense of religious diversity, conflict, and perplexity still quite foreign to Bali. Thus, if one comes, as I did, to Bali after having worked in Java, it is the near total absence of either doubt or dogmatism, the metaphysical nonchalance, that almost immediately strikes one. That, and the astounding proliferation of ceremonial activity. The Balinese, perpetually weaving intricate palm-offerings, preparing elaborate ritual meals, decorating all sorts of temples, marching in massive processions, and falling into sudden trances, seem much too busy practising their religion to think (or worry) very much about it (Geertz 1973:175–176).

Geertz then remarks that "to say that Balinese religion is not methodically ordered is not to say that it is not ordered at all," and goes on briefly to describe three "relatively well-defined *ritual* complexes which exhibit, in turn, a definite approach to properly religious issues no less respectable for being implicit" (my italics). It is a pity that Geertz has not pursued the study of these ritual complexes on their own terms, and instead has constructed from his own imagination (that is, religious background) the allegedly implicit but "properly religious" issues. But now we see something surprising happen. In the *Negara* book, these issues are no longer religious but turn out to be political. It is difficult to reconstruct the meanderings of other minds, but can it be that we witness the result of a merger between two erroneous assumptions, viz., (1) ritual must express something and (2) ritual must express religion, in the manner, say, of a "hermeneutic circle?" That would explain the "hopping back and forth between the whole conceived through the parts that actualize it and the parts conceived through the whole that motivates them" (Lieberson 1984:40, apparently after Geertz). It might also explain the contradiction between ritual expressing political teachings—the main thesis of the book—and such expressions as "a royal cremation was not an echo of a politics" (page 120) or "to construe the expressions of the theatre state, to apprehend them as theory" is "prejudice" (page 136).

So let us return to things "properly religious." Any reader would expect such things to possess at least a proper religious affiliation. But in Bali, as in Sri Lanka, Burma, Thailand, the other countries of Southeast Asia, and indeed in Nepal and on the Indian subcontinent itself, it is often impossible to make a sharp distinction between Hindu, Buddhist, and "animist." Geertz had noted this with respect to Javanese Islam, which is permeated by Hindu and animist notions, and even though he sometimes refers to "Hindu Bali," he is careful when mentioning Hinduism ("is that what the Balinese great tradition should be called?" page 46). What we actually find in Bali is a *ritual* in which features that can be differently labelled when one looks at their historical origins have merged—just as in Sri Lanka (see Obeyesekere, *passim*), and just as in Thailand where we meet with an amalgam of Buddhism and "animism" as Tambiah pointed out in his refutation of Spiro's attempt to keep the two distinct.

One reason that labels such as Hinduism and Buddhism are not to be taken too seriously is that doctrines and beliefs are not as important as in Western religion; what counts instead is ritual affiliation, lineages, initiation, cults and practice (see AGNI II: xiv–xv). This is precisely what was missing in Geertz' observation quoted above page 327, and explains why things that appear incompatible from a doctrinal point of view are easily combined: they are not doctrinal, but ritual. If Geertz had pursued his study of Balinese ritual complexes and not persisted in his search for religious meaning, he would not have missed a discovery that would have been a fitting climax to his two earlier findings, viz., that the "religion" of Java is not like a religion in the Western monotheistic sense, and the "religions" of Indonesia and Morocco, though both labelled "Islam," are not a single religion in that sense either. For in Bali, Geertz was on the verge of making an even more momentous discovery, viz., that there, as in many of the traditional societies of South, Southeast and East Asia, rituals are not necessarily associated with doctrinal superstructures or belief systems; that is, they are *rituals without religion*.

The use of such words as "proper" and "properly" is very revealing about the prejudices of an author. Part of what Geertz apparently had in mind before he ever set foot on Balinese soil, although he need at no time to have been fully aware of it, is that the Balinese *must* have a *proper religion*. It is ironic that Hooykaas made a similarly revealing slip in his own domain; and Geertz did not fail to notice it. Amin Sweeney drew my attention to the memorable exchange (memorable, that is, if one tends to remember abusive oratory) that took place between Geertz and Hooykaas in the French journal *Archipel* (1976) on the occasion of Hooykaas' review of the Geertzes' book *Kinship in Bali* (1975). Hooykaas demonstrated in subtle, not so subtle, and downright awkward ways that the Geertzes had many facts wrong and were not very familiar with the scientific literature on Bali. Anyone who checks the list of alleged mistakes will concede that Hooykaas was right in almost every case; but Geertz, declaiming eloquently on anthropology and philology in his felicitous style, got the better of his adversary and the uncritical reader's sympathy will rest with him. In two cases (pages 25 and 134), Hooykaas' criticism is simply lost on Geertz because when the latter wrote his rebuttal he still did not know he did not know the sources that Hooykaas criticized him for not knowing.

In the course of his review, Hooykaas quoted the third sentence of the Geertzes' book in the following context:

> Several years ago a team of TV reporters interviewed the Paris public, trying to find out what it still knew about Stalingrad after a quarter of a century. The results were devastating. I have only to remind the author of the third clause of his own book: 'Two fully cooperative and intelligent Balinese from the same village may give completely variant accounts on matters that the ethnologist believes to be crucial for his formulations.' Quite so, but then why not consult proper books? (page 241).

Geertz replied that his sentence "states the conditions of an ethnographer's work, the very shape of the 'fact' he is investigating, and the challenge and possibility his subject offers him, not something to be got round by consulting 'proper books' " (page 225).

That Hooykaas' bias is "books" is not surprising; but that Geertz' bias is "religion" is. For, as an anthropologist, Geertz should be especially cautious when it comes to projecting concepts from his own culture. We have seen that Geertz was cautious in his Java book, despite its easily misleading title; in the Bali book he is less prudent although the Western concept of religion is even less applicable there.

At a closer look, the exchange between Geertz and Hooykaas demonstrates that the two fighting cocks agree at least to some extent on the importance of written sources; and this agreement reveals a shared bias which might not mar our understanding of, say, Islam or China, but which is another obstacle to the understanding of Balinese—and indeed, most South and Southeast Asian—culture. The issue is an interesting one. Hooykaas quotes Geertz at some length, and I shall do the same especially because the quote comes from an earlier (1964) paper that in the meantime has become well-known and has been reprinted in Geertz 1973 (where the quote now occurs on page 185). Hooykaas writes (page 237) with reference to this 1964 paper:

> Here Geertz tells us about post-war Bali, to be exact the year 1957, that new era (after centuries of manuscript copying) of mimeographed and sometimes even printed pamphlets. Some of them are done in Balinese and others in Roman script, some of them in Balinese language and others in Indonesian. Nearly weekly they were produced by publishers, in the island-capital Denpasar mainly, but also in the provincial capitals Gianyar, Klungkung and Tabanan (names not to be forgotten). 'When I bought some books of this sort,' Geertz writes on p. 297, 'and left them around our house in the village, our front porch became a literary center where groups of villagers would come and sit for hours on end and read them to one another, commenting now and then on their meaning, and almost invariably remarking that it was only since the Revolution that they had been permitted to see such writings, that in the colonial period the upper castes prevented their dissemination altogether. This whole process represents, thus, a spreading of religious literacy beyond the traditional priestly castes—for whom the writings were in any case more magical esoterica than canonical scriptures—to the masses, a vulgarization, in the root sense, of religious knowledge and theory. For the first time, at least a few ordinary Balinese are coming to feel that they can get some understanding of what their religion is all about; and more important, that they have a need for and a right to such understanding.'

If I had to review this passage I would probably comment on those righteous, anti-colonial and democratic Americans with their open houses and canonical scriptures. Perhaps I would add that it is at least conceivable that the visiting anthropologist's house was more comfortable and spacious than many others in the village; or remark on the, at least apparent, inconsistency inherent in the notion of a priestly class that does not understand the meaning of the very writings they themselves composed. But Hooykaas, who was more knowledgeable about Bali than I shall ever be, and also more kindly disposed even under duress, reacted as follows:

> The painful reality is that the author here straight-away believed a few young village lads, probably not yet born when in 1928 the Kirtya Foundation for palmleaf manuscripts was created in the then capital Singaraja. Soon it had its own modest building: a spacious room for clerks and European books of reference on Bali and Lombok, a very sufficient store for the well-preserved manuscripts, a well-visited room for anybody interested, opened by the then acting Governor-General.

Hooykaas continues in this vein, informing us how that Kirtya library, which now lodges some 3700 manuscripts and which during the colonial period wrote and financed a dozen publications, was a standard reference library on Bali and Lombok. About the frequent visits he made there in the late thirties and early forties, Hooykaas says, "I cannot remember that the readers' room was ever unoccupied."

Geertz replied that the "young village lads" who spent time on his porch were in fact "men of all ages, including ones born not only before 1928 but even before Hooykaas" . . . and so on it goes. One hopes that, should his essay be reprinted again, Geertz will not withhold from his readers this information on the Kirtya library (about which he wrote in his reply that it "has done invaluable work"). It is tempting to say more about this exchange, especially about colonialism—for example, that the Dutch, British and French, whatever their atrocities, left a splendid scholarly record of the cultures, languages, and histories of the countries where they committed them, whereas the Americans, who were almost successful in destroying the country, never even left room in their system of higher education for studying Vietnam (see Staal 1970b).

In the present context, the important issue is the following. Geertz' assumption that the Balinese could never get any understanding of "what their religion is all about" until they could read their canonical scriptures clearly shows that he does not understand at all what Balinese "religion" is. Hooykaas does not commit such a basic mistake, although both he, the philologist, and Geertz, the anthropologist, share the same Western prejudice in favor of written books. But Hooykaas objects at least to the expression "holy writings" (page 239) which Geertz uses freely. In fact, Hooykaas objects on several counts to Geertz' uses of "holy" and "sacred"—expressions that Hooykaas quite rightly says are "highly laden technical terms from the field of divinity/theology and should not be used easily." All these errors are amusing and entertaining, but Geertz' error has in addition far-reaching implications. For if a people can get no understanding of what their religion is all about without reading their canonical scriptures, the Indians must have been ignorant about their religion for the better part of 2,500 years.*

We have seen that Tambiah was not averse to introducing a bit of technical jargon even if it is not always clear what good it does. Geertz goes much further and likes to flirt with contemporary ideas whatever their nature or provenance. The "hermeneutic circle" is as dear to him as "deep structure," though "deep play" has nothing to do with the latter; for "deep structure" is a technical term with a very precise meaning whereas "deep play" is a nice way of expressing the claim Geertz first made and then abandoned, as we have just seen. In linguistics, a "deep structure" is an abstract underlying syntactic structure, which has to meet certain conditions of well-formedness, and which is postulated in order to provide a starting point for derivations of "surface structures" with the help of rules that also meet specific conditions of well-formedness. In Geertz, "deep play" is an activity that seems innuocuous and irrelevant, but that in fact expresses important issues (such as, in the case of the Balinese cockfight, honor and status). However, this terminology has no interesting implications as in the case of linguistics: for while Chomsky and his followers studied deep structures in order to find universal structures, which underlie all human languages, on Geertz' view "there may be no interesting general laws of culture, or of anthropology, to discover" (Lieberson 1984:45; cf. Geertz 1985). "Thick descrip-

* Even in Islam, "reading canonical scriptures" is not a prerequisite for being a good Muslim: Quran means "recitation" and "the main stress is always on recitation and on the rote learning necessary to it" (observed by Geertz himself in Morocco: 1983:110–112).

tion," similarly, is a spin-off from Gilbert Ryle, as Geertz acknowledges, but without the subtleties that Ryle attached to what is after all a piece of semantic observation that stands in need of a theoretical analysis—an analysis that neither Ryle nor Geertz made any attempt at providing.

The emphasis on religion and accordingly on *meaning* that we meet with in Geertz' later work raises a host of philosophical problems. We have seen in Chapter 3 how logicians and linguists have tried to come to terms with problems of meaning. This can be done provided we are working within a theoretical framework that is well developed—as are logical syntax and semantics. But ideas or phrases taken out of their (theoretical) context will never be helpful, as even a minimum of analysis can demonstrate.

Let us consider the idea from the confines or suburbs of communication theory that has especially appealed to Geertz, as we have already seen, of "a message sunk in the medium." Now, a message is always sent in order to convey meaning; a meaningless message is no message. A message also needs a medium, by means of which it is conveyed—e.g., a telephone. Let us take the simple example of a message left on my telephone answering machine, saying: "Mr. W. will not come this afternoon." What would it mean, in such a context, to refer to that message as "sunk in the medium?" It seems to convey something like: there is no message apart from and beyond the medium. In other words, the message that Mr. W. will not come has disappeared in the medium, viz., the telephone. Ordinarily, a telephone message is a message sent *through* a telephone. The expression "sunk in the medium" suggests that the telephone message is not independent of the telephone; in fact, in the limiting case, when the message is completely "sunk," the telephone is all of the message. There are not two entities, message and medium; there is only one left. But this does not make any sense, unless it merely means that there *is* no message, but that we have a substance that is interpreted as a medium but that is not a medium through which anything passes: the telephone interpreted as a message by itself. Like someone arriving home, seeing his telephone and exclaiming: it must be that Mr. W. has telephoned and left the message that he will not come this afternoon! But since there is no message, this exclamation is mere fantasy—an expression of disappointment, perhaps, or a wish—that has nothing to do with either medium or message.

It is likely that Geertz did not have telephones in mind when he invoked the idiom; but the communication engineers who introduced the terminology were very much concerned with such media. It is accordingly unclear to what extent any part of their theory applies to anthropology. Why, then, should Geertz wish to make use of such unhelpful constructions, that become obscure as soon as they are detached from their original context? There are several possible answers, but the best one can do is study illustrations he provides himself. Geertz refers to *poiesis*, "making" or "doing," as such an activity where the message is "sunk in the medium." What he means, apparently, is that it is impossible to do justice to a poem by formulating its meaning as something separate from the particular form in which it has been expressed in the poem. But why emphasize meaning at all? Why not accept what poets say themselves, namely, that poems are made not with ideas (meanings) but with words? If one starts with the primacy of meaning, and then picks on a particular way of expressing it, one is finally forced to insist that, in some cases, the meaning is not to be separated from its particular expression. It is obviously preferable from a methodological point of view to proceed differently, and to accept a poem as a datum that may be interpreted on one or more levels, as the need arises, and without ignoring the concrete formal structure which is in any case part of it. That method has been put to good use by linguistic interpreters of poetry, e.g., Roman Jakobson. Such interpretations show that the formal structure of a poem makes a specific contribution to the explanation of its expressive power. Each piece of analysis that Jakobson has given contains such a specific discovery.

Geertz believes that art cannot be understood by a formal structural analysis of "sounds, images, volumes, themes, or gestures'' (1983:96). Such statements, however, are uninteresting as well as unconvincing. They are uninteresting because they can never be demonstrated, and unconvincing because in specific cases they have already been refuted. Moreover, such positive cases of analysis as were given, for example, by Jakobson, may lead to a general theory, unlike any belief that ''it cannot be done.''

I have spent some time on this discussion about poetry because it throws light on the problems in anthropology we have been discussing. The study of ritual deals with *activities*, and *poiesis* is the general word in Greek for ''activity.'' *Poiesis* corresponds to Sanskrit *karman*, from the root *kṛ-*, ''do,'' ''make,'' which signifies ''activity'' and in particular ''ritual activity.'' The corresponding Latin is *actum*, ''done,'' the past passive participle of *agere*, ''to do.'' The plural *acta*, ''(things) done,'' corresponds to Greek *dromena*, ''activities,'' which also refers to ritual activities.

In ritual we are primarily dealing with sounds and acts, and these correspond to each other. Our main confusions in this area are due to the facts that ''sound'' reminds us of language, and that ''act'' seems to be something simple. About sound and language I have said enough, but with regard to acts it should be emphasized that they are not simple. I can illustrate this no better than by quoting Austin (1961:126–127): ''The beginning of sense, not to say wisdom, is to realize that 'doing an action,' as used in philosophy, is a highly abstract expression—it is a stand-in used in the place of any (or almost any?) verb with a personal subject, in the same sort of way that 'thing' is a stand-in for any (or when we remember, almost any) noun substantive, and 'quality' a stand-in for the adjective . . . So we come easily to think of our behaviour over any time, and of a life as a whole, as consisting of doing now action A, next action B, then action C, and so on, just as elsewhere we come to think of the world as consisting of this, that and the other substance or material thing, each with its properties. . . . If we are to continue to use this expression in sober philosophy, we need to ask such questions as: Is to sneeze to do an action? Or is to breathe, or to see, or to checkmate, or each one of countless others? . . . Further we need to realize that even the 'simplest' named actions are not so simple—certainly are not the mere making of physical movements, and to ask what more then, comes in (intentions? conventions?) and what does not (motives?), and what is the detail of the complicated internal machinery we use in 'acting''—the receipt of intelligence, the appreciation of the situation, the invocation of principles, the planning, the control of execution and the rest." And in another essay, published in the same volume (page 224), Austin writes: "Philosophers at least are too apt to assume that an action is always in the last resort the making of a physical movement, whereas it's usually, at least in part, a matter of convention."

It might seem at first sight that anthropologists would be the last to make the latter mistake; after all, they are not (or rarely) inspired by the physical sciences and are professionally interested in "conventions." However, they do tend to assume, mistakenly, like many other practitioners of the humanities and the social sciences, that actions must be done intentionally, purposefully, and meaningfully, and must therefore possess a meaning or even incorporate a message that someone wishes to send us. This is precisely what contradicts the chance-like association between mantras and acts discussed in Chapter 24, to which I referred as "inner chance development."

The anthropological studies discussed in the present chapter exhibit another chance-like development which supplements the former and to which I shall refer as "outer chance development." It corresponds to the *accretion* referred to by Schipper (see Schipper and Staal, forthcoming), and is found in each of the three anthropological studies as when Obeyesekere writes with respect to mythology (above page 324): "Any mythological tradition comes from historically diverse sources." As we noted, this is characteristic of ritual traditions as well. It is obvious that the result of chance encounters cannot be meaningful in the manner ritual is generally described and always conceived. To assume that we are dealing with a meaningful unit would be just as unreasonable as to suppose that the Christmas tree refers to or is the same as the tree of knowledge of good and evil mentioned in the paradise story of *Genesis*.

Outer chance developments arise when different cultures or features of different cultures come together by chance and combine into new structures. We have seen such elements—"Hindu," "Buddhist," "Muslim," "animist"—come together and form "mixtures," "amalgams," "totalities," "syncretisms"—whatever scholars have called them—in Thailand, Sri Lanka, Java and Bali, and we could adduce similar instances from other areas of South, Southeast and East Asia. Although these combinations can sometimes be explained from or at least against a historical background, they are obviously not developments that may be described as intentional or meaningful activities. They are chance encounters. That they can be combined at all is due to the fact that the resulting structures are ritual. There are hardly any restrictions as to the combination of ritual acts with each other. We can combine the making of an oblation with the singing of a song, the killing of an animal, the lighting of a candle or the crossing of a bridge. Doctrines or beliefs, on the other hand, do not equally easily combine because they have to be consistent with each other in order to do so. We shall study this in greater detail in Chapter 28A, but we can already conclude that the development of ritual structures from *external* elements is often due to chance.

Inner chance developments arise within a ritual tradition as in the cases discussed in Chapter 24 where the verse of Rigveda 9.1.1 with its various ritual applications yielded different examples of chance events, which cannot be explained in terms of intentions, purpose or meaning. In each case the verse was associated with a rite for no apparent reason—like the windblown seed that settles on a particular spot. One could not go so far as to claim that, on each of these three occasions, *any* other verse would do; but there are certainly many verses that could be used. We conclude that the development of ritual structures from both *external* and *internal* elements is often due to chance.

Discussions on culture and nature are more often inspired by metaphysical issues than by empirical data. In some cases, however, definite conclusions have been established, and they do not always point in the same direction. The recent debates on animal language have clearly led to the conclusion that animals, although certainly capable of communication with each other and thus of conveying messages and information, do not possess language in the human sense. The human animal, thus characterized by language, is often actually obsessed by it; but that does not imply that every activity he engages in is language-like, and accordingly meaningful. Unless we can show that in all cases they are not, we must therefore allow the possibility that some human activities are meaningless and governed by chance. To construct a world of meaning where there is none is mythology and not a substitute for finding the truth. Ritual ceremonies provide the unbiased observer with so many unexplained mysteries, that is it likely that we should conclude that some are simply due to chance. We have found two kinds of evidence that clearly supports such a conclusion.

Our evidence has been drawn from Asia, but if relevant, it must also occur elsewhere. Geertz' Bali book provides an example, together with a final illustration of his own bias. For Geertz does not like chance, and when the evidence clearly points at it, he looks the other way. In a note in the Bali book (page 216), he quotes the following passage from Giesey (1960), a student of royal funerals in fifteenth- and sixteenth-century France: "Time and time again . . . I have emerged with the conviction that some crucial innovation in the ceremonial first occurred quite haphazardly . . . and later generations when re-enacting it embellished it with clear-cut symbolism. This is to say, on the level of events themselves, chance frequently reigned; but symbolic forms affected the thought. . . ." Geertz agrees with this "picture of irregular evolution . . . regularized by post hoc interpretation and adjustment," but he adds, significantly: " 'chance,' I think, is not quite the right word."

What is remarkable about Giesey's formulations (which include "haphazardly'.' as well as "chance") is not that they simply picture "irregular evolution," but that they closely resemble biological explanations—presumably without any knowledge of such types of analysis on the part of Giesey (since otherwise he would doubtless have mentioned it). For "crucial innovations in the ceremonial first occurring quite haphazardly . . . later embellished with clear-cut symbolism" is strikingly similar to "variations arising by chance . . . later selected in accordance with the demands of the environment." The latter expression has been used to characterize those fundamental tenets of Darwinism that have not been modified or abandoned in the expanded versions of Darwinism that took shape in the 1930's and 1940's (Stebbins and Ayala 1985:72). When a *biological* explanation of a *ritual* fact is so plausible in terms of available methodologies, it makes good scientific sense to pursue it and not to take refuge in semantic theories that are unsubstantiated.

Our conclusion that chance plays an important role in ritual is now well established but it is not altogether new. Jonathan Smith (1982:53) quoted two stories from Kafka and Plutarch, respectively, each illustrating the same:

> Leopards break into the temple and drink the sacrificial chalices dry; this occurs repeatedly, again and again; finally it can be reckoned on beforehand and becomes a part of the ceremony.

> At Athens, Lysimache, the priestess of Athene Polias, when asked for a drink by the mule drivers who had transported the sacred vessels, replied, "No, for I fear it will get into the ritual."

Part IV

The Human Sciences

26

The Science of Ritual

To most Western scholars and Westerners generally, science is a characteristically Western achievement. Whether science is considered a panacea or a curse, it is the West that receives the praise or blame. Confirming the myth of "le miracle grec", the origins of science have been sought and found in Greece. It has long been customary to claim that Greek science, especially geometry, in its abstract and pure forms, presents a basic contrast to the practical concerns of the ancient Egyptians, who had to partition lands along the Nile, but never obtained more general insights or searched knowledge for its own sake. True, both Egyptians and Greeks knew how to construct a right angle with the help of a triangle with sides of 3, 4, and 5 units' length; but while the Greeks derived this as a theorem, to the Egyptians it allegedly remained a mere carpenter's rule. In this miserable role, the Egyptians have been appointed as representatives of all non-Greek civilizations of this world.

Modern research on the history of science has shown that such a picture is neither adequate nor justified. Babylonian mathematics and astronomy, for example, have been proved to be subjects of considerable interest. It is true that modern science, as it developed in the West since the sixteenth century, far surpasses almost anything that came before. However, it neither follows from this that science originated only in the West, nor that its later achievements took place only there. That the early developments of science are not confined to Europe has been established beyond any doubt in numerous publications. Though Neugebauer's work on the Ancient Near East may be pronounced a close second, this is nowhere put forward more impressively than in Joseph Needham's volumes on 'Science and Civilisation of China', a series that is still in progress. Many volumes of this monumental work deal with the physical or 'positive' sciences, though a fair amount of space is taken up by what we would regard as technology. For India, we do not possess any such standard work. There are numerous monographs in the field, from early attempts such as Brajendranath Seal's 'The Positive Science of the Ancient Hindus' of 1915, to contemporary publications of the Department of Mathematics and Astronomy of the University of Lucknow, comprising a series of texts edited by Ram Ballabh, Kripa Shankar Shukla and others, also in progress; an ongoing series of publications by the National Institute of Science at New Delhi, and another ongoing project of manuscript inventories entitled *Census of the Exact Sciences in Sanskrit* by David Pingree. For comparisons between Greek, Indian and Babylonian mathematics, see Seidenberg 1962, 1972, 1978 and 1983.

Most of these publications deal with the so-called "positive" sciences, but we have seen in Chapter 5 that the ancient Indians developed also a science of a different kind: the science of linguistics. The present section deals with another Indian science: the science of ritual. I could have called it "The Indian Science of Ritual" were it not for the fact that no other culture or civilization has developed any such science, as far as I know: the only science of ritual mankind has evolved is the Indian science of ritual. Both sciences—of language and of ritual—are, at least apparently, "human sciences." If we assume that there is a hierarchy among the human sciences, we should expect that the science of language is situated at the base of this hierarchy, for it studies the most basic feature in which humans differ from the other animals. At the top of the hierarchy one would hope for sciences to deal with the more lofty features and expressions of the human spirit such as religion, art, mysticism, and ritual. The two sciences of ritual and language at the opposite ends of such an as yet entirely hypothetical hierarchy hold promise for the development of a full range of intermediate sciences that deal with the human animal in all its richness and complexity.

It has been claimed that many of the characteristic features of man cannot be dealt with by scientific methods; an argument that we shall subject to closer scrutiny in Chapter 29. So far we have found (in Chapter 2) that science is not as narrow as many empiricists, positivists, phenomenologists and hermeneuticians have assumed. It is not confined to behavior, appearances, quantities, tangibles, or measurable entities. As for "scientific method," almost anything goes, provided we arrive at hypotheses that account for the data. To support the claim that the ancient Indians did not only develop a science of language, but also a science of ritual, it is necessary to say more about the concept of science that underlies such a claim. The following sketch is not a philosophy of science, but lists a few rules of thumb intending to show that, if it is justified to call chemistry, economics, archeology, or demography sciences, it is justified also to regard the occupation with ritual that we find in the Śrauta Sūtras as such.

I regard the following four features as characteristics of science, and present, though in varying degrees, in the sciences I am familiar with:

(1) A science consists in part of a body of statements, rules, theorems, or theories which aim at the true description and analysis of some part of the world. There must be a measure of empirical adequacy to these, which can be established, not necessarily for all of them, by tests, verifications, or falsifications, directly, indirectly, or at least in principle.

(2) Complementing and extending this empirical adequacy, there are abstract statements that go beyond the data, and may be hypothetical, postulated, or speculative. Such statements may include predictions, and be based upon anything (e.g., a scientist's intuitions or dreams).

(3) This entire edifice of descriptions and generalizations should be consistent to some extent; in particular, contradictory statements can never be regarded as final. However, in most cases it is not easy to ascertain whether two statements, even if fully explicit, are contradictory.

(4) There is a methodology of argument which addresses itself to different viewpoints and propositions, and proceeds to a shifting of options so as to reach a generally accepted conclusion. The abstract statements mentioned under (2) are sometimes arrived at through such a process. Logical derivations within a theory may be regarded as formalized specimens of such argumentation.

These characteristics are fairly vague, not operational, and not free from redundancy. There may be sciences that are not in accordance with some of them (e.g., mathematics). However, these characteristics are sufficient for my present purpose. As a fifth one might add a feature that emphasizes the pure and theoretical nature of science. This feature was much admired by the Greek philosophers. Aristotle commented favourably upon the notion of *θεωρία* as 'desinterested contemplation'. Since some of my colleagues who claim to be scientists also claim that they deal with what they deal with because it is ultimately useful or relevant, I shall not include this feature. When necessary, we may simply distinguish between 'pure' and 'applied' science.

The Indian disciplines of ritual and grammar, which I have come to regard as sciences, were in ancient India called *śāstra*. This term has been translated as 'traditional discipline' or 'traditional science'. However, I would not regard everything that used to be called *śāstra* as 'science'. At an earlier period, ritual and grammar were considered *vedāṅga*, or '(disciplines) auxiliary to the Vedas'. There existed a certain complementarity between these two. In order to explain this, we need some conceptual and terminological clarification.

Grammar, Sanskrit: *vyākaraṇa*, is a discipline which has language for its object. In the work of Pāṇini, the object-language is to some extent *chandas*, 'the metrical portions of the Vedas', viz., *mantras*; and to some extent *bhāṣā*, the spoken language of Pāṇini's time, which has been shown to be co-extensive with the domain of Vedic prose (primarily, the Brāhmaṇas, Āraṇyakas, early Upaniṣads, and Śrauta Sūtras).

Ritual is an ambiguous term. On the one hand it refers to a

discipline, the 'science of ritual', which is embodied, in the Vedic realm, in the Gṛhya and Śrauta Sūtras; and on the other hand it refers to the *object* of this discipline. The two chief types of ritual text correspond to the two chief types of object-ritual (page 66): the *gṛhya* or domestic ritual which comprises so-called life-cycle rites or sacraments and the *śrauta* ritual, which is more abstract and complex. Like in the rest of this book, I am mainly concerned with the latter, because it exhibits the general features of ritual more clearly and explicitly, and has also been studied in the Śrauta Sūtras in a more thorough and scientific manner.

The main technical device that the Indian sciences of language and ritual introduced and continue to use is the concept of *sūtra* that corresponds to the contemporary concept of *rule* developed in contemporary linguistics especially since Chomsky (Chapter 6). The convergence of these two concepts is remarkable for although both operate with linguistic evidence, the Western notion was partly inspired by the mathematical sciences and logic, whereas the Indian notion originated in the context of ritual. The related abstract concepts that contributed to the development of Indian linguistics: categories such as meta-rules, other meta-linguistic markers, features and elements, ordered sequences and systems of rules of Chapter 5 also originated in a ritual context. These devices and mechanisms enabled the Indian ritualists to describe and analyze the complex structures discussed in Chapters 10 through 12.

The art of composing in sūtra style originated in the Śrauta Sūtra of Baudhāyana (not later than the sixth century B.C.E.: Caland 1903:11) and culminated in Pāṇini, who went farthest in the direction of formalization (Renou 1963:180,198). The "meta-rules" (*paribhāṣā*) of Indian science also occur for the first time in Baudhāyana. They were grouped together at the end of his Śrauta Sūtra in a special section called *karmānta*, "end of the *karman* section" (cf. the Vedānta or "end of the Vedas," which came into being much later). Gonda has recently translated and summarized the beginning of this section (Gonda1977:509–510). According to Gonda, this section illustrates the original meaning of *paribhāṣā* as a "discourse round the text." The following excerpts are based upon Gonda's renderings:

> One should understand the ritual procedure from a group of five, viz. from the metrical texts of the Veda (*chandas*, i.e. the *mantra* portions of the Taittirīya Saṃhitā), the *brāhmaṇa*, conviction or certainty as a ground or means of action, by means of the method (*nyāya*), and by means of the structure (*saṃsthā*). When we say 'From the metrical texts of the Veda' that means that one should, in accordance with the order of the *mantras* observed in the tradition, conclude: 'this act must be performed first, this later'. Moreover, the very *mantra* announces the ritual act, and explains the act . . . What one cannot execute by means of the metrical texts one should try to execute by means of the *brāhmaṇa*, for the *brāhmaṇa* prescribes with authority the purport of the undefined *mantras*, viz. 'he performs this act with this mantra, that with that'. For example, if the text mentions the *mantra* 'For refreshment (food) thee, for strength thee' (TS 1.1.1a) he cuts off a certain branch . . . Moreover, a *brāhmaṇa* prescribes also the purport of acts that are not accompanied by *mantras*, when for instance it reads: 'At a distance of eight steps a brahmin should establish the sacred fire . . . .' ([Taittirīya Brāhmaṇa] 1.1.4.1) . . . As to the expression 'by means of structure', when the Soma has been stolen one should extract juice from *ādāra* or *phālguna* plants.

The last phrase seems to refer to substitutions, which are always justified provided the structure of the ritual is retained. Gonda continues with paraphrases of the text:

> Section 2 deals with some fundamental concepts relating to *mantras*, sacrificial rites etc. which are different in practice and applicability (*adhikaraṇa*) . . . In Section 3 an explanation is offered of the distinction between the 'warp' (*tantra*) and the 'woof' (*āvāpa*) of a sacrificial rite, that is of the framework, standing model, or those components which it has in common with other rites, and those that vary from ritual to ritual and are therefore the special characteristic features. In Section 4 the author deals with certain basic forms . . . defines and explains terminology, etc. . . . The seven Soma rituals are enumerated . . . Section 5 answers the question of the difference between the two terms used in the Baudhāyana corpus *pūrvā tatiḥ* and *uttarā tatiḥ* 'the antecedent and the subsequent series of ceremonies'. The standard ritual is *pūrvā tatiḥ* and what one arranges (modifies) is *uttarā tatiḥ*; e.g., the establishment of the ritual fires is *pūrvā tatiḥ*, the re-establishment *uttarā tatiḥ*; of the vegetarian sacrifices (*iṣṭi*), the full and new moon sacrifices are the *pūrvā*

> *tatiḥ*, all the optional rites *uttarā tatiḥ* . . . In Section 6, the author turns to the use of *mantras*, for instance: "One should not, for the sake of a ritual act, interrupt a *mantra*". In case of the immolation of a victim the *mantra* that is handed down is short, the act long, in other cases however the act is short but the *mantra* long . . . .

Baudhāyana is still relatively verbose, but his meta-rules, like all other rules, are formulated more succinctly in the later ritual Sūtras. As a simple illustration of the Indian science of ritual, I provide here a translation of a portion of the twenty-fourth section of the Āpastamba Śrauta Sūtra of the fifth or fourth century B.C.E., first translated into German by Caland (1928), which primarily lists meta-rules:

Āpastamba Śrauta Sūtra 24.1.1–26

(1) *yajñaṃ vyākhyāsyāmaḥ* 'We shall explain that ritual',
(2) *sa trayāṇāṃ varṇānāṃ brāhmaṇarājanyayor vaiśyasya ca* 'it pertains to the three classes, brāhmaṇa, kṣatriya, as well as vaiśya',
(3) *sa tribhir vedair vidhīyate* 'it is enjoined with the three Vedas',
(4) *ṛgvedayajurvedasāmavedaiḥ* 'with the help of Ṛgveda, Yajurveda, and Sāmaveda',
(5) *ṛgvedayajurvedābhyāṃ darśapūrṇamāsau* 'the full and new moon rituals with Yajurveda and Ṛgveda',
(6) *yajurvedenāgnihotram* 'the Agnihotra with the Yajurveda',
(7) *sarvair agniṣṭomaḥ* 'the Agniṣṭoma with all (three)',
(8) *uccair ṛgvedasāmavedābhyāṃ kriyate* '(the rites) are performed with Ṛgveda and Sāmaveda (recited and chanted, respectively) with a loud voice',
(9) *upāṃśu yajurvedena* 'with Yajurveda softly',
(10) *anyatrāśrutapratyāśrutapravarasaṃvādasampraiṣaiś ca* 'except with the ritual call (*o śrāvaya*), answering call (*astu śrauṣaṭ*), *pravara* (lineage), *saṃvāda* (ritual dialogues) and commands',

(11) *antarā sāmidheniṣu anūcyam* 'in the case of the firewood verses the utterance is intermediate',
(12) *mandreṇa prāg ājyabhāgābhyāṃ prātaḥsavane ca* 'at a low pitch before the *ājyabhāga* oblations (in an *iṣṭi*) and at the morning pressing',
(13) *madhyamena prāk sviṣṭakṛto madhyandine ca* 'at a middle pitch before the *sviṣṭakṛt* oblation and at the midday (pressing)',
(14) *kruṣṭena śeṣe tṛtīyasavane ca* 'at a high pitch elsewhere and at the third pressing',
(15) *vāksaṃdravaś ca tadvat* 'and the pace of the voice is similar',
(16) *ṛgvedena hotā karoti* 'the Hotā performs with the Ṛgveda',
(17) *sāmavedenodgātā* 'the Udgātā with the Sāmaveda',
(18) *yajurvedenādhvaryuḥ* 'the Adhvaryu with the Yajurveda',
(19) *sarvair brahmā* 'the Brahman with all (three)',
(20) *vacanād vipratiṣedhād vānyaḥ kuryāt* 'when it is stated explicitly or in case of contradiction another should perform',
(21) *brāhmaṇānām ārtvijyam* 'the priestly functions belong to brahmins',
(22) *sarvakratūnām agnayaḥ sakṛd āhitāḥ* 'in all rites the fires are set up once',
(23) *juhotīti codyamāne sarpirājyaṃ pratīyāt* 'when 'he makes an oblation (*juhoti*)' is enjoined, 'of ghee' should be understood',
(24) *adhvaryu kartāram* 'as agent the Adhvaryu (should be understood)',
(25) *juhūṃ pātram* 'as implement (ladle) the *juhū*',
(26) *vyāpṛtāyāṃ śruveṇa* 'when (the *juhū* is already) used, with the śruva'.

Most of these rules and metarules are clear but some are of a more technical nature. The first serves as a heading or caption for the section that follows, a customary practice in Indian "texts" because they are not texts but oral compositions.

Metarules 2 through 9 are straightforward, and 10 deals with specific exceptions, several pertaining to the Iṣṭi (Chapter 9A). 12–14 capture a generalization that applies at the same time to three subdivisions of the Iṣṭi and to the three pressings of Soma. 15 in its brevity announces the later sūtra-style which is more formulaic: it states, when expanded (as is done in *vṛtti*, "expansion" glosses) that the pace of the voice on the three occasions in both rites (the Iṣṭi and the Soma pressing) is, respectively, slow, medium and fast.

Metarules 16–19 pertain to the "users": they are "pragmatic" rules, if we decide to extent the usage of the term in this manner. With 20 we reach a special case of the principle of contradiction that recurs in similar form and with numerous applications in linguistics, logic, philosophy, and other disciplines (see Staal 1988a:109–128). Metarules 21 and 22 are self-evident. In 23–26, lastly, we have a striking parallel to the structure of Pāṇini's grammar: when nothing else is stated, the entities mentioned (ghee or clarified butter, the Adhvaryu priest, the *juhū* ladle) are understood. When something else is stated, it prevails. For example,

> "he makes the X oblation"

always means:

> "the Adhvaryu makes the X oblation of ghee with the *juhū*."

But if the Sūtra text states, for example,

> "the Pratiprasthātā makes the X oblation"

it means:

> "the Pratiprasthātā makes the X oblation of ghee with the *juhū*."

This is parallel to Pāṇini's metarule 2.3.1 (*anabhihite*: page 44), which states that, in the *kāraka* theory, nothing is expressed more than once. The ritual parallel is more or less obvious.

While in grammar, the rules block an ungrammatical sequence by preventing its derivation, in ritual it prevents impossibilities like two different priests or ladles doing the same thing at the same time and place.

Harold Arnold has drawn attention to another metarule which occurs somewhat later in Āpastamba's *paribhāṣā* section: 24.2.13: *antarāṇi yajñāṅgāni bāhyāḥ kartāraḥ* "the ritual limbs should be inside, the officiating (priests) outside". "Limbs" refers primarily to the implements, and "inside" and "outside" mean closer and less close to the fire. The Śrauta Sūtra of Satyāṣāḍha uses similar expressions. Kātyāyana's Śrauta Sūtra (1.8.31–32) expresses similar restrictions, but in a different way:

(31) *haviṣpātrasvāmyṛtvijāṃ pūrvaṃ pūrvam antaram* 'with respect to closeness to the fire, each comes before the next in the sequence oblation-implement-patron-priest',

(32) *ṛtvijāṃ ca yathāpūrvam* 'and the order of the priests is the order of their election' (viz, in which they were elected at the beginning of the performance).

These distinctions, introduced by the ritualist Kātyāyana, are related to an important distinction introduced by the grammarian Kātyāyana (perhaps the same as the ritualist: Thieme 1937–1938) between the concepts of *antaraṅga* and *bahiraṅga*. These apply in linguistic morphology to internal and external constituents. For example, a rule applicable *within* a word is *antaraṅga* with respect to a rule which applies across word boundaries. The general principle which governs the use of these concepts is defined in terms of the technical concept of *asiddha*, itself defined as follows:

> "Rule A is *asiddha* with respect to rule B" if and only if "Rule A is to be regarded as not having taken effect when rule B is to take effect."

This concept and the specific order of rules to which it applies play a crucial role in grammar (see, e.g., Joshi and Kiparsky 1979). Having defined *asiddha*, we define the use of the pair *antaraṅga/bahiraṅga* by means of a metarule:

> *Bahiraṅga* rules are *asiddha* with respect to *antaraṅga* rules.

Renou has studied the terminological and stylistic similarities between ritual and grammar in an important article (Renou 1941–1942, republished in Staal 1972:434–469). He deals not only with rules and metarules, but also with the use of particles expressing generalizations, options, exceptions or implications, the role of substitutions, primary and derived elements, prototypes and extensions or variations, the distinction between essentials and incidentals, the construction of larger entities from smaller elements, systems of relations, etc. Anyone who wishes to obtain an idea of the connexions between the Indian sciences of ritual and grammar will benefit from this study.

Renou's conclusions with regard to the terminological and stylistic similarities between the two sciences can be extended to the structural, logical and methodological connexions we are concerned with in the present context:

> These stylistic and terminological parallels between ritual and grammatical theory show that we are dealing with disciplines which originated in the same circles, but which answered complementary needs. Both pertain to the practice of the *śiṣṭa*, the specialists . . . When dealing with a particular term, it is not easy to establish whether it originated with the grammarians or the ritualists: in the absence of a fixed chronology of texts, and with the general parallelism of techniques in ancient India, such a search becomes arbitrary. However, in the majority of cases it is clear that the point of departure lies in the religious texts. Grammar appears as a specialized investigation within the larger domain of explicit ritual science. The extent and importance of the religious literature, the undeniable priority of the *mantras* and of the ritual forms which they presuppose, invite us to look for origins in that domain.

Renou's views (which make better sense if we substitute "Vedic" for the two occurrences of the all-too Western term "religious": see Chapter 28) suggest that the Indian science of ritual was earlier than the Indian science of language.

What remains to be shown is that the Indian traditional *śāstra* disciplines of ritual and grammar are indeed sciences in accordance with the four characteristics of science laid down at the outset of this section, viz., empirical adequacy, abstraction, consistency, and methodology. I shall take up these features one by one.

(1) Empirical adequacy. In the Introduction to his Mahabhāṣya, Patañjali has formulated the 'potter's principle' (page 40): 'if you want pots, you go to a potter, but if you want words, you don't go to a grammarian'. Where do you go? To *loka*, the world, for example, the market place where people speak the language. Grammar is a curious enterprise, that may appear circular to those who do not understand it: the grammarians try to derive correct forms, but the correctness of the forms is already known from those who know the language. In fact, in case of conflict, it is the speakers of the language who decide. If grammar provides a derivation of a form that is not used, it is grammar that is wrong. Thus grammar aims at empirical adequacy, and all its efforts are aimed at reaching this goal. Note that this is not different from the situation in physics, that paragon of modern science: physics tries to account for facts with which we are already familiar—e.g., that apples fall.

Ritual science is in precisely the same position. The Śrauta Sūtras account for rituals and rites that are performed in accordance with specific traditions. Accordingly, neither grammars, nor ritual manuals are teaching manuals. They can only be understood by people who are already familiar with the subject. They are composed for the sake of the subject only. Other reasons given are mostly rationalizations.

This characterization implies further that both the Aṣṭādhyāyī and the Śrauta Sūtras are primarily descriptive and not prescriptive. But at this point we have to keep in mind, that what was originally descriptive, has become increasingly prescriptive. Pāṇini's grammar originally reflected the usage of the *śiṣṭas*, those who spoke Sanskrit properly; but to later generations, its expressions became law, and thus contributed to the fixation of Sanskrit. The ritual sūtras have similarly become prescriptive. Some contemporary ritual performances have been revivalistic in precisely this sense: attempts have been made to *follow* particular Śrauta Sūtras. However, there are also living śrauta traditions in India. The Nambudiris, for example, follow their own tradition. When told that Baudhāyana describes certain rites differently, they say 'Interesting', but would not for a moment consider a change in their own proceedings.

The transition from description to prescription indicates increasing dogmatism. We found this already indicated by the *jñāpaka* notion, and the resulting *jñāpakasiddhaparibhāṣās*. The general reverence of the later grammarians for the *trimuni*, 'the three sages', Pāṇini, Kātyāyana, and Patañjali, illustrates this further. Even Patañjali himself accepts Pāṇini as an authority, in whose grammar no single element may be without meaning or purport (*anarthaka*). However, Ojihara (1978:227) has rightly pointed out that this does not imply that Pāṇini's rules are beyond criticism, but that they have to be subjected to a thorough examination in order to find out what is their ultimate motivation (*prayojana*). Wherever precisely we draw the line, the claim that ritual and grammar were sciences in ancient India pertains to the earliest works, the Aṣṭādhyāyī and the Śrauta Sūtras. It does not hold true of the later developments, which did become increasingly dogmatic and scholastic.

One feature of description that has contributed to the development of ritual and grammar in India is the *formal* nature of these disciplines. Emphasis on form is a general characteristic of Indian civilization. The Vedas refer more to the forms of language and rites, than to their meanings or function. The Brāhmaṇas introduce large scale interpretations of ritual, but these can often be shown to be failures. Language is of course concerned with meaning, and semantics is basic to Pāṇini's grammar; however, once the derivations start, they are fully explicit and formal. The Śrauta Sūtras do not provide the rites with any meaning. This inherent formality has contributed significantly to the scientific character of the study of ritual in India.

(2) If grammar, physics and ritual accounted only for what we knew already, the accounting might be interesting but the results would not fail to disappoint us. It is here that abstraction

becomes significant. Much of the discussions around the texts initiated by the *paribhāṣās* are concerned with this dimension. In another famous passage in the Introduction to his commentary, Patañjali has explained that the forms of language are infinite, and so cannot be enumerated; only general rules and exceptions can account for them (page 40). He elucidates this with a reference to ritual, which is equally significant: For the same holds for the *sattras*, or rituals of indefinite duration (page 89). Hillebrandt had ridiculed these thousand-year performances, which obviously no human being can engage in. But they give expression to the recursive procedures which constitute the essence of the ritual of the Śrauta Sūtras, and without which they would constitute not a science, but a mere inventory.

The principle of brevity, expressed by a famous metarule about the saving of half a mora, may contribute to the expression of generalizations, but it is at best a mnemonic device or a game, not a scientific principle. Buiskool, Cardona, and others have shown that Pāṇini's grammar is not actually governed by this principle, but formulates rules through functional generalizations. The minimization of syllables has been an end in itself only among minor grammarians.

(3) Consistency is a matter of description or a feature of a theory; facts are always consistent. In grammar, I have already referred to the rule *vipratiṣedhe paraṃ kāryam*, which would have safeguarded the consistency of the grammar if it had been universally applicable. Whether the Aṣṭādhyāyī is indeed consistent is a matter of continuing discussion. Attempts to save it can be made from various points of view: recourse may be had to emendations of the text, to postulating interpolations, to decomposing and dissecting the text into various layers and portions, or to the *jñāpaka* gymnastics of the later commentators. It is important to note that any of these strategies can only be fruitful when we are dealing with a text such as the Aṣṭādhyāyī, which is basically set up as a logical and rational account of a specific area of experience.

In ritual, the situation is different. There is less scope for inconsistencies to appear because of the variety of options and schools. The Śrauta Sūtras do not recommend or argue for specific options; they merely describe and analyze the tradition they have selected and opted to follow. Do they not then accept the Vedic injunctions (*vidhi*) enjoining certain rituals for certain purposes? No, not explicitly, for the matter has been entirely ritualized. The Vedic *vidhi* is described only in as far as it is part of the formal declaration of intent (*saṃkalpa*) which the yajamāna makes at the outset of a ritual performance. Ritual options, moreover, are compatible, unlike some articles of faith, religious convictions, or philosophical doctrines.

This compatibility is consistent with the characteristics of *outer chance* developments (page 344) and with the explicit declarations of Indian philosophers, e.g., Śaṅkara in the Introduction to his *Vedānta Sūtra Bhāṣya* where he stated that opposing injunctions prompting rites are compatible as options, but opposing truths are incompatible since they contradict each other:

> There is no option as to whether a thing is thus or thus, is or is not. Option depends on human notions. Knowledge of the nature of a thing does not depend on human notions. It depends only on the thing itself. To say with regard to a pillar "it is a pillar or it is a man or it is something else" does not result from correct knowledge. To say that it is a man or something else results from false knowledge. To say that it is a pillar results from correct knowledge, because it depends on the thing itself. Therefore the means of knowing objects, that are existent things, depend on the things themselves (quoted in Staal 1988a: 119).

(4) Methodology, lastly, is implicit in Śaṅkara's observation just quoted: the principle of non-contradiction which is alluded to here and explicitly formulated elsewhere in Indian logic and philosophy was first stated as a metarule in Āpastamba Śrauta Sūtra 24.1.20. Other logical distinctions and principles were formulated in Patañjali's *Mahābhāṣya* or "Great Commentary" on Pāṇini's grammar. It must be assumed that several of these technical insights and devices were known to ritualists and grammarians before Patañjali: for the latter, including Pāṇini, confined themselves to formulating rules and did not adopt the

more discursive commentorial style which Patañjali introduced. In India, logic developed from ritual and grammar; its history, though as checkered as the history of Western logic, developed along different lines (Staal 1988a, pages 37–48). Ritual rules and metarules were subsequently transmitted, via the Mīmāṃsā philosophy of ritual, to other sciences and to the legal systems of the Dharmaśāstra whence they entered Indian jurisprudence.

It is clear that we are entitled to conclude that the Indian works and disciplines dealing with ritual and language may be regarded as specimens of science. The degree of scientificality in all these works need not be the same, and their efficiency and successfulness may vary, but this applies to sciences and scientists everywhere.

There are three final observations to be made. It may come as a surprise to many that ritual has anything to do with science. Is ritual not pervaded by magic and superstition? Is the great achievement of science not that it has emancipated from ritual? In India itself there is ample historical reason for such feelings of ambiguity with respect to ritual. The Upaniṣads, Buddhism, the Vedānta, as well as modern secularism—all declare unanimously that ritual is useless and in fact unworthy. By contrast, the authors of the Śrauta Sūtras obviously believed in the efficacy of ritual. At this point we have to pay attention, however, to a remarkable fact: whatever were the beliefs of the authors of the Śrauta Sūtras, these beliefs did not interfere with their science *at all*. I would go further than this, and claim, that there is no modern or contemporary scholar of ritual—whether a student of religion, a social scientist, or a psychologist—who is as little influenced in his studies by his beliefs as the authors of the Śrauta Sūtras were by theirs. However, what is true of the Śrauta Sūtras, is neither true of the Brāhmaṇas, nor of the later Mīmāṃsā. The Brāhmaṇas indulge in unhampered speculation, and are as arbitrary as contemporary trends in the study of religion. The Mīmāṃsā, on the other hand, is a system of philosophy that adheres to the axiom that the Vedic *dharma* as expressed by the *vidhi* injunctions is conducive to the highest good. The Mīmāṃsā has paid much attention to specific ritual problems; but the Indian tradition is on the whole right in classifying it as *darśana*, 'philosophy'. It became increasingly philosophical when it took to arguing with the Buddhists. The Śrauta Sūtras are different from the Brāhmanas and Mīmāṃsā both, and I regard only their efforts and achievements as scientific in nature.

The mixture of scientific and un- or less scientific works and activities is characteristic of almost any period of the history of science or civilization. It explains Hermann Oldenberg's expression *vorwissenschaftliche Wissenschaft*, "pre-scientific science," which was intended as a characterization of the Brāhmaṇa literature (Oldenberg 1919). Brian Smith (1986:93, note 3) has written that my "science of ritual" "would seem to be an updating of Oldenberg's term." In fact, I have tried to show that the Śrauta Sūtras are scientific, and the Brāhmaṇas un-(rather than: pre-) scientific. Of course, the distinction between the two classes of works is not as hard and fast as the characterization suggests, but this is not at issue. Whether *vorwissenschaftliche Wissenschaft* is a *contradictio in adjecto* is another question. In any case, the term "science" should be confined to what is scientific and not pre-scientific. If Smith were right, Pāṇini's grammar would also have to be regarded as "pre-scientific."

At the outset of this chapter I referred to attempts that were made to establish that science is exclusively Western. In the course of the chapter I have not shown that science in the conventional English sense—that is, "positive" science—did actually originate in India. The reason is simple: it didn't. India has produced great mathematicians and astronomers, and has evolved chemistry, botany, medicine, and other natural sciences. In all these respects, India is on a par with other great civilizations. However, with respect to the human sciences of ritual and grammar, the Indian contributions have not only been outstanding, but unique.

In our contemporary world, the human sciences have been much neglected. It has become a cliché to state that man understands the stars but not himself. The strength of contemporary science lies in the mathematical, physical, and biological sciences. The contributions made by the contemporary humanities and social sciences are comparatively dismal. The best that some of them have evolved is a narrow empiricism. Rational speculation has generally been absent, and theories have been rare and haphazard. There is excitement about fashions but no sense of progress. It has in fact been argued that the sciences of man cannot be sciences, and that they require unique categories such as "Verstehen" that conflict with all rational approaches—as if man could in principle not be studied objectively, that is, studied at all (Chapter 29).

Linguistics is the only field of study that has finally escaped from the traditional humanities and the behavioristic biases of the social sciences, and has emerged as a scientific discipline. It is therefore not in the least surprising that in recent years significant similarities have been discovered between contemporary linguistics and the Indian science of grammar.

In the field of ritual the situation is different. There is nothing in contemporary research that resembles or even approaches the scientific achievements of the Śrauta Sūtras unless it is derived from these sūtras, such as Hubert and Mauss (1897–1898). This is not due to the fact that humans do not engage any longer in ritual. We do, and so do our animal relatives, whose rituals have actually been neglected less. What we lack is not rituals, but ritualists, and a science of ritual. For these reasons it is not merely interesting that the ancient Indians had a science of ritual. Nor is it simply a fact that may help us to better understand India and Indians. The science of the Śrauta Sūtras is the only science of ritual that we are in a position to study and contemplate. It will inspire us once we realize ourselves that we need to create and develop such a science.

The third and last observation I wish to make is this. It is clear that no science of ritual would easily fit into the customary subdivisions of academic disciplines. Though Sanskritists have greatly contributed to the study of ritual, its science does not belong to the humanities as it is independent of language and is moreover concerned with other animals than only people. Nor is it a natural or a social science. Social sciences lack the tools to analyze it (Chapters 14 and 25). Some of these comments apply to linguistics. In the United States, linguistics has been incorporated among the social sciences partly because these were at one time believed to attract financial support more easily than the humanities. Practical considerations aside, the case of ritual demonstrates that existing classifications of the sciences—and especially the alleged distinction between sciences and humanities—lack a serious foundation.

27

Oral Traditions

The human sciences could have originated anywhere and under any circumstances, but from the available evidence it seems that it happened in India some time between 1,000 and 600 B.C.E.. We can now pinpoint some of the reasons. Indians were careful observers of what was going on inside them: thus they discovered that different sounds were produced by different movements of the mouth and the tongue (page 36). They also paid attention to breathing, an attention that sometimes turned into an obsession, and that pertains to the pronunciation of sounds of language, the recitation and chanting of mantras, Yoga, and pulmonary development in general. Long breath and the breathing of mantras such as OṂ and HIṂ (page 275) are therefore not only probable precursors of the sounds of language but also conducive to health—in any case, not worse than jogging.

Other civilizations have also paid attention to breath. In Sufism, mystics speculated on *dhikr* although they rarely went beyond the ascertainment that the term was used in eighteen senses in the Koran. In Taoism, speculations on respiration techniques went farther (see, e.g., Maspero 1950:107–114; Schipper 1982:182,202,206) and empirical observations resulted in sexual gymnastics and healing techniques connected, for example, with accupuncture. In India, similar speculations on *prāṇa* led to similar techniques, connected with diet, massage, Yoga, and sexual gymnastics. Historical connections between China and India, across the (eastern?) Himalayas, have to be assumed. According to Filliozat 1946, followed by Eliade 1969: 413, the influence went from south to north, or west to east, according to Needham 1956:427–428, the other way round. But such isolated techniques, cures, and speculations do not make a science as does a system of structured explanations of the kind characterized in Chapter 26. These observations, therefore, do not refute the idea that the earliest known examples of human sciences are the Indian sciences of ritual and language.

How and why did these sciences originate? "Introversion" is not enough. To explain their origins in detail would be a large undertaking (for more details see Staal 1986b), but the historical development in India shows that their origins are closely related to the fact that ritual and mantras, like language, were orally transmitted and that safeguards for the dependability and fidelity of their transmission with exclusive emphasis on *formal* correctness were required. Both sciences originated from the twofold analysis of the continuous recitation of the Vedas into their "word-for-word" recitation called Padapāṭha (Jha 1973,1975, 1976) and the setting to music of that Padapāṭha immediately after its constitution, that is, around 1,000 B.C.E. (Chapter 5). These investigations led to the analysis of mantras in their ritual setting and to formulating a system of sandhi and other phonological rules. Both types of analysis made use of rules and led to general, theoretical discussions on the notion of rule.

We can only understand this development and what happened subsequently when we take note of a remarkable fact: the art of writing was not known in ancient India. It is possible that a writing system had existed in India before the Indo-European semi-nomads arrived and composed the Vedas. For in the course of excavation of the remnants of the earlier Harappa civilization, a few hundred seals were found which contain symbols or symbolic shapes that could be interpreted as a form of script. At the present state of our knowledge these symbols, which have not been deciphered, may be regarded as a script, ownership marks, astrological formulas, or something else. Whatever their nature, it is clear that there are no links between these 'inscriptions' and the later Indian scripts that are based upon forms introduced into India from the Near East, probably not long before the third century B.C.E It is also clear that there were originally no connections between the semi-nomadic Indo-European groups that entered India from the northwest and composed the Rigveda, and these large and sedentary indigenous city civilizations of earlier centuries and millenia of which only material remnants are left.

The earlier literature contains several references to script, but we do not know what kind of writing the authors had in mind. What is clear is that the first Indian uses were confined to royal edicts and commercial transactions. Writing was alright for keeping accounts but it continued to be emphatically and meticulously excluded from the ancestral traditions which were considered too pure to be written down. The low evaluation of what was regarded as an alien and barbaric invention is illustrated in a variety of quotations, some assembled by Ghurye 1950, others by Staal 1961 (I,1). For example, *Aitareya Āraṇyaka* 5.5.3: a pupil should not recite the Veda 'if he has eaten flesh, or seen blood, or a dead body, or done what is unlawful . . . or had intercourse, or written . . .'.

The most remarkable feature of the Indian scripts is not their shapes but their scientific arrangement which is basically the same in all the many forms with which we are familiar. Instead of the haphazard ABC's of the West, the Indian scripts begin with the series of vowels—basically *a*, *i*, *u*, *e*, *o*, *ai*, *au*—followed by the consistently ordered consonants beginning with *ka*, *kha*, *ga*, *gha*, *nga*, etc. It has been noted long ago that this arrangement shows that the scientific analysis of the sounds of language was completed in India *before* any script was introduced, and was so widely known that the newly introduced invention was adapted to this analysis as a matter of course. Renou and Filliozat (1953:668) went one step further: 'On doit même remarquer à ce propos qu'une écriture alphabétique du type sémitique aurait pu entraver les études phonétiques si elle eût alors existé dans l'Inde, car elle aurait donné le modèle d'une analyse commode mais non scientifique des sons du langage' ('One is forced to observe in this context that a Semitic type of writing would have hindered phonetic studies if it had existed at the time in India, because it would have provided a model of analysis of the sounds of language that was practical but not scientific').

Ritual is not only often transmitted without the help of *writing*; it is often transmitted without the help of *language*. Like many other features of culture and civilization—cutting, digging, aiming or planting; features of musical scales and melodies, visual patterns, motifs and shapes, dances, stellar constellations, cooking, the construction of ploughs, weapons and altars, the elements of arithmetic and geometry—ritual is often transmitted by *demonstration*: see Frontispiece and above page xv. Language is remembered together with meaning but mantras are remembered from their sound and a demonstration or oral exposition of their ritual setting.

The oral transmission of the Vedas inspired many special techniques. In addition to the Padapāṭha and Saṃhitāpāṭha, the Prātiśākhya literature introduces 'modifications' (*vikṛti*) that are based upon the Padapāṭha, and that 'strengthen' the oral tradition, that is, minimize the chance of a single word being lost. The first of these is the Kramapāṭha, in which each word is repeated once but in such a way, that it is first linked through sandhi with the word that preceeds, and then with the word that follows. In other words, if the separate words of the Padapāṭha are referred to by numerals as follows:

1 / 2 / 3 / 4 / 5 / . . .

the Kramapāṭha becomes:

12 / 23 / 34 / 45 / . . .

It is clear that sandhi combinations of the Saṃhitāpāṭha are reintroduced here, for they obtain within each of these pairs, but not between the pairs. At the same time, it becomes more difficult to forget a single word: for if a pair were forgotten, the continuity between the succession of pairs would show a break. Note that this does not apply to the recitation of the Saṃhitā or Padapāṭha themselves: if a word is forgotten in their recitation, it does not leave a trace. 'The study of the Kramapāṭha,' says the Prātiśākhya of the Atharveveda (4.108), 'has for its object the fixation (*dārḍhya*) of Saṃhitā and Pada.'

Subsequent modifications render the oral transmission even more firm and stable by introducing methods that resemble the scanning of a tape by a computer, e.g.:

Jaṭāpāṭha:

1 2 2 1 1 2 / 2 3 3 2 2 3 / 3 4 4 3 3 4 / 4 5 5 4 4 5 / . . .

Ghanapāṭha:

1 2 2 1 1 2 3 3 2 1 1 2 3 / 2 3 3 2 2 3 4 4 3 2 2 3 4 /
3 4 4 3 3 4 5 5 4 3 3 4 5 / . . .

Such techniques of oral transmission introduce new sandhi combinations (e.g., '2-1', '3-2') that did not occur in the Saṃhitāpāṭha and thus further minimize the probability of a single word being lost. It is not surprising that as a result of these widely practised mnemonic techniques of oral transmission, there is less variation among the oral traditions of the Vedas than among the manuscripts of much later date that Western scholars have used and that are themselves based upon these oral recitations.

The Kramapāṭha is fully explained in the Ṛkprātiśākhya and is mentioned by Pāṇini; it must therefore be at least as old as the 6th century B.C.E. The other modifications are of later date. All survive at the present day and can still be heard in many parts of India (cf. Staal 1961, Chapters 2, 5 and 6: Levy-Staal 1968).

The fixation of the oral tradition by these mnemonic techniques pertains only to the *form* of the mantras; there is no corresponding tradition that fixes and preserves their *meaning*. The interpretations of the tradition of ritual and mantras, and the meanings assigned to them have therefore always changed. This succession of interpretations is part of the history of the philosophies of India. The exclusive emphasis on form also explains the doctrine of the ritualist Kautsa, according to whom the mantras were meaningless (*anarthakā mantrāḥ*: above page 112). This view should not be interpreted in terms of scepticism, positivism, or behaviorism. It is a purely ritualistic stance that limits the function of mantras to the ritual use which is their proper home, just as language is the proper home of meaning.

Kautsa's position is easier to understand when we remember a feature of the Vedic compositions that is closely connected with the emphasis on their form and the ensuing techniques of their formal transmission: their obscurity. Unlike epic descriptions, which are explicit and full of attention to detail, the Vedas, and especially the Rigveda, were allusive even in their original context. Thieme has shown that in apparently simple songs such as Rigveda 1.32, which extolls the heroic deeds of Indra, the poet does not describe events in detail and in their natural succession, but refers and alludes to them in order to show how heroic they were, how deadly to the enemy, how memorable for the future, and so forth (Thieme 1957:88–89). Such descriptions, addressed to insiders and presupposing specific knowledge soon begin to be misunderstood.

Forms that are not understood tend to be transmitted with emphasis on their formal properties, a feature that is also connected with their ritual use. That a formal analysis developed from this formal transmission is related to another difference between the transmission of the epics and that of the Vedas: the former were transmitted by bards, addressing villagers in open settings; the latter were handed down from father to son or from teacher to pupil in strict and often secret isolation. Such facts and others (Staal 1986b) prevent the facile application of concepts that elsewhere have been successfully applied to more popular oral epics. They also show that the thesis that science and literacy are necessarily connected (Goody 1968) is not generally valid, and throw doubt on the distinction between literate and non-literate forms as a significant distinction between advanced and less advanced forms of civilization.

To understand Kautsa let us visualize—or rather: imagine the audition—of an actual ritual performance. When the blindfolded Grāvastut priest recites his Rigveda verses at the midday pressing of the Soma (page 76), he seems in fact—as his name indicates—to be addressing the pressing stones (*grāvastut*). Contemporary scholars of religion are prone to accept strange or exotic facts without question as possibly endowed with spiritual value—a variant, at first sight, of Quine's "principle of charity": we should always interpret statements in such a manner that they make as much sense as possible (Quine 1981:41; above, page 26). Such "tolerance" may signal a kindly disposition but is not necessarily flattering to the ritualist. It is more reasonable to assume that ritualists are rational beings who *do* things that make sense. That is the real import of Quine's principle, and it is exactly what Kautsa did.

Kautsa did not question the Grāvastut's act, but its customary interpretation: for how can a person in his right mind address inanimate objects? He pointed out that mantras do not merely seem to address stones or herbs: they also seem to refer to things that do not exist (e.g., a being with four horns, three feet, two heads and seven hands) and be redundant and self-contradictory (e.g., one mantra asserts: "There is only one Rudra, there never was a second," and another refers to "the innumerable thousands of Rudras"). Finally, he emphasized what we have just observed: that there is a tradition for mantras to be learned by heart, but no corresponding tradition to teach their meaning.

All these contradictions are based upon the assumption that mantras refer or convey meaning like the declarative statements of ordinary language. Kautsa concluded that the assumption is wrong and that mantras are meaningless although they have to be recited on the proper occasion. Though Kautsa's views are in accordance with the Śrauta Sūtras, they were criticised in an early work on etymology, the Nirukta, and also in the later Mīmāṃsā Sūtra. Yet Kautsa's views exhibit the orthopraxy or insistence on right practice that characterizes most Indian traditions. The philosopher Śaṅkara, for example, approvingly quotes a text which declares: "he who teaches a mantra or officiates at a ritual with mantras without knowing their composer-seer, meter, deity and brāhmaṇa, will run his head against a pole or fall into a pit" (Vedānta Sūtra Bhāṣya 1.3.30). In this list of requirements, Śaṅkara does not include knowledge of meaning: all he demands are formal data transmitted together with the recitations. The composer-seer, meter and deity are all recited names. The brāhmaṇa is merely another recited text.

An oral transmission that excluded meaning and emphasized form created ideal conditions for the origination of science. Max Weber called attention to this "formal rationality" and regarded it as "the essential differentiating factor of Western civilization" (Goody 1968:65). But India and China refute his contention. In the Indian science of ritual the formalities are even more formidable than in grammar. Within the long ritual recitations of the Soma sequences (Chapter 9B), the order of mantras is always different from the order in which they originally occurred in the Veda from which they were taken. This is either due to chance (Chapter 24) or follows from the application of formal criteria pertaining to sound, length, meter, etc. We thus find that the original meaning has disappeared and that the resulting assemblage conveys no meaning either.

A prerequisite for the traditional study of ritual is that the student knows his own Veda by heart. He must know it thoroughly, from beginning to end. When given any couple of words, he must be able to continue the recitation from there. If he is good or takes pleasure in games, he can recite it backward; recite every other word; do with the words anything that a computer can be programmed to do; single out or count their occurrences, group them together according to certain criteria; in brief, perform precisely the kinds of exercise of which the *vikṛti* 'modifications' are simple examples. *On this foundation* he can learn to *change* the traditional order that he has committed to memory; and here we witness the beginning of those extraordinary exercises that are the bread and butter—or rice and ghee—of Vedic ritual. Most of these make no sense in terms of meaning, and often little sense even in terms of form; because many of them were, at the outset and at least in part, either due to intuitions that are no longer recoverable, or simply due to chance. Once put together, these exercises can be learnt. There may be elements that facilitate their study, for example, the occurrence of certain words; such as the word for dawn—*uṣas*—that the pupil will be familiar with even if he need not know what it means. Or 'Agni,' for that matter; much more common and familiar; yet to the young scholar who is beginning to find his way in the ritual maze, primarily nothing but a sound. Mantras recognizable because of a name or term they contain are the "perfect form" mantras that *address* (page 196).

To illustrate the formal complexity of ritual recitation, I shall discuss the "Morning Litany" (*prātaranuvāka*) recited by the Hotā priest before dawn on the Soma pressing day. This recitation lasts about an hour and consists (in the Kauṣītaki recension: AGNI I:600–601) of 360 mantras. I shall not list them all but the following assemblage lists the first 158 mantras (all references are to the Rigveda by "circle," "hymn," and verse):

10.30.12 (three times)	7.16.1–12
1.74.1.–9	3.16.1–6
1.1.1–9	3.10.1–9
6.16.15–27	8.23.1–30
2.5.1–8	1.150.1–3
4.7.2–11	1.140.1–7
4.2.1–20	5.11.1–6
7.12.1–3	5.6.1–10

Committing the 360 mantras of the "Morning Litany" to memory in the right order is not the end, but the starting point of what comprises ritual competence. For now the student has to know the ritual 'application:' that is, he has to know when, where and by whom the Litany is to be recited. He has to know what the other priests are doing at the same time, what other acts, recitations or chants may have to be engaged in earlier, at the same time or later, and who is responsible for all of these. Moreover, all this knowledge often constitutes an element treated as a complex unit by means of which larger ritual structures are constructed at another time. The 'Morning Litany' is a case in point. For toward the end of the Agnicayana ritual, which was performed by Nambudiri brahmins in 1975 and is the object of AGNI, another recitation takes place which incorporates a modification of the Morning Litany. This is the

'Recitation for the Aśvins' (*āśvinaśastra*) performed also by the Hotā priest and long before dawn, but on the final day of the ritual. It contains 1,000 verses instead of 360, and there is a close relationship between the two recitations. This may be described in approximate terms as follows: a specific number of mantras are omitted from each group of metres of the Morning Litany, and others are inserted in order to arrive at the number that is required for the Aśvin Recitation.

The description of this latter recitation in AGNI proceeds in the customary artificial fashion of modern scholarship; it refers to the verses by the numbers that Western scholars have assigned to the various elements. But AGNI also specified the verses that were *omitted* from the Morning Litany, because these alone make the enterprise intelligible. Since the issue that is relevant in the present context has been treated at some length in AGNI I, I will quote from that book:

> It might be asked why *omitted* mantras should be part of the description of the 1975 performance . . . Only the omission and insertion of particular mantras can explain the extraordinary feat of memory that is here on display. The hotā knows thoroughly the Ṛgveda Saṃhitā, from beginning to end. Throughout the recitation, he never hesitates when he is within a hymn, or at the end of a hymn when he is about to recite the next hymn. But when he is about to recite *another* hymn, or *other* verses than the ones that traditionally follow, he pauses at his last breathing pause, i.e., in the middle of the last verse. At that time, obviously, he concentrates on what is to be done next. Once he remembers it, he continues with the next part of the verse, and continuous immediately, without taking breath, with the other hymn or verses that are prescribed. . . . The Recitation for the Aśvins is similar to the Morning Litany. Since he has learnt how to recite the Morning Litany by deviating from the order of the Ṛgveda Saṃhitā as it is handed down, he has learned to further deviate from the litany when he recites the Recitation for the Aśvins (AGNI I:685–686).

The entire procedure that is described here exemplifies the general structure of Vedic learning that has been outlined at the outset of the same work. It relates several concepts we have already met with to each other and places them in their proper perspective:

> The oral transmission of the Vedas from father to son or from teacher to pupil is known as *adhyāya*, 'learning' or 'recitation.' This is contrasted with *prayoga*, 'ritual application,' which refers to the general use of Vedic texts in ritual, or *viniyoga*, which refers to the recitation of a particular mantra at a particular point in the ritual. Vedic ritual is primarily characterized by the recitation, by one or more priests, of Vedic passages. The structure and organization of this recited material follows the requirements of the ritual. As a result, sentences and verses are often taken out of their original context (which is preserved in the *adhyāya* only) and adapted to new surroundings. A reciter who is familiar with the *prayoga* has learned different arrangements of fragments of the oral tradition that he has already memorized, and knows where to insert them into ritual structures. This new dimension of learning may be handed down orally too, and without any connection with ritual activity. And so we meet with three kinds of knowledge, handed down orally, each presupposing the former. Most reciters preserve the Vedic texts in their original, or presumedly original, order. Some among them have, in addition, learned how recitations have to be modified and rearranged for use in the ritual. A few have preserved the ritual practice itself, and know what, how, where, and when to act as well as to recite (AGNI I:31–32).

The sciences of ritual and grammar were born in the context of these oral traditions and it is likely that they were also created without the help of writing. That the Rigveda itself was orally composed—no one has ever doubted it. That the science of ritual, which relies so heavily on memory, might have been orally composed, can be imagined, though barely—depending on who does the imagining. But that Pāṇini's grammar, 'one of the greatest monuments of human intelligence' (Bloomfield 1933:11), could have been orally composed is an idea that has never appealed or even made sense to Western scholars. The only important exception was Max Müller—an exception not easily brushed aside for he was one of the greatest pioneers of precisely these studies that are at the heart of the Indian oral tradition. It is well known that Max Müller was one of the great nineteenth century polymaths, not only a Sankritist but also the pioneer of the new 'Science of Religion (page 258).' But he was also the first editor and translator of the Rigveda, which he published in six volumes that appeared between 1849 and 1873, and in which he included the Ṛkprātiśākhya.

Boehtlingk discussed the part that writing may have played in the composition of Pāṇini's grammar in the Introduction to his edition and translation. But Boehtlingk did not say: 'may have played;' he said: 'must have played.' Boehtlingk was also a great scholar; he did not only know a great deal, but possessed an original and disciplined mind; moreover, he relied on argument and not on hearsay or fashion. When such a person feels strongly that something must be the case, but has no real argument to support it, he relies on a device that serious scholars rarely use: the exclamation mark. The exclamation mark occurs once in Boehtlingk's Introduction; it is used on the one occasion when no argument is given and when he refers to Max Müller's opinion that the Brāhmaṇa's and Sūtras 'ohne Kenntnis der Schrift verfasst worden seien!' ('were allegedly made without the knowledge of writing!')

Sixteen years after Boehtlingk's edition, Caland demonstrated that the Sūtra of Baudhāyana was an oral composition (Caland 1903, reprint 1966:3). This has been universally accepted (e.g., Kashikar 1968a:43, Gonda 1977:514). Pāṇini's grammar is also a Sūtra work; in fact, it has been called (by Renou), 'l'apogée du genre.' Max Müller does not explicitly refer to Pāṇini when he refers to 'the Sūtras;' but he did, of course, include him. The difficulty of his implicit assumption that the grammar was an oral composition is that the sūtras are interdependent in an extraordinary complex manner—more so than the ritual sūtras. One change in a sūtra in any of its chapters will necessitate numerous changes in several other sūtras in several other chapters. Even a change in the order of two sūtras—a simple inversion, for example—would have far reaching implications and consequences. A circumstance, incidentally, that exemplifies an important linguistic fact: the inversion of two rules in the deep structure of a grammar may have the most dramatic effects on its surface manifestations—just as an inversion of the amino-acids within a gene may lead to diametrically opposed characteristics in the phenotype.

Let us consider a simple example of the effects of such an inversion of rules and describe it in general and abstract terms. In a system in which the rules are ordered in such a way that each rule has to be applied before the next, the sequence of rules:

$$\left.\begin{array}{l} a \rightarrow b \\ b \rightarrow c \end{array}\right\} \quad (1)$$

has the same effect as the single rule:

$$a \rightarrow c. \quad (2)$$

But if the rules are interchanged, as in:

$$\left.\begin{array}{l} b \rightarrow c \\ a \rightarrow b \end{array}\right\} \quad (3)$$

not (2) but something quite different results: there are now two kinds of 'b': one that was already present but is now replaced by 'c'; and another that is 'new' for it comes into being whenever we start with 'a'. The second 'b' might as well be given another name, say, 'd', so that the sequence of rules (3) becomes:

$$\left.\begin{array}{l} b \rightarrow c \\ a \rightarrow d. \end{array}\right\} \quad (4)$$

Now, if we reverse the order again to see what difference it makes, we obtain something that is quite different from (1), viz.:

$$\left.\begin{array}{l} a \rightarrow d \\ b \rightarrow c. \end{array}\right\} \quad (5)$$

I have little doubt that a mind like Pāṇini's could solve these kinds of problems that lesser minds would find difficult or impossible to handle without pencil and paper, and that in our letter-bound culture cannot even be imagined: he would do it, in principle, by combining the uncommon analytical gifts he undoubtedly possessed with the extraordinary feats of memory that were part of his culture, having strenghtening this powerful combination further by exercising it through constant and regular practice. After all, Pāṇini was a trained grammarian who must from his early days have been steeped in the knowledge of the grammatical works of his preceptors and predecessors—works of which at present and thanks to him only the names survive.

Of course one cannot prove a theory that makes the most of the elusive notion of genius; I can only try to argue that it is a reasonable and promising hypothesis, and therefore quite feasible to pursue it. But if it would ultimately run into serious problems or not find favor, I can still think of another explanatory scenario: Pāṇini worked in close collaboration with some colleagues or, more likely, pupils. Let us assume, for example, that he had more or less completed the rules of vowel sandhi, and provisionally formulated these in a consistent manner and to his satisfaction. Now there appears a problem elsewhere in the grammar; and the only way in which it can be given a simple solution is by inverting two of the sandhi rules he had just formulated. Immediately a host of problems arise, and the rule system begins to generate ungrammatical forms. How to save it, safely modify and keep track of it without losing the thread?

The solution is simple: Pāṇini asked his favorite pupil to memorize the rules for vowel sandhi he had provisionally formulated. He turned his attention elsewhere, and returned to effect the required inversion. The student who was given the special assignment heard it, and knew precisely how to react to it by reformulation. Other pupils who had memorized other portions of the grammar were eagerly listening in order to find out how any proposed modification would affect their domain; and if trouble arose, they immediately took steps to overcome the problem by changing the rules, their order, their formulation, or whatever else had to be changed. This led to other revisions elsewhere in the grammar, supervised and synthesized by Pāṇini himself. There are many *ad hoc* devices for patching up rules that must have been resorted to on such occasions and that can in fact explain certain oddities that we meet with in the corners of Pāṇini's grammar.

Is the idea of such team-work alien to Indian civilization which is depicted, after all, as a culture of solitary navel-gazers? Not at all, for that picture is nothing but a caricature. The Ṛkprātiśākhya was the first composition to describe the teaching of Veda recitation to a group of students. A few decades ago, when the Jaiminīya branch of the Sāmaveda was on the verge of extinction—for it had been transmitted in its full breadth only in Kerala and only in twenty Nambudiri families (see Staal 1961: 86)—one of the foremost Sāmavedins belonging to that school, Itti Ravi Nambudiri, rose to the occasion and set out to *remember* and finally *write down* the entire Jaiminīya tradition *with the help of his pupils*. Does this phrase indicate that his pupils helped him with the transcription? No, not at all; he would not entrust that to anyone. What he did is chant the songs together with the others, going over them again and again. Sometimes one would stop, because he could not remember; at other times another. Sometimes it was Itti Ravi himself who seemed to have forgotten an uncommon chant even though it was he who had originally taught it to the others—but that had, in some cases, been several decades earlier. It should be noted that we are dealing here with the ritual domain of the so-called *gāna* songs that is much more specialized than the Sāmaveda Saṃhitā; there is no such thing as a Padapāṭha, not to mention modifications such as Krama or any of the others (cf. AGNI I: 276–278). In these rarified chants, a pupil might remember what the master himself had forgotten; only if it was recognized by several others including himself would Itti Ravi accept it as authentic.

I believe that it would be profitable for Western psychologists who are studying memory to learn Sanskrit. This would enable them to go to India and study the mnemonic techniques and practices of those increasingly rare traditional *paṇḍits* that are in popular parlance referred to as 'walking encyclopedias.' It would be interesting to enquire into a phenomenon that I can only explain by introducing a notion of 'collective memory': I am referring to a practice that is common among Vedic reciters and chanters. Vedic brahmins always prefer to recite in pairs: for two do not only know more than one; two that recite together know more than the same two reciting separately. At first I did not understand or like this practice; it does not make for clear recordings—especially since the Vedic chanters do not seem to favor the musical notion of singing in unison. However, I finally understood that reciting together does not only increase the confidence of the chanters; it also leads to the recovery of a larger portion of the oral tradition than could ever be recovered by single performers.

And so we return from ritual to grammar and attribute to Pāṇini the masterminding of an art that is exclusively *mental* and *oral*. It explains, among other things, the extraordinary Indian insistence on the importance of the *guru*. (The importance of the guru is deeply ingrained in the counterculture. However, since the invention of writing and especially of printing, gurus are much less relevant and rarely expound a doctrine that is not already known from texts. Their importance is now confined to the teaching of practices that cannot be easily learned from books, such as meditation.)

The Indian art of scientific composition is ultimately explained by the requirements of the ritual. For ritual requires precision, accuracy and an extreme degree of formality. The *form* of the mantras is all that counts and it is their form that had therefore to be preserved. The emphasis on formality that characterizes the science of ritual was equally important to the science of language. The latter science was also inextricably linked to oral transmission: for grammar exists *rakṣārtham*, 'for the sake of preservation', as Pāṇini's commentator Patañjali formulated it unambiguously in the Introduction to his *Mahābhāṣya* or 'Great Commentary.' The insistence on formal accuracy, the exclusion of meaning, and the extraordinary precautions that were taken to preserve the Vedas; the concomitant sciences of ritual and grammar—all of these were therefore rooted in ritual. In the final resort, we have to extend this conclusion beyond the confines of India: for Western philology and linguistics would not exist without the Rigveda and Pāṇini, and these were only preserved because of the ritual tradition. Thus came into being the two sciences of ritual and language, one still exclusively Indian;

paradigms of what Max Weber called 'formal rationality.' These sciences, however, were not only Indian; they also were, from beginning to end and throughout their development, *oral*.

The strength of oral tradition is extraordinary and in the case of India the invention or introduction of writing would have detracted from the substance of Indian culture in its formative period. If writing had been known, two human sciences would not have come into being at such an early period. Much of the strength of oral tradition survives, especially in tribal culture where it has least been studied and where the historical continuity often remains hidden. It is unlikely that we shall ever know how long oral traditions have been maintained in Africa, Australia, or the Americas. But in India and China, where the past is known as well as the present—and sometimes better known—solid results can be attained provided the data are studied thoroughly and with an open mind as far as methodology is concerned. Jyotirindra Jain (1984) has shown that the Rathvas, a West Indian tribe, maintain in their ritual paintings a cult of Indra that preserves Vedic features extinct in Hinduism since at least a thousand years. The Rathvas probably adopted this cult from the people from whom they learnt farming and agriculture. The study of such living artistic traditions requires a combination of the methods of anthropology and of art history, a synthesis like that between anthropology and the human sciences without which neither ritual and mantras, nor Asia can be understood (Chapters 14 and 25).

28

Religions

28A. Seeking Religion in Asia

The study of religion ought to play an important part in the human sciences, for while language provides the foundation for most intellectual activity of the human animal, religion hovers around the loftier realms of human expression and belongs to a domain that lies beyond language. Religion consists in part of oral traditions that tend to develop not merely into literary, but into *scriptural* traditions. The oral traditions of religion are generally of the loosely organized epic type that are particularly suitable for the expression of changing interpretations. When scriptural, these traditions become fixed, but not in the sense of the tightly organized Vedic type of tradition that led, at least in India, to formal analysis and the human sciences. Religious traditions do not lead to science because interpretations, instead of being questioned or changed, tend to harden into doctrine.

For the understanding of religion, our point of departure remains the extended form of Durkheim's account of religion (above page 126). Durkheim distinguished two categories of religious phenomena, beliefs and rites, and assumed that the latter depend on the former. The assumption is unpersuasive because rites do not depend on beliefs: they lead a life of their own, which is determined by rules, as we have seen. In many cases, beliefs depend on rites because they are interpretations of rites. Durkheim's account is also incomplete because it omits mystical experience. Nevertheless, his account is a good point of departure because of its classic succinctness. Durkheim has logically pursued his preconceptions, and what Quine wrote about Austin also applies to him:

> Historians of science tell us that science forges ahead not by an indiscriminate Baconian inductivism but by pursuing preconceptions, even mistaken ones. I see in Austin's work this kind of progress (Quine 1981:91).

We extend and modify Durkheim's account by distinguishing three categories: rites, mystical experiences and beliefs. There are several dependencies between specific members of these three classes, especially of beliefs on the two others, but basically the three are independent. Extending Durkheim's analogy we say accordingly that the "religious" categories of rite, mystical experience and belief are interrelated like the "ordinary" categories of action, perception and thought.

Among these three categories, rites are primary because they are almost always independent and can be accounted for on their own terms. They also possess a longer background of evolutionary development: ritualization is common among nonhuman animal species. Both human and non-human animal rituals can be described in the ethological terms of "FAP" ("Fixed Action Pattern": Thorpe 1951) and "MAP" ("Modal Action Pattern": Barlow 1977). Rites become "religious" when they are provided with a religious interpretation. We have accordingly referred to Asian rituals as rituals "without religion." This expression, however, stands in need of an explanation because it is contradictory if we follow Durkheim and regard ritual as a necessary feature of religion.

Mystical experience is another category that goes beyond the confines of what is generally regarded as religious. I have discussed this at greater length in another book (Staal 1975) and shall mention here only one feature of the argument given there. Mystical experiences are generated not only by so-called religious practices such as ritual, recitation, and meditation, but also by practices that are nonreligious, at least in their primary sense, for example, fasting, breathing or drugs. Indian texts like the Yogasūtra or the Buddhist Abhidharmakośa enumerate such causes without distinction, and sometimes add others: for example, the grace of a deity that is conducive to visions and incorporates mystical experiences into an existing tradition; or "birth" to account for those we might call natural mystics, people who fall into mystical experiences without training or expectation.

Mystical phenomena possess physiological as well as psychological features and appear to be biologically determined. How this can be explained will have to be determined by future research. Some early beginnings were discussed in my 1975 book, but the field is still wide open, and several promising avenues of research have not been touched or even imagined. Whether nonhuman animal species experience mystical phenomena, for example, is unknown. This is probable since drugs affect many species of animals, sometimes in unexpected ways. Such questions are not beyond the pale of scientific investigation: much information is available on the perception of color among animals, to mention one example.

It is safe to conclude that the two categories of ritual and mysticism are independent from the doctrinal component of religion. This is in accordance with Geertz' statement that "religious life" in Java includes "etiquette, art, and mystical practice," combined with the observation that it excludes the dimension of doctrine or belief (page 327). It also fits the well known fact that Indian religious traditions emphasize correct practice more than correct doctrine, so that we need the concept of "orthopraxy" in many contexts where, in the West, "orthodoxy" would be required. A Hindu may be a theist, pantheist, atheist, communist and believe whatever he likes, but what makes him into a Hindu are the ritual practices he performs and the rules to which he adheres, in short, what he *does*.

To understand "religion" in its fullest sense we should now turn to the third category of religious phenomena. Doctrines and beliefs are regarded as religious when they involve belief in a god or gods, in paradise and hell, faith, salvation, and similar religious concepts that are characteristic of the three monotheistic religions of the West. But now we meet with a difficulty. It is gradually becoming more widely known that most of the other "religions" of mankind are deficient in one or another respect when studied within this perspective: in Buddhism and Jainism there is no belief in a god or gods; in Taoism immortality is not located in a hereafter; in Yoga, Mīmāṃsā and several other Indian traditions, gods are accessories or otherwise subordinate; in Confucianism none of these concepts or ideas exist in even remotely similar forms. The main reason, however, that Asian traditions do not fit the Western pattern of religion is that their emphasis is not on doctrines or beliefs, but on ritual, mysticism, or both. In so far as doctrines or beliefs are mentioned at all, they are not primary but added: they are of the nature of secondary interpretations, often rationalizations and generally after-thoughts. Not infrequently the doctrinal dimension, allegedly incorporated into a sacred book, has been created in response to Western demands and expectations. This is in accordance with the fact that terms for religion that refer to its doctrinal content are relatively rare in the languages of Asia and are invariably of recent date. Hajime Nakamura expanded on this during a 1984 conference (Staal 1985b:54, note 24): in India, the term *dharma* has been used in the sense of "religion" in expressions like *hindū dharma*, *bauddha dharma*, *jaina dharma* only during the last few centuries. The same holds for the Chinese *tsang-chiao* and the Japanese *shūkyō* (宗 教). The concept of "Hinduism," incidentally, came up in the thirties of the nineteenth century in English literature on India (Heesterman 1985:207, note 19).

Matters of doctrine or belief range over a wide spectrum. Mythology, for example, resembles ritual in that it often develops and grows by incorporting arbitrary elements following an "*outer chance* development" (pages 324, 344). Doctrine, on the other hand, possesses a philosophic dimension that prevents unlimited growth: consistency has to be preserved. To the belief in a single god or in transmigation one cannot add the belief in another two gods or in a day of judgment. Kautsa excluded mantras from the category of meaningful statements for precisely this reason: for if they were, some of them would affirm the existence of one Rudra, others of many, and this is contradictory (page 375).

Amalgams of religious phenomena are also found in Western

religion, but play a minor role because of the insistence on doctrine. Major incorporation of "foreign" material would lead to conflict. Obvious examples of ritual elements that are not felt to be inconsistent with existing tenets of belief are the incorporation of "Christmas" trees or "Easter" eggs in the Christian calendar and in Christian practice. In Asia, such amalgamation is found on a much larger scale. Before looking at Asian traditions from a more systematic point of view, I shall discuss five examples, some already met with in other contexts.

(1) The rudiments of Vedic ritual were brought to India by the Indo-European intruders who had already added to their Indo-European fire cult the Indo-Iranian ritual of Soma. To the resulting mixture they added the art of building large altars from kiln-fired bricks which was inherited from the Harappan or Indus Civilization (Converse 1974; Staal 1978a; 1982:39–53; AGNI I: 125–166).

(2) The Vedic fire cult with many of its mantras spread all over Asia together with Tantrism although its relationship with other Tantric rites is tenuous. We find accordingly, even at present, Vedic rites and mantras, in Tibet, Japan and Bali (Skorupski 1983; Strickmann 1983; Hooykaas 1983 a and b; Payne 1986). In Bali, the majority of these are classified as Hindu but some are regarded as Buddhist; elsewhere they are looked upon as Buddhist if the need for a label is felt at all.

(3) The Balinese *mumukur* ceremony takes place after the cremation of a deceased's body and intends to separate the soul from the physical remnants of the body. This rite is related to the Javanese shadow play of *wayang kulit*, originally a summoning of ancestors for magical purposes. It also corresponds to similar ceremonies found in other parts of Indonesia and used to be enacted after the entombment of the ancient Javanese kings. Many large monuments on Java were originally built as dwelling places for the king's soul. Subsequently they were interpreted

and constructed as "Hindu-Javanese" temples although they are neither Hindu, nor temples (Stutterheim 1931).

(4) In Japan, the government separated Shinto and Buddhist divinities during the Meiji Restoration of 1868. Grapard (1982) has shown that prior to this separation, Shinto and Buddhist elements had entirely fused. At many cultic centers, what had begun as a Buddhist cult, became and remained syncretic throughout the middle ages and became "Shinto" only in 1868. At Tonomine, for example, where the ritual cycle had been mostly Tendai Buddhist, food offerings began to be made to the Shinto deity Kamatari starting from an auspicious day in 1465, chosen by divination and transmitted to the Buddhist authorities by an imperial messenger. Dances and sumo wrestling were also offered, and Kamatari was regarded as an "avatara" of the "Pure-Name" Buddhist lay master Vimalakīrti. Here as elsewhere, ritual, political and cultural features and elements were inextricably merged.

(5) Taoism has incorporated Buddhist Tantric rites and concepts that came from India although they may originally have been of Chinese origin. Whatever the historical relationship (page 369), "it is possible to find detailed parallels of much precision between Taoism and Tantrism," although "the field has been so uncultivated that much research will be required" (Needham 1956:427–428). That there is not merely parallel growth but a historical connexion is clear especially in those cases where the similarities are based not upon factual relationships but upon fantasy. The most telling example is a practice on both sides of the Himalayas still advocated by contemporary gurus and swamis. The latter associate this practice with the belief in the possibility that "the entire seminal fluid accumulated in the testicles starts flowing upwards toward the heart. Then it gets purified by the gastric fire and moves on into the brain, strengthening all the sensory nerves and greatly enhancing a yogi's powers of memory and intelligence" (Muktananda 1974:98; Staal 1978b). The Taoist practice consists of exerting pressure

"on the urethra between the scrotum and the anus, thus diverting the seminal secretion into the bladder, whence it would later be voided with the excreted urine" (Needham 1956:149).

The inapplicability of Western notions of religion to the traditions of Asia has not only led to piecemeal errors of labeling, identification and classification, to conceptual confusion and to some name-calling. It is also responsible for something more extraordinary: the *creation* of so-called religions. This act was primarily engaged in by outsiders and foreigners, but is sometimes subsequently accepted by members of a tradition. The reasons lie in the nature of Western religion, which is pervaded by the notion of exclusive truth and claims a monopoly on truth. It is professed by "People of the Book" in the apt phrase the Koran uses to refer to Jews, Christians and Muslims. In most parts of Asia, such religions do not exist, but scholars, laymen and Western converts persist in searching for them. If they cannot find them, they seize upon labels used for indigenous categories, rent them from their original context and use them for subsequent identification of what is now called a "religious" tradition. Thus there arises a host of religions: Vedic, Brahmanical, Hindu, Buddhist, Bon-po, Tantric, Taoist, Confucian, Shinto, etc. In Asia, such groupings are not only uninteresting and uninformative, but tinged with the unreal. What counts instead are ancestors and teachers—hence lineages, traditions, affiliations, cults, eligibility, and initiation—concepts with ritual rather than truth-functional overtones.

Several baffling consequences follow from this stage of affairs. Conversion, for example, is different in Asia from its Western counterpart and a person may adhere to two or more "religions." Conversions, moreover, are not confined to the religious domain; they are well-known in the comparative study of ritual. They resort under that subdivision of rites that has been referred to as "rites de passage" or "liminal," because they seem to constitute, effect or accompany a transition from one state to another. In the realm of Vedic ritual, such rites are called *gṛhya* or "domestic" rites. One of them is *upanayanam*, the ritual through which a member of one of the three highest castes becomes "twice-born." Its successor in the history of Indian ritual is the Buddhist *upasampadā*, which transfers a layman (*upāsaka*) to the monastic life so that he becomes a monk (*bhikṣu*). These two rites are similar in many respects, and there are further similarities with the *dīkṣā* or "consecration" ceremonies that exist in Vedic as well as Tantric forms (cf. Staal 1982b: 47, and AGNI, I: 317–333), and with initiation rites of the Indo-European sodalities and secret brotherhoods that left many traces in the monastic communities of Jainism and Buddhism (cf. Bollée 1981). The prototype or paradigm of all these ceremonies is Shamanistic initiation, which is labelled variously but remains essentially the same in accordance with the maxim: rites are invariant under religious transformation.

Though mass initiations are occasionally met with (a new variant in Madras City is group *upanayanam* for poor brahman boys), a characteristic feature of most of these rites is that they pertain to a single individual. In Asia, the ritual character of these "conversions" predominates, and this was often the case in the West, as is shown, for example, by the similarities between the Jewish circumcision ceremony and Christian baptism in the early centuries C.E. to which attention has been drawn by Jonathan Z. Smith. These similarities also illustrate the invariance of rites under religious transformation. In more recent centuries, we still hear from time to time that practice is more important than preaching. Said Dr. Johnson: "Sunday should be different from other days; people may walk but not throw stones at birds." However, the individual and subjective experiences that accompany conversion rites have on the whole been increasingly emphasized in the West. We find here a wide range of possibilities. At one end of the spectrum there is Ian Barbour's solemn declaration which is intelligible only within an existentialist-Christian perspective: "Religious commitment . . . is a self-involving personal response, a serious decision implicating one's own life, a willingness to act and suffer for what one believes in" (Barbour 1980: 239). At the other end of the spectrum there is the flirtation with Rome that was fashionable in

Oxford during the days of Oscar Wilde, who wrote about it in a letter:

> If I *could hope* that the Church would wake in me some earnestness and purity I would go over *as a luxury*, if for no better reason. But I can hardly hope it would, and to go over to Rome would be to sacrifice and give up my two great gods "Money and Ambition" (quoted by Auden 1974: 305).

In the modern West, conversions such as these are considered witty when they occur in literature, but Americans raise an eyebrow when they are real. Not so in Asia, where conversion has never been merely psychological or "spiritual." A good example is that of the Thakali, a group of traders living in the valley of the Kali Gandaki, one of the deepest gorges in the world which runs roughly north-south between the mountain massifs of Annapurna and Dhaulagiri in Nepal (cf. Jest, 1964/65). This community was engaged in the trade between Tibet and India via Kathmandu. One of their traditional transactions was to purchase thousands of goats in Tibet, and sell them in the central valley of Kathmandu where they were then sacrificed during the festival of Dasaiñ. Originally a variety of Tibetan Buddhists with a strong admixture of Bon-po and local rites and deities, the Thakali learned Nepali and adopted Hinduism when they found that this earned them the respect of their trading partners in Kathmandu. However, with the increase of the power and prestige of the Buddhist kingdom of Mustang, which is situated at the northern end of the gorge and protrudes into Tibet, they reverted to Tibetan and Buddhism. When the trade with Tibet stopped as the border was closed, Mustang lost its prominence, they became Hindus again, and had *saptāha*, "weekly rites", performed for them by brahmans. Presently, with the new popularity of Tibetan and everything Buddhist especially among tourists, mountaineers and other foreign visitors, the Thakali are once more in the forefront of Tibetan Buddhist culture.

Such repeated transitions are not easy. Said Churchill, speaking from experience: "Anyone can rat once; but it takes a certain ingenuity to rat twice." Nor should these transitions be brushed aside as mere opportunism. They are no more opportunistic than is the desire to live close to one's work. Gods, Buddhas, ritual transitions and political parties are there to assist man in his endeavors and occupation. Todd Lewis (personal communication) visited Thakali homes in Pokhara and saw their domestic shrines which display Tibetan lamas as well as Hindu and other local deities. This is not a rare form of syncretism; such phenomena are common in all parts of Asia.

Adherence to more than one "religious" tradition is especially common in China. I confine myself to a quotation from Michel Strickman:

> What then *are* China's religions? So far we have taken notice of Buddhism, an import, and Taoism, a native creation. The oft-mentioned "Confucianism" is, in my opinion, best seen as something else, not strictly comparable—more a Paideia, a system of culture and its graduated inculcation, rather than a faith professed by a guild of ritual technicians claiming otherworldly authority. The paradigm later styled "Confucian" was simply a broad base of Sinic letters, a fundamental view of cosmos and society which we might better term "common Chinese," for it was also fully shared by Taoist priests and Chinese Buddhist monks. Indeed, in mediaeval times, Taoist abbeys and Buddhist monasteries often sheltered academics providing training in this common Chinese literary culture, full assimilation of which, whatever one's regional or even ethnic origins, certified a man as civilised: respectably Chinese. The embarrassment of modern scholars who retain the old Chinese rubric of the "Three Teachings" is apparent when they have to deal with the cult of the dead ("ancestor worship"), and sacred sciences such as divination and geomancy. It is customary to vacillate, assigning these wayward phenomena now to one of the great Three, now to another. But in fact they belong to none of them exclusively, and are freely used, when needed, by all. This might also serve to describe the attitude of most Chinese to Buddhist and Taoist institutions, and for the mediaeval period, as well as the modern, a functional rather than sectarian approach to the question of religious identity might best serve for the great majority of the population. (Strickmann 1982:55)

Though India has always been regarded as a land of religion, the situation is very similar to what we find in China. Most of the alleged differences between India and China are due to Western projections. India became fashionable during the Romantic Period, and has therefore always been expected to respond to religious yearnings. China, on the other hand, was a favorite of the Enlightenment, and has therefore been expected to be without religion. In the Indian cultural area, however, Hinduism and Buddhism often overlap (Staal 1982b, with special reference to the Himalayas). This was true in Southeast Asia, characterizes much of Tantrism (where there is often a one-one-correspondence between Hindu and Buddhist notions), and is still widespread in Nepal or Bali (where we meet, for example, with "Buddhist Brahmans": Hooykaas 1973). If "Vedism" is regarded as a separate "religion," we have to record that in many parts of India, especially in the South, "Hindus" continue to perform "Vedic" rites (AGNI, II:199–251).

In India, the chief conceptual tangle is proffered by Hinduism itself. For Hinduism does not merely fail to be a religion; it is not even a meaningful unit of discourse. There is no way to abstract a meaningful unitary notion of Hinduism from the Indian phenomena, unless it is done by exclusion, following the well-worn formula: a Hindu is an Indian who is *not* a Jaina, Buddhist, Parsi, Christian, Muslim, Sikh, Animist, . . . (the list is indefinite). I used to know a Hindu who considered himself a Seventh-Day Adventist. When faced with such data, should we abandon the concept of religion altogether? Basically, there are two possible procedures. We can either start with a rather narrow concept of "religion," based upon the three Western monotheisms, and see to what extent such a concept can be used in Asia. Or else we can try to formulate a wider and more flexible concept, and see just where that leads us. In either attempt the result may be positive, in which case the term "religion" may be fruitfully employed; or negative, in which case it is best discarded.

I shall begin with the *first* procedure. To start with a definition would be rash: definitions come in the end, when a domain of experience has been subjected to systematic analysis and conceptual issues have been fruitfully discussed (page 63). Not even the area of Western religion is such a domain. However, even if we do not seek to provide a precise definition, it is not entirely unclear what would be involved in a concept of religion based upon Judaism, Christianity, and Islam. It would involve such notions as a belief in God, a holy book, and (at least in two cases out of these three) a historic founder. Taking our cue from this last exception (the fact that Judaism has no historic founder), we can meaningfully ask whether it is feasible to apply to Asia a concept of religion that requires the presence of at least two of these three characteristics. What we find, even with these relatively flexible characteristics, is that none of the so-called religions of Asia is a religion in this sense. Buddhism, for example, has a founder, but neither a belief in God, nor a holy book. Even Ruegg, who is inclined to consider Buddhism a religion (though *dharma*, according to him, expresses a concept that applies to more levels than "religion"), writes:

> It is a well known fact that for Buddhism, both 'early' and Mahayanist, gods, like all other beings, are subject to Karma and its ripening and they accordingly also belong to one of the five (or six) forms of transient existence in Buddhist cosmology. In Buddhism there is no supernatural and supreme God who creates the world and beings and who presides over or modifies Karma in favour of beings (Ruegg 1981:424).

As for holy books, the attempt to assign such a role to the *Dhammapada*—like the similar attempt with regard to the *Bhagavad Gītā* in "Hinduism"—is nothing but a response to Western missionaries or an attempt to meet Western expectations. Taoism does not have a belief in God, but is alleged to have a founder and a holy book; however, the latter is but a small fragment of the Taoist Canon. Tantrism does not appear as an independent movement. It is allied with Buddhism or Śaivism, and shares characteristics with the Yoga which enters into similar alliances. Shintoism lacks all three characteristics. Confucianism possesses only one: it has a founder. And so our conclusion can only be that any notion of religion that is based upon characteristics of the three Western monotheistic religions is inapplicable in Asia.

Turning now to the *second* procedure we can try to introduce a more general and flexible concept: the extended Durkheim account with which we started this chapter. Any definition based upon its three categories should be sufficiently flexible to be applicable to at least some of the Asian phenomena. To begin with, almost all Asian phenomena that have been regarded as religious are replete with ritual. It may be objected that Buddhism does not pay much attention to ritual, for the Buddha declared that the Vedic ritual of his brahman countemporaries did not assist in the attainment of *nirvāṇa*. But whatever the opinion of the Buddha on this point (a topic to which I shall revert), it is clear that ritual has always played an important part in Buddhism. Buddhist monks have always spent a large amount of their time performing rituals, whether for their own benefit, or for the benefit of others. This can still be observed throughout the Buddhist world, e.g., in Sri Lanka, Burma, the Tibetan areas of India and Nepal, Bhutan and Japan. The category that is least important in Buddhism is the category of belief. Buddhism is "an intensely practical religion, inclined to treat doctrinal definitions . . . with some degree of unconcern" (Conze 1969:11). Snellgrove (1959,I:40) declares similarly: "For it is not the philosopher who gives life to a religion, but the man who succeeds in practising it, and in India the practiser *par excellence* has always been the *yogin*." And specifically about Tantric Buddhism: "To any who conceive of Buddhism as just philosophy, this preoccupation with ritual and techniques of yoga may well appear a riot of degeneration, but to a Buddhist who conceived of his religion primarily as an art of yoga and who had never neglected the use of ritual, it might very reasonably have appeared as the most effective teaching ever sponsored under the name of Buddha."

Though Western scholars and believers have paid much attention to Buddhist doctrines, (and Buddhist philosophy does not lag behind any other system of thought in the proliferation of its concepts, ideas and theories), the Buddha himself either kept silent or was not forthcoming when he was asked a purely theoretical or doctrinal question. The parable of the man who was hit by a poisonous arrow, and then asked who had shot it, what was his caste and occupation, and what wood the arrow was made of and from which plant the poison had been extracted, is there to illustrate the point: that man would die before his questions could be answered. Such questions that deal with irrelevant theoretical problems belong to the category of "unanswerable questions" or "inexpressibles" (*avyākṛtavastūni*). Buddhist aspirants are dissuaded from taking them too seriously.

Like the other so-called religions of Asia, Buddhism is characterized by the fact that ritual (in which all the monks engage) is more important than mystical experience (which only a few attain), which is in turn more important than belief or doctrine (a matter confined to philosophers, scholarly monks or reserved for Western converts, anthropologists, and tourists). I shall not try to determine in the present context whether meditation constitutes a fourth "fundamental category," or whether it is a variant of the ritual category, or even a category that falls somewhere in between the ritual and the mystical. Meditation, at any rate, is not gazing upon nothing (except in the limiting case), but is closely related to ritual and mantras.

How is it possible for ritual to occupy such an important place in Buddhism when the Buddha himself was sceptical about its efficacy? We can only arrive at a satisfactory answer to this question if we abandon the view that ritual is symbolic, and depends on doctrine or belief, and accept that ritual is something-to-be-done. We have studied several Asian illustrations of the fact that rituals are transmitted without interpretation or with constantly changing interpretations, and are engaged in for their own sakes. In India, this is particularly clear from the Brāhmaṇa literature (Chapter 13A). But even in the Upaniṣads, Jainism and Buddhism, the situation remains similar. In Heesterman's words (1964:27 = 1985:42):

> The question that occupies religious thought appears not to be: sacrifice or rejection of sacrifice, but rather what is the true sacrifice. Equally the question does not turn on brahmin superiority or its rejection, but on the point who is the true brahmin. On these points both orthodox and heterodox thinkers seem to agree.

The contribution of the Upaniṣads is less often the replacement of *karman*, "ritual activity," by *jñāna*, "insight," than the insistence that *karman* should be performed with *jñāna*. The implications of these facts confirm what we have observed before. Rituals are not merely remarkably persistent *within* so-called religious traditions, where they are provided with constantly changing interpretations; rituals remain the same even across so-called religious boundaries: they are *invariant under religious transformation*. This is demonstrated by the fact that the same rites occur in Vedic, Hindu and Buddhist forms, not only in India but also in China, Japan, Tibet, and Indonesia. This explains why Buddhist monks engage in rituals, for many of their rituals, e.g., rites of oblation into a fire, are independent of Buddhism. The same holds for the numerous initiatory, seasonal and exorcistic rites that Buddhist monks engage in and that are as independent of Buddhism as the Christmas tree is independent of Christianity.

We arrive at the following conclusions. If we adopt the "extended-Durkheim" concept of religion. which incorporates the categories of doctrine (belief), ritual, mystical experience and meditation (the latter either as a fourth category or as a subcategory of one or two of the others), we have a concept on our hands that has all the characteristics of pathological, if not monstrous growth, tumorous with category blunders. It is worse than a spider with a submarine, a burning bush, an expectation, and a human head. We have found that the trio of ritual, meditation and mystical experience consists of categories that are more fundamental than the category of religion itself. Only doctrine or belief may be in a position to constitute a religious category *per se*. We have thus arrived at a point where we should clarify the situation by making a terminological decision. The simplest decision would seem to involve a return to our *first* procedure, make "doctrine" a defining characteristic of "religion," and confine the term "religion" to Western monotheism. This is what I shall do for the time being. As we shall see, this is not an inconsequential decision, and the notion of religion will still turn out to have applications in Asia.

When we return to the empirical domain to see whether these conceptual clarifications may be relevant, we find that many other considerations have to be taken into account as well. Buddhism is often regarded as something special even within the Asian context, and in this respect closer to religion in the Western sense, comparable—if not in rivalry with—Christianity. It is clear that Buddhism and Christianity are in some respects similar. Both have a single historical founder and are spread over large parts of the world. However, we have to be careful not to interpret Buddhism as a religion within a Christian perspective. This has not only been done by Western missionaries, scholars and converts, but also by Buddhists themselves. The challenges of the Christian missions, combined with colonialism and the alleged superiority of the West, have led to representations of Buddhism by Asian Buddhists that have little to do with Buddhism in any of its genuine manifestations. The only way in which we can arrive at an adequate understanding of Buddhism is by approaching it first in the Asian context from which it arose and in which it obviously still fits. Once we do this we discover that some of the similarities between Buddhism and Christianity acquire a different meaning, or vanish.

I have already mentioned that the assignment of a single holy book to Buddhism is nothing but a reaction to Christian and Western expectations. The next point of similarity that is often mentioned is the missionary activity that has led to the world-wide spread of both traditions. These activities are similar to some extent, but the differences are equally significant. The spread of Buddhism from India to Central Asia, China and beyond, is in many respects different from the Christian conversion of Europe. The diffusion was not just of Buddhism, but included the exportation of Indian philosophy, logic, science, medicine, astronomy, grammar, and Sanskrit legends, lore and literature. These events have been collectively referred to, not without justification, as Indianization. The immense effort of translation (from Sanskrit into Chinese, Korean, Japanese, Tibetan, etc.) that these processes involved is comparable only to a limited extent to the relatively simple effort of translating the

Bible into several European languages (an activity that was undertaken in the wake of Protestantism). These activities are more on a par with the vast translation efforts from Greek into Latin and other European languages that took place during and especially after the Middle Ages. These European translations were chiefly concerned with the non-religious domain, for religion had been excised from the Greek heritage. The arts and sciences that came to China together with Buddhism had also nothing to do with religion: they were simply Indian.

We are now in a position to note another significant difference between not only the Buddhist and the Christian expansions, but also between the translations from the Greek and from the Sanskrit: the European and Asian recipients were not equally backward or barbarian. When Greek science reached northern and Western Europe through the intermediary of the Arabs, it filled what was almost a vacuum. The northwest European barbarians had nothing that even resembled the civilization to which they were beginning to be exposed. But when Indian medicine, for example, reached China, it came face to face with a traditional system of medicine that had been thriving for centuries. That such meetings did not always lead to violent clashes is due to partial similarities between the Indian and Chinese systems that still stand in need of explanation. Summarizing the difference, we should say that, in Europe, a religion that had no links with civilization swept over an uncivilized area long before civilization arrived from elsewhere. In Asia, on the other hand, Buddhism came as part of a package that contained mostly civilization and that met with a civilization in all respects its equal. The contrast is between religious mass conversion on the one hand and a meeting of civilizations on the other.

There is yet another significant fact that we cannot fail to note when we try to interpret the Buddhist expansion in Asia in the Asian perspective that is its natural home. When Buddhist practices and ideas went from India to *Southeast* Asia, they were not only connected with many non-religious ideas and techniques, but they were also linked with the expansion of Hinduism. In most of Southeast Asia, Hindu expansion preceded the advent of Mahāyāna Buddhism. The two merged to some extent, as we have seen, and then, in countries such as Burma and Thailand, were replaced by Sinhalese Theravāda Buddhism after the twelfth century. This process can also be referred to as Indianization, but it took on forms that are to some extent different from the ones that characterize the Indianization of Central and East Asia. As Coedès and others have shown, the Indian idea that was most influential in Southeast Asia was the concept of divine kinship. In Cambodia and Thailand, the King came to be regarded as a God on earth—whether it was a Hindu God or a living Buddha. The concept of Indianization cannot do justice to the historical processes and transformations that actually took place. In Cambodia, Burma and Fu-nan (on the lower Mekong valley) there had long been ceremonies during which a "Lord of the Mountain-Top" was set up to represent the unification of territories conquered by the king. The cult of the divine king, therefore, was originally animistic (using that term in deference to Coedès 1966: 143, and for lack of a better one), then received Hindu and finally Buddhist labels—if one insists on using labels in spite of the fact that they are less informative and significant than the entities to which they are attached (cf. also Stutterheim 1931).

The gradual importation of Buddhism from India into China is especially instructive for being in many respects totally unlike a religious conversion. I can do no more than refer to some of the facts that Strickmann has recently collected and analyzed in his study "India in the Chinese Looking-Glass" (Strickmann 1982) from which I have already quoted. We should first of all take into account what the Chinese were looking for. They were not waiting for a "religion." They had long regarded the Western regions as a paradise where the Mother Queen of the West dwells "in a splendid palace amid the peach orchards, ringed with tigers and other heraldic beasts." They were always fascinated by the exotic, the marvellous and the fantastic, and anything that emerged from the Western regions was first of all measured against those standards. If it was frightening, like most of the demonic apparitions that plagued travellers on the silk route, it could perhaps be propitiated or avoided; in some cases, it could simply be eaten. "Ingestion (rather than expulsion) as a means of dealing with otherwise troublous phantoms has always recommended itself to the economical and food-obsessed Chinese."

Another need was therapeutic ritual. "There is copious testimony to Buddhist professional activity in the treatment of disease." The treatments were herbal as well as ritual, and extended to rites for the salvation of the dead, which developed as a compromise between the monastic requirement that the monks should leave their families, and the all-embracing grip of the Chinese family system: these rites "satisfied not only the family's past, but also guaranteed its beatific future. . . Chinese Buddhist monks and Taoist priests quickly perceived and responded to this demand." Another Chinese interest was caves, and this could easily attach itself to the tradition of cavern-sanctuary, already well attested in early Buddhist India. The obsession with mountains-with-caves or pebbles-with-holes is Indian as well as Chinese, and probably of Central Asian origin (see AGNI, I:139–166). The Chinese interest developed Taoist as well as Buddhist forms: "Both Chinese Buddhist and Taoist sources state that the moutains and their cavern-paradises will serve as sacrosanct places of refuge during the world's final apocalyptic convulsions."

Strickmann's essay is rich in information that is relevant in the present context. I shall conclude with a final quotation that may serve as a summary: '"In Chinese, religious conversion is styled "transformation" (*hua*). What was the role of religion in this great Babel of peoples? If the overlooming monoliths of race, language, and state were heaved aside, should we in fact find that religion offers a master key to understanding, a straightaway through the maze of ethnic profusion? Such has not been the view of historians of China writing in English. It is regularly implied that religion, for the Chinese, was at best a distinctly marginal phenomenon, at worst a form of low-class self-indulgence."

All these considerations on the non-religious nature of most

Asian traditions that are generally called religions, explain some baffling facts of Asian history, for example, why Buddhism is often undistinguishable from Hinduism, why Buddhism disappeared from India and was exported all over Asia where it fused with different civilizations, and in general, why we find so many *outer chance* "syncretisms" in Asia. Even Buddhism, which is in some respects more similar to Christianity than any other Asian tradition, is basically a ritual-mystical cult that pays little attention to doctrine or belief. That it has made such a different and misleading impression in the West is largely due to the fact that Western seekers and students have confined themselves mainly to the study of Buddhist philosophy, and have not heeded the Buddha's advice that philosophic speculation does not lead anywhere.

28B. Seeking Out the Buddha

If it is true that Buddhism pays little attention to doctrine, this raises an important question: did Buddhism introduce a separate doctrine? The answer is generally assumed to be in the affirmative as a matter of course; but the facts are far from obvious. Unlike the early Christian missionaries in northern and western Europe, who addressed peoples that can only be described as savages, the Buddha did not preach in a vacuum. His teachings were not only preceded by those of Jainism, but they formed part of the general intellectual ferment that characterizes the seventh and sixth century B.C.E. context in India. In that context it should be simple to determine what *doctrinal* innovations the Buddha offered. In fact, they are surprisingly difficult to find and formulate.

If the Buddha preached that there is an endless cycle of transmigration from which it is possible to escape—it had already been done in the Upaniṣads and in Jainism. If he preached that the true brahman is not he who is born in the highest caste, but he who is fearless, controlled, free from sins, etc.—the Upaniṣads had already stated that a brahman is only he who speaks the truth, or knows brahman (see Bhattacharya 1973; 88–89), and the Jaina *Uttarādhyayana-sūtra* had declared:

> He who is exempt from love, hatred and fear, and who shines forth like burnished gold, purified in fire, him we call a brahman . . . (Jaini 1979: 75).

If the Buddha preached that the true sacrifice is not that in which oblations are made into the fire—the Upaniṣads had already declared that only fools engage in such sacrifice, while a much earlier Vedic Brāhmana regarded as the highest sacrifice, the sacrifice to *brahman* which consists in study (Bhattacharya 1973:115–116). According to the Jaina *Uttarādhyayana-sūtra*, true sacrifice is "guarding one's purity by means of the restraints of a Jaina monk" (Jaini 1979:76).

If the Buddha said anything against the Veda—the Upaniṣads themselves had not merely done it, but it is nowhere formulated in more radical terms than in the *Bṛhad Āraṇyaka Upaniṣad* (4.3.21-22), which is one of the two earliest and most venerable Upaniṣads: "His is a condition beyond all desire, free from evil, without any fear. Like a man in the embrace of his beloved knows of nothing outside, nothing inside, that person in the embrace of the self which is wisdom (*prājñena ātmanā*) knows of nothing outside, nothing inside. His is the condition of bliss when all desires are fulfilled, where there is only the desire for *ātman*, or no desire at all. There, the father is no father, the mother is no mother, the worlds are no worlds, the gods are no gods, the Vedas are no Vedas."

If the Buddha denounced the sacrifice of animals—it had already been done in the Upaniṣads, and, more emphatically, in Jainism. The killing of sacrificial victims by ritualists was ridiculed in the earliest Vedic texts. It occurs in a verse of the *Rigveda* (10.82.7), which returns in the *Taittirīya Saṃhitā* of the Black Yajurveda (4.6.2.2.e):

> You will not find him who has created
> some obstacle is in your way.
> Enveloped in mists and stammering,
> taking life, the reciters wander (cf. AGNI, I:547).

Heesterman has shown, in a series of articles (1962, 1964, 1983), that the trend away from animal sacrifice, which culminated in the Upaniṣads, Jainism and Buddhism, is found throughout Vedic ritual itself: it is not a radical movement, but an unmistakeable, gradual tendency to move away from bloodshed and violence. The "interiorization" of ritual is part of this general development.

It might be said that all these points are not doctrinal but ideological: that is, replete with social, political and religious implications. So let us revert to pure metaphysics. Did not the Buddha propose a major new theory at least in this rarified domain of speculation: the doctrine of non-self (*anātmavāda*)? And did not this doctrine stand in absolute contrast to the Upaniṣadic doctrine of self (*ātmavāda*) which was further developed in the Vedānta? Here our authorities seem to agree unanimously. The picture has been drawn, with broad but magisterial strokes, by T.R.V. Murti in *The Central Philosophy of Buddhism* of 1955.

Yet even here caution is necessary, and the situation is more complex than it appears at first sight. It is not open to doubt that many of the later Indian Buddhist philosophers advocated the *anātmavāda*; they are quite explicit on this count. The Nāgārjuna who was the author of the *Mahāprajñāpāramitāśāstra*, made accessible through its monumental translation from the Chinese version by Etienne Lamotte, wrote for example:

> Look for the *ātman* on heaven or earth, inside or outside, in threefold time or in the ten regions, but you will not find it anywhere. Only the meetings of the twelve supports (viz., the six sense organs and their objects) produces the six cognitions. The meeting of the three (organ, object and cognition) is called contact. Contact produces sensation, idea, attention, and the other mental dharmas. In our system, ignorance leads to the belief in the personality. Because of that belief, people believe that the *ātman* exists. But that belief is destroyed by the vision of the truth regarding suffering and the relative knowledge with respect to suffering. When belief in the personality is destroyed, the *ātman* is no longer seen. (Lamotte 1949:747;1976:2005).

What did the Buddha himself have to say on this topic? He indicated that the five *skandhas*, and more generally, all dharmas, are *anātmā* (see Lamotte IV, 1976:2005; Bhattacharya 1973, 12, *passim*). But in the Upaniṣads, the corresponding five *kośas* are equally ephemeral: they do not survive after death and they do not transmigrate. In the Upaniṣads, the *ātman* is different from the *kośas*, and is real. In Buddhism, the *skandhas* are *anātmā*, which implies, in Sanskrit, that they are different from the *ātman*. But that *ātman* itself, is it real or unreal?

The few early passages in which the Buddha is quoted as expressing himself on these issues have been discussed by scholars for over a century, and both interpretations have been defended. Those who have adduced reasons for a specific interpretation comprise some of the greatest Orientalists of the past, the very same scholars to whom we owe in fact almost all the basic information we now possess on the Upaniṣads and on early Buddhism. How then are *we* to decide?

The obvious answer to such a question is that we should go back to the texts, and try to read and understand them in the light of all the information that is presently available. However, we should critically assess the sources of our information and the channels through which it has been obtained. These requirements are obvious, but taking them into account in the area we are discussing leads to several preliminary observations. First of all, we will discover an astonishing schism for which there exists no intrinsic or scientific justification: the schism between "Indologists" and "Buddhologists". It might seem that this division corresponds to the schism between Hindus and Buddhists, but this begs the question we are asking, and "Indology" would need to encompass a great deal more than "Hinduism" in any case. It might be argued that the schism between Indologists and Buddhologists exists for good reason because of necessary specialization, and ensuing differences in background and education between different specialists: a scholar who deals with Vedic and Hindu texts needs primarily Sanskrit (though a smattering of other Indo-Iranian or Indo-Aryan languages is helpful), whereas a scholar who deals with Buddhist texts needs in addition to Sanskrit not only Pali, but Chinese (for primary sources, primarily), and Japanese (for primary as well as secondary sources), and if possible Korean, Tibetan, Mongolian and a handful of other languages. Scholars of the latter type are extremely rare, obviously. Even if we include Japanese scholars who possess advantages of language and culture, they can still be counted on the fingers of one hand.

The schism between Indologists and Buddhologists, however, is not only based upon the presumed need for specialization; it is also based upon at least one unproven assumption. That assumption is that Buddhism is a religion, and that there is therefore a certain unity to the subject. We have seen in the preceding section that the concept of religion is not easily applicable to Buddhism or to any other Asian tradition. That unity is therefore imposed from the outside and *a priori*. The unities presumed to cover early and late Buddhism, or Indian, Chinese, and other forms of Buddhism, are functions of the same unproven assumption. Of course, one is bound to see unity when one is convinced that it must exist. But such an approach will not lead to adequate evaluations. It is not open to doubt that Chinese Buddhism has been influenced by Indian Buddhism. But in particular cases, that influence might be small and insignificant in comparison to other influences. For scholarship to be adequate, it should not be based upon such assumptions. Only if we abandon them are we in a position to discover whether, and to what extent, such a unity may in fact exist.

Another circumstance complicates the issues we are dealing with. When Buddhism became first known in the Western world, it was the Pali sources that were almost exclusively relied upon. The picture that emerged was that of a simple religion, replete with ethical notions and similar to Protestantism. The Mahāyāna insofar as it was referred to at all was regarded as a deterioration: at best a fresh development in the Far East, at worst a decadent manifestation influenced by Tantrism and other debased Hindu notions of later date. As it happens, the same specialization that I mentioned has led to a reversal of this former picture, which has been beneficial because it represents a step forward in our knowledge and understanding: it has been found that the Mahāyāna is much older and that the Chinese translations from the Sanskrit provide reliable information on much earlier stages of Indian Buddhism than had been assumed at first, not only in the domain of the Mahāyāna, but also in that of the Theravāda. Because of these sources we now have a more reliable picture of the history of Indian Buddhism than could ever have been reached if we had confined ourselves to Indian sources.

Another qualification has yet to be taken into account when we evaluate these sources and their significance: they do not take us back to the time of the Buddha. During the early period of what has been called "original Buddhism," the order was hardly organized and there were few monasteries. "The life of Buddhist ascetics in its incipient stage was fairly different from the monastic life of monks in later days. It was quite close to the life of hermits as is mentioned in great epics, such as the *Mahābhārata* and the *Rāmāyaṇa*" (Nakamura 1980:58). The schism that gave rise to the Mahāsaṃghika sect took place during the period of Aśoka in the third century B.C.E. The points of difference that were discussed at that time were largely minor matters of monastic discipline. In addition, five theses defended by these first "heretics" were directed against the traditional Arhats: they were declared to be subject to certain impurities, mental as well as physical (e.g., nocturnal emissions). These heretical views were supported by laymen (*upāsaka*) who, according to the traditional doctrine had no access to *nirvāṇa* (Lamotte 1958:312–319). More important doctrinal differences that characterize some of the Mahāyāna theories, such as emptiness (*śūnyatā*) are of much later date, and were referred to as *pratirūpakadharma* ("imitation-doctrine": Lamotte 1973:39–40; cf. Nakamura 1964b).

Even with these new developments on the doctrinal level, there was no split in the monastic community: monks with different views continued to live together in the same monastaries and were subject to the same discipline—if we except *minutiae*. When Hiuen-tsiang visited India around 630 C.E., he found several monasteries, especially in north-west India, where the monks devoted themselves to different schools at the same time. Lamotte comments memorably on this and on the later splits within the Mahāyāna: "In India, tolerance and accommodation are more important than differences of doctrine; for belief has only relative value. In the West, this would be inconceivable; among us, each difference of opinion leads to a serious dissension. For a Buddhist, salvation does not come from faith, but from renouncing the world and bringing peace to the spirit" (Lamotte 1973:12–13). Lamotte speaks here with double authority: until his recent death, he was the most distinguished member of that tiny band of scholars who can be counted on the fingers of one hand; and he was at the same time a Catholic priest.

With all these considerations and qualifications we are now sufficiently armed to discuss a simple example. At the second sermon in Banaras, as referred to in the *Anattalakkhaṇa-Sutta* and other sources (see Bhattacharya 1978:12 sq.), the Buddha is reported to have declared with reference to the aggregate of the five *skandhas*: "This is not mine, I am not this, this is not myself" (*n'etaṃ mama, n'eso 'ham asmi, na m'eso attā*). Even a person without Pali can see how the thought in the final clause is expressed: this aggregate (*eso*) is not (*na*) my (*m'*) self (*attā*). The first thing that strikes us is that the term *anattā* is not used. The second fact we should bear in mind is that *attā/ātman* is used in Sanskrit and Pali as the reflexive pronoun which functions in the same manner it does in other languages such as English. "Self," in other words, is nothing but a reification of "self." A person who knows nothing about these doctrinal controversies would therefore translate: "this is not myself." A person less innocent is tempted to translate: "this is not my self," and a translator who wishes to press a point: "this is not my Self."

There are several similar passages in the earliest sources. A scholar familiar with later Buddhism will not see any problem: he will take such statements to mean that the *skandhas* are not real, with the implicit understanding that the *ātman* is also not real. A scholar familiar with the Upaniṣads will not see any problem either: he will take such statements to mean that the *skandhas* are not real, and naturally different from the *ātman* which *is* real. I do not pretend to offer a solution to this difficulty in the context of the present chapter. My purpose is different: I want to show that there *is* a difficulty. Many contemporary scholars have simply disregarded it: "Buddhologists" assume that the *anātma* doctrine is indissolubly connected with the Buddhist religion; "Indologists" are afraid to touch Buddhism, and so have said nothing.

In the last generation, two great Orientalists conducted a controversy on this issue: Hermann Oldenberg defended the view that the Buddha accepted the *ātman*, and Louis de la Vallée-Poussin defended the opposite view. Oldenberg was one of the last Indologists who wrote authoritatively on Sanskrit, Vedic, Hindu, as well as on Buddhist matters, whereas de la Vallée Poussin was one of the first Buddhologists, albeit *avant la lettre*, who eschewed non-Buddhist topics.

In the present generation there are at least five scholars who are familiar with early Buddhist as well as Upaniṣadic literature, and have expressed themselves on the issue: Bhattacharya, Frauwallner, Lamotte, Murti and Nakamura (in alphabetical order). I have already referred to Murti: his book dealt chiefly with the *Mādhyamaka*, but he also argued that the original Buddhist doctrine was *anātmavāda*. Nakamura defends the opposite view, though with qualification: "In early Buddhism, they taught avoidance of a wrong comprehension of non-*ātman* as a step to the real *ātman* . . . Therefore early Buddhists never maintained the non-existence of *ātman*. They merely opposed the substantial permanence of anyone's *ātman*. As for the metaphysical question whether an absolute *ātman* exists or not, early Buddhists kept silence" (Nakamura 1964a:90–91). Nakamura devoted a separate study to the problem of self in Buddhist philosophy (Nakamura 1977), which he summarized as follows: "Buddhism did not deny the self as such, contrary to the general assumption by many scholars who tend to regard the theory of Non-Self as a sort of nihilism" (Nakamura 1980:63–64). Frauwallner agrees with Nakamura, but is more explicit: "The

Buddha never ceases to emphasize that none of the five heaps (*skandha*), which make up the mundane personality, should be taken for the I. It was far from him, however, to deny the existence of the soul'' (Frauwallner 1956:63).

Bhattacharya is the most explicit among contemporary scholars: his book *L'Ātman-brahman dans le bouddhisme ancien* of 1973 is largely devoted to the issues we are discussing, and I have taken many quotations from this work. Bhattacharya defends the view that the Buddha accepted the *ātman*.

What, finally, did Lamotte have to say on the issue? He is careful, as one would expect, if not over-cautious. After briefly referring to Frauwallner, Oldenberg, de la Vallée Poussin and Bhattacharya, he emphasizes that we have no explicit statement attributed to the Buddha in which he affirms the existence of the *ātman*. We should therefore, says Lamotte, confine ourselves to the golden rule laid down by the Buddha himself: ''What I have not declared, take that to be non-declared, and what I have declared, take that to be declared.'' (Lamotte 1976, IV:2004–2005).

Earlier (Staal 1985b:44), I concluded from this passage that Lamotte did not explicitly affirm that the Buddha taught the non-self. In a footnote, I criticized de Jong's review of Lamotte, 1976, for rejoicing that ''M. Lamotte categorically rejects all attempts at discovering in Buddhism the belief in a Vedāntic ātman'' (de Jong 1978:168). In his reply, de Jong (1987:151) drew attention to other statements by Lamotte showing that according to the Buddha there is no *ātman*. Lamotte must accordingly be classified with Murti. But the main question remains unresolved: why was the Buddha so ambiguous and unclear with respect to what we are inclined to regard as a central issue that the leading specialists arrive at opposite interpretations of his statements? A substantial part of the answer must lie in the Buddha's lack of interest in doctrinal matters, a lack of interest he explicitly affirmed in the parable of the arrow and elsewhere. This is important in the present context because it shows that even in Buddhism, the Asian tradition that is in many respects most religion-like, doctrine plays a subordinate role and mystical experience and rites are basic.

We must conclude that the concept of religion is not a coherent concept and therefore misleading. It does not hang together like a concept should and should either be abandoned or confined to Western traditions. This conclusion is to be drawn with caution and is not without qualifications. For example, ritual is more important in Judaism than in Christianity, and in Catholicism than in Protestantism; and the reverse holds, accordingly, for doctrine. Much of the emphasis on doctrine in the study of non-Western traditions is, in fact, connected with the rise of Protestantism (cf. Nyberg 1953).

A phenomenon more like religion in the Western sense appears in the later phases of development of several Asian traditions. Śaivism and Vaiṣṇavism, for example, though often referred to as "Hindu sects," may therefore be called "religions" (as is done in Gonda 1954 and elsewhere). They should perhaps be regarded as the first two indigenous religions of India. They are closely related and not entirely distinct, but that holds for the three Western monotheistic religions, too.

Whereas Śaivism remained orthodox in its insistence on *jñāna* and orthoprax like all preceding Indian traditions, including Buddhism, Vaiṣṇavism introduced a new concept epitomized by the term *bhakti* or "devotion." The sources can be traced to a more distant past: the late Śvetāśvatara Upaniṣad (Oldenberg 1915:238; Lauenstein 1943:86–89). With *bhakti*, a more purely "religious" element in the Western sense is introduced for the first time, and dogmas and religious squabbles come to the fore. A Hindu is no longer an Indian concerned about what he must do while thinking anything he likes. A Hindu becomes a believer in God equipped with faith and a holy book. The development of the Bodhisattva ideal in Buddhism is connected with this notion of *bhakti*. Thus Mahāyāna also came to incorporate religion—or perhaps we should say two religions, one in India and one in the Far East. That Shinran's "Pure Land Buddhism" was influenced by the Indian *bhakti* cults and not, for example, by Christianity, has long been known (Otto 1930:7–9). The traditions of "Buddhist" temples in Japan also became indistinguishable from the cults of various divinities in the so-called "Shinto" shrines (page 392). Buddhists have finally turned into believers, not in God but in the Buddha. But such developments are no longer inspired by the original outlook of the founder, which was the hallmark of classical Buddhism:

> Adhesion to the Buddhist faith does not require that the adept rejects his ancestral beliefs or denounces the religious practices that are current in his *milieu*. Through one of those compromises of which India has given so many examples, everyone is free to worship apart from the "Three Treasures," the deities of his region, caste or choice and perform the appropriate rites. Throughout history one meets with famous Buddhists who continue their worship of spirits. Nāga and Suparṇa, Yakṣa, Vajrapāṇi, Women and Fairies. Householders, benefactors of the Sangha, remain loyal to the gods of their class: Kuvera, spirit of riches; Hāritī, the fairy with the children; the tutelary Couple, etc. The higher castes continue to demand for the great Vedic and Brahmanic deities: Indra, Brahmā, Māra, etc. The advent of Buddhism has never produced a "twilight of the gods." Śākyamuni does not oppose the pagan gods of Hinduism. He recognizes that "the deities, honored and worshipped by man, will in turn honor and worship him." He does not condemn pagan rites: he disapproves of sacrifice in which living beings are killed; he recommends peaceful offerings devoid of cruelty; certain practices based upon pure superstition, ritual baths, etc. are practically without value. What is important is to put everything in its place: gifts to pious monks are better than the cults of the gods; taking refuge in the Three Treasures is better than giving gifts; the highest achievement of sacrifice is to enter the order (Lamotte 1958:74–75).

28C. Mythology

Students of religion have increasingly had an inkling of the fact that "religion" in the Western sense, with its emphasis on doctrine, is not a single, coherent concept. This insight has led to a gradually increasing attention to non-doctrinal phenomena such as mysticism and ritual, to "popular" religion and "little traditions." But anthropologists have failed to render the much needed assistance in unravelling the resulting conceptual tangles and confusions. Instead of being critical of the Western concept of religion with its concomitant emphasis on doctrine or belief, they have continued to search for features that fit into Durkheim's category of "thought." This has led to the preoccupation with myths and symbols that still characterizes cultural anthropology and the study of religion. The process has been facilitated by the incorporation of ideas from (various schools of) psychoanalysis (cf. page 153).

One reason for the interest in mythology is that "one can prove almost anything of the nature of myths if one selects only a part of the data and refuses to look at the context" (Ingalls 1960:196). Scientific method is then replaced by a panacea: take myths, psychology, add a little of anything you like, and you can get whatever you want. I have paid little attention to mythology partly because of this elasticity, and partly because myths are already overdone.

In India, mythology developed from the Brāhmaṇas just as science developed from the Śrauta Sūtras. The relation between Brāhmaṇas and Śrauta Sūtras—long disputed—was correctly estimated by Caland, tested by Tsuji (1952) and has been expressed by Gonda (1977:497) in terms that are no longer controversial:

> The authors of the Brāhmaṇas endeavoured to explain the origin, meaning and raison d'être of the ritual acts etc., and to prove their validity; the compliers of the Sūtras, on the contrary, aimed at a systematic description of every ritual in its natural sequence.

I have tried to show, in addition, that the Śrauta Sūtras embody a science, and that the Brāhmaṇas offer interpretations that are generally arbitrary and ad hoc. Their authors undoutedly *knew* the ritual; but they did not know "what it meant."

From some scholarly writings (Lévi-Strauss', for example) it would seem that the concept of religion has already been quietly buried. Its critical assessment in the light of all available data, and possible excision from scientific usage remains a task for the future. Departments of religion, programmes of study involving religion in a historical, comparative or phenomenological perspective, and many related institutions and efforts remain relevant to the study and understanding of Western traditions. It is unlikely that they are very helpful in the study of non-Western peoples and civilizations. The work that has been done under such headings has to be re-evaluated or redone after the concepts have been scrutinized and purified, renewed or replaced. Mythology within or without religion is still a promising subject, but it goes beyond our present investigation and is treated elsewhere (Staal 1988b).

28D. Philosophy of Religion

It would stand to reason to expect that conceptual analysis is the primary task of a discipline traditionally called "philosophy of religion," taught in most English speaking countries in departments of religion or philosophy. In this field of studies, however, the current approach is generally outmoded. The philosophy of religion is not only exclusively taught in terms of doctrines and beliefs, but almost entirely confined to what Western philosophers and theologians have written about Christian doctrines. Thus attention is paid to the existence of god and alleged proofs of that existence, to good and evil, reason and faith or belief, and so forth. Anselm's ontological proof and its discussion by Western philosophers, culminating in Kant's discovery that existence is not a predicate, predominate in these courses. That Kant's discovery does not even make sense in Chinese was established by A. C. Graham (1959, 1965, 1967).

The real objection to the manner this discipline is taught is that it has little or nothing to do with the so-called religious traditions of mankind. A philosophy of religion worthy of its name should begin with a discussion of the concept of religion and an investigation into the status of a possible science of religion based upon what is presently known about the religions or so-called religions of mankind. Ritual, mantras and mysticism should occupy at least as important a place in such an investigation as matters of doctrine or belief. Should it turn out that concepts of Western philosophy are not appropriate for fruitfully dealing with such topics, the subject is all the more interesting and worthy of discussion. The philosophy of religion is important for that reason and also because the imposition of the Western concept of religion on the rest of the world illustrates how Western imperialism continues to thrive in the realms of thought.

A philosophy of religion based upon Indian philosophy would be equally parochial but more adequate because Indian philosophers were familiar with the science of ritual. This holds especially for the Mīmāṃsā which is at the same time the most Indian and least studied of the six classical systems. Out of 159 metarules of the twenty-fourth section of Āpastamba Śrauta Sūtra quoted in Chapter 26, nearly a hundred correspond closely to sūtras of the Mīmāṃsā Sūtra (Garge 1952:54). The vārttikas of grammar, which are often metarules too, are also closely related to these sūtras (Paranjpe 1922:72), which is not surprising in view of the fact that the Mīmāṃsā is often regarded as an analysis of sentences (*vākya*). Since they are either based upon it or react against it, many Indian philosophies, including Buddhist systems, the philosophies of language and especially the Advaita Vedānta of Śaṅkara cannot be adequately understood or evaluated without knowledge of the Mīmāṃsā. Within such a philosophic perspective, a philosophy of religion could attain substantial results.

29

The Myth of the Two Cultures

In 1867, William James wrote from Germany to his sister about a person he had met at a dinner party at the house of Hermann Grimm:

> A soft, fat man with black hair (somewhat like the Renan of the photograph) of uncertain age between twenty-five and forty, with very small green eyes, he wore the obligatory frockcoat with *an exceedingly grimy shirt and collar and a rusty old rag of a cravat.* The professor overflowed with information about everything knowable and unknowable. *He is the first man I ever met of a class of men to whom learning has become as natural as breathing.* He talked and laughed incessantly at the table and gave Mrs. Grimm the whole story of Buddhism, and I don't know what other bits of the history of religion. After dinner Grimm and the professor got involved in a heated controversy about the primitive form of natural religion. I noticed that the professor's answers became somewhat tired and then his massive head suddenly fell forward. Grimm called out that he'd better have a proper sleep in his chair. He eagerly consented. Grimm gave him a clean handkerchief which he threw over his face and appeared to go to sleep instantly. After ten minutes Grimm woke him with a cup of coffee. He rose like a giant refreshed, and continued to argue with Grimm about the identity of Homer (quoted from Rickman 1979:26–27 after W. Nohl; the italicised part of the letter was written in English, the rest in German).

The person James described was Wilhelm Dilthey. If a single person had to be held accountable for historicism, the reinvention of hermeneutics, and the introduction of the distinction between sciences and humanities into contemporary Western culture, it should be him. The terminology of the "two cultures" was later introduced by the British author and physicist C. P. Snow. Dilthey's distinction between *Naturwissenschaften* ("sciences of nature" or "natural sciences") and

Geisteswissenschaften (literally, "sciences of the spirit") was accepted without question by most continental philosophers, from Heidegger to Foucault, including all existentialists and almost all phenomenologists with the exception of their founder, Edmund Husserl. Though Anglo-American philosophers have been less sanguine about embracing it explicitly, the distinction is now a fact of academic life on both sides not only of the Channel but of the Atlantic, and is generally felt to be not merely due to an unavoidable division of labor (as in the "National Science Foundation" and the "National Endowment for the Humanities"), but to deep and intrinsic differences of organization, method and nature. The myth of the two cultures is now so deeply ingrained that it might be called the Prejudice of Twentieth Century Research.

That it *is* a prejudice and not based upon facts or a serious demonstration becomes clear as soon as we look at the matter more closely. Dilthey was unfamiliar with the sciences and attributed to them the caricature of "scientific method" I have discussed in Chapter 2. He introduced a special faculty, *Verstehen*, "understanding" or "empathy," characterized vaguely but abundantly illustrated and exemplified, always in such a manner as if it were exclusively appropriate to the study of man.

I have already touched upon this subject in Chapter 3 and cannot, in the present context, give a full account of this notion which has been very influential not only in the humanities but also in the social sciences (it was adopted, for example, by Max Weber). I shall quote a few phrases from the sympathetic account given by H. P. Rickman in *The Encyclopedia of Philosophy* (1967,II:405–406):

> *Das Verstehen* is a technical term with a definite meaning that must be clearly distinguished from its general use as a synonym for any kind of comprehension. It is the comprehension of some mental content—an idea, an intention, or a feeling—manifested in empirically given expressions such as words or gestures.
>
> In his later writings (when "How is meaningful experience possible?" became his central question: page 404), Dilthey placed increasing emphasis on two additional conditions.

> The first of these two conditions for understanding expressions is knowledge of the particular concrete context in which they occur. A word is better understood, sometimes only understood, in its verbal setting; an action, in the situation that gave rise to it. From this condition Dilthey derived the methodological principle that to understand an expression we must systematically explore the context in which it stands. For example, to understand a religious movement or philosophic doctrine better, we must relate it to the climate of opinion and the social conditions of the time. For example, the philosophy of Spinoza can be better understood against the background of the rise of science and the conflict between different religious sects in the sixteenth and seventeenth centuries.
>
> The second of these conditions is knowledge of the social and cultural systems that determine the nature of most expressions. To understand a sentence we must know the language; to understand a chess move, the rules of the game.

I shall not attempt to subject these expressions to a detailed analysis; they are second hand descriptions from a general work of reference. I have used them because Dilthey is never clear on central issues ("Dilthey himself never gave a systematic treatment of these 'ideas,' but only what may be termed preludes for such a treatment, with the topics of life, life context, expression, interpretation, and understanding as the leading themes": Spiegelberg 1965,I:122). It is not clear, for example, what the difference is between the two "additional conditions," and many of the explanations are so obvious as to be trivial. The "method" of *Verstehen*, moreover, is not different from the point of departure of any scientific account, whether in the "natural" sciences or in the humanities. Out of context, facts, data and phenomena cannot be understood (Vedic ritual, for example, was placed in such a context in Chapter 7). But this is only a point of departure, a first step, which corresponds to the "phenomenology" of physics (pages 12–13): science becomes interesting when phenomenological description is followed by *abstraction* from the concrete context and when a general hypothesis is formulated. That this is rarely done in the humanities is a matter of fact; but that it *cannot* be done has never been demonstrated.

In the social sciences, more attention has been paid to "theory" than in the humanities. It is common, however, for social scientists to insist that ritual is "embedded" in society. It is, but interesting results are obtained when we abstract from this context and observe that the same ritual forms and structures are associated with different social events and are embedded in different societies. The same holds for the embedding of ritual in religion. By insisting upon context and prohibiting abstraction, the nature of ritual and mantras has remained inaccessible.

Dilthey's distinction between the sciences and the humanities, therefore, reduces to a chimera based upon the caricature of scientific method discussed in Chapter 2: what he describes as characteristic of the sciences of man is also found in the sciences of nature; only, the latter go beyond it in all interesting cases. The same holds for most discoveries in the human sciences: this applies to Jakobson, Chomsky or Lévi-Strauss—to mention a few names of authors whose work we have discussed.

In some of Dilthey's work, and in other publications (specifically in Heidegger who repeatedly refers to him in the context of hermeneutics and historicity), the uniqueness of the humanities is related to the unicity of man, which is, in turn, related to a tradition of discussions on "subjectivity" in modern philosophy. The argument runs, briefly, as follows. "Man" is so different from stars, rocks, molecules and even other animals that he cannot be studied by the same methods by which these other things are studied. He is, after all, not a thing: he is the unique studying subject himself. This conviction explains, among other things, Heidegger's effort to introduce "existentials" into the study of "Dasein" (page 26).

The argument is not simple and I shall not attempt fully to unravel it in the present context. But we must recognize, to begin with, that every star is also unique. The sun, "our" star, is particularly important to us, and so close, relatively speaking, that we can learn more from it than from any other star. But we learn more from it not only about it; we learn more from it about other stars, too. This leads to hypotheses that are general or universal and that can be related to other data. The unicity of man, or any other entity, is similar. The only apparent examples of entities that do not have a unique individuality are certain subatomic particles which seem to be interchangeable and undistinguishable in principle.

It is true that we ourselves are not only objects, animals, and beings, but also subjects. Being subjects means that we are in a position to evolve a general theory or hypothesis about subjectivity—a theory that aims at "objectivity" like anything else that aims at being true. Dilthey did not accept this, and was bound to accept relativism. Heidegger, following in his wake, rejected it explicitly when he asserted that every truth depends on *Dasein* (page 28). But whatever they say, most statements made by philosophers, scholars and scientists aim at truth. Dilthey or Heidegger do not wish to be interpreted as claiming that what they say is false. They may deal with unique entities but they try to say something about them that is not unique but general, universal and true.

Dilthey is noted for his work in history. Historians seem especially concerned with what is unique. There was only one Hitler. What historians provide, in fact, are illustrations of the problems to which Dilthey drew attention. I shall briefly discuss two illustrations from Huizinga's *Herftsttij der Middeleeuwen* ("The Autumn Tide of the Middle Ages") of 1919. The first example concerns context. As his title indicates, Huizinga adopted a particular perspective by placing the period of his investigation (the fourteenth and fifteenth century in France and the Netherlands) in the context of an age of completion rather than a new beginning. But this is not different from the astronomer who chooses to describe a star as having evolved from a gaseous cloud rather than as developing into a red giant, or a biologist who describes the development of an animal species as the end of an evolutionary movement rather than the beginning of a new species.

Norbert Elias has criticized the limited time perspective of sociology by comparing sociology and cosmology in a similar spirit:

> For sociologists, processes and structures of the nineteenth or eighteenth century often appear as events of little significance for what happens today. What happened one thousand or two thousand years ago may appear to many contemporary sociologists not worth speaking of, something of no interest whatsoever for sociologists. Cosmologists, on the other hand, may well be equally interested in what happens today and what happened millions of years ago. They see clearly the connection between past and present. They are able to perceive such events together as aspects of a unitary process. Their time perspective, in other words, is dictated not by their personal involvement but by the facts themselves, whose connection with each other they try to unravel and to represent by means of testable theoretical models, mostly of process models. If the time perspective of sociologists too were fact oriented, they too would have the task of bringing to light the processes connecting past events with each other and with present times (Elias 1987:xvi–xvii).

That history cannot be objective is just as unpersuasive a proposition as that it deals with unique things. Chapter XI of Huizinga's book describes the churchyard of the Innocents at Paris, with its skulls and bones in open charnel-houses along the cloisters that surround the burial ground on three sides. Huizinga uses this and other descriptions to evoke the medieval image of death. The description is as objectively true as any other scientific hypothesis: it represents the facts as best the author knew them, and may have to be reviewed, modified or rejected in the light of later findings. The same holds for the hypothesis about the image of death that the author presents.

In the present context it is relevant to recall that Huizinga was also the author of *Homo ludens* (1938), a theoretical and speculative work that attempts to determine the "play element of culture" (*het spelelement der cultuur*). In American universities, this is prescribed as a textbook not in philosophy or history but in departments of physical education because it deals with games and sports and emphasizes the body, an entity often neglected by theoreticians (Sartre included it in *Being and Nothing*, an ingenious Cartesian adaptation of Heidegger's *Being and Time*, which had omitted it). The body is as important in ritual as it is in most of the games that Huizinga deals with and that illustrate a greater variety of "language games" than were discussed by Wittgenstein, who introduced this notion. In Wittgenstein, "language games" remain so vague that they can be identified with the most diverse entities. In ritual, the mantras of Kashmir Śaivism were interpreted by Harvey Alper as "Śiva's Language-game" (Alper 1988:249–294). The importance of Huizinga's *Homo ludens* is that he characterized play precisely and enumerated a number of its features, including the circumstance that it is generally engaged in for its own sake. He included ritual in this characterization.

If even a cursory inspection of a historical text suggests that Dilthey's approach is not applicable to his own discipline, it should not surprise us that the allegedly fundamental distinction between the sciences and humanities is not supported by any of the illustrations or theoretical considerations offered in its support. Dilthey was a fascinating scholar, but even Husserl, the founder of phenomenology, "considered him chiefly as a man of genius for intuition, but not of rigorous science and theory" (Spiegelberg 1965,I:123 referring to Husserl 1952:173). Dilthey was the son of a clergyman and his biography includes a case of puritanical idealism that his sympathetic exponent Rickman (1979:28–30) regards not only as "a little repugnant today" but, even for a contemporary of Queen Victoria, as "a mystery." Dilthey's ideas are religious in the sense of the Western notion (Chapter 28) as was established in 1929 by Fritz Heinemann.

Heinemann (1929:178–208) describes the "religious coloring" of the approach to history found throughout the Romantic period, in Schleiermacher, Hegel, Carlyle and Dilthey. He shows how the freedom which Dilthey attributes to *Verstehen*, by which one raises above the limitations of place and time through a creative identification with other eras and personalities, is described in terms of a religious experience. Dilthey commented on a variety of religious values:

> "Germany is a nation which, since the end of the middle ages, has responded to each strong intellectual impulse with a change in its religious outlook" (*Deutschland ist eine Nation, die seit Ausgang des Mittelalters auf jeden starken intellektuellen Impuls mit einer Veränderung des religiösen Weltansicht antwortete*: in Heinemann, page 187).

> "My vocation is to grasp the innermost religious life in history and to express it in dynamic terms at the present time when we are moved exclusively by the state and by science" (*Mein Beruf ist, das Innerste des religiösen Lebens in der Historie zu erfassen und zur bewegenden Darstellung zu bringen in unseren von Staat und Wissenschaft ausschliesslich bewegten Zeiten*: in Heinemann, page 191).

Heinemann, who praises Dilthey's contribution to philosophy as the first understanding of life and history that is free from "abstract thinking," characterizes it at the same time as "historical pantheism." Such "pantheism" is different from Christian theism but conforms to the Western notion of religion which stresses doctrinal content. Whatever the value of this vision, it does not provide a solid foundation for a distinction upon which not only much contemporary research is based, but also the modern understanding of man and his place in the universe—at least in the Western world.

The study of ritual and mantras undertaken in the present book and the conclusions and corollaries derived from this study do not support nor are they supported by the idea that the humanities and the sciences are fundamentally different from each other. We have seen that other areas of the humanities have also been studied without depending on the assumption of the two cultures, notably in the science of language: this applies to the work of Jakobson—the scholar who has "done most to revitalize the human sciences" (Frank 1984:29)—of Chomsky and his followers, and includes much of Lévi-Strauss' anthropology. The distinction between sciences and humanities is not clearly appropriate to the study of history, and clearly inappropriate in areas of natural science such as biology. This is obvious from the work of Konrad Lorenz and the development of ethology which ensued, along with attempts at "socio-biology" and the work of scholars like Jacques Ruffié in France or Stephen Jay Gould in the United States. It would be surprising if methods of study that work in science and in the areas of language, ritual, philosophy, music, literature, anthropology and history could not be profitably used in all areas of the humanities. Our conclusion must be that the human sciences are simply a group of sciences.

Dilthey was right that history is a necessary component of the study of man. The importance of history explains, but does not justify the enduring popularity of historicism or more recent relativisms such as "post-structuralism" or "post-modernism." It is clear that theories that emphasize an exclusively synchronic approach are incomplete unless they are supplemented by diachronic theories which include hypotheses on origins. In linguistics, this has been accepted again after long hesitation: the strictures of the Linguistic Society of Paris, which prohibited at the beginning of the century the study of the origin of language, are no longer in force (see, for example, Parts II and III of the *Proceedings* of the conference on "Origins and Evolution of Language and Speech": Steklis, ed., 1976).

Although neglected by anthropologists, history, which includes the study of origins, is relevant to the study of ritual (Chapter 14). Burkert, originally a classicist, is perspicuous in this respect. Despite the fact that he is hesitant when stating what he does:

> I once wrote that one should forbid the use of the term "origin," and I try, sometimes without success, to avoid the word in my own usage. What I am trying to find is what I would call *formative antecedents*, which of course implies the notion that the earlier is a formative power for what is latter . . . (Burkert 1987:212).

he is very interesting when speculating about origins, provided we look at what he actually does (see, e.g., Burkert 1987:152).

To adopt, like Burkert, a biological approach, is to adopt an evolutionary, that is, Darwinian perspective, whether developed along orthodox lines or in a more revolutionary vein. For a theory about the origin of language, for example, Eldredge and Gould's 1972 proposals for "punctuated equilibria" are more promising than the traditional "phyletic gradualism." For Donald Davidson, speaking at the conference just referred to (1976:18–19), is right in saying that a language is only a language when it is similar to the most highly developed languages (the only ones we happen to know).

Jonathan Smith's distaste for origins is much more marked than Burkert's although he, too, has advanced speculations about origins, adding that they have to be regarded as a *jeu d'esprit* (Smith 1987:206). His stated, theoretical position is uncompromising:

> These considerations underscore the position that a theory of sacrifice cannot be found in a quest for origins, but can only be found through the detailed examination of elaborations (1987:195).

Later, after discussing interesting hypotheses about things that might have happened "before which," he writes:

> but there comes a point where the nature of the sources simply will not let you go any farther. In other words, my nervousness on the subject of "originating," "origins," "original" has to do in part with a stance. In another sense, it has very much to do with the nature of the reports that I, at least, am dependent on—reports designed precisely not to ask the question that's been asked, namely, the question about history, about origin (1987:208).

In 1978 I published an article in which I speculated about features of the Agnicayana that must be regarded as pre-Vedic (Staal 1978). Kashikar argued that it is impossible and unnecessary to engage in such speculations (Kashikar 1979). He objected to hypotheses that go beyond the data and that are not absolutely certain. My reply (Staal 1982a:44–47) referred to scientific speculation about the origins of life, the earth, the planetary system and the universe. Such speculations are among the most interesting contributions of contemporary science and are, of course, not "absolutely certain." They go beyond the observed data and resort under the domain of the unobservable. In paleontology, a class of microscopic beings, called *archibacteriae*, have been postulated to have existed for the last three and a half billion years, although no one has seen them. Astrophysicists theorize about what happened during the first few seconds of the "history" of the universe. Why should humanists be prohibited from doing the same within their own disciplines?

Some speculations are, probably, no more than wild dreams. They have value only if they are treated as hypotheses amenable to rational discussion. Since they are liable to being improved, they are not final. Final truth is sought in religion but does not exist in science. This does not imply that one should avoid unobservables. Kashikar or Jonathan Smith simply deprive themselves and their readers of hypotheses that are of interest because they contain possible explanations. We shall not make progress unless we supplement synchronic studies with diachronic studies that do not eschew origins. In all these respects the human sciences are like the exact sciences and there is no foundation for the myth of the two cultures.

Dilthey's historicism is a forerunner of Kuhn's *Structure of Scientific Revolutions* (1970) and both lead easily to relativism although Kuhn himself has not accepted relativist interpretations of his work. To followers of anti-scientific ideologies, science is as arbitrary as faith and a scientific hypothesis is no better than a myth. The distinction is, that hypotheses, unlike myths, are refuted or rejected by considerations of logic or fact. The difference is illustrated by Stephen Toulmin's *The Return to Cosmology* (1982), which argues, following Kant, that hypotheses concerning "the universe as a whole" cannot be scientific and must therefore be myths. Toulmin supports this argument with a critique of two French biologists, Jacques Monod and François Jacob, who had used their discoveries in molecular biochemistry to bolster the already well entrenched central tenet of Darwinism, that variations arise by chance and selection is based upon the demands of the environment.

Toulmin diminishes the importance of chance with which, says he (page 145), Monod has made "excessive play." He criticizes Monod's and Jacob's "Biological Structuralism" for depending on "mechanistic Cartesianism." Rhetorical force is added by attributing a "peculiar Frenchness" ("not meant frivolously": page 15) not only to Monod and Jacob, but also to the mystic dreams of Teilhard de Chardin. Not being a biologist,

I may be wrong in failing to detect any difference between this "Biological Structuralism" and Darwinism apart from the fact that the former is further developed. But one need not be a biologist to be able to perceive that hypotheses about anything "in its entirety" (Kant's phrase) are scientific provided they depend on data and argument, are liable to rational discussion, and can be refuted by considerations of fact and logic. Toulmin has not shown that there is a point where the theories of science must end and make room for mythology.

We have seen that the myth of the two cultures crossed the Channel and the Atlantic. Let us pray that it does not settle on the Pacific Rim.

30

Conclusions

30A. The Origin of Language

The previous chapter has thrown doubt on the doctrine that there is a fundamental difference between science and the humanities. Developments in linguistics, biology and other sciences, and the investigations on ritual and mantras in Parts II and III combine to show that the general scientific method of gathering data and formulating hypotheses to account for these data can be fruitfully adopted in all these kinds of research. The final blow to the myth of the two cultures is delivered by the existence of Indian sciences of language and ritual (Chapter 26), which originated from an oral tradition (Chapter 27) without depending on any form of natural science. These Indian sciences show that the distinction of the two cultures is not only unfounded but lacks universality: for science is not confined to the natural sciences as they developed in the West. This conclusion is supported negatively by the religious nature of *Verstehen* and of the privileged status claimed for it: for the underlying notion of religion is not universal but Western (Chapter 28). All these conclusions support the idea that the human sciences are scientific in nature and universal in scope.

We are now in a position to provide the provisional definition of ritual that could not be given at the outset (page 61). Ritual may be defined, in approximate terms, as a system of acts and sounds, related to each other in accordance with rules without reference to meaning. The qualification implies that neither ritual nor mantras constitute a "language." Ritual rules are sometimes the same, and sometimes different from the rules of language discovered in linguistics. Two features characterize them: (1) they are recursive and can generate infinitely many structures; and (2) they correlate sounds and acts in such a manner as to approximate a one-one-correspondence, even though we find in actual fact numerous deviations from this principle. This second feature implies that Parts II and III have dealt with different sides of the same coin: both "ritual" and "mantras" fall under "ritual" in a wider sense. Since ritual is not a system of symbolic representations that refer to something else, it cannot be explained in terms of religion or society. Though embedded in various contexts and applied to a variety of events, it adheres to its own rules, follows its own course and leads its own life.

The independence of ritual from religion and society has been perceived before. The late Naoshiro Tsuji, for example, who was not only Japan's leading Sanskrit scholar but also a specialist of Vedic ritual in the tradition of Hillebrandt and Caland, regarded the traditional intepretations of ritual as irrelevent to its understanding. Familiar with the full breadth of Indology and Sanskrit literature, he once remarked that nothing reminded him more of Vedic ritual than the Japanese tea ceremony (Minoru Hara, personal communication).

To what extent is our working definition of ritual applicable to other data? To answer this question would require a large undertaking with ramifications leading us in different directions. In some contexts, rites and mantras must be kept distinct; in others, the concept of ritual will include both. The definition needs to be tested in non-Asian civilizations and among non-human animals. I have generally assumed that animal ritualization is akin to the human, following the results of ethology (Lorenz 1963 = 1966, 1965, 1967, Eibl-Eibesfeldt 1971, 1975, Hinde 1982 with the literature cited; cf. also Chapter 23) and the research of such scholars as Burkert (1979, especially Chapter II), Fehling (1974), and so forth. The notions of "FAP" ("Fixed Action Pattern": Thorpe 1951) and ("Modal Action Pattern": Barlow 1977) are helpful in understanding ritual structure among many animal species. I shall illustrate the relevance of ethology for the study of human ritual with one example from Vedic ritual.

According to Heesterman (1962, 1983), Vedic ritual must be explained against a background of battle, the agonistic elements of which are "identified away" by abstract liturgical elements. Other explanations of ritual from violence have been given elsewhere, specifically by Burkert (1972) and Girard (1972). They are the subject of a recent publication entitled *Violent Origins: Ritual Killing and Cultural Formation* (Hamerton-Kelly, ed., 1987).

Ritual as a replacement for aggression is not uncommon among nonhuman animals. It is found in *tournaments*, a term used by Konrad Lorenz and other ethologists to refer to ritualized battles. Here is an example:

> During the breeding season the male marine iguanas become territorial. They defend a small area of lava rock against other males, whilst females are allowed to stay. If a male rival approaches the territory, its owner displays. He opens his mouth, nods with the head and walks stiffleggedly up and down in front of the rival, showing his lateral aspect. The dorsal crest is erected and the gular regions extended. If the rival answers by the same display, fighting is initiated. The opponents rush at each other. But in spite of the biting intentions shown during the display they never bite each other, but instead lower their head and butt. The hornlike scales on the roof of the head interlock and the animals try to push the other away. This can continue for a while, with pauses in between, during which the opponents display frontally. The struggle ends when one of the rivals is pushed from the rock or when he gives up by assuming a submissive posture (lying flat on his belly). The winner then stops fighting and waits in threat display for the rival to leave. The fight is a highly ritualized tournament in the course of which the stronger wins, without hurting the loser.
>
> * * *
>
> Ritualized fighting is fairly widespread in animals that are capable of inflicting serious damage to the conspecific. Poisonous snakes never bite each other, but the rivals wrestle according to fixed rules. Cichlid fishes have developed various forms of mouthfighting and thus avoid mutual damage. In a number of species, e. g. in wolves, fighting starts as a damaging fight, but ends by a submissive posture of the loser, which inhibits further aggression (Eibl-Eibesfeldt 1966:475–476; referring to Lorenz 1963).

At this point a problem arises: if ritual as defined, or defined along similar lines, occurs among nonhuman animals, the science of ritual is not a component of the human sciences, but a link between those sciences and other biological sciences. The solution to this problem depends on the extent to which human and other animal rites are different. My present guess is that human ritual differs from animal ritual in the greater degree of its involvement with mantras. For this there is empirical support and it would explain that humans evolved language and other animals did not. It is too early to propose a solution to this problem which would depend on many details about which little is known; but it is worth pointing out that any solution would have implications for the concept of culture. For if culture is a system of meanings and symbols (the "Chicago doctrine" in the words of Edmund Leach 1985:156), ritual is not part of culture (as it is not part of religion), and a wide gap subsists between humans and other animals (this is in accordance with Western religious speculation following *Genesis*: see Staal 1979c). The alternative is to incorporate ritual in culture along with language, but regard only language as exclusively human. Available data support this latter option. The definitions of ritual and culture affect the problem of the origin of language, whether it coincides with the origin of the human animal or whether it constitutes merely an important event in its evolution, as seems more likely.

Ritual data from human and other animal species suggest that both prehuman animals and humans who had not yet evolved language, performed rituals basically of the nature we have studied. I assume that complex ritual systems evolved in which there were several types of sound and act and numerous deviations from the principle of one-one-correspondence. This labyrinth of correspondences became more prominent when sounds that correspond to acts were uttered even at times when the acts themselves were *not* performed. We need assume no more than that our ancestors sang, hummed and voiced sounds while *imagining* or *thinking* of rites. These latter faculties are available to many animals: they imagine (danger, for example) or think (of food or sex). This stage survives or is re-enacted in the otherwise unexplicable phenomenon of mantra recitation and meditation outside ritual context. Language originated when sound-meaning correlations were selected out of the abundance of sound-act correspondences that exist in animal ritual.

The phonological pattern extracted from Jakobson (page 275): *oṃ*, *mama*, *papa* illustrates this development from mantras to language. Sounds did more than accompany rites; they developed into a language that *refers* to rites. This survives in the idea of one-one-correspondence between mantras and rites that is otherwise difficult to explain. Acts, already distinct, were now classified by sounds. This system of reference generated *meanings* that were stand-ins for acts and other entities. Since the correlation between rites and mantras constituted a complex system, meanings developed by further extension, accretion and systematization until language was born with the full complexity of its features—a complexity that cannot be explained by assuming that it gradually developed as a rational system for the sake of reference, expression, or communication. Born by chance, language was selected and retained, despite its cumbersome complexity, because of its uncanny power to relate a great variety of sounds to a great variety of meanings. Like elsewhere in biology, traces of its origin remain. For although language correlates sounds and meanings, large chunks of arbitrary ritual structures survive in it which play no part in this correlation. They explain the syntax of human languages and other features of language that are similarly intricate, nontrivial, nonfunctional and determined by highly restrictive principles.

If this sketch correctly characterizes the development from ritual via mantras to language, it provides an immediate explanation for the hypothesis that ritual and mantras are not languages: they are not languages because they originated prior to language in the scheme of evolution. This hypothesis has other implications of which I shall mention three.

(1) It is incorrect to assume that mantras are meaningless because their meaning was forgotten. It would be extraordinary for any intelligent creature to continue to engage in meaningless

activities and remember the extremely complex structures constructed out of mantras, whilst forgetting the simple meanings presumably assigned to them in their original context. The untenability of this assumption is supported by an analysis of one of the more sophisticated hypotheses about such forgetting. Paul Thieme (1957) distinguished between the explicit descriptions of the epic and the allusive nature of the Rigveda. According to him, meaning was forgotten because the verses of the Rigveda were, by their very nature, allusive and obscure (page 374). Thieme also proposed that Vedic ritual originated from a *feast*: it is a "stylized feast" (*stiliertes Gastmahl*). It is not clear whether there is any connection between these two theories.

Like other reductionist theories (Smith 1987:196 mentions three types: sacrifice, New Year and initiation), the "feast" hypothesis does not explain the data. Thieme attributes the belief in the magical power of mantras to the nature of *brahman*, a problem he had dealt with elsewhere. He explains the survival of mantras and acts without their original meaning, which has been "forgotten," by the fact that "the element of the irrational, unintelligible, even contradictory plays, after all, in magic a necessary role" (*Das Element des Irrationalen, Unverständlichen, ja Widersinnigen spielt ja in der Magie eine notwendige Rolle*: Thieme 1957: 91). But this "necessary" role cannot serve as an explanatory hypothesis. It merely states in different terms ("magic") what we are trying to explain.

Puzzling about ritual is not the belief in "magical power" held only by a minority of those who continue to engage in its performance. Its mystery lies buried in the apparently innocent notion of "stylization." This is not different from the "ritualization" of activity that is the object of the science of ritual. Burying problems in an apparently simple notion is reminiscent of the exchange in linguistics to which I referred on page 54: Charles Hockett (1968) had argued that Chomsky's "transformations" were unnecessary because the "subtle facts about various languages" (Hockett 1968:3) they had brought to light could be explained by *analogy*. Lakoff's review article of 1969 showed that the notion of "analogy" could account for the data

Chomsky had dealt with, provided the "theory of analogy" would incorporate all the devices Chomsky had used to define transformations, including rule order, recursiveness, variables, exceptions, cyclical application, and so forth. A theory of "stylization" that explains all the rules of ritual so far discussed would for the same reason be an adequate theory of ritual.

(2) A second implication of the hypothesis of the ritual origin of language is that it explains the emergence of logic. The redundancy of language was gradually discovered—a process that still continues. This led to attempts to expunge these ritual survivals and construct more effective and rational systems of expression and communication. This explains the construction of the artificial languages of logic and mathematics. If language reflected meaning in a straightforward manner, it would be logical to begin with and there would be no need for logic.

(3) The assignments of meanings to ritual sounds had been an arbitrary but successful process. Not surprisingly, it picked up momentum and could not be stopped. Meanings were now assigned to all kinds of entities. Not only were sounds, arbitrarily but systematically, interpreted as meanings, thus producing language; but trees, mountains, rivers, the universe, animals, man himself were also endowed with meanings that were believed to be intrinsic. Everything became meaningful. These extrapolations from language explain the origin of many features of magic, mythology, religion, and philosophy itself. They place Max Müller's and Wittgenstein's views on these features as "diseases of language" in their evolutionary context.

We are now in a position to discuss the origins of hermeneutics—a topic that is more interesting than hermeneutics itself. The development from ritual via mantras to language demonstrates the insufficiency of any approach that treats ritual and mantras as languages. But if they are not languages, they certainly are not texts. We have seen that the *Modistae* and other medieval grammarians prevailed over the "authors" who emphasized texts (page 35), and that contemporary linguistics similarly prevailed over the emphasis on texts and finite corpora in Whitney, Bloomfield and others (page 52). A more ancient and venerable European speculation holds that the entire universe is a book that needs to be deciphered. In his famous work on European literature and the Latin middle ages, Ernst Robert Curtius devoted a chapter to this *topos* of "the book as symbol." We recognize here the impact of canonical books in the Western monotheistic religions which the Koran aptly characterized as "religions of the book." Today such speculation is no longer found in scientific theory though it survives in metaphorical expressions such as "the book of nature."

In the human sciences the metaphor has survived much longer and is more than a metaphor whenever we really deal with *texts*—as in philology. To look upon other manifestations of culture as texts, however, reflects the particular nature of Western religion. To this belief hermeneutics adheres, and it explains all its foibles. It is found elsewhere in an attenuated form, especially among scholars concerned with textual interpretation. Jonathan Smith, for example, although untainted by the irrationalities of hermeneutics, looks for a text whenever he seeks support for an argument. This self-imposed restriction prevents him from looking for a global theory of universals. It is less fatal, yet misleading when it occurs in a metaphor, for example: "ritual is primarily a matter not of nouns and verbs, but of qualifiers—of adjectives and adverbs" (Smith 1987:194).

To sum up—*ritual* originated when the compound activity of doing things and making sounds grew into a system. This happened early, after the emergence of the phylum *Chordata*. *Language* was born when that system was used to express meaning, probably late in the evolution of *homo sapiens*. *Texts* originated as expressions of language when writing was invented during the historical period. Like most other features of nature, ritual, therefore, is not a language; *a fortiori*, it is not a text.

Hermeneutics is confined to texts and text-like objects. As a corollary I conclude that attempts to bridge the gap between "Anglo-Saxon" and "Continental" philosophies by attempting a synthesis between analytical philosophy and hermeneutics are fruitless and misguided. This could be shown with reference to Richard Rorty or Charles Taylor, but I shall illustrate it with reference to the philosopher who has done most to interpret the history of the human sciences within a philosophic perspective.

30B. Michel Foucault

Foucault's *Les mots et les choses* (1966), an "archeology of the human sciences," shows, like Quine's *Word and Object* (1960)—not to mention *Words and Things* (Gellner 1959), *Words and Objections* (Davidson and Hintikka 1969), or *Words* (*Les mots*: Sartre 1963)—that the chief concern of contemporary philosophy is with the relationships between language and reality. One way to study these relationships is by concentrating on how existing languages refer. Since it is unlikely that language came into being to enable human beings to philosophize about reality, it is more promising to devise new languages that can do better than the existing ones. The artificial languages of logic and mathematics are such languages. Their development is due to the insight that the objects of reference need not possess the structure of ordinary language—the mistake exemplified by the simple illusion that, whenever there is a word, there must be a thing to which it refers. Another example is the belief that reality must consist of substances that possess attributes because language possesses nouns qualified by adjectives. The entities to which language refers need not be languages or even language-like even if human beings are predisposed to look upon them as such.

Even at the relatively early point of his short career when he wrote *Les mots et les choses*, Foucault would not say that philosophy deals primarily with the relationships between language and reality. But he says something similar, in inimitable Foucaultian, and after referring to Nietzsche and Mallarmé: "the whole curiosity in our thought now resides in the question: What is language, how can we find a way round it in order to make it appear in itself, in all its plenitude?" (I quote from the

English translation: Foucault 1970:306). Foucault's primary aim was not to overcome the opposition between analytical and continental philosophies. Rather, he attempted to go, as the title of a monograph about him (Dreyfus and Rabinow 1982) puts it: "beyond structuralism and hermeneutics." Concern with this problem is similar but more firmly rooted in the French intellectual climate; it was the chief topic of the dispute between Lévi-Strauss and Sartre (page 259) which focused on structuralism and phenomenology. Foucault also formulated it first with reference to phenomenology, long before hermeneutics had become fashionable in the English speaking countries.

There are important differences between phenomenology and hermeneutics but they are insignificant in the present context. That Foucault was concerned with developments on both sides of the Channel, affecting the main concerns of modern philosophy, is clear from his attempt to show that both structuralism and phenomenology have a common ground in a nineteenth century development in the course of which "language became an object." This view is largely based upon a discussion devoted to Franz Bopp (pages 280–294 of the English translation). The preceding sections of the same chapter (Chapter 8 of Part II) dealt with the British economist David Ricardo and the French anatomist Georges Cuvier. In the next chapter, Foucault discusses "the vast play of language contained within a single space" as "a leap toward a wholly new form of thought" and notes: "Only those who cannot read will be surprised that I have learned such a thing more clearly from Cuvier, Bopp, and Ricardo than from Kant or Hegel" (page 307).

According to Foucault, the objectification of language led to three related developments: the study of the Indo-European languages by Bopp; logical algebra or the formalism of thought by Boole and Russell; and the discovery of the unconscious by Freud. Many phrases and passages in which this is formulated in *Les mots et les choses* are, at least at a first reading, obscure. I shall therefore quote the French originals along with their (anonymous and occasionally free) translation:

> At the archeological level, the conditions of possibility of a non-verbal logic and of a historical grammar are the same. The ground of their positivity is identical (page 297 of the English translation: *au niveau archéologique, les conditions de possibilité d'une logique non verbale et celle d'une grammaire historique sont less mêmes. Leur sol de positivité est identique*: 1966:310).

> The critical elevation of language . . . implied that it had been brought nearer both to an act of knowing, pure of all words, and to the unconscious element in our discourses. It had to be either made transparent to the forms of knowledge, or thrust down into the contents of the unconscious. This certainly explains the nineteenth century double advance, on the one hand towards formalism in thought and on the other towards the discovery of the unconscious—towards Russell and Freud. It also explains the tendency of one move towards the other, and of these two directions to cross: the attempt, for example, to discover the pure forms that are imposed upon our unconscious before all content; or again, the endeavour to raise the ground of experience, the sense of being, the lived horizon of all our knowledge to the level of our discourse. It is here that structuralism and phenomenology find, together with the arrangements proper to them, the general space that defines their *common ground* (page 299; *La surélévation critique du langage . . . impliquaît qu'il soit rapproché à la fois d'un acte de connaître pur de toute parole, et de cela qui ne se connaît pas en chacun de nos discours. Il fallait ou le rendre transparant aux formes de la connaissance, ou l'enfoncer dans les contenus de l'inconscient. Ce qui explique bien la double marche du XIXe siècle vers le formalisme de la pensée et vers la découverte de l'inconscient—vers Russell et Freud. Et ce qui explique aussi les tentations pour infléchir l'une vers l'autre et entrecroiser ces deux directions: tentative pour mettre au jour par exemple les formes pures, qui avant tout contenu s'imposent à notre inconscient; ou encore effort pour faire venir jusqu'à notre discours le sol d'expérience, le sens d'être, l'horizon vécu de toutes nos connaissances. Le structuralisme et la phénoménologie trouvent ici, avec leur disposition propre, l'espace général qui définit leur* lieu commun: 1966:312).

These phrases are not merely occasionally puzzling; they are, when clear, so demonstrably mistaken that the argument collapses. One problem is that the formalization of logic in Boole and Russell was not only foreshadowed by Leibniz, but is connected with the medieval logicians and goes clearly back to Aristotle. Its advance in the nineteenth century is due to mathematics, the science of formalization *par excellence* and the first science that Foucault intentionally omitted from his account (since it is already given "pride of place" in the history of science and thought: page ix of the "Foreword to the English edition").

The weakest link in Foucault's account is the inclusion of historical grammar or comparative grammar of Indo-European in this trinity of "positive unconscious knowledge" which marks the beginning of the modern age and constitutes the chief subject of Foucault's work (pages xi-xii). Bopp could only develop these disciplines because he had been influenced and inspired by the Indian grammarians (Chapters 5 and 6). The entire convergence of disciplines took place in the nineteenth century as a matter of fact, but is due to chance: its roots are diverse and have nothing in common in terms of their "historicity." If it were true that these diverse disciplines express a unified "positive unconscious knowledge," we must assume that the sea-faring nations of Western Europe that initiated the colonization of Asia were driven by an unconscious desire to discover a theory of language.

The "objectification" of language that Foucault deduces from these considerations as the common ground of structuralism and phenomenology was the foundation upon which the Indian grammatical tradition rested. It was explicitly formulated by the Sanskrit grammarians in terms that happen to exemplify the structure of the Sanskrit language. We have seen that the most commonly used Sanskrit term for Pāṇini's notion of rule, which goes back to the science of ritual, is *sūtra*. But there is a synonym that is widely used, for example by Patañjali in his account of the infinity of language (page 40): *lakṣaṇa*. This formation consist of a stem "*lakṣ*" and a suffix "*(a)na*" which together denote an activity directed at an object. The object is formed, in accordance with the general structure of Sanskrit, by the suffix "*ya*" being attached to the stem. This results in *lakṣya* which means: "the object of *lakṣ*." The Sanskrit grammarians accordingly refer to the rules of grammar as *lakṣaṇa*. The objectification of language, therefore, is not a discovery of early nineteenth century Europe, but of ancient India. It was the *ground* upon which the edifice of the Sanskrit grammarians rested, and was explicitly formulated as such. Because of Charles Wilkins, Franz Bopp and others it was incorporated into traditional philology and led to the origination of linguistics in the West.

Foucault is to be applauded for including in his philosophic investigations studies of the history of science, especially of the often neglected human sciences. This inclusion distinguishes him from many other philosophers who confine themselves to philosophy. It might seem unfair to blame Foucault for not having included the study of Indian science in a perspective that is already so vast. I am not blaming Foucault but merely pointing out that the history of science cannot be confined to the West. The separation between East and West, which turned into an almost unbridgeable gap after the European Renaissance, is artificial and counterproductive especially in the domain of science. The prejudice that science and rational thought are only Western is not only pernicious but an obstacle to the understanding of any scientific development. Science is not the product of a peculiar European development; it is universal. For a historian of science or of ideas, trying to account for Bopp without referring to Pāṇini is like a historian of logic studying Tarski without mentioning Aristotle, or an archeologist digging at Istanbul without knowing that it is built on Byzantium.

That Foucault accepts the prejudice that rational thought is only Western is clear from the Preface to his book which quotes from Borges' imaginary Chinese encyclopedia a taxonomy of categories "that lack all life and place, but are rooted in a ceremonial space, overburdened with complex figures, with tangled paths, strange places, secret passages, and unexpected communications" (page xix). That such a confused assemblage amuses Foucault is only to be expected—but why would he assume that an Asian would not be equally amused? I have shown elsewhere that such taxonomies constitute a literary genre that has nothing to do with Chinese or Indian logic or scientific thought, which have both evolved rational taxonomies like the Western. The common prejudice that Oriental thought is irrational, exotic and weird lacks a serious foundation (Staal 1975: Chapters 1–3; 1988a:20–22, *passim*).

It might still be claimed that this criticism is unfair because Foucault's search for historicity is, after all, a relativist undertaking. Elsewhere Foucault has written that: "effective history differs from traditional history in being *without constants* . . . history becomes effective to the degree that it introduces discontinuity into our very being" (Foucault 1977:153–154).

Philp (1985:78), who quotes this passage, adds: "At the heart of Foucault's work lies the conviction that there is no constant human subject to history—that there is no valid philosophical anthropology—and thus no basis for claiming that we can identify a coherent and constant human 'condition' or 'nature.' " This passage comes from a later work, and Foucault has, as he has repeatedly noted, often changed his mind. This is a mark of sincerity, but the latter view is unfortunately false. It is obvious that humans have changed throughout history and are different in different parts of the world; but whatever the changes and differences, it is equally obvious that humans have features in common which they do not share with monkeys, fish, trees or stars.

Foucault's speculation about the *common ground* of phenomenology and structuralism shows no trace of relativism or of this later theory of "absence of constants." It is a hypothesis about events that took place in the nineteenth century and is argued for with detailed information and sustained (though not always perspicious) argument. Since he obviously wishes to be taken seriously, Foucault is open to serious criticism.

A final question arises in this context. Is the "structuralism" Foucault refers to in fact related to what I have generally called "science" and tried roughly to characterize in Chapters 2 and 26? Dreyfus and Rabinow have tried to pinpoint the kind of structuralism Foucault has in mind and how he himself differed from it. They distinguish two kinds of structuralism (1982:53–55): the *atomistic* in which the elements are completely specified apart from their role in a system, and the *holistic*, "in which what counts as a *possible* element is defined apart from the system, but what counts as an *actual* element is a function of the whole system of differences in which the given element is involved." Dreyfus and Rabinow state that Foucault addresses the second, but rejects it in favor of yet another *ism* that is more radical and referred to as *pragmatic holism*. Here, even the *identity* of a statement depends on the use that is made of it: "Not only can the identity of *the statement* not be located once and for all in relation to that of the sentence, but *it* is itself relative and oscillates according to the use that is made of *the statement* and the way in which *it* is handled" (quoted from the 1972 English translation of Foucault 1966, page 104). Though this passage is imprecise (for example, to *what* can the expressions I have italicized refer if not to an identical "statement"?), the state of affairs that Foucault attempts to express is not uncommon in science. In some sciences the basic concepts are defined beforehand; in others, they are not. Chomsky's symbol "S," for example, which stands for "Sentence," is not defined in advance but is contextually defined by the entire system of linguistics in which it occurs. The notion of ritual provisionally used in the present study and not defined, approximately, until now, has a similar status as do, indeed, Sanskrit terms for ritual such as *kriyā* and *karman*. Foucault's *pragmatic holism*, which sounds like something wonderfully new, refers in fact to a common feature of science.

30C. Concluding Generalities

What remains to be carried out is a systematic, formal analysis of the rules of ritual. This will be an extensive project of research for which I have only tried to pave the way. In the absence of solid results to which such an analysis might lead, no general conclusion can be drawn and there is only room for scattered remarks.

The regard for unicity on the part of many phenomenologists and hermeneuticians has a religious origin. Oscar Cullmann has shown that the word and the concept for "once" occur with characteristic frequency in the Bible. His book starts with the statement: "Original Christian faith and thought are not based upon the spatial distinction between this world and a world beyond, but upon the temporal distinction Once—Now—Then" (Cullmann 1946:1). In Christianity there is not only one God, who has one son; God has created the world *once*, sent his son *once*, and there is *one* day of judgement. The notion of progress, that hallmark of the West, partly derives from these ideas. Many Oriental systems, on the other hand, stress repetition, transmigration or reincarnation, numerous worlds and world periods. This distinction between East and West is related to that between rectilinear and circular time. The present relevance of Asian ideas is connected with the need for a future based on balance and stability rather than unlimited growth.

Uniqueness is often related to chance, for the products of chance are generally unique. If a native of Beijing marries a Sioux from Minnewaukan, North Dakota, their child is likely to be unique. Its characteristics, on the other hand, need not be unique at all. Everything is unique to some extent, but nothing is unique in all respects. Many things are similar in one respect, fewer in two, still fewer in more, and no two things are similar in all respects. Things that are relatively unique may be of special interest only on account of features that are themselves non-unique.

A possible objection to the theories sketched in this book is that the structural complexities of Vedic ritual should perhaps be dismissed for being unique, anomalous and hence of limited use to the general theory of ritual. I briefly addressed this question in the General Introduction to AGNI (I:16):

> Perhaps Vedic ritual is too sophisticated, highly developed, and intellectual. This may be so—I could not tell without a major comparative survey of rituals. However, I suspect that such criticism is on a par with saying that it does not matter that a certain theory of language does not apply to Sanskrit or English, because Sanskrit or English are too sophisticated, highly developed, and intellectual. If anyone were to make such a claim, the conclusion would be simple and immediate: his theory of language is itself insufficiently sophisticated, developed, and intellectual. The same verdict must apply to the theories of ritual we have reviewed. If they cannot account for Vedic ritual, they must go.

The theories I had reviewed in the General Introduction to AGNI were rather general; they could probably not account for *any* ritual. Moreover, I had not, at the time of writing, undertaken any comparative study of ritual, although the second volume of AGNI itself contained data that were intriguing in this respect (especially in the articles by Hooykaas, Skorupski and Strickmann).

These questions about uniqueness are empirical and can only be definitively answered when we make detailed comparisons of Vedic ritual with other rituals that appear similarly complex and sophisticated. Students of comparative ritual face certain problems, however, for they cannot do fieldwork all over the world and must accordingly consult the scientific literature, which is almost entirely preoccupied with problems of semantics. The only way to overcome this obstacle is by reading between the lines. This can be done, provided the fieldwork reports of an author are very explicit and rich, and replete with what is nowadays called "thick description." In that case we may try to achieve what Malinowski required that an anthropological book should enable its readers to do: construct a theory that accounts for the author's data but is different from his own theory.

Attempts of this sort have been made in Chapter 25. Subsequently, similarities were found between the historically unrelated Vedic and Taoist ritual traditions. These will be studied in a forthcoming publication by Kristofer Schipper and myself.

Several anthropologists have remarked that the Agnicayana ritual is unique and that what counts in anthropology is the "common" rites of "ordinary" people. Burkert has voiced a similar objection to Jonathan Smith and myself:

> Your paradigms seem to be of a different character. I think for Jonathan it is mainly rabbinic; for Frits it is the brahmanic tradition. But both are special cases, because you have there groups of people who really spend their lives meditating on ritual or doing ritual, and they keep their own identity just by this, in my view, nearly obsessive concentration on ritual. I am looking at more humane kinds of ritual that are communicative and are understandable to a certain degree, though perhaps not totally understandable (Burkert 1987:233).

The question is: how different is a special case? The obsessiveness with ritual that Burkert pinpoints sheds as much light on ritual as Mozart's or Euler's obsessions shed on music or mathematics. It is clear that musicologists should study symphonies as well as lullabies, and mathematicians cylindrical algebra as well as fractions. It is unlikely that it would be fruitful to confine our science to what is ordinary, human, and more or less intelligible. The most curious and challenging things are neither average, nor immediately intelligible. It is unlikely that a theory of ritual, if adequate, will be simple. There will be complaints about its myriad rules as there have been about Chomsky and Halle's *Sound Pattern of English*, Euclid's *Elements*, or the Śrauta Sūtras.

Science includes analysis of the apparently unique, but accounts for it in terms of its opposite: the general and universal. To make something intelligible is to relate it to general and universal features. Universality characterizes the best work also in the human sciences. Jakobson discovered the simplest and at the same time most well-established universals—distinctive features. For Chomsky, the search for universals of language is the essence of linguistics. For Lévi-Strauss, anthropology seeks universals of the human mind.

Universals need not be universal in the sense that they must be found everywhere. The issue, at first sight puzzling, is discussed in "Universals" (Staal 1988a) with special reference to logic and linguistics, but is straightforward within phonology itself. The click sounds of Xhosa and Hottentot are described in terms of universal distinctive features but these sounds occur only in a few language families. Ritual and mantras are particularly well developed in Asia. Mantras seem to be common in Africa, too, but one has to read between the lines (Dammann 1963:116–131, 228–233). The modern West preserves little more than *abracadabra*, *amen*, *aleluja* and *hosanna*, although Pentecostals add uncounted numbers of meaningless sounds almost every day. That these ritual sounds involve musical patterns that we now recognize as recursive was pointed out by the founder of the phenomenology of religion, G. van der Leeuw. In a chapter on "Music and Religion" he drew attention to the schema ABA in: "Kyrie eleison—Christe eleison—Kyrie eleison" (van der Leeuw 1948:378).

Although the term *mantra* is of Sanskrit origin, I have tried to show that the study of mantras deals with features that are universal. We can now speculate and even predict—other features of science not absent from the human sciences. When I first visited Bali, I predicted that I would hear Vedic mantras. Within a few days after my arrival, I heard a priest at a temple ritual recite a fragment of the Gāyatrî (page 306). In subsequent conversation, it turned out that he knew the entire mantra. I thus obtained a verification of my prediction. Later I learned that the Gāyatrî in its entirety is not used in traditional Balinese ritual, but had been recently introduced from India by a Hindu missionary. My hypothesis was falsified—and the episode illustrates that we should not rush to conclusions.

Hypotheses may be suggested by negative facts, for example, the fact that the Old Testament does not contain ritual texts. This does not imply that there was no ritual: the biblical texts are "what whoever wrote them wanted you to know, as opposed to what they might know" (Smith 1987:210). Although there is no information on biblical rites, Smith adds (ibid.): "The rabbis gleefully will supply that lacuna for you, but they don't know any more than I do on the subject." It is true that an *argumentum e silentio* does not prove much, but a hypothesis may be established with a good measure of probability if it is supported by a general theory of ritual and a sound knowledge of a particular context—in this case, the Bible and whatever data have been made accessible by the biblical sciences.

In anthropology, "language" occupies the pride of place. This is as it should be for language is the most characteristic feature of the human animal, more important, for example, than a prohibition on incest, variable as to content. The importance of language, however, does not justify the emphasis on meanings and symbols adopted in anthropology and religious studies. Mantras are not sounds of an unknown language that has to be deciphered, and neither mantras nor ritual acts are symbols that express meanings. Both are governed by rules, but they are rules without meaning. Our confusions in interpreting ritual systems are largely caused by the disconcerting concatenation of two independent and unrelated facts: ritual systems are like language in that they are governed by rules, but unlike language in that they do not express meanings. For their study, understanding and analysis, such systems accordingly require syntactic theories that deal with rules, not semantic theories that deal with meanings. The Indian Śrauta Sūtras have paved the way.

Indian and Western civilization have been characterized by their emphasis on linguistics and mathematics, respectively (e.g., Ingalls 1954, Ruegg 1978, Staal 1963a, 1965b). It would be more accurate to say that the originality of Indian science lies in the discovery of rule-governed activity. The importance of rules is that they express regularities, similar to the regularities of nature and the non-human universe in general—whether the latter are regarded as "laws of nature" or as mathematical formulas. An important distinction between rules that govern *activities* and rules that describe other regularities is that agents who perform activities may be aware of the rules they follow or observe. This is not confined to humans; dogs know where they may not go. A distinction must be made between *following* a rule and *knowing that* (*or knowing what*) *rule one follows*. The planets go around the sun in accordance with regularities described by rules, but do not know or consciously follow any of these rules.

When they are aware of the rules they follow, men and other animals *add* a feature to patterns of regularity that already exist in the universe. If we adopt the distinction of Indian philosophy between *pradhāna* or "principal entity" and *guṇa* or "subordinate entity" (page 230), following a rule is *pradhāna*, being aware of it, *guṇa*. This particular *guṇa* exhibits the nature of consciousness, that much overrated philosophers' pet (E. W. Beth called it "het troetelkind der traditionele wijsbegeerte"), a kind of tracing in the mind or brain as yet unexplained. For us individuals such awareness does not only make a difference; it may be a matter of life and death. In the development of the species it plays a less important role or no role at all. The limited relevance of Wittgenstein's remarks about following rules (Chapter 6B) is connected with this difference between individuals and the species. Innate knowledge of rules is the result of a process that may have gone on for millions of years. It may be unconscious because it may reflect knowledge acquired by the species that never became conscious in any individual.

Awareness of rules is not only a subordinate feature; it also varies with individuals and circumstances. In the use of language, some speakers or hearers are more clearly aware of the grammatical rules they follow than others. No speaker who is not a linguist is aware of complex features such as rule order or the rules that account for the difference between "John's eagerness to please" and *"John's easiness to please" (page 25). In ritual, Heesterman(1962:18;above, page 154) has discussed a case that exhibits similar features. When the victim is tied to the sacrificial pole, "the cord is fastened to the right foot, goes round the left side of the neck and is then wound round the right horn and finally fastened to the stake." This explains the origin of the rite: originally, the victim's head was cut off while it was tied to the stake. In the present context, we make a different observation: most ritualists who conform to the rule are unlikely to be aware of the historical origins of what they are doing. Some might recognize their plausibility if they were pointed out to them; in some individuals, an awareness or semi-awareness of their original motivation may be lingering. Whatever the degree of awareness, what counts in ritual is what the ritualist *does*.

The meaninglessness of ritual and the myth of the two cultures are two tips of the iceberg of human nature. What remains under water is not only the roots of religion, but an even more ancient and archaic obsession with language and its symbol-generating and mythopoeic functions. This reflects the nature of man as the unique creature that is endowed with language and loves to talk. The origination or discovery of language was the most momentous step the human animal took in the course of its evolution. It also threw him into immediate and profound confusion. To attach meanings to sounds in order to express oneself or establish communication opens up a world of new possibilities. To attach meaning indiscriminately is by the same token profoundly disorienting. This explains Wittgenstein's remark that philosophical problems have an aura of profundity because they are as deep as our language (*Philosophical Investigations* §111).

Although every zoologist knows that an elephant does not have meaning, students of the humanities and social sciences attach meaning to many expressions and manifestations of humanity as if they were linguistic expressions. An artificial gap between us and the rest of the universe is created by myths that have solidified into doctrines, e.g., that man is unique, created in the image of a deity, or beyond rational understanding. Underlying such ideas is the assumption that man must make sense. To an unbiased observer, much of that sense seems arbitrarily assigned, evanescent, or due to chance. The available evidence suggests that man can make as much sense as he likes, but does not make intrinsic sense. Like our language, and all other creatures, we humans originated by chance. The thought may have occurred to King Solomon when he was contemplating ants (*Proverbs* 6:6). It must have been in the mind of the poet of Rigveda 10.129.7:

> Whence this creation has arisen—perhaps it formed itself, or perhaps it did not—the one who looks down on it, in the highest heaven, only he knows—or perhaps he does not know (translation O'Flaherty 1981:25–26).

Excursus

"Writing in the Sky"

Hermeneutics and Astrology:
A Neoplatonic Parallel

The *Enneads* of Plotinus are called after the number (*ennea*, "nine") of chapters in each of its books just as the *Aṣṭādhyāyī* of Pāṇini is called after the number (*aṣṭa*, "eight") of its chapters. In a passage of the fourth *Ennead*, the great Neoplatonic philosopher, who was born in 205 A.D. in Upper Egypt and studied in Alexandria, stresses the ritualistic nature of prayer and argues that its effect is neither due to a deity or heavenly body nor based on the intention of the person who prays but derives from the correctness with which it is performed:

> In the stars (that is, the gods) there is no will to answer our prayers . . . their powers are used without will, whether they are provoked (by us) or not, through a scientifically effective procedure (τέχνη) . . . The performer may be a bad person (κακός)—it need not surprise us: bad people fetch water from the rivers. The being that gives does not know that it gives; it simply gives (IV 4.42.3–4, 6–8, 14–17 Bréhier).

The explanation of the efficacy of prayers lies in the fact that the entire universe is like a single organism:

> Prayer is effective because one part of the universe sympathizes with another, as in the stretched string of a lyre when the vibration moves from low to high. Often, when one string vibrates, another perceives it, as it were, because they are tuned in concord and harmony. Vibrations move even from one lyre to another, showing how far the "sympathy" goes. In the universe, too, there is one universal harmony even if it consists of contraries (IV 4.42.11–14).

This picture is more attractive than Cartesian dualism, but it does not explain how particular heavenly bodies influence our destiny. This is the topic of the third chapter of the second *Ennead*:

> If heavenly bodies signify (σημαίνουσιν) future events, like we say of many other things that they are signs (σημαντικά) of the future, whence comes this quality? How does order come about? For nothing could announce events that are not arranged in order. The stars must be like letters that are constantly being written in the sky, or that have been written once and for all, and that move; while performing another activity, they also, through that same activity, convey meaning (σημασία) (II 3.7.1–7).

The fifth century Roman Neoplatonist Macrobius referred to this view and explicated it further in his *Commentary* on Cicero's *Scipio's Dream*:

> In his treatise *Do the stars act?*, Plotinus declares that nothing happens to man because of the force or power of heavenly bodies; but the events that destiny has in store for us are announced by the seven wandering stars by means of their locations and retrogradations. Similarly, birds signify future events of which they are unaware by the way they fly or alight, and by their wings or songs. Hence we are right in saying that Jupiter is auspicious or Mars inauspicious, since happy events are signified (*significantur*) by the former and unhappy events by the latter (translated from the French translation in Duhem 1914, II:310).

Duhem places this discussion in its philosophic context by quoting an observation due to Bréhier (1907:1). The Greek philosophers discussed the nature of causation by specifying what kind of entity can be a cause. The Pre-Socratics recognized only causes that are material and visible; Plato and Aristotle sought the principles of things in elements that are perspicuous to clear thought, that is, intelligible things; the Stoics and Epicurians returned to the Pre-Socratic view that causes must be material; the Neoplatonists reacted against this and returned to Plato by again accepting only intelligible causes. Pre-Socratics, Stoics and Epicurians were all in a position to accept the claims of astrology according to which stars are causes of terrestrial events. Their disbelief in unseen and immaterial causes resembles that of the modern empiricists and positivists discussed in

Chapter 2, but is, in the case of astrology, not based upon empirical facts. Plotinus did not accept material causation, but interpreted the stars as endowed with meaning or significance: they inform us about events that are caused by other agencies.

The naive astrological view, that the stars cause events, runs parallel to the naive view that rites cause events. Some Brāhmaṇas declare that the rising and setting of the sun is caused by the performances of the morning and evening Agnihotra. But if one does not believe that stars or rites cause or influence events,—and neither Plotinus, nor contemporary hermeneuticians do—then what is there left to believe? Skirting the obvious answer ("Nothing") what we need is an explanation for the fact that people entertain such beliefs. Both Neoplatonists and hermeneuticians felt that there must be something left to believe in. They accordingly postulated "meanings" or "significations," a scientific procedure provided it is supported by empirical data. Neoplatonists and hermeneuticians justify their belief by treating a variety of entities as if they were texts. Hermeneuticians stop short of stars, which Plotinus included without compunction.

That Plotinus did not believe in rituals is related by his pupil Porphyry in his *Life of Plotinus* (10.33–38):

> Amelius was a lover of rituals (φιλοθύτος). He would never miss the New Moon Ceremonies or any other recurring festivals. Once he wanted to take Plotinus with him, but the latter said: "the gods should come to me, not I go to them." We did not understand the mentality underlying these proud words, and we did not dare to ask.

The Neoplatonic parallel indicates that the urge to attach meanings to what is essentially meaningless is a common feature of the human animal. It occured in the Brāhmaṇas and re-appared in hermeneutics and related philosophies like "symbolic anthropology." This extrapolation from the systematic reference to meanings that characterizes language must have come into being—probably not very long—after the origin of language.

Bibliography

A. Texts

The texts are listed without particulars regarding editions, translations, commentaries, etc., which are known to specialists. Non-specialists may derive comfort from the thought that mantras should be *heard*, not *read*.

Aitareya Āraṇyaka
Aitareya Brāhmaṇa
Anattalakkhaṇa Sutta
Āpastamba Śrauta Sūtra
Aṣṭādhyāyī
Āśvalāyana Gṛhya Sūtra
Atharvaveda Prātiśākhya
Atharvaveda Saṃhitā
Baudhāyana Śrauta Sūtra
Bṛhad Āraṇyaka Upaniṣad
Chāndogya Upaniṣad
Jaiminīya Araṇyageyagāna
Jaiminīya Ārcika
Jaiminīya Grāmageyagāna
Kauṣītaki Brāhmaṇa
Kātyāyana Śrauta Sūtra
Kauthūma-Rāṇāyanīya Grāmageyagāna
Mahābhāṣya
Maitrāyaṇi Saṃhitā
Mīmāṃsā Paribhāṣā
Mīmāṃsā Sūtra
Mīmāṃsā Sūtra Bhāṣya
Nārada Śikṣā
Nirukta
Pañcaviṃśa Brāhmaṇa
Prapañcasāra
Puṣpasūtra
Ṛgveda Prātiśākhya
Ṛgveda Saṃhitā
Sāmaveda Saṃhitā
Śatapatha Brāhmaṇa
Stobhānusaṃhāra

Taittirīya Āraṇyaka
Taittirīya Brāhmaṇa
Taittirīya Prātiśākhya
Taittirīya Saṃhitā
Ūhagāna
Vājasaneyi Prātiśākhya
Vedānta Sūtra Bhāṣya

B. Other Publications

Aarsleff, H. (1970). "The History of Linguistics and Professor Chomsky." *Language* 46:570–585

AGNI: see Staal 1983a

Alper, H. P. (1988). "Śiva's Language-game," in: Alper, ed.: 249–294

Alper, H. P. (ed.) (1988). *Understanding Mantras*, Albany, N.Y.

Anscombe, G. E. M. (1959). *An Introduction to Wittgenstein's Tractatus*, London

Apel, W. (1970). *Harvard Dictionary of Music*, Cambridge, Mass.

Aristotle, *Categoriae et Liber de Interpretatione*, ed. L. Minio-Paluello, Oxford 1949

Aristotle, *Categories and De Interpretatione*, transl. J. L. Ackrill, Oxford 1963

Aristotle, *Metaphysics*, ed. W. D. Ross, I-II, Oxford 1924

Arnold, Harold (forthcoming). "The Hinduization of Vedic Ritual," in: Strickmann (ed.) 1988

Auden, W. H. (1974). *Forewords and Afterwords*, New York

Austin, J. L. (1961). *Philosophical Papers*, Oxford

Austin, J. L. (1962). *How to do Things with Words*, Oxford

Ayer, A. J. (1936) *Language, Truth and Logic*, New York

Balasooriya, S. *et al.* (1980). *Buddhist Studies in Honour of Walpola Rahula*, London and Sri Lanka

Baptista, Luis (unpublished), "On Parallels between Bird Song and Speech Development."

Barbour, Ian (1980). "Paradigms in Science and Religion," in: Gutting, Gary (ed.) 223–245

Barlow, George W. (1977). "Modal Action Patterns," in: Sebeok (ed.) 98–134

Beck, Leslie (ed.) (1962). *La philosophie analytique*, Paris

Benfey, Th (1874). *Einführung in die Grammatik der vedischen Sprache*, Göttingen

Beth, Evert W. (1959). *The Foundations of Mathematics: A Study in the Philosophy of Science*, Amsterdam

Bethel, T. (1976). "Darwin's Mistake," *Harpers* (February)

Bharati, Agehananda (1965). *The Tantric Tradition*, Garden City

Bhattacharya, K. (1973). *L'ātman-brahman dans le bouddhisme ancien*, Paris

Bleeker, C. J., G. W. J. Drewes and K. A. H. Hidding (eds.) (1951). *Proceedings of the 7th Congress for the History of Religions*. Amsterdam

Bloomfield, L. (1933). *Language*. New York

Bloomfield, M. (1906). *A Vedic Concordance*. Cambridge, Mass. Reprint 1964.

Boehtlingk, Otto (1887). *Pāṇini's Grammatik*. Leipzig. Reprint 1964.

Bokenkamp, Stephen R. (1983). "Sources of the Ling-pao Scriptures," in: Strickmann 1981–1983, II:434–486

Bollée, W. B. (1981). "The Indo-European Sodalities in Ancient India." *Zeitschrift der deutschen morgenländischen Gesellschaft* 131:172–191

Boulez, Pierre (1966). *Relèves d'apprenti*, textes réunis et présentés par Paul Thevenin, Paris

Bowra, Sir Maurice (1966). "Dance, Drama, and the Spoken Word," in: Huxley, ed. 387–392

Bradley, F. H. (1893). *Appearance and Reality*, London

Bréhier, Emile (1907). *La théorie des incorporels dans l'ancien Stoicisme*, Paris

Brough, J. (1950). "The meaning of ni$\sqrt{\text{hnu}}$ in the Brāhmaṇas." *Siddheshwar Varma Commemoration Volume*, I:126–130

Brough, J. (1953). *The Early Brahmanical System of Gotra and Pravara*, Cambridge

Brough, J. (1971). "Soma and *Amanita muscaria*." *Bulletin of the School of Oriental and African Studies* 34:331–362

Brown, W. N. (1965). "Theories of Creation in the Ṛgveda." *Journal of the American Oriental Society* 85:23–34

Brunner, Hélène (1986a). "Les membres de Śiva." *Asiatische Studien/Etudes Asiatiques* 40:89–132

Brunner, Hélène (1986b). "*Maṇḍala* et *Yantra* dans le Sivaisme Agamique: Definition, description, usage rituel," in Padoux (ed.) 11–35

Brunner-Lachaux, Hélène (1963–1977). *Somaśambhupaddhati*, I–III, Pondichéry

Burghardt, Gordon M. and Bekoff, Marc (1978). *The Development of Behavior: Comparative and Evolutionary Aspects*, New York

Burkert, Walter (1972). *Homo Necans: Interpretationen altgriechischer Opferriten und Mythen*, Berlin

Burkert, Walter (1979). *Structure and History in Greek Mythology and Ritual*, Berkeley

Burkert, Walter (1983). *Anthropologie des religiösen Opfers*, Munchen

Burkert, Walter (1987). see: Hamerton-Kelly

Bursill-Hall, G. L. (1974). "Toward a History of Linguistics in the Middle Ages, 1100–1450," in: Hymes (ed.) 77–92

Caland, W. (1903). "Uber das rituelle Sūtra des Baudhāyana." *Abhandlungen für die Kunde des Morgenlandes* 12:1–65. Reprint 1966.

Caland, W. (1904–1913). *Baudhāyana-śrauta-sūtra*, Calcutta, I–III

Caland, W. and V. Henry (1906), *L'Agniṣṭoma: description complète de la forme normale du sacrifice de Soma dans le culte védique*, I–II, Paris

Caland, W. (ed.) (1926), *Ziegenbalg's Malabarisches Heidenthum*, Amsterdam

Carnap, Rudolf (1936–1937), "Testability and Meaning," *Philosophy of Science* 3:419–471 and 4:1–40

Carnap, Rudolf (1947), *Meaning and Necessity*, Chicago

Carnap, Rudolf, Charles Morris and Otto Neurath (1936–1962), *International Encyclopedia of Unified Science*, Chicago

Cassirer, Ernst (1925), *Philosophie der symbolischen Formen*, Berlin, I-II

Cherry, C. (1974), *Pragmatic Aspects of Human Communication*, Dordrecht-Boston

Chomsky, Noam (1957), *Syntactic Structures*, The Hague

Chomsky, Noam (1961), "On the notion 'rule of grammar'," *Structure of Language and its Mathematical Aspects, Proceedings of symposia in applied mathematics* 12:6–24

Chomsky, Noam (1964), *Current Issues in Linguistic Theory*, The Hague

Chomsky, Noam (1965), *Aspects of the Theory of Syntax*, Cambridge, Mass

Chomsky, Noam (1966), *Cartesian Linguistics. A Chapter in the History of Rationalist Thought*, New York and London

Chomsky, Noam (1968), *Language and Mind*, New York

Chomsky, Noam (1975), *Reflections on Language*, New York

Chomsky, Noam (1980), *Rules and Representations*, New York

Chomsky, Noam (1981), *Lectures on Government and Binding*, Dordrecht-Cinnaminson

Chomsky, Noam (1986), *Knowledge of Language: Its Nature, Origin and Use*, New York

Chomsky, Noam and Morris Halle (1968), *The Sound Pattern of English*, New York

Coedès, G. (1967), *The Making of South East Asia*, Berkeley-Los Angeles

Converse, H. S. (1974), "The Agnicayana Rite: Indigenous Origin?" *History of Religion* 14:81–95

Conze, Edward (1969), *Buddhist Meditation*, New York

Coward, H. and Sivaraman, K., (eds.) (1977), *Revelation in Indian Thought. A Festschrift in Honour of Professor T. R. V. Murti*, Emeryville

Cullmann, Oscar (1948), *Christus und die Zeit. Die urchristliche Zeit- und Geschichts-Auffassung*, Zurich

Curtius, Ernst Robert (1948), *Europäische Literatur und lateinisches Mittelalter*, Bern

Dammann, Ernst (1963), *Die Religionen Afrikas*, Stuttgart

Dandekar, R. N. (1946–1973), *Vedic Bibliography*, Poona, I–III

Dandekar, R. N. (1982), "Some Aspects of Vedic Exegesis," *Indologica Taurinensia* 10:71–81

Dandekar, C. G., Kashikar, C. G. and others (1958–1973), Śrautakoṣa: *Encyclopaedia of Vedic Sacrificial Ritual*, Poona

Darwin, Charles (1872), *The Expression of the Emotions in Man and Animals*, London

Davidson, Donald (1976), "Introduction," to Part II in: Steklis, etc. (ed.) 18–19

Davidson, Donald and Hintikka, Jaakko (1969), *Words and Objections: Essays on the Work of W. V. Quine*, Dordrecht

Davison, A. T. and Apel, W. (1974), *Historical Anthology of Music*, Cambridge, Mass, I–II

Demiéville, P. (1930), "Bombai," *Hôbôgirin. Dictionnaire encyclopédique du bouddhisme d'après les sources chinoises et japonaises* 1:93–113

Demiéville, P. (1980), "Notes on Buddhist Hymnology in the Far East," in: Balasooriya, ed.

Diehl, C. G. (1956), *Instrument and Purpose: Studies on Rites and Rituals in South India*, Lund

Dilthey, Wilhelm (1949), *Grundriss der allgemeinen Geschichte der Philosophie*, ed. by H.-G. Gadamer, Frankfurt am Main

Drewes, G. W. J. (1925), *Drie Javaansche Goeroe's*, Leiden

Dreyfus, Hubert L. and Rabinow, Paul (1983), *Michel Foucault. Beyond Structuralism and Hermeneutics*, Second Edition, with an Afterword by and an Interview with Michel Foucault, Chicago

Duhem, Pierre (1914), *Le système du monde: histoire des doctrines cosmologiques de Platon à Copernic*, Paris

Dumont, Louis (1959), "Le renoncement dans les religions de l'Inde," *Archives de sociologie des religions* 7:45–69

Dumont, Louis (1966), *Homo hierarchicus: Essai sur le système des castes*, Paris

Dumont, P.-E. (1939), *L'Agnihotra*, Baltimore

Dumont, P.-E. (1957), "The Full-Moon and New-Moon Sacrifices in the Taittirīya-Brāhmaṇa," Part I, *Proceedings of the American Philosophical Society* 101:216–243

Dundes, Allan (1978), "Into the Endzone for a Touchdown," *Western Folklore* 37:75–88

Durkheim, Emile (1915), *Les formes élémentaires de la vie religieuse. Le système totemique en Australie*, Paris. English translation 1915, London and New York

Edwards, Paul (ed.) (1967), *The Encyclopedia of Philosophy*, New York - London, I–VIII

Eggeling, Julius (1882–1900 = 1966), *The Śatapatha Brāhmaṇa*, I–V, New Delhi

Eibl-Eibesfeldt, I. (1966), "The Fighting of Marine Iguanas," in: Huxley, ed. 475–476

Eibl-Eibesfeldt, I. (1971), *Love and Hate*, New York

Eibl-Eibesfeldt, I. (1975), *Ethology*, New York

Eldredge, Niles (1982), "An Ode to Adaptive Transformation," *Nature* 296:508–509

Eldredge, Niles and Gould, Stephen Jay (1972), "Punctuated Equilibria: An Alternative to Phyletic Gradualism," in: Schopf, ed.

Eliade, Mircea (1958), *Yoga: Immortality and Freedom*, Princeton

Eliade, Mircea (1964), *Shamanism: Archaic Techniques of Ecstasy*, London

Elias, Norbert (1987), *Involvement and Detachment*, Oxford

Faddegon, B. (1927), "Ritualistic Dadaism," *Acta Orientalia* 5:177–195

Fehling, Detlev (1974), *Ethologische Uberlegungen auf dem Gebiet der Altertumskunde: Phallische Demonstration—Fernsicht—Steinigung*, München

Filliozat, Jean (1946), "Les origines d'une technique mystique indienne," *Revue philosophique* 136:208–220

Filliozat, Jean (1965), "Kailāsaparamparā," in: *Felicitation Volume of Southeast Asian Studies presented to His Highness Prince Dhaninivat*, Bangkok

Findly, E. B. (1988), "Mántra Kaviśastá: Speech as Performative in the Ṛgveda," in: Alper, ed. 15–47

Firth, Raymond (1967), *Tikopia Ritual and Belief*, Boston

Foucault, Michel (1966), *Les mots et les choses*, Paris, Translated as:

Foucault, Michel (1970), *The Order of Things. An Archaeology of the Human Sciences*, New York

Foucault, Michel (1977), *Language, Counter-Memory, Practice*, Oxford

Frank, Joseph (1984), "The Master Linguist," *The New York Review of Books*, April 12

Frauwallner, Erich (1956), *Die Philosophie des Buddhismus*, Berlin

Freud, Sigmund (1907), "Obsessive Acts and Religious Practices," *Collected Papers* 2:25–35

Fung Yu-Lan (1952), *A History of Chinese Philosophy*, transl. Derk Bodde, Princeton, I

Gadamer, H.-G. (1965), *Wahrheit und Methode*, Tübingen

Gardner, Martin (1987), "Giving God a Hand," *The New York Review of Books*, August 13, 17–23

Garge, D. V. (1952), *Citations in Śabara-Bhāṣya*, Poona

Geertz, Clifford (1960), *The Religion of Java*, Glencoe, Ill.

Geertz, Clifford (1964a), " 'Internal Conversion' in Contemporary Bali," *Malayan and Indonesian Studies Presented to Sir Richard Winstedt*, Oxford, 282–302, reprinted in: Geertz 1973:170–189

Geertz, Clifford (1964b), "Tihingan: A Balinese Village" *Bijdragen tot de Taal-, Land- en Volkenkunde* 120.1–33

Geertz, Clifford (1968), *Islam Observed*, New Haven

Geertz, Clifford (1972), "Deep Play: Notes on the Balinese Cockfight," *Daedalus* 101:1–37, reprinted in: Geertz 1973:412–453

Geertz, Clifford (1973), *The Interpretation of Cultures*, New York

Geertz, Clifford (1976), "Hooykaas on (the) Geertz(es): A Reply." *Archipel* 12:219–225

Geertz, Clifford (1980), *Negara: The Theatre-State in Nineteenth Century Bali*, Princeton

Geertz, Clifford (1983), *Local Knowledge: Further Essays in Interpretive Anthropology*, New York

Geertz, Clifford (1985), "Waddling In," *The Times Literary Supplement*, 4.288 (June 5) 623

Geertz, H. and C. Geertz (1975), *Kinship in Bali*, Chicago

Gellner, Ernest (1959), *Words and Things. A Critical Account of Linguistic Philosophy and a Study in Ideology*, London

Gennep, A. van (1909), *Les rites de passage*, Paris

Gennep, A. van (1911), "De la méthode à suivre dans l'étude des rites et des mythes," *Revue de l'Université de Bruxelles*, 502–523. *Dutch translation*: Wetenschappelijke Bladen 3:97–110. English translation in: Waardenburg 1973 I:287–300

Ghurye, K. G. (1950), *Preservation of Learned Tradition in India*, Bombay

Giesey, R. E. (1960), *The Royal Funeral Ceremony in Renaissance France*, Geneva

Girard, R. (1972), *La violence et le sacré*, Paris

Gombrich, Richard (1971), *Precept and Practice*, Oxford

Gombrich, Richard (1974), "Eliade on Buddhism." *Religious Studies* 10:225–231

Gombrich, Richard (1985), "Knowledge of the Unknowable." *The Times Literary Supplement*, 4,278 (March 29) 359–360

Gonda, J. (1954), *Aspects of Early Viṣṇuism*, Utrecht

Gonda, J. (1963a), *The Vision of the Vedic Poets*. The Hague

Gonda, J. (1963b), "The Indian Mantra," *Oriens* 16:244–297

Gonda, J. (1965), *Change and Continuity in Indian Religion*. The Hague

Gonda, J. (1977), *The Ritual Sūtras*, Wiesbaden

Gonda, J. (1979), "Śatarudriya," *Sanskrit and Indian Studies: Essays in Honor of Daniel H. H. Ingalls*, Dordrecht 75–91

Gonda, J. (1980a), *The Mantras of the Agnyupasthāna and the Sautrāmaṇī*. Amsterdam

Gonda, J. (1980b), *Vedic Ritual: The Non-Solemn Rites*. Amsterdam

Gonda, J. (1981), *The praügaśastra*, Amsterdam

Gonda, J. (1982), *The Haviryajñāḥ Somāḥ: The interrelations of the Vedic solemn sacrifices. Śāṅkhāyana Śrautasūtra 14,1–13. Translation and Notes*, Amsterdam

Gonda, J. (1985), *The Ritual Functions and Significance of Grasses in the Religion of the Veda*, Amsterdam

Goodman, Nelson (1955), *Fact, Fiction and Forecast*. Cambridge Mass.

Goody, Jack (ed.) (1968), *Literacy in Traditional Societies*, Cambridge

Goody, Jack (1977), "Against 'Ritual': Loosely Structured Thought on a Loosely Defined Topic," in: Moore and Myerhoff, eds. 25–35

Goris, Roelof (1926), *Bijdrage tot de Kennis der Oud-Javaansche en Balineesche Theologie*, Leiden

Goudriaan, T. (1986), "Kubjikā's *samayamantra* and its manipulations in the Kubjikāmata," in: Padoux, ed., 141–167

Goudriaan, T. and Gupta, S. (1981), *Hindu Tantric and Śākta Literature*, Wiesbaden

Gould, Stephen Jay (1977), *Ever Since Darwin: Reflections in Natural History*, New York

Graham, A. C. (1959), Being in Western Philosophy compared with *Shih/Fei* and *Yu/Wu* in Chinese Philosophy," *Asia Major* (new series) 7:79–112

Graham, A. C. (1965), " 'Being' in Linguistics and Philosophy," *Foundations of Language* 1:223–231

Graham, A. C. (1967), " 'Being' in Classical Chinese," in: *The Verb "Be" and its Synonyms. Philosophical and Grammatical Studies*, ed. J. W. M. Verhaar, Dordrecht, I:1–39

Grapard, Allan G. (1982), "Japan's Ignored Cultural Revolution: The separation of Shinto and Buddhist divinities in Meiji (*shimbutsu bunri*) and a case-study: TŌNOMINE" (mimeographed)

Gray, J. E. B. (1959a), "An Analysis of Ṛgvedic Recitation," *Bulletin of the School of Oriental and African Studies* 22:86–94

Gray, J. E. B. (1959b), "An Analysis of Nambudiri Ṛgvedic Recitations and the Nature of the Vedic Accent," *Bulletin of the School of Oriental and African Studies* 22:499–530

Green, Douglas, M. (1965), *Form in Tonal Music*, New York

Gren-Eklund, G. (1978–1979), "An upaniṣad of sāman," *Orientalia Suecana* 27/28: 148–158

Gulik, R. H. van (1980), *Siddham: An Essay on the History of Sanskrit Studies in China and Japan*. Nagpur

Güntz, Th. (1861), *Der Geisteskranke in seinen Schriften*, Thonberg bei Leipzig

Gutting, Gary (1980), *Paradigms and Revolutions. Appraisals and Applications of Thomas Kuhn's Philosophy of Science*, Notre Dame

Güttinger, Hans Rudolf (1970), "Zur Evolution von Verhaltnisweisen und Lautäusserungen bei Prachtfinken (Estrilididae)," *Zeitschrift für Tierpsychologie* 27/8:1011–1075

Halle, Morris (1957), "In Defense of the Number Two," *Studies Presented to Joshua Whatmough on his 60th Birthday*, The Hague, 65–72

Halle, Morris (1975), "Confessio Grammatici," *Language* 51:525–535

Halle, Morris (1983), "On the Origins of the Distinctive Features," *International Journal of Slavic Linguistics and Poetics*, 27:Supplement, 77–86.

Hamerton-Kelly, Robert G. (ed.) (1987), *Violent Origins: Walter Burkert, René*

Girard, and Jonathan Z. Smith on Ritual Killing and Cultural Formation, Stanford

Hammel, E. A. and Simmons, W. S. (1970), *Man Makes Sense: A Reader in Modern Cultural Anthropology*, Boston

Harman, G. (1968), Review of Chomsky 1966, *Philosophical Review* 77:229–235

Harnad, Stephen R., Steklis, Horst D. and Lancaster, Jane (eds.) (1976), *Origins and Evolution of Language and Speech, Annals of the New York Academy of Sciences* 280:1–914

Hartshorne, Charles (1973), *Born to Sing: An Interpretation and World Survey of Bird Song*, Bloomington

Harvard Dictionary of Music (1970), ed. W. Apel, Cambridge

Hayes, E. Nelson and Hayes, Tanya (1970), *Claude Lévi-Strauss: The Anthropologist as Hero*, Cambridge, Mass and London

Heesterman, J. C. (1957), *The Ancient Indian Royal Consecration*, 's-Gravenhage

Heesterman, J. C. (1962), "Vrātya and Sacrifice," *Indo-Iranian Journal* 6:1–37

Heesterman, J. C. (1964), "Brahmin, Ritual and Renouncer," *Wiener Zeitschrift fur die Kunde Sud- und Ostasiens* 8:1–31

Heesterman, J. C. (1983), "Other Folk's Fire" in: AGNI II:76–94

Heesterman, J. C. (1984), "The Ritualist's Problem," in: Joshi, S. D., ed. 167–179

Heesterman, J. C. (1985), *The Inner Conflict of Tradition: Essays in Indian Ritual, Kingship and Society*, Chicago

Hegel, G. W. F. (1985), *Lectures on the Philosophy of Religion, III: The Consummate Religion*, transl. R. F. Brown, P. C. Hodgson and J. M. Stewart with the assistance of H. S. Harris, Berkeley

Heidegger, Martin (1953), *Sein und Zeit*, Tubingen

Heinemann, Fritz (1929), *Neue Wege der Philosophie: Geist/Leben/Existenz. Eine Einführung in die Philosophie der Gegenwart*, Leipzig

Helms, L. V. (1882), *Pioneering in the Far East and Journeys to California in 1849 and to the White Sea in 1848*, London

Hill, Jane H. (1972), "On the Evolutionary Foundations of Language," *American Anthropologist* 74:308–317

Hillebrandt, A. (1880), *Das altindische Neu- und Vollmondsopfer in seiner einfachsten Form*, Strassburg

Hillebrandt, A. (1897), *Ritual-Literatur, Vedische Opfer und Zauber*, Strassburg

Hinde, Robert A. (1982), *Ethology. Its Nature and Relations with Other Sciences*, New York

Hockett, Charles F. (1968), *The State of the Art*, The Hague

Hoogt, J. M. van der (1929), *The Vedic Chant studied in its Textual and Melodic Form*, Wageningen

Hooykaas, C. (1964), *Āgama Tīrtha: Five Studies in Hindu-Balinese Religion*, Amsterdam

Hooykaas, C. (1966), *Sūrya-Sevana: The Way to God of a Balinese Śiva Priest*, Amsterdam

Hooykaas, C. (1973), *Balinese Bauddha Brahmins*, Amsterdam

Hooykaas, C. (1976), "Social Anthropology, A Discipline of Theories and Hear-Say? (A Propos of Geertz on Bali)" *Archipel* 11:237–243

Hooykaas, C. (1983a), "Agni Offerings in Java and Bali," in: AGNI II:382–402

Hooykaas, C. (1983b), "Homa in India and Bali," in: Strickmann, ed. II:512–591

Howard, Wayne (1977), *Sāmavedic Chant*, New Haven and London

Howard, Wayne (1983), "The Music of Nambudiri Unexpressed Chant (*aniruktagāna*)," in: AGNI II:311–342

Hubert, H. and M. Mauss (1899), "Essai sur la nature et la fonction du sacrifice," *L'année sociologique* 2:29–138

Hughes, H. Stuart (1968), "Structure and Society," in: Hayes and Hayes 1970.22–46

Huizinga, J. (1919), *Herfsttij der Middeleeuwen*, Haarlem

Huizinga, J. (1938), *Homo ludens: Proeve eener bepaling van het spelelement der cultuur*, Haarlem

Humboldt, Wilhelm von (1836), *Uber die Verschiedenheit des menschlichen Sprachbaues und ihren Einfluss auf die geistliche Entwickelung des Menschengeschlechts*, Berlin

Husain, Yusuf (1929), *L'Inde mystique au moyen age: hindous et musulmans*, Paris

Husserl, Edmund (1952), *Ideen zu einer reinen Phänomenologie und phänomenologische Philosophie*, II, in: *Husserliana* IV.

Huxley, J. (ed.), (1966) "A Discussion on Ritualization of Behaviour in Animals and Man," *Philosophical Transactions of the Royal Society of London*, Series B, No. 772, 251:247–526

Hymes, Dell (ed.) (1974), *Studies in the History of Linguistics: Traditions and Paradigms*, Bloomington

Ikari, Yasuke (1975), "Ukhā to Mahāvīra," *Journal of Indian and Buddhist Studies* 23:1057–1046

Ikari, Yasuke (1983), "Ritual Preparation of the Mahāvīra and Ukhā Pots," in: AGNI II:168–177

Immelmann, K. (1962), "Beiträge zur einen vergleichenden Biologie australischer Prachtfinken," *Zoologisches Jahrbuch* 90:1–196

Ingalls, D. H. H. (1954), "The Comparison of Indian and Western Philosophy," *Journal of Oriental Research* 22:1–11

Ingalls, D. H. H. (1960), "On the Study of the Past," *Journal of the American Oriental Society* 80:191–197

Jacob, François (1981), *Le jeu des possibles. Essai sur la diversité du vivant*, Paris

Jain, Jyotirindra (1984), *Painted Myths of Creation: Art and Ritual of an Indian Tribe*, New Delhi

Jaini, Padmanabh S. (1979), *The Jaina Path of Purification*, Berkeley-Los Angeles-London

Jakobson, R. (1962), "Why 'Mama' and 'Papa'?" *Selected Writings*, The Hague, I:538–545

Jakobson, Roman and Halle, Morris (1960), *Grundlagen der Sprache*, Berlin

James, E. O. (1917), *Primitive Ritual and Belief. An Anthropological Essay*, London

Jay, P. C. (1968), *Primates*, New York

Jayatilleke, K. N. (1963), *Early Buddhist Theory of Knowledge*, London

Jest, Corneille (1964/1965), "Les Thakali," *Etnographie* 58/59:26:49

Jha, G. (transl.) (1933–1936), *Shabara-Bhāṣya*, I-III, Baroda

Jha, G. (1942), *Pūrva-Mīmāṃsā in its Sources*, Benares

Jha, V. N. (1973), "Śākalya and Pāṇini," *Bulletin of the Deccan College Research Institute* 33:223–226

Jha V. N. (1975), "Iti-karaṇa in the Ṛgveda-Padapāṭha," *Bulletin of the Deccan College Research Institute* 35:49–54

Jha, V. N. (1976), "Stages in the Composition of the Ṛgveda-Padapāṭha," *Bulletin of the Deccan College Research Institute* 35:47–50

Jong, J. W. de (1978), Review of Lamotte 1976, *T'oung Pao* 44:168–173

Jong, J. W. de (1987), "Lamotte and the doctrine of non-self," *Cahiers d'Extrême-Asie* 3:151–153

Joos, Georg (1934), *Theoretical Physics*, London

Joshi, S. D. (ed.) (1984), *Amṛtadhārā: Professor R. N. Dandekar Felicitation Volume*, Delhi

Kane, P. V. (1941, 1962), *History of Dharmaśāstra* Vol. II, Pt. II; Vol. V, Pt. II

Kashikar, C. G. (1968a), *A Survey of the Śrauta Sūtras*, Bombay

Kashikar, C. G. (1968b), "Presidential Address," *Vedic Section, All-India Oriental Conference, XXIVth Session*, Varanasi

Kashikar, C. G. (1979), "Agnicayana: The Piling Up of *svayamātṛṇṇā*," *Annals of the Bhandarkar Oriental Research Institute* 60:215–218

Kiparsky, Paul (1979), *Pāṇini as a Variationist*, Cambridge-London-Poona

Kiparsky, Paul (1982), *Some Theoretical Problems in Pāṇini's Grammar*, Poona

Kiparsky, Paul and Staal, Frits (1969), "Syntactic and Semantic Relations in Pāṇini," *Foundations of Language* 5.83–117

Klimburg-Salter, D. E. (1982), *The Silk Route and the Diamond Path: Esoteric Buddhist Art on the Trans-Himalayan Trade Routes*, Los Angeles

Kosambi, D. D. (1950). "On the Origin of Brahmin Gotras." *Journal of the Royal Asiatic Society, Bombay Branch* 26:21–80

Koster, Jan (1983). "Karel, Darwin en Chomsky. Over taal en evolutie." *Hollands Maandblad* 3–21

Kraemer, H. (1921). *Een Javaansche primbon uit de zestiende eeuw*, Leiden

Kripke, Saul (1982). *Wittgenstein on Rules and Private Language*, Cambridge Mass.

Kroodsma, Donald E. (1974). "Song Learning, Dialects, and Dispersal in the Bewick's wren." *Zeitschrift für Tierpsychologie* 35:352–380

Kroodsma, Donald E. (1978). "Aspects of Learning in the Ontogeny of Bird Song: Where, From Whom, When, How Many, Which, and How Accurately?" in: Burghardt and Bekoff, 215–230

Kuhn, Thomas S. (1970). *The Structure of Scientific Revolutions*, Second Edition, Chicago

Kunjunni Raja, K. (1963). *Indian Theories of Meaning*, Madras

Lakoff, George (1969). "Empiricism Without Facts," *Foundations of Language* 5:118–127

Lakoff, Robin (1969). Review (indirectly) of Chomsky 1966. *Language* 45:343–364

Lamotte, Etienne (1944–1980). *Le traité de la grande vertu de sagesse de Nāgārjuna (Mahāprajñāpāramitāśāstra)*, I–V, Louvain

Lamotte, Etienne (1958). *Histoire du bouddhisme indien*, Louvain

Lamotte, Etienne (1973). "Der Verfasser des Upadeśa und seine Quellen," *Nachrichten der Akademie der Wissenschaften in Göttingen, I. Philologisch-historische Klasse*, 31–50

Lancaster, J. B. (1968). "Primate Communication Systems and the Emergence of Human Language," in: Jay, ed. 439–457

Lauenstein, Diether (1943). *Das Erwachen der Gottesmystik in Indien*, München

Leach, Edmund (1970). *Lévi-Strauss*, Glasgow

Leach, Edmund (1985), Review of Singer 1984, *American Ethnologist* 12:154–156

Leeuw, G. van der (1948). *Wegen en Grenzen*, Amsterdam

Lévi, Sylvain (1898, 1966). *La doctrine du sacrifice dans les Brāhmaṇas*, Paris

Lévi-Strauss, Claude (1962). *La pensée sauvage*, Paris

Lévi-Strauss, Claude (1964). *Mythologiques I: Le cru et le cuit*, Paris. English translation 1969, New York and Evanston

Lévi-Strauss, Claude (1966). *The Savage Mind*, Chicago

Lévi-Strauss, Claude (1968). *Tristes tropiques*, Paris

Lévi-Strauss, Claude (1971). *L'homme nu*, Paris

Levy, John and Staal, Frits (1968). *The Four Vedas*, LP Album, New York

Lieberson, Jonathan (1984). "Interpreting the Interpreter," *The New York Review of Books*, March 15, 39–46

Liebich, Bruno (1891), *Pāṇini. Ein Beitrag zur Kenntnis der indischen Literatur und Grammatik*, Leipzig

Ligeti, L. (1978), *Proceedings of the Csoma de Kőrös Memorial Symposium*, Budapest

Lorenz, Karl (1951), "Uber die Enstehung auslösender 'Zeremonien'," *Die Vogelwarte* 16:9–13

Lorenz, Karl (1963), *Das sogenannte Böse. Zur Naturgeschichte der Agression*, Wien. English translation:

Lorenz, Karl (1966), *On Aggression*, London

Lorenz, Karl (1967), *Evolution and Modification of Behavior*, Chicago

Lüders, H. (1959), *Varuṇa II: Varuṇa und das Ṛta*, Göttingen

MacFarland, Pamela and Staal, Frits (1988), "Ritual Language Dismantled," in: *Le rituel. Actes du Colloque du Centenaire de l'Ecole Pratique des Hautes Etudes, Section des Sciences Religieuses*

Mâche, François-Bernard (1983), *Musique, Mythe, Nature; ou les Dauphins d'Arion*, Paris

Malamoud, Charles (1967), "Village et forêt dans l'idéologie de l'Inde brāhmaṇique," *Archives européennes de sociologie* 17:3–20

Malamoud, Charles (1977), *Le svādhyāya: récitation personelle du Veda. Taittirīya-Āraṇyaka Livre II*, Paris

Malamoud, Charles (1983), "Exégèse de rites, exégèse de textes," *Puruṣārtha* 7:17–38

Malinowski, B. (1948), *Magic, Science and Religion*, New York. Fragment in: Waardenburg 1973 I. 546–559

Mann, Thomas (1948), *Doktor Faustus: Das Leben des deutschen Tonsetzers Adrian Leverkühn, erzählt von einem Freunde*, Stockholm

Maspero, Henri (1950), *Le taoïsme*, Paris

Mauss, Marcel (1969), *Oeuvres*, III, Paris

May, L. C. (1956), "A Survey of Glossolalia and Related Phenomena in Non-Christian Religions," *American Anthropologist* 58:75–96

McAllister, David P. (1949), *Peyote Music*, New York

Merlan, Philip (1953), *From Platonism to Neoplatonism*, The Hague

Michael, Tara (1986), "Le Śrī-Cakra dans la *Saundarya-Laharī*, in: Padoux, ed. 127–137

Miller, G. A. (1964), "The Psycholinguists," *Encounter* 23:29–37

Miller, G. A. and Chomsky, N. (1963), *Handbook of Mathematical Psychology*, II, New York and London

Monod, Jacques (1970), *Le hasard et la nécessité. Essai sur la philosophie naturelle de la biologie moderne*, Paris

Montague, Richard (1968), "Pragmatics," reprinted in: Thomason, ed., 1974:95–118

Montague, Richard (1970), "Pragmatics and Intensional Logic," reprinted in: Thomason, ed., 1974:119–147

Moore, S. F. and Myerhoff, B. G. (eds.), *Secular Ritual*, Amsterdam

Morris, Desmond (1957), " 'Typical Intensity' and its Relation to the Problem of Ritualization." *Behavior* 11:1–12

Muktananda Paramahansa, Swami (1974), *The Play of Consciousness (Chitshakti Vilas)*, California

Muller, F. Max (1867), *Chips from a German Workshop I: Essays on the Science of Religion*, London

Munson, T. N. (1962), "Wittgenstein's Phenomenology." *Philosophy and Phenomenological Research* 23:37–50

Murti, T. R. V. (1955), *The Central Philosophy of Buddhism*, London

Mylius, Klaus (1976), "*Die vedischen Identifikationen am Beispiel des Kauṣītaki-Brāhmaṇa*." *Klio. Beitrage zur alten Geschichte* 58/1:145–166

Mylius, Klaus (1977), "Potṛ, potra. Charakteristik eines vedischen Opferpriesteramtes." *Ethnographisch-Archäologische Zeitschrift* 18:219–232

Mylius, Klaus (1982), "Acchāvakīya und Potra: Vergleich zweier vedischer Opferpriestamter." *Alt-Orientalische Forschungen* 9:115–131

Mylius, Klaus (1986), "*Acchāvakīya* und *potra*—ein Vergleich." *Sanskrit and World Culture*, Berlin: 471–474

Naess, Arne (1965), *Four Modern Philosophers: Carnap, Wittgenstein, Heidegger, Sartre*, Chicago

Nagatomi, M., Matilal, B. K., Masson, J. M. and Dimock, E. (eds.) (1980), *Sanskrit and Indian Studies, Essays in Honor of Daniel H. H. Ingalls*, Dordrecht

Nakamura, Hajime (1964), "A Critical Survey of Mahāyāna and Esoteric Buddhism." *Acta Asiatica* 6:57–88, 7:36–94

Nakamura, Hajime (1977), "The Problem of Self in Buddhist Philosophy," in: Coward and Sivaraman, eds., 99–118

Nakamura, Hajime (1980), *Indian Buddhism: A Survey with Bibliographical Notes*, Tokyo

Needham, Joseph (1954-1976), *Science and Civilisation in China*, I–V:3, Cambridge

Nettl, B. (1953), "Observations on Meaningless Peyote Song Texts." *Journal of American Folklore* 66:161–164

Neugebauer, O. (1957), *The Exact Sciences in Antiquity*, Providence

Nietzsche, Friedrich (1871), *Die Geburt der Tragödie aus dem Geiste der Musik*, Basel

Nieuwenhuijze, C. A. O. van (1945), *Śamsu'l-Dīn van Pasai: Bijdrage tot de kennis der Sumatraansche mystiek*, Leiden

Nottebohm, Fernando (1970), "Ontogeny of Bird Song." *Science* 167/2:950–956

Nyberg, H. S. (1953), "Das Studium des Orients und die europäische Kultur." *Zeitschrift der deutschen morgenländischen Gesellschaft* 103:9–21

Obeyesekere, Gananath (1981), *Medusa's Hair: An Essay on Personal Symbols and Religious Experience*, Chicago

Obeyesekere, Gananath (1984). *The Cult of the Goddess Pattini*, Chicago

O'Flaherty, Wendy Doniger (1981). *The Rig Veda. An Anthology*, Harmondsworth (Penguin Books)

Ojihara, Y. (1978). "Sur une formule Patañjalienne: *na cedanīm ācāryaḥ sūtrāṇi kṛtvā nivartayanti*." *Indologica Taurinensia* 6:9–234

Oldenberg, H. (1915). *Die Lehre der Upaniṣaden und die Anfänge des Buddhismus*, Gottingen

Otto, Rudolf (1930). *Indiens Gnadenreligion und das Christentum*, Gotha

Padoux, Andre (1963). *Recherches sur la symbolique et l'énergie de la parole dans certains textes tantriques*, Paris

Padoux, A. (1978). "Contributions a l'étude du mantraśāstra." *Bulletin de l'ecole française d'extrême-orient* 65:65–85

Padoux, A. (ed.) (1986). *Mantras et diagrammes rituels dans l'hindouisme*, Paris

Padoux, A. (1988). "MANTRAS—What are they?", in: Alper, ed. 295–318

Paranjpe, V. G. (1922). *Le Vārtika de Kātyāyana. Une étude du style, du vocabulaire et des postulats philosophiques*, Paris

Parpola, Asko (1981). "On the primary meaning and etymology of the sacred syllable OṂ." *Proceedings of the Nordic South Asia Conference Held in Helsinki*, June 10–12.

Parpola, Asko (1983). "Jaiminīya Śrauta Sūtra on the Agnicayana, with Bhāvatrāta's Commentary," in: AGNI II:700–736

Parret, Herman (ed.) (1976). *History of Linguistic Thought and Contemporary Linguistics*, Berlin

Payne, Richard K. (1986). *Feeding the Gods: The Shingon Fire Ritual*, Delhi : International Academy of Indian Culture

Penner, Hans H. (1985). "Language, Ritual and Meaning." *Numen. International Journal of the History of Religions* 32:1–16

Philp, Mark (1986). "Michel Foucault," in: Skinner, ed., 65–81

Piston, W. (1947). *Counterpoint*, New York

Piston, W. (1962). *Harmony*, New York

Plotin (1924—1954). *Ennéades*, texte établit et traduit par E. Bréhier, I–VI, 2, Paris

Pott, P. H. (1966). *Yoga and Yantra: Their Interrelations and Significance for Indian Archeology*, The Hagne

Porphyre (1924). *La vie de Plotin et l'ordre de ses écrits*, texte établit et traduit par E. Bréhier in: *Ennéades*, I, Paris

Preisendanz, K. (1973–1974). *Papyri Graeci Magicae. Die griechischen Zauberpapyri*, herausg. A. Henricks, Stuttgart

Proclus (1873). *In Primum Euclidis Elementorum librum commentarii*, ed. G. Friedlein, Leipzig

Quine, W. V. (1953). *From a Logical Point of View*, Cambridge, Mass.

Quine, W. V. (1960). *Word and Object*, Cambridge, Mass.

Quine, W. V. (1981), *Theories and Things*, Cambridge, Mass.

Renou, Louis (1931), *Bibliographie védique*, Paris

Renou, Louis (1941–1942), "Les connexions entre le rituel et la grammaire en sanskrit," *Journal asiatique* 233:105–165, reprinted in: Staal 1973:434–469

Renou, Louis (1942, 1957), *Terminologie grammaticale du sanskrit*, Paris

Renou, Louis (1947), *Les écoles védiques et la formation du Véda*, Paris

Renou, Louis (1949), "La valeur du silence dans le culte védique," *Journal of the American Oriental Society* 69:11–18

Renou, Louis (1953), *Religions of Ancient India*, London

Renou, Louis (1954), *Vocabulaire du rituel védique*, Paris

Renou, Louis (1956), *Histoire de la langue sanskrite*, Paris

Renou, Louis (1960), *Le destin du Véda dans l'Inde. Etudes védiques et pāṇinéennes*, VI, Paris

Renou, Louis (1963), "Sur le genre du *sūtra* dans la litterature sanskrite," *Journal asiatique* 251:165–216

Renou, Louis (1978), *L'Inde fondamentale*, ed. C. Malamoud, Paris

Renou, Louis and Filliozat, Jean (1953), *L'Inde classique*, II, Paris

Renou, Louis and L. Silburn (1954), "*Nírukta* and *ánirukta* in Vedic," *Sarūpa Bhāratī, Lakshman Sarup Memorial Volume*, Hoshiarpur

Revzin, I. (1974), "From Animal Communication to Human Speech," in: Cherry, 15–26

Rickman, H. P. (1967), "Wilhem Dilthey," in: Edwards, ed., 2:403–407

Rickman, H. P. (1979), *Wilhelm Dilthey: Pioneer of the Human Studies*, Berkeley

Rinkes, D. A. (1909), *Abdoerraoef van Singkel: Bijdrage tot de kennis van de mystiek op Sumatra en Java*, Heerenveen

Ripley, Sidney Dillon (1982), *A Synopsis of the Birds of India and Pakistan*, Bombay

Robin, Leon (1908), *La théorie platonicienne des Idées et des Nombres d'après Aristote*, Paris

Robins, R. H. (1976), "Some Continuities and Discontinuities in the History of Linguistics," in: Parret (ed.) 31–31

Rorty, Richard (1979), *Philosophy and the Mirror of Nature*, Princeton

Ruegg, D. S. (1969), *La théorie du Tathāgatagarbha et du Gotra*, Paris

Ruegg, D. S. (1973), *Le traité du Tathāgatagarbha de Bu ston Rin chen grub*, Paris

Ruegg, D. S. (1978), "Mathematical and Linguistic Models in Indian Thought: The Case of Zero and *Śūnyatā*," *Wiener Zeitschrift für die Kunde Südasiens* 22:171–181

Ruegg, D. S. (1981), "On the Supramundane and the Divine in Buddhism," in: Katz, N. (ed.), *Buddhist and Western Philosophy*, New Delhi, 421–424

Ruffié, Jacques (1983), *De la biologie à la culture*, Paris, I–II

Russell, Bertrand (1953), *Mysticism and Logic*, London

Ruwet, Nicolas (1966), "Méthodes d'analyse en musicologie," *Revue belge de musicologie* 20:65–90. Reprinted in: Ruwet 1972.100–134

Ruwet, Nicholas (1972), *Langage, musique, poésie*, Paris

Salmon, W. (1969), Review of Chomsky 1966, *Journal of Linguistics* 5:165–187

Sarma, Neelakanta (1972), *Textes sanskrits et tamouls de Thailande*, Pondichéry

Sarma, E. R. Sreekrishna (1983), "Kauṣītaki Brāhmaṇa on the Atirātra," in: AGNI II:676–699

Sartre, Jean-Paul (1943), *L'être et le néant*, Paris. English translation: *Being and Nothingness*, New York 1956

Sartre, Jean-Paul (1960), *Critique de la raison dialectique*, Paris

Sartre, Jean-Paul (1963), *Les mots*, Paris

Scharfstein, Ben-Ami (forthcoming), *Like the Song of a Bird: On Art and the Esthetic Universal*

Schechner, R. (1986), Review of AGNI, *Journal of Asian Studies* 45:355–363

Schechner, R. (1987), "A 'Vedic Ritual' in Quotation Marks," *Journal of Asian Studies* 46:108–110

Schipper, Kristofer (1982), *Le corps taoïste*, Paris

Schipper, Kristofer and Frits Staal (1988), "Vedic and Taoist Ritual," in: Strickmann, ed. 1988

Schipper, Kristofer and Frits Staal (forthcoming), *Ritual Structure*

Schipper, Kristofer and Wang Hsiu-huei (1986), "Progressive and Regressive Time Cycles in Taoist Ritual," in: *Time, Science and Society in China and the West*, Amherst: 185–205

Schoenberg, Arnold (1970), *Fundamentals of Musical Composition*, New York

Schopenhauer, Arthur (1818), *Die Welt als Wille und Vorstellung*, Dresden

Schopf, T. J. M. (ed.) (1972), *Models in Paleobiology*, New York

Schrieke, B. O. J. (1916), *Het boek van Bonang*, Leiden

Schwab, J. (1886), *Das altindische Thieropfer*, Erlangen

Searle, John R. (1969), *Speech Acts. An Essay in the Philosophy of Language*, Cambridge

Sebeok, Thomas A. (ed.) (1966), *Portraits of Linguists*, I–II, Bloomington

Sebeok, Thomas A. (ed.) (1977), *How Animals Communicate*, Bloomington

Seidenberg, A. (1962), "The Ritual Origin of Geometry," *Archive for History of Exact Sciences*, 1:488–527

Seidenberg, A. (1972), "On the Area of a Semi-Circle," *Archive for History of Exact Sciences*, 9:171–211

Seidenberg, A. (1978), "The Origin of Mathematics," *Archive for History of Exact Sciences*, 18:301–342

Seidenberg, A. (1983), "The Geometry of the Vedic Rituals," in: AGNI II:95–126

Silburn, L. (1955), *Instant et cause. Le discontinu dans la pensée philosophique de l'Inde*, Paris

Simon, R. (1908). *Das Puṣpasūtra mit Einleitung und Ubersetzung*, München

Singer, Milton (1984). *Man's Glassy Essence: Explorations in Semiotic Anthropology*, Bloomington

Skinner, Quentin (1986). *The Return of Grand Theory in the Human Sciences*, London

Skorupski, Tadeusz (1983). "Tibetan Homa Rites," in: AGNI II:403–417

Smart, J. J. C. (1965). "The Methods of Ethics and the Methods of Science," *Journal of Philosophy* 62:344–349

Smith, Brian K. (1986). "The Unity of Ritual. The Place of the Domestic Sacrifice in Vedic Ritualism," *Indo-Iranian Journal* 29:79–96

Smith, Jonathan Z. (1978). *Map Is Not Territory: Studies in the History of Religion*, Leiden

Smith, Jonathan Z. (1987), see: Hamerton-Kelly (ed.)

Smith, W. Robertson (1889). *Lectures on the Religion of the Semites*, London

Smith, F. and Miller, G. A. (eds.) (1966). *The genesis of Language: A Psycholinguistic Approach*, Cambridge, Mass.

Snellgrove, David (1959). *The Hevajra Tantra*, I–II, London

Spiegelberg, H. (1965). *The Phenomenological Movement. A Historical Introduction*, Princeton, I–II

Spiro, Melford E. (1970, 1982). *Buddhism and Society: A Great Tradition and its Burmese Vicissitudes*, Berkeley

Sreekrishna Sarma, E. R. (ed.) (1968–1976). *Kauṣītaki Brāhmaṇa: Text and Vyākhyā of Udaya*, Wiesbaden, I–III

Sreekrishna Sarma, E. R. (1983). "Kauṣītaki Brāhmaṇa on the Atirātra," in: AGNI II:676–699

Staal, J. Frits (1961). *Nambudiri Veda Recitation*, The Hague

Staal, J. Frits (1963a). *Euclides en Pāṇini. Twee methodologische richtlijnen voor de filosofie*, Amsterdam

Staal, J. Frits (1963b). "Sanskrit and Sanskritization." *The Journal of Asian Studies* 22:261–275. Reprinted 1972.

Staal, J. Frits (1965a). "Context-sensitive Rules in Pāṇini," *Foundations of Language* 1:63–72

Staal, J. Frits (1965b). "Euclid and Pāṇini," *Philosophy East and West* 15:99–116

Staal, Frits (1966). "Analyticity." *Foundations of Language* 2:67–93

Staal, Frits (1967a). *Word Order in Sanskrit and Universal Grammar*, Dordrecht

Staal, Frits (1967b). "Review of Hans-Georg Gadamer's *Wahrheit und Methode: Grundzüge einer philosophischen Hermeneutik*," *Foundations of Language* 3:203–205

Staal, Frits (1968), "The Twelve Ritual Chants of the Nambudiri Agniṣṭoma," *Pratidānam: Indian, Iranian and Indo-European Studies Presented to F. B. J. Kuiper on his Sixtieth Birthday*, 409–429

Staal, Frits (1969, reprinted 1976), "Sanskrit Philosophy of Language." *Current Trends in Linguistics* 5:499–531

Staal, Frits (1970a), "Performatives and Token-Reflexives." *Linguistic Inquiry* 3:373–381

Staal, Frits (1970b), "Cambodia: Sanskrit Inscriptions." *The New York Review of Books* July 2, 15

Staal, Frits (1971), "What was left of pragmatics in Jerusalem." *Language Science* 14 (February): 29–32

Staal, Frits (1973), *A Reader on the Sanskrit Grammarians*, Cambridge-London

Staal, Frits (1975a, 1988[2]), *Exploring Mysticism. A Methodological Essay*, Berkeley-Los Angeles-London; also Harmondsworth (Penguin Books)

Staal, Frits (1975b), "The Concept of Metalanguage and its Indian Background," *Journal of Indian Philosophy* 3:315–354

Staal, Frits (1978a), "The Ignorant Brahmin of the Agnicayana," *Annals of the Bhandarkar Oriental Research Institute*, 59:337–348

Staal, Frits (1978b), "On and Around Yoga," *Journal of Indian Philosophy* 6:177–187

Staal, Frits (1979a), "Ritual Syntax," *Sanskrit and Indian Studies: Essays in Honor of Daniel H. H. Ingalls*, Dordrecht 119–142

Staal, Frits (1979b), "The Meaninglessness of Ritual." *Numen. International Journal of the History of Religions* 26:2–22

Staal, Frits (1979c), "Oriental Ideas on the Origin of Language." *Journal of the American Oriental Society* 99:1–14

Staal, Frits (1980), "Rites That Make No Sense." *The Communication of Ideas: 10th International Congress of Anthropological and Ethnological Sciences*, eds. J. S. Yadava and V. Gautam, New Delhi, 3:145–154

Staal, Frits (1982a), *The Science of Ritual*, Poona

Staal, Frits (1982b), "The Himalayas and the Fall of Religion," in: Klimburg-Salter, ed., 38–51

Staal, Frits (1983a), *AGNI. The Vedic Ritual of the Fire Altar*, I–II, Berkeley

Staal, Frits (1983b), "Moon Chants, Space Fillers and Flow of Milk." *Surabhi: Professor E. R. Sreekrishna Sarma Felicitation Volume*, Tirupati, 17–30

Staal, Frits (1984a), "The Search for Meaning: Mathematics, Music and Ritual," *American Journal of Semiotics* 2:4.1–57 = "Ritmo nel rito," *Conoscenza Religiosa* 2:197–247

Staal, Frits (1984b), "Ritual, Mantras and the Origin of Language." in: Joshi, S. D., ed. 403–425

Staal, Frits (1984c), "Abacadabra voor Intellectuelen," in: *De brandende kwestie*, Amsterdam 2:151–177

Staal, Frits (1985a), "Mantras and Bird Songs." *Journal of the American Oriental Society* 105:549–558

Staal, Frits (1985b), "Substitutions de paradigmes et religions d'Asie." *Cahiers d'extrême Asie*, 1:21–57

Staal, Frits (1986a), "The Sound of Religion." *Numen: International Journal for the History of Religions* 33.33–64, 185–224. French translation by Michèle Garlati: "Le son de la religion." Maîtrise de Linguistique, Université de Paris X, Nanterre

Staal, Frits (1986b), "The Fidelity of Oral Tradition and the Origins of Science," *Mededelingen der Koninklijke Nederlandse Akademie van Wetenschappen, Afd. Letterkunde*, n.r. 49/8:251–288. French translation by Michèle Garlati: "La fidélité de la tradition orale et les origines de la science," Maîtrise de Linguistique, Université de Paris X, Nanterre

Staal, Frits (1987), "Professor Schechner's Passion for Goats." *The Journal of Asian Studies* 46:105–108

Staal, Frits (1988a), *Universals: Essays in Indian Logic and Linguistics*, Chicago

Staal, Frits (1988b), *Kailas: Center of Asia*, Chicago

Staal, Frits (1988c), "Vedic Mantras." in: *Understanding Mantras*, ed. H. P. Alper, New York, 48–95

Staal, Frits (1988d), "The Center of Space: Construction and Discovery," *Inner and Outer Space*. New Delhi

Staal, Frits (1988e), "An Outline of Vedic Ritual," in: Strickmann (ed.)

Staal, Frits (1989), *Jouer avec le feu. Pratique et théorie du rituel védique*, Paris

Stebbins, G. Ledyard and F. J. Ayala (1985), "The Evolution of Darwinism," *Scientific American* 253:1.72–82

Steever, S. B. (1985), Review of Obeyesekere 1984, *Journal of the American Oriental Society* 105:186–187

Steiner, George (1965), *Language and Silence*, New York

Steinitz, Paul (1978), *Bach's Passions*, New York

Steinkellner, E. (1978), "Remarks on Tantristic Hermeneutics," in: Ligeti, ed., 445–458

Steklis, Horst B., Harnad, Stevan R. and Lancaster, Jane (eds) (1976), *Origins and Evolution of Language and Speech, Annals of the New York Academy of Sciences* 280:1–914

Strickmann, Michel (1981–1983), *Tantric and Taoist Studies in Honour of R. A. Stein*, I–II, Bruxelles

Strickmann, Michel (1982), "India in the Chinese Looking-Glass," in: Klimburg-Salter (ed.) 52–63

Strickmann, Michel (1983), "Homa in East Asia," in: AGNI II:418–455

Strickmann, Michel (ed.) (1988) *Classical Asian Rituals and the Theory of Ritual*, Berlin

Stutterheim, W (1931), "The Meaning of the Hindu-Javanese caṇḍi," *Journal of the American Oriental Society* 51:1–23

Tambiah, S. J. (1968a), "Literacy in a Buddhist Village in North-east Thailand," in: Goody (ed.) 85–131

Tambiah, S. J. (1968b), "The Magical Power of Words," *Man* 32:175–208

Tambiah, S. J. (1979), "A Performative Approach to Ritual," *Proceedings of the British Academy* 65:113–169

Tambiah, S. J. (1984), *The Buddhist saints of the forest and the cult of amulets*, Cambridge

Taylor, Charles (1984), *Philosophical Papers*, Cambridge, I–II

Thielcke, Gerhard (1964), "Zur Phylogenese einiger Lautäusserungen der europäischen Baumlaufer (*Certhia brachydactyla* Brehm und *Certhia familiaris* L.)," *Zeitschrift für zoologische Systematik und Evolutionsforschung* 2:383–413

Thieme, Paul (1931), "Grammatik und Sprache, ein Problem der altindischen Sprachwissenschaft," *Zeitschrift für Indologie und Iranistik* 8:23–32

Thieme, Paul (1935), *Pāṇini and the Veda*, Allahabad

Thieme, Paul (1957), "Vorzarathustrisches bei den Zarathustriern und bei Zarathustra," *Zeitschrift der deutschen morgenländischen Gesellschaft* 107:67–104

Thieme, Paul (1982–1983), "Meaning and Form of the 'Grammar' of Pāṇini," *Studien zur Indologie und Iranistik* 8/9:3–34

Thomason, R. H. (ed.) (1974), *Formal Philosophy: Selected Papers of Richard Montague*, New Haven-London

Thorpe W. H. (1951), "The definition of terms used in animal behaviour," *Bulletin of Animal Behaviour* 9:34–40

Toulmin, Stephen (1982), *The Return to Cosmology: Postmodern Science and the Theology of Nature*, Berkeley

Tsuji, N. (1952), *On the Relation Between Brāhmaṇas and Śrautasūtras*, Tokyo (in Japanese, with English summary)

Turner, Victor (1975), *Revelation and Divination in Ndembu Ritual*, Ithaca and London

Varenne, Jean (1962), "Mantra védiques dans le Raurava-Āgama," *Journal asiatique* 250:185–189

Von Schroeder, L. (1887), *Indiens Literatur und Cultur in historischer Entwicklung*, Leipzig

Waardenburg, Jacques (1974), *Classical Approaches to the Study of Religion*, I–II, The Hague-Paris

Wasson, R. Gordon (1968), *Soma: Divine Mushroom of Immortality*, New York.

Waismann, F. (1965), "Notes on Talks with Witgenstein," *The Philosophical Review* 74:12–16

Wayman, A. (1976), "The Significance of Mantras, from the Veda down to Buddhist Tantric Practice," *Indologica Taurinensia* 3:483–497

Weber, Max (1922), *Religionssoziologie*, Tubingen. English translation 1963.

Weir, R. (1970), *Language in the Crib*, The Hague

Westergaard, N. (1841), *Radices linguae sanscritae*, Copenhagen

Wheelock, W. T. (1982), "The Problem of Ritual Language: From Information to Situation, "*The Journal of the American Academy of Religion* 50:49–71

Wheelock, W. T. (1985), "Patterns of Mantra Use in Vedic Ritual," *Numen. International Review for the History of Religions* 32:169–193

Wheelock, W. T. (1988), "The Mantra in Vedic and Tantric Ritual," in Alper, ed. 96–122

Whitehead, A. N. (1942), *Adventures of Ideas*, Harmondsworth

Whitehead, A. N. and Russell, B. (1925), *Principia Mathematica*, I, Cambridge

Whitney, W. D. (1879, 1889), *Sanskrit Grammar*, Leipzig

Whitney, W. D. (ed., transl.) (1871), "The Taittirīya-Prātiçākhya, with its Commentary, the Tribhāṣyaratna," *Journal of the American Oriental Society*, 9:1–469

Whitney, W. D. (1872), "Steinthal and the psychological theory of language," *North American Review*, 114. Reprinted in *Oriental and Linguistic Studies*, New York 1874

Wittgenstein, Ludwig (1961), *Tractatus Logico-Philosophicus*, with transl. by D. F. Pears and B. F. McGuinness, London

Wittgenstein, Ludwig (1958), *Philosophical Investigations*, with transl. by G. E. M. Anscombe, Oxford

Wittgenstein, Ludwig (1966), *Lectures and Conversations on Aesthetics, Psychology and Religious Belief*, ed. C. Barrett, Oxford

Ziegenbalg, B., see: Caland, ed. 1926

Zimmer, H. (1926), *Kunstform und Yoga im indischen Kultbild*, Berlin

Zimmer, K. H. (1968), Review of Chomsky 1966, *International Journal of American Linguistics*, 34:290–303

INDEX OF NAMES